BACK
TO
REALITY

**A Critique of
Postmodern Theory
in Psychotherapy**

BACK
TO
REALITY

A Critique of
Postmodern Theory
in Psychotherapy

Barbara S. Held

Professor of Psychology
Bowdoin College

W. W. NORTON & COMPANY
NEW YORK • LONDON

Library of Congress Cataloging-in-Publication Data

Held, Barbara S.
  Back to reality : a critique of postmodern theory in psychotherapy
/ Barbara S. Held.
      p.   cm.
  "Norton professional book."
  Includes bibliographical references and index.
  ISBN 0-393-70192-1 :
    1. Psychotherapy—Philosophy. 2. Postmodernism. 3. Eclectic
psychotherapy. 4. Constructivism (Psychology) 5. Subjectivity.
I. Title.
RC437.5.H44 1995
816.89′14′01—dc20   95-13740 CIP

W. W. Norton & Company, Inc., 500 Fifth Avenue, New York, NY 10110
W. W. Norton & Company, Ltd., 10 Coptic Street, London WC1A 1PU

1 2 3 4 5 6 7 8 9 0

For David

Contents

Preface

This is not a book about how to do psychotherapy. It is a book about how to think about psychotherapy—more precisely, how to think as clearly as possible about the theory and the practice of psychotherapy. If we accept as inevitable a link between thought and action (as do the many postmodernists I examine throughout this book), then my ideas should affect the actual doing of therapy to the extent that they have indeed affected the thinking of those readers who are themselves practicing therapists.

I do not use the expression "as clearly as possible" lightly. From start to finish the writing of this book has been a struggle to be as clear as possible about matters that in some cases still elude my understanding. I hope for a reader who is willing to struggle along with me in those places where I am obviously reaching for something that may be just beyond my grasp. Nowhere was that struggle more real for me than in the creation in Chapter 3 of my version of a generic model of therapy systems. There is some irony for me in the fact that the highly abstract philosophical nuances of realism and antirealism—although by no means easy to take on—posed fewer problems in the final analysis than my attempt to make sense of the component parts of therapy systems. After all, I am a psychologist, not a philosopher, by profession.

At the outset I had not planned to create this or any other generic model. But in coming to terms with the full impact of the postmodern influence on therapy, I came to realize that what I have called the "antisystematic" aspirations of many within that movement were as central to its constitution as its antirealist insistence that we all make rather than discover reality. Hence the generic model was born of necessity: it guided me, and, if it serves its intended purpose, will guide the reader in comprehending the points of convergence and divergence between so-called postmodern and modern therapy systems. Nonetheless, the model is a work in progress for me—one that I know will be a source of much disagreement among therapists and that I suspect will continue to plague me for years to come.

In addition to warning the reader of the difficulties that will be experienced in coping with my attempt at a generic model, I feel compelled to provide a few guidelines about approaching the book in general. Most important is my use of many quotations to document and critique the arguments put forth by members of what I have come to call the postmodern narrative therapy movement. Besides being prepared to read the quotations carefully, the reader should note my use of bracketed comments of my own internal to some quotations. I use that convention in order to show the reader just where in the words of the authors I quote the most critical ideas (in terms of my own argument) reside.

Although I have tried to be as precise as possible throughout my analysis, I have tried not to seek more precision and clarity than is possible, given my decision to examine theory and philosophy within psychotherapy. In short, I hope I have managed to follow Aristotle's call not to seek more precision than the subject matter under scrutiny will allow. If the reader judges me on balance to have fulfilled that dictum more often than not, I will consider my work successful in at least that one important regard.

* * *

There are many who shared my struggle in producing this book, and I am happy to acknowledge them for their contributions here.

Most of the book was written while I was a visiting scholar in the Department of Psychology at Tufts University during my 1992–1993 sabbatic leave from Bowdoin College. I am grateful first to Robert Guertin, Dean of the Graduate School of Arts and Sciences, and Joseph DeBold, then Chair of the Psychology Department, for making this position possible. Jackie Ellis and Cynthia Goddard made many of the arrangements that expedited my work during that year. I am also grateful to other members of that department who spent many hours discussing my ideas and giving me much needed critical feedback. John Kounios and Richard Chechile were always ready to listen and to offer excellent ideas in return. I am particularly grateful to Zella Luria, with whom I exchanged wide-ranging thoughts about the intellectual movement known as postmodernism. She became a supportive friend and colleague in the process, and I continue to learn much from her about psychology in particular and science in general. Sarah Patterson in philosophy was most gracious in allowing me to take her illuminating course in the history of modern philosophy.

Others outside of Tufts helped me throughout my year in the Boston area, especially in my understanding of work done in the humanities that pertained to my own work. At Wellesley College Mary Lefkowitz in classics and Owen Flanagan in philosophy were helpful in may ways, but especially so in giving me the chance to air the ideas contained in this book at a colloquium there. My discussions with the classicists Hugh Lloyd-Jones and Richard Thomas were always enlightening. Henry Grunebaum of family psychotherapy training at Cambridge City Hospital gave me much food for thought. I am especially grateful to him for the opportunity to speak before the members of his training program.

Closer to home are my many friends and colleagues at Bowdoin College, without whom this project might never have happened. In my own department, I owe thanks to Paul Schaffner and Suzanne Lovett for reading parts of the manuscript and for sharing their reactions and thoughts with me in many hours of discussion. Donna Trout and Alfred Fuchs provided necessary technical and moral support. Outside psychology, Barbara Weiden Boyd in classics has, in our many discussions over the last ten years, given me much material about the postmodern influence (and other trends) in the humanities; her astute knowledge about this influence made it possible for me to understand something about the humanist's perspective. Joanne Feit Diehl in English pointed me toward relevant texts of literary theory and criticism, and for that I am grateful. Turning to the physical sciences, Carey Phillips in biology, George Schmiedeshoff in physics, and Peter Trumper in chemistry allowed me to enter directly the world of their own research projects; these were experiences that made my formulation of a science/humanities distinction possible. All of my students have, by virtue of their incisive questions, contributed to this book, but my research assistants contributed in more direct and painstaking ways. I thank Mara Savacool, Richard Lucas, Kari Primo, Leigh Perry, Bridget Christiano, Joshua Baron, and Audrey Snowden for their dedicated efforts in locating references and helping to prepare the manuscript for publication. Bowdoin College itself was generous in awarding me grants that permitted me to take a full year's sabbatic leave and also paid for reference materials and manuscript preparation.

Although he taught at Bowdoin for most of his career as a philosopher, and so is surely part of that community, Edward Pols deserves a paragraph of

his own. Friend, colleague, and mentor, he has worked with me since 1982 —
we published some papers together in the 1980s — to help prepare me for
what ultimately became this book, although neither of us had any idea at the
time that our lengthy discussions about science and philosophy, including the
commonsense world of knowing, would culminate in this project. In addition, he read many drafts of the book manuscript, and helped to unscramble
my thinking on more than one occasion. I am deeply indebted to him for the
greatest gift of all: he helped me to know, but also to have the courage to
acknowledge that I *do* know — as well as *what* I know. His influence throughout this book is explicit, and needs no further discussion here.

Friends, colleagues, and family outside of Bowdoin also deserve mention.
Michael Boyd gave me advice that was always at once both intellectual and
practical, and I owe much to him for that. Donald Freedheim, Alan Gurman,
Rachel Hare-Mustin, Barry Duncan, and Harold Goolishian supported this
project from the start. The reader will find that the words of some of these
distinguished psychologists are criticized in the pages of this book. That they
encouraged me nonetheless is testament to their own intellectual integrity.
My parents, Harriette and Milton Held, my sister, Roberta Held, and my
husband's parents, Louise and Chandler Bellows, were supportive in every
way imaginable. Were it not for the love and support of my husband, David
Bellows, also a clinical psychologist, I would not have had the courage I
needed to see this project through to its completion.

Finally, I cannot thank enough those who gave countless hours to reading
and commenting upon prior drafts of the entire book manuscript. Larry Fader
of Dialogue Center in Portland, Maine, Richard Flanagan of the Delaware
Family Center, and John Lehnhoff of Methodist Richard Young Hospital in
Omaha, Nebraska all had much to say that sometimes changed but always
encouraged and engaged my thinking. Although they were not "official readers," the comments on the full book manuscript that I received from Edward
Pols and David Bellows were of no lesser value to me. Susan Barrows Munro
of Norton raised all the right questions, kept me on track, and with expert
efficiency turned my manuscript into a book. I consider myself fortunate to
have had her guidance.

BACK
TO
REALITY

**A Critique of
Postmodern Theory
in Psychotherapy**

CHAPTER 1

An Introduction to Postmodern Theory and Its Use in Psychotherapy

There is no consensus about how to answer the most fundamental questions of psychotherapy. More striking is the absence of a clear consensus about what constitutes those most fundamental questions. Nonetheless, most psychotherapists would surely agree that the two obvious questions—what causes problems and what causes solutions—are among the most fundamental, provided we define the terms "problem" and "solution" broadly enough to incorporate any undesirable or desirable state, respectively. Given this diversity of opinion, then, it is noteworthy that many disparate movements within psychotherapy—family/systemic, constructivist/constructionist, psychoanalytic, cognitive, and some feminist therapies—have begun to employ a common rhetoric, one that articulates a particular philosophical doctrine: that therapy is a linguistic, narrative, or storied enterprise. It is my purpose in this book to explore that doctrine—its essence, the reasons for its adoption, and its manifestations and consequences.

A fundamental thesis of this book is that this emerging linguistic "paradigm" can be understood only in the context of a broader intellectual movement that has swept the humanities in the last two decades and is now working its way into the social sciences, in which psychotherapy provides just one instance of a general intellectual trend (Rosenau, 1992). In its broadest sense, this intellectual movement is called "postmodernism." And since a good many therapists use that ambiguous, ambitious, and controversial term themselves to characterize their own theoretical underpinnings, I shall apply that same term to the psychotherapy movement I examine in this book (e.g., Anderson & Goolishian, 1988, 1992; de Shazer, 1991; de Shazer & Berg, 1992; Frank, 1987; Gergen & Kaye, 1992; Hare-Mustin & Marecek, 1990a; Howard,

1

1991; Lax, 1992; McNamee & Gergen, 1992; Neimeyer, 1993; Omer & Strenger, 1992; Parry, 1991; Polkinghorne, 1992; White & Epston, 1990). In what follows I call these therapists "narrative therapists" or "postmodern narrative therapists," depending upon my intended emphasis. My inquiry focuses upon postmodern or poststructural literary theories and criticisms, since it is to those literary approaches that postmodern narrative therapists have turned. Insofar as that type of literary theory is founded upon the antirealist doctrine that the knower, rather than discovering reality as it is, creates or constructs his or her own "reality" in language, I also scrutinize the use of certain (postmodern) antirealist philosophical doctrines by narrative therapists.

The discerning reader will note that my purpose is in part a critical one, as I assess the use of postmodern theory within psychotherapy, an assessment that attends to its many flaws and shortcomings for that purpose. It is not, however, a monolithically negative evaluation. For I also argue that the emergence of that movement reflects an attempt to solve a problem within the discipline of psychotherapy that has eluded resolution despite many attempts to provide one. Viewed as an attempt to solve a recalcitrant problem in psychotherapy theory and practice, the postmodern narrative therapy movement must be assessed with an open mind; indeed, if psychotherapy — working within the confines of a traditional, or modern, scientific enterprise — had successfully solved that problem, the need for alternative solutions would not be so compelling. Thus, just as the narrative therapy movement must be understood in the broader context of the postmodern humanistic[1] trends it adopts, so must it also be understood in the context of the modern scientific approaches to therapy that were obviously found inadequate by postmodern proponents in the first place. The integrative/eclectic therapy movement, which adopts a modern scientific approach and tries to solve the same recalcitrant problem to which the narrative movement responds, provides that context. It therefore serves as a basis for comparison.

But my assessment of these postmodern trends within psychotherapy is a critical one nonetheless. First, they have, in my experience, been all too widely and uncritically embraced by many psychotherapists, and so their internal workings and theoretical and applied implications have not heretofore received the kind of comprehensive, serious scrutiny I think they warrant. Second, to determine whether postmodern literary theories and philosophies exert a positive influence on therapy, we must examine them in the same clear light of critical reason that we would use to examine the basis for any major psychotherapy movement. Only then can we determine whether these ideas have relevance for therapy, and so begin to make rational, informed decisions about the proper application of these revolutionary trends to the therapeutic enterprise. In order to provide this critical evaluation, I have had to develop a generic model of therapy systems that can be used to compare and contrast any and all systems of therapy. This generic model can therefore be used independently of the postmodernism issue to analyze the workings of therapy systems.

In this book I have more than a critical purpose. That additional purpose is to provide an alternative to postmodern theory as it now functions in therapy, an alternative that addresses the unresolved problem within psychotherapy I have only alluded to. As my title suggests, that alternative—contrary to postmodern theory—promotes the adoption of realism in psychotherapy, although it is a modest, or limited, realism that I call for. But I do not dispense indiscriminately with all the ideas behind postmodern therapy; rather, my aim is to provide a more coherent and consistent approach to psychotherapy theory—and, of course, practice—than can now be found in the postmodern narrative therapy movement.

WHAT IS POSTMODERN THEORY?

The concept of postmodern theory is a controversial one. In the first place, it is misleading to speak of just one such theory, since there are many competing postmodern theories that are not necessarily consistent with one another (see Best & Kellner, 1991; Kvale, 1992a; Rosenau, 1992, for a complete account). Rosenau (1992), for instance, distinguishes between affirmative and skeptical postmodernists, assigning to the latter the more extreme and radical breaks with the views of modernity. Moreover, there is still considerable disagreement about whether we have actually left behind a modern era and entered a postmodern one.

Although I define the term "postmodern" just below, it is not my purpose to provide an overview of developments in postmodern theory, a task that has already been performed by others. Because I am both a theorist and a practicing clinician, it is my purpose to consider how and why some of those developments have found their way not only into the theory of psychotherapy but also into its practice. To characterize therapy as a linguistic and literary matter, postmodern narrative therapists have called upon the linguistic philosophy of Wittgenstein (1953) and Rorty (1979) as well as the poststructural literary theory and philosophy of such writers as Foucault, Derrida, and de Man. Hence, the ideas derived from these two humanistic movements provide the focus of my evaluation.

It is my claim that a central, defining feature of linguistic philosophy and poststructural literary theory—and indeed of all postmodern theory itself—is the explicit adoption of a fundamental antirealism. Thus, if there is one position that unites the many manifestations of postmodern thought, I believe it is the rejection of a realist epistemology in favor of an antirealist one (e.g., Best & Kellner, 1991; Chaiklin, 1992, pp. 197–202; Gergen, 1992, pp. 23–25, 1994; Kvale, 1992b, p. 2, 1992c, pp. 32–35; Polkinghorne, 1992, pp. 148–149; Rosenau, 1992). Since I organize my assessment of how postmodern theory has affected psychotherapy around the distinction between realism and antirealism, let us first turn our attention to that distinction.

The Realism/Antirealism Distinction

The nature of realist and antirealist epistemological doctrines has occupied philosophers for a good many centuries—consider Descartes, Hume, and Kant, to name only three. The distinction itself is therefore a matter of enormous complexity. Nevertheless, there has emerged in this century a defining feature of the realist/antirealist distinction that is most relevant to my analysis. It is also, when put in its most fundamental terms, accessible to those without a formal philosophical background.

The realist doctrine, simply put, states that the knower can attain knowledge of an independent reality—that is, reality that is objective in the sense that it does not originate in the knower, or knowing subject.[2] The expression "independent reality," then, refers to the independence of the thing known from the knower—more precisely, from the knower's cognitive operations and the theoretical, linguistic, or narrative constructions produced by those operations. Thus, for the realist, nothing—no theory, for instance—*necessarily* intervenes between the knower and the known, or between the knower and the (mind-independent) object of the knower's inquiry. The knower can therefore get at—attain awareness of—some objects of inquiry (e.g., an apple, a tree, person, house, painting, poem, story, or scientific proposition) without imposing a theory, language, idea, construct, or narrative that alters or distorts in experience the real nature of that object, or reality. Moreover, in those cases when the knower does need to use some theory to understand some aspect of reality (e.g., the physics of the very small or causality in general), that theory does not *automatically* alter or distort the real/independent reality it purports to explain. Thus, according to the realist doctrine, *knowable* reality—indeed *reality* itself—is not merely a theoretical, cognitive, or linguistic construction on the part of the knower, a construction that tells us something about the knower and his or her cognitive operations, but little, if anything, about the object of inquiry, that is, about the independent reality to be known. A typical realist epistemology, then, implicitly acknowledges the existence of an independent ontological reality—a real "thing in itself"—that can be known to some extent. In therapy, for example, the therapist can be certain that the person who sits before her, saying he feels threatened by some life experience—and behaving as if he indeed is threatened, is not *merely* a by-product of the therapist's own theoretical or linguistic construction on the basis of some utterly unknowable stimulus.

But the waters are already deeper than they seem, for a realist doctrine does not commit one to the epistemological doctrine of the passive knower (i.e., the so-called spectator theory of knowing). Rather, as I argue in Chapter 6, the knower employs an active rational or cognitive process in the act of knowing. That active process permits direct (i.e., unmediated by theory) awareness of an independent reality in some, but not all, instances of knowing.

Thus, we can already begin to notice that the doctrine of realism may itself reflect different epistemological positions. In its most simplistic form—sometimes called naive realism—the knower is said to attain all aspects of an independent reality. But in the alternative to naive realism that I adopt, knowers may, in many instances, only be able to approximate the real nature of some independent reality that is not directly observable. They may do so by means of theories, hypotheses, explanations (e.g., in science or in therapy) that may in the end turn out to be inadequate to the reality under investigation—that is, they may turn out to be incorrect. The therapist in the example I just provided was not likely to have witnessed the emotional abuse that the adult client complains of and says is the cause of his feeling threatened. But in a therapy session she can nonetheless attend directly to the client's descriptions of that abuse and to the client's actual in-therapy behavior. Perhaps, with his consent, she can even talk to others who were in a position to observe the abusive events directly. The therapist can therefore make some judgment about whether those events indeed occurred and whether they play some causal role in the client's current difficulties. The fact that the therapist arrives at, or constructs, such a *theory* about the client does not, according to a realist doctrine, prevent that theory from reflecting, to some extent, the extratheoretic, or true, reality of the client's life.

To provide another illustration, the therapist can have direct (i.e., unmediated by theory) awareness of a client pacing during a session, waving her arms about, and uttering sentences about how agitated she feels. These sentences may or may not tell the therapist something true about the client's psychological state, which the therapist cannot observe directly. But based on what he has observed directly and on his knowledge of psychological principles, the therapist can nonetheless develop, or construct, a theory about what is causing that behavior, what the client's intent in so behaving is, and so forth. For the realist, that theory can in *principle* give some accurate approximation of the client's actual psychological state. Similarly, the physicist cannot have direct awareness of events that are very small, such as subatomic ones, or events that are very large, such as cosmological ones. But the physicist can nonetheless develop a theory, based on what is available to direct observation, that gives some correct approximation, that is, some *indirect* (or theory-mediated) knowledge, of what is actually going on at those levels of reality that cannot be observed directly. That the physicist's theory may evolve as technology becomes more sophisticated, allowing more precise measurements, does not mean that the enterprise was anything less than realist at any point along the way. So too the doctrine of realism means that the science of psychology, with its evolving theories, can tell us something real about what causes problems, and what causes solutions.

The form of realism that I have just illustrated describes the scientific enterprise, among other rational activities. There is nothing about science, as it has been pursued over the ages, that commits the knower to an antirealist epistemology (Held & Pols, 1985a, p. 513). In this book, I advocate the adoption of this form of non-naive realism. This modest realism, as I will now call it, does not preclude the articulation, striving for, and, sometimes, the attainment of certain independent truths, whether in science, in therapy, or in life. Indeed, it is essential for the scientific or any other rational enterprise, including psychotherapy, that we be capable in many circumstances of attaining a reality that is independent of the knower and the knower's subjectivity. As I explain in Chapter 6, it is precisely because we have *direct* (unmediated by theory) awareness of some things that we can construct theories, based on what we have observed directly, that give us indirect (theory-mediated) knowledge of an independent reality that we cannot observe directly.

I shall return to the realist doctrine in due course. For now let us turn our attention to the antirealist doctrine, since its use in psychotherapy is the focus of my assessment. The antirealist doctrine, which has also been called constructivism or constructionism in psychotherapy circles (e.g., Efran, Lukens, & Lukens, 1990; McNamee & Gergen, 1992), states that the knower cannot, under any circumstances, attain knowledge of a reality that is independent of the knower; rather, knowers make, invent, create, constitute, construct, or narrate, in language, their own subjective realities or, in the usual terminology, antirealities or nonrealities (see Held, 1990, 1992; Held & Pols, 1985a, 1987a; Pols, 1992a).

For antirealists, then, a theory, language, construct, or narrative always intervenes, or mediates, between the knower and the known—that is, between the knower and the targeted independent reality that is usually presumed to exist.[3] Therefore, the knower can never have direct awareness of an independent (of the knower) reality. Moreover, the theory, language, construct, or narrative that intervenes between the knower and the known *always*, according to antirealists, prevents unaltered or undistorted awareness of an independent reality. That is because for antirealists the knower's own cognitive operations and the theoretical, linguistic, or narrative constructions produced by those operations always alter or distort in experience the true nature of the object of knowing (the targeted independent reality), thereby making all knowledge inescapably subjective or relative. For example, the therapist cannot know the true nature of the client and his struggles as they really exist, no matter what the therapist observes in the therapy sessions. Rather, the antirealist doctrine insists that the therapist's theories, language, constructions, or narratives about the client always determine just what the therapist observes, and so preclude any direct (i.e., theoretically unmediated), undistorted, or even any indirect (i.e., theoretically mediated), undistorted knowledge of the client's true condition.

Thus, according to the antirealist, the therapist who, for instance, holds a psychoanalytic theory will, no matter what the client says or does, always observe certain forms of intrapsychic conflicts in the client.[4] That therapist will, moreover, attribute the client's difficulties to those conflicts, whether or not those conflicts actually exist and play some real causal role in the client's problem. Similarly, the antirealist doctrine means that the science of psychology, including the theories developed within that science, cannot tell us anything real about problem causation and problem resolution. For the antirealist, then, the theory one holds literally makes or constitutes or brings into being the "reality," or nonreality, one finds; one's theory can never reflect the reality that is actually there.

The antirealist doctrine is at the core of linguistic philosophy, or what Pols (1992a) calls the linguistic consensus within philosophy (Wittgenstein,

Quine, Sellars, etc.). It is also the philosophical basis for poststructural literary theory, which I discuss in Chapters 4 and 7. Antirealism is therefore a defining feature of the postmodern narrative therapy movement, which makes explicit use of poststructural literary theory and linguistic philosophy. To the extent that postmodern theory in general defines itself by way of "discourse analysis,"[5] the antirealist doctrine is also a defining feature of the many manifestations of postmodern theory (Best & Kellner, 1991, p. 213; de Shazer, 1991; Hare-Mustin & Marecek, 1990a; Rosenau, 1992; Wetherell & Potter, 1988, pp. 170–172; White & Epston, 1990).

For the postmodern narrative therapist, then, all experiences of the world are mediated by the (reality-distorting) theory, language, discourse, narrative, or story that clients and therapists, who inhabit *particular* (linguistic or discursive) contexts, adopt (e.g., Anderson & Goolishian, 1988, 1992; de Shazer, 1991; de Shazer & Berg, 1992; Efran, Lukens, & Lukens, 1990; Epstein & Loos, 1989; Frank, 1987; Gergen & Kaye, 1992; Hare-Mustin & Marecek, 1990a; Hoffman, 1990; Howard, 1991; Lax, 1992; McNamee & Gergen, 1992; Neimeyer & Feixas, 1990; Omer & Strenger, 1992; Parry, 1991; Polkinghorne, 1992; Sluzki, 1992; White & Epston, 1990). Thus, according to the antirealist doctrine that postmodernists in general propound, one's view of, or discourse about, reality can never reflect the true or independent (of the knower) nature of that reality.

Put differently, according to the antirealist doctrine, we can never get outside of language to attain knowledge of an independent – or extralinguistic[6] – reality. As Polkinghorne (1992), a self-proclaimed postmodern therapist, succinctly puts it, "A common theme of the postmodern epistemology is that linguistic systems stand between reality and experience (Rorty, 1989[a]). Each language system has its own *particular* way of *distorting, filtering and constructing experience* [all italics added]" (pp. 149–150); "Our experience is always filtered through interpretive schemes" (p. 149). McNamee and Gergen (1992) also offer, in the name of a postmodern approach to therapy, a similar argument:

> Our formulations of what is the case are guided by and limited to the systems of language in which we live. What can be said about the world – including self and others – is an outgrowth of shared conventions of discourse. Thus, . . . one cannot describe the history of a country or oneself on the basis of "what actually happened;" rather, one has available a repertoire of story-telling devices or narrative forms and these devices are *imposed* [italics added] on the past. (p. 4)

These statements have important implications for the postmodern narrative therapist, because the antirealist doctrine they reflect radically alters what is commonly understood to be the nature of truth. For the postmodern therapist in particular, as well as the postmodern theorist in general, there is no way of knowing that can give us *any* true, independent reality. All "truths," therefore, are *merely* constructions in language made by knowers situated in *particular* discursive contexts. And each particular discursive context allegedly precludes, in its own unique way, the attainment or experience of any reality that is independent of the knower and therefore independent of the knower's (reality-distorting) theory or linguistic/discursive context.

The antirealist doctrine, like the realist one, contains more than one formulation. "Notice that it is a more radical claim to say . . . that *reality* does not exist independently of the knower than it is to say . . . that our *experience* of reality, being structured by ourselves, may be different from what reality in fact is" (Held & Pols, 1985a, p. 513). This distinction may be important for some constructivists/antirealists: they could argue that their theory, language, construct, or narrative does not alter or distort anything, since, according to them, there *exists* no independent reality to be mediated/altered by theory in the act of knowing. Rather, for these more extreme antirealists, the only reality that exists is the reality of their own mental constructions (see Note 3). But whether the antirealism is of the more or the less radical sort, it always precludes any access (direct or indirect) to an independent reality, and *that* is the point of all antirealist doctrines. So it is also the point of postmodern theory itself.

The Modern/Postmodern Distinction

With this understanding of the realism/antirealism distinction, we are now in a position to summarize briefly some basic differences between modern and postmodern views as they have recently been put forth (Best & Kellner, 1991; Kvale, 1992a; Rosenau, 1992). Because it adheres to a realist doctrine, the modern position can be characterized as follows: (a) general laws and truths may be attained by way of reason, science, and technology, and so progress is possible (see Chaiklin, 1992, p. 197; Gergen, 1992, pp. 18–25); (b) there is determinacy of meaning in any text or event; and (c) the subject/self/individual has a real ontological status or existence.

The determinacy of meaning in texts or events refers to the idea—which runs counter to poststructural literary theory—that a text has a true or objective meaning which can be determined by the reader through the use of proper literary methods. Whether that true meaning is the one intended by the author is a debatable point within literary theory. The answer to that question is a function of whether one adopts a traditional theory of literary interpretation, which allows authorial intention, or the new theory of criticism, which is based on the structuralist view that the text is structured only by language and so is itself independent of the author. Nonetheless, in structuralism the text is said to retain an underlying internal form, system, or structure that determines its meaning—a structure and meaning that can be revealed by the reader who uses proper structuralist methods (see Kugler, 1988; Suleiman, 1980; Tompkins, 1980).

The equation of texts and events is a poststructural literary theory move, based on the notion that all phenomena—the self, mind, and all happenings in life—are themselves nothing more than texts. Thus, all phenomena supposedly consist solely in linguistic or literary constructions made by "readers"/observers. And these constructions, it is claimed, can be "deconstructed," altered, "rewritten," or rearranged, often without limits or constraints on the obtained meanings (see Culler, 1980; Ellis, 1989; Fish, 1980, cited in Tompkins, 1980, p. xxii; Krieger, 1987). Thus, any experience—the contraction of a fatal disease, for instance—can have an infinite variety of interpretations or meanings, an infinite variety of manifestations and consequences, depending upon who is doing the reading, observing, or interpreting.

The poststructural literary theory that equates texts and events is the one most prominently adopted by postmodern narrative therapists, and I shall therefore return to it in Chapter 4. At a later point in the present chapter, I shall also consider the ontological status of the subject/self/individual, including the distinctions between those three terms. But for now it is important to remember that this text/event equation, which reflects a postmodern sentiment, runs counter to any sort of modernist,[7] realist doctrine.

We turn now to the postmodern view, which, because it includes a fundamental antirealist doctrine, can be characterized as follows: (a) it rejects general laws and truths, and so the idea of progress itself, in favor of local, unique, personal, contextualized "truths" (e.g., Chaiklin, 1992; Polkinghorne, 1992); (b) it claims that there is an indeterminacy, or a plurality, of meaning in texts/events; and (c) it proclaims the "death" of the subject/self/individual—that is, it denies the subject's real ontological status or existence.

Regarding the first point, recall that all knowledge, or "truth," is for the postmodernist highly transitory or context dependent, so that generalities of any sort cannot be made. As Best and Kellner (1991, p. 4) put it, "all cognitive representations of the world are historically and linguistically mediated." Also recall that the belief that "theories mirror reality" is a modernist, realist belief (Best & Kellner, 1991, p. 4) that postmodernists reject (see Rorty, 1979). What we are plainly dealing with in the first quotation, then, is a version of the antirealist doctrine that theory/language[8] *always* intervenes between the knower and the known so as to alter or distort in experience, as a function of the knower's *particular* historical/linguistic context, the true or independent nature of the known. Therefore, the knower can never claim access to any true or independent (of the knower) reality. Rather, the belief that all knowledge is theory/language bound means that an individual's *idea* of reality is always dependent upon—constituted by—the *particular* theory/ language (or discourse) the individual is adopting or responding to in any particular place and time, that is, in any particular context. Thus, because individuals are constantly subjected to changing physical and interpersonal and, hence, linguistic or discursive contexts, what is "true" for one moment, place, or person may not be "true" for the next moment, place, or person. In particular, what is "true" for a person at Time 1 and Place 1 may not be "true" for that same person at Time 2 and Place 2. Similarly, what is "true" for a person at Time 1 and Place 1 may not be "true" for a different person in that same time and place. It all depends on the *particular* theory/language that constitutes one's experience of the world in any given moment, however fleeting that moment may be. Therefore, "truth"/knowledge must by definition be fragmented, nonunitary/nonglobal, local, specific, ephemeral, transitory (and so forth) within a postmodern framework.

This idea is also central to postmodern narrative therapy, which attempts to use only each client's unique or personal experience, rather than to employ general categories of problems (e.g., depression) to which clients get assigned for intervention purposes (e.g., Anderson & Goolishian, 1988). But that is a matter I shall take up in due course. For now, let us return to the idea of the indeterminacy and plurality of meaning in texts/events. In contrast to the modernist view described above, postmodern/poststructural literary theory— especially the currently popular "reader-response" criticism—denies that the text (or event) has any existence independent of the reader or observer/ listener (see, e.g., Brooks, 1992; Culler, 1980; Fish, 1980; Krieger, 1987; Suleiman, 1980; Tompkins, 1980). Therefore, the reader herself (within her *particular* historical/linguistic context) determines what the text means. In its more radical and extreme form, there are no constraints on the meanings that the reader can obtain—no constraints imposed by the author or even by the structure of language itself (Ellis, 1989). It must be said that not all poststructuralists adopt a position that is so extreme.[9] But it is nonetheless evident that if a text/event can mean whatever a particular reader/knower or even a particular group of readers/knowers, however large, finds in it, there can be no one true (independent of the knower or group of knowers) meaning that can be discovered through the use of proper methods. The relativism of this position is surely antithetical to any sort of realist doctrine, no matter how modest it may be. It is therefore clear that here we are dealing with an antirealist doctrine of a profound and fundamental sort.

The Science/Humanities Distinction[10]

It is noteworthy that accounts of postmodernism express a suspicion of reason/rationality, science, and technology as a means of attaining truth and achieving progress. The reader should keep this suspicion in mind, since it affects arguments about how psychotherapy theory, practice, and even research should proceed from modern and postmodern perspectives. In particular, this suspicion affects the way the disciplines of the sciences, as opposed to those of the humanities, can or should be used to answer questions that pertain to psychotherapy. In the recent past, for example, members of the family/systemic and other therapy movements appealed to quantum physics and biology (e.g., Doherty, 1986; Goldberg & David, 1991; Speed, 1991) to legitimate their antirealist leanings, whereas now, in the name of antirealism, they invoke the humanities, despite the epistemological controversy between realists and antirealists that rages there. Indeed, that controversy is behind the recent creation of a distinct form of the humanities known as "postmodern humanities."

Determining the merits of a scientific vs. humanistic approach to psychotherapy is, to be sure, a complex undertaking in itself. Further complications arise from the fact that postmodernists, who reject the use of traditional (i.e., modern or realist[11]) science, also profess to be antihumanistic: they denounce any traditional humanistic belief in the subject's or individual's capacity for agency and centrality in the world. Nonetheless, postmodernists find a home within the disciplines (such as philosophy, languages, and literature) that constitute what has traditionally been called the humanities, by pursuing only so-called postmodern forms of inquiry (see Rosenau, 1992, pp. 47–49, for a more complete account). The science/humanities distinction also raises the not-so-new question about whether therapy is best viewed as an art or an applied science, a question I discuss in the final chapter of the book.

WHY A POSTMODERN (ANTIREALIST) THEORY OF PSYCHOTHERAPY NOW?

Having considered how fundamental the doctrine of antirealism is to any conceptualization of postmodern theory, we must now ask why members of so many disparate therapy movements are turning, as if in an orchestrated effort, to postmodern philosophy and literary theory. There may well be as many answers to that question as there are therapists, since psychotherapy is a discipline that has resisted any broad consensus. Let us therefore first consider a variety of answers to that question, before I present the one that I find to be the most substantive and persuasive.

In a cynical and ungenerous spirit, we can attribute this postmodern turn to the fact that psychotherapy tends to be, at least in some of its more popular manifestations, a trendy business. Consider, for instance, the proliferation of books in the so-called "self-help" movements, including those that promote the "co-dependency" and "dysfunctional family" movements. Books about co-dependency now abound. And although I have yet to find a definition of that term that makes its meaning clear and distinct, it has nonetheless been adopted as a core explanatory construct by more than a few reputable therapists. This is all the more troubling because the term has been used to account for all psychological problems. Like these self-help movements, postmodernism is a trendy enterprise these days, as anyone can judge by perusing the titles now appearing in the literary theory, critical and cultural theory, and philosophy sections of bookstores, as well as the titles in the sections devoted to social science itself. So we may conclude, in our cynical spirit, that psychotherapists are simply trendy types who, by definition, seek novelty for novelty's sake—an explanation that is admittedly neither satisfying nor uplifting.

Another explanation for the importation into therapy of postmodern theory is somewhat less cynical. It rests on the fact that therapy is now and always has been a highly complex enterprise, one in which precise, preformulated theories and methods are not easily applied in practice because of the unique, individuated nuances of each and every therapy case. But the complexity of therapy also derives from the vast number of formulations about problem causation and problem resolution that permeate its many distinct schools: this is a knowledge base that certainly exceeds what any earnest therapist can hope to know, let alone manage systematically and rationally in practice. This is a reality that proponents of the eclectic therapy movement, many of whom seek to reduce the sheer magnitude of information by means of an integrative "metatheory" (e.g., Prochaska & DiClemente, 1984), know only too well.

What the antirealism of the postmodern movement affords therapists, then, is a legitimate way to diminish the discipline's complexity, by diminishing if not eliminating what therapists need to know in advance of each case. For if, as the antirealist position states, there is no way to know what really has caused the client's problem, then no one (school of psychotherapy's) theory of problem causation or psychopathology (e.g., a maladaptive cognitive style to explain depressive symptoms) can be said to be truly necessary for problem resolution; rather, all such knowledge is dispensable, leaving the clinician free to focus on the unique nuances of each case without the imposition of general, predetermined theories of problems/pathology to constrain his practice. As we shall see in the next chapter, this solution is opposed to those offered by both technical and integrative eclectics, who wish to retain the information therapists need to and can know, by providing a system that makes the knowledge base of therapy more manageable.

We may therefore conclude that the use of postmodern theory in therapy serves a dual purpose: it rids the practitioner of the burden of having to know and apply a vast amount of theory and research about psychopathology (i.e., problem causation) and psychotherapy (i.e., problem resolution)—an amount which certainly exceeds the capacities of any one practitioner. But it simultaneously encourages the therapist to attend vigilantly to the unique specifics of each therapy case, thereby enhancing the fit between the therapist's usual or preferred theoretical formulations and the case at hand (Held, 1991a, 1992).

Historically, psychotherapy has also turned to other disciplines to define and legitimate itself. In the past, at least since the time of Freud, who was himself no stranger to physics and biology, those disciplines tended to be the physical sciences, such as (quantum) physics (e.g., Doherty, 1986; Goldberg & David, 1991) and biology (e.g., Dell, 1985). Now we find a "linguistic turn" to the humanities in the form of the narrative therapy movement. But in either case, psychotherapy has never seemed quite comfortable inhabiting its own domain. Perhaps what accounts best for this (linguistic) turning to other disciplines is a pervasive realization that the "grand narrative" (to use a postmodern term) of therapy has simply not succeeded: despite almost 50 years of the scientific study of psychotherapy, there is still surprisingly little consensus about what causes problems and what causes solutions. It is therefore not surprising that many therapists are now abandoning the physical sciences—with their "grand narratives" or "unified theories"—as a proper model for therapy, and are instead taking refuge in the postmodern humanities, which defy grand narratives and the idea of progress in the first place.

The Problem of Individuality:
An Alternative Explanation

Although each of these explanations may have some validity, I believe there is an explanation for the current and pervasive use of postmodern theory in therapy that is more substantive, and so less cynical, than the explanations I presented above. I suggest that therapists who adopt postmodern theory are attempting to solve the problem I only alluded to in the opening pages of this book; let me now define that problem explicitly. The problem is this: how can we construct a theoretical system of psychotherapy such that, when it is used to guide the practice of therapy, there is both attention to the unique individuality of each client *and* preservation of a systematic, rule-governed, replicable enterprise? Put differently, how can the practice of therapy be individualized, and at the same time also be consistent, replicable, or generalized—that is, systematic—across cases? This is a problem that has plagued psychotherapy for countless years, despite many attempts at resolution. The magnitude of the problem was seen by many to be embodied by the strict, deindividualizing constraints of Freudian psychoanalysis, with its highly formalized theory of personality and psychopathology (i.e., its theory of problem causation), and its highly formalized, rigid method of therapy (i.e., its theory of and approach to problem resolution). Indeed, most post-Freudian therapy movements—most notably, humanistic, gestalt, cognitive, interpersonal, and systemic therapies—have emerged in either implicit or explicit reaction to that problem.

Because this problem has been a defining focus of many therapy movements, it will also serve as an organizing theme of *Back to Reality* and the arguments I advance here. I therefore intend to show just how the postmodern narrative therapy movement is yet another response to that intractable problem—even though, like some other therapies that preceded it, it does not explicitly define itself in that way. Still, it is a response that must be evaluated in light of that pervasive problem.

Returning now to the assertion that the postmodern narrative therapy movement is in fact a response to the problem of keeping therapy individualized and yet systematic, we are immediately confronted with a difficulty, or rather a contradiction. On the one hand, the postmodern narrative therapy movement attempts to maximize individuality in therapy in the context of its adoption of postmodern theory; on the other hand, postmodern theory has for the most part rejected any traditional understanding of the existence of the individual (Rosenau, 1992). Let us therefore first turn our attention to that problem.

In postmodern theory, there is much talk about the "death of the subject," that is, of the one who experiences the world or object. Hence, there is talk about the "death" of the individual and her identity, as well (for a complete account, see Best & Kellner, 1991; Kvale, 1992a; Rosenau, 1992). Although there is some disagreement within the postmodern movement about the lengths to which this view should be taken, there is also some consensus that in the postmodern world we must relinquish our claim to any unique, coherent, consistent self/identity. Rather, the modern notion of the individual/self with a consistent identity is replaced by the concept of a postmodern, "decentered subject." This means that the individual in particular and humanity in general can no longer conceive of itself as existing at the center of the world. Instead, the postmodern subject becomes—by way of some variant of the text/event equation—"part of the text of the world" (Kvale, 1992b, pp. 14–15; Løvlie, 1992, pp. 124, 132). Thus, whatever self or identity exists is constituted solely in language by means of the ever-shifting interpersonal (linguistic) interactions that define social roles in language (Gergen, 1991a, 1992; Kvale, 1992b, 1992c; Løvlie, 1992, p. 125). Rosenau puts it as clearly as any when she states, "Subjects are actually 'contingent effects' of language . . . in a particular historical context" (1992, p. 47).

This view demands that the subject/self/individual be conceived, if at all, as fragmented, ephemeral, inconsistent, fluid, fluctuating—in short, devoid of any "single form or personality" (Rosenau, 1992, p. 57).[12] For example, the person characterized (i.e., perceived) as dominant in one interpersonal/ linguistic context is suddenly characterized as submissive in a different context. Neither characterization, however, gives us the person as he or she truly *is*, a notion that this view in any event dismisses. At best, what we have is a "nonreality" created by the observer doing the observing or characterizing in a particular context. Moreover, with few exceptions,[13] this "selfless," or "nonself," condition is seen as positive, that is, as a good thing toward which we should all strive (e.g., Gergen, 1991a; Gergen & Kaye, 1992).

But this postmodern demise of the traditional subject/individual poses a problem for my thesis. How can the use of postmodern theory in psychotherapy be an attempt to solve the problem of preserving the unique individuality of each therapy client if that same theory rejects the very concept of the individual? The answer lies in what I perceive to be two incompatible positions within postmodern theory. On the one hand, there is no longer a coherent individual, or unique self, that differentiates one individual from the next in any consistent way. But on the other hand, there is a clear exaltation of the "local and specific," that is, of "contextually bound knowledge" (Chaiklin, 1992, pp. 198, 203; Polkinghorne, 1992, p. 149) that defies the formation of universal truths, or general laws, including a consistent, true or lawful self, as we saw in the illustration just provided.

This second position would not necessarily be problematic for postmodernism's "death of the subject," except for the fact that the terms "local," "specific," "particular" and so forth often get translated to mean the *individual's* unique perspective, or experience, at a particular time and place (i.e., a contextualized, individuated perspective). So, on the one hand postmodern theory eliminates the individual; but on the other hand it exalts individuality in its attempts to avoid universal truths, laws, and generalities. As Rosenau (1992, p. 53) aptly puts it, "The invention of the [fragmented] post-modern individual provides a means for post-modernists to abandon the [modern] subject while retaining an individualist perspective." Best and Kellner (1991, p. 284) seem to be saying something similar when they state, "A contradiction of some postmodern theory is that while theoretically it dispenses with the individual, it simultaneously resurrects it in a post-liberal form, as an aestheticized, desiring monad." Rosenau believes ambivalence is the explanation for this contradictory stance: "There is a certain ambivalence about eliminating the subject in post-modern social sciences. . . . [an ambivalence that has resulted not in] readopting the subject so much as repositioning [i.e., redefining] it" (1992, p. 52). More specifically, she discusses the postmodern concept of "habitus" to reinforce this view:

> Habitus, a summary term, refers to the cumulative, durable totality of cultural and personal experiences that each human being carries around as a result of life experiences (speech, mannerism, style of dress, table etiquette, posture, body shape). All these are found to have an impact on how one is perceived, on the patterns of interaction involving others, and on the formation of the parameters that govern social outcomes. Habitus, a subject-specific concept, cannot be structuralized or aggregated: *it is unique to each individual; it requires a specific, noncollective subject.* [italics added] (Rosenau, 1992, p. 59)

This concept, which certainly implies consistency at the level of the individual, is self-contradictory in the context of a theory that rejects any concept of an enduring, consistent, individual self.

In the discipline of psychotherapy, the importation of such postmodern ideas has meant that each therapy client must be viewed as a unique individual, with his own unique history or set of experiences (i.e., "habitus"). Therefore, predetermined categories such as diagnoses (e.g., depression), categories that have traditionally played a role in selecting the proper intervention, can no longer apply to the therapeutic enterprise (see Anderson & Goolishian, 1988, and other references from the narrative therapy movement). Hence, with the blessing of postmodernism's emphasis on that which is local, unique, and specific, each therapy case starts anew, with as few prior, or predetermined, conceptions or generalizations—and so with as much attention to the unique nuance of each particular case—as a systematic, rule-governed enterprise will tolerate.

This approach to therapy, then, ensures that the unique individuality of each client will not in any way be compromised. I do not, therefore, believe it is mere coincidence that the postmodern agenda translates into an emphasis on individuality in therapy: indeed, it is my primary assertion that what attracted many therapists to postmodern theory in the first place was their frustration with therapies whose general, predetermined explanatory concepts (e.g., oedipal struggles in psychoanalysis) diminished individuality. It is therefore my claim, for which I provide evidence in Chapters 3, 4, 5, and 7, that the postmodern, or linguistic, turn in therapy is a response to the seemingly intractable problem of achieving a theoretical system of therapy that generates a practice that is individualized and yet systematic, rule-governed, or replicable.

That postmodern theorists, when discussing therapy, emphasize the individuality of the client can be demonstrated simply enough by quoting them. Polkinghorne (1992), for instance, in a chapter titled "Postmodern Epistemology of Practice," states, "In making clinical judgments in their work with clients, they [practitioners] evince a postmodern belief in individual differences and the need for *particularized* [italics added] understanding" (p. 155). And in applying the postmodern assumption of "fragmentariness" to therapy he goes on to say:

> Psychological practice [in contrast to academic psychology] emphasizes the uniqueness of each client. Because the meaning clients experience is a function of their interpretive schemes . . . , and because these schemes are developed in the context of their cultural environments and *personal* [italics added] histories, therapists' knowledge of clients is attuned to the particular and diverse. (p. 159)

Speaking more generally, Best and Kellner (1991) describe the postmodern emphasis on individuality by stating, "With their emphasis on the individual and singularity, many postmodernists reject collective struggle and large-scale social transformation" (p. 222). Best and Kellner also call attention to the postmodern desire "to preserve particularity and to engage in microanalysis" (p. 227). But what is important here is that when they emphasize individuality, postmodern theorists/therapists cannot avoid reinstating the subject/individual—however fragmented, nonunitary, linguistically constituted, and contextualized that postmodern subject is considered to be (cf. Best & Kellner, 1991, p. 284; Rosenau, 1992, pp. 53–56).

I suppose I could "dodge" the whole problem of emphasizing individuality in therapy in the context of a postmodern outlook by substituting, as I have already done, the term "individualized" for the term "individuality." That maneuver might appear to take the emphasis off the client's enduring (ontological) status as an individual, and instead put it squarely on the process of tailoring, that is, *individualizing*, therapy to whatever particularities the therapist finds in each momentary encounter. But that would indeed be a dodge, because the latter still presumes an actual *individual* to whom the actual therapy must be tailored. Put differently, something that is individualized must be individualized in reference to some existing individual. There is, it seems, no way around the need to take seriously the notion of the individual, at least when one does or speaks about psychotherapy.

When I argue that the postmodern narrative therapy movement seeks to preserve uniqueness or individuality, I therefore do *not* mean the preservation of a fragmented, decentered subject/individual in any postmodern sense. Rather, I speak to the uniqueness, meaning the nongeneralizability or non-universality, of each individual's life situation as it is discussed in therapy. And that uniqueness certainly extends to individuals who might share some common attribute considered particularly relevant to the therapeutic endeavor, such as clinical diagnosis. For instance, no two "schizophrenics" are alike, at least not for *all* problem resolution—therapeutic intervention—purposes. Thus, speaking from what some might consider a modernist framework, I certainly agree with such theorists as Rosenau (1992, pp. 54–55), Glass (1993, pp. 12, 14, 25–27), and Sass (1992, pp. 174–175), who are critical of the idealization of such postmodern qualities as "decentered," "fragmented," "incoherent," "relativized," "floating," when they are applied to the self/individual (cf. Gergen, 1991a). In my opinion, this is certainly no ideal of mental health—itself a seemingly global, modern construct—to which any serious practicing clinician, *modern or postmodern*, would in all good conscience subscribe.

Throughout this book I use the term "individuality" interchangeably with "uniqueness" and so employ either or both terms, depending on the emphasis I intend. I believe that the individual's expression of his uniqueness or individuality in therapy reflects something enduring to his self/identity as it really exists; indeed, in my view that uniqueness is precisely what constitutes the individual's true self. Let us call this the traditional, ontological view of individuality. As a practicing clinician myself, I aim at attaining a therapeutic practice that is both individualized (in this traditional sense) and systematic/ replicable. Achieving those twin goals is difficult, for they indeed are in conflict, as I have already stated. Nonetheless, I hope to show in the course of this book that if we make clear, explicit distinctions among the component parts common to all theoretical systems of therapy, we can reach a reasonable compromise or balance in achieving those two goals.

Since my view of individuality is just the one that postmodernists reject, the reader might suppose that I would be totally dismissive of narrative therapy, which has adopted postmodern theory as its guide. Still, a consistent theme of this book is that the adoption by narrative therapists of a pervasive postmodern antirealism constitutes nothing less than a serious, albeit self-contradictory, attempt to preserve in therapy the very individuality (in the traditional, ontological sense of that term) that the adopted postmodern theory denies. That attempt is grounded on the problematic assumption of narrative therapists that the client's own, unique views of her unique life experiences are necessarily antirealist (or subjective). I return to that problematic assumption in Chapter 3. But just here, in noting the narrative therapy movement's real attempt to preserve real individuality in therapy by appealing to antirealism, we catch a glimpse of the problematic oscillation between realism and antirealism that I focus upon in my critique of the postmodern narrative therapy movement. I develop that critique fully in Chapter 5.

A COMPARATIVE (REALIST)
CONTEXT FOR THE NARRATIVE
THERAPY MOVEMENT

Postmodern narrative therapy is not the first therapy movement to concern itself with the preservation of each client's uniqueness or individuality. Indeed, every therapy movement, from psychoanalysis through client-centered humanism and behaviorism, has wrestled with ways to tailor its general theoretical formulations about problem causation, as well as its theories and methods[14] of problem resolution, to the unique nuances of each clinical case. Still, those generalities were always assumed to be realist, or objective—that is, to reflect some independent, extratheoretic reality. As Polkinghorne (1992, p. 155) states, "Freud and Jung wrote as if they were providing descriptions that *accurately* reflected the actual inner workings of the psyche; Rogers, as if he were describing the *actual* operations of a substantial self; and Skinner, as if the mechanisms of learning he presented were precise descriptions of *real* human dynamics" [all italics added]. It therefore seems that postmodern narrative therapy is the first to argue explicitly for the elimination of *all* general categories of problems (e.g., diagnoses) embedded within general laws of problem causation and problem resolution. These categories and laws are themselves denounced by postmodern therapists as misleading, misguided, and irrelevant to the therapeutic process precisely because of their generality and because they lay claim to objectivity, which postmodern therapists take to be unattainable.

Thus, the postmodern narrative therapy movement is the first to take a strong antirealist position about what we can objectively know about any domain, including the domain of therapy. As I noted above, even the humanistic therapy movement advanced by Rogers, a movement which emphasizes the unique, subjective (or phenomenal) perspective of each individual therapy client, nonetheless propounds perfectly general laws of problem causation and problem resolution, laws that are, moreover, taken to be fully realist. For example, that movement makes reality claims about how the failure to symbolize and integrate experience in awareness damages the self-concept and thus leads to a host of problems (Rogers, 1961). So, too, the gestalt and existential therapy movements concern themselves with the ill effects of the failure to integrate diverse aspects of emotional experience, or the failure to find meaning in life, respectively. These failures are posited by each theoretical system as nothing less than the real or true (general) cause of all problems defined within that system.

But there is at present another broad therapy movement that has, like the postmodern narrative movement, striven explicitly to attain theoretical conceptualizations of therapy (and methods based on those conceptualizations) that enhance the likelihood of a flexible and therefore individuated practice. That other movement has, therefore, also sought to solve the problem of attaining an individualized yet systematic approach to the practice of therapy. As I mentioned earlier, that movement is the integrative/eclectic (hereafter, eclectic) therapy movement. It is important to consider that movement's efforts, because they have assumed a very different shape from those of the narrative therapy movement. The eclectic therapy movement—with both its successes and failures in its 25 (or so) year quest—therefore provides an historical context in which to understand the emergence and struggles of the narrative therapy movement. It also provides a point of comparison by which to consider the three fundamental distinctions that I have related to psychotherapy theory: the realism/antirealism distinction, the modern/ postmodern distinction, and the science/humanities distinction.

The narrative and eclectic therapy movements find themselves in perfect agreement on the point that no one theoretical system of therapy can adequately or properly fit all clients and all therapists. But in their pursuits of a more individualized approach to the practice of therapy, their respective responses to that belief have taken opposing forms. The narrative movement rejects the use, or "imposition," in practice of all general theories—for instance, generally applied theories of problem causation, such as how irrational thinking can cause depression in many or all people. The narrative movement rejects all such generalities because they are alleged to contain no independent truth, and so their use only serves to hamper the individualization of therapy practice. The eclectic therapy movement, by contrast, embraces many such general theories (and the methods derived from them—see Note 14), since it believes that each formulation, to the extent that it has shown itself to have some scientific standing or validity, has enough truth or reality in it to merit its use. For eclectics, then, the problem is to determine which generality or formulation to apply to which type of client, to achieve (in reality) the most beneficial outcome possible. Because of their opposing stances on the potential truth status of therapeutic generalities, then, the eclectic and narrative therapy movements occupy opposite sides of a realist/antirealist dichotomy.

To be more precise, many members of the eclectic therapy movement (e.g., Beutler, 1991) advocate the flexible selection of variables from client, therapist, and treatment categories, a process that permits the systematic, rule-governed yet individualized approach to therapy practice that they seek. Thus, in what is called the "matrix paradigm," which I discuss in Chapter 2, clients are assigned to general, predetermined[15] categories such as diagnosis or coping style. These categories allegedly reflect the real or true state of the client as it pertains to his or her problem, and so they help to determine the best type of treatment for a client. For example, if a client is diagnosed as phobic, then, according to the available treatment research, systematic desensitization, but not psychoanalysis, would be indicated. Moreover, there is usually some (theoretical) speculation about the possible reasons for that type of finding (although that is a point of contention within the eclectic movement).

Thus, the eclectic movement adopts a traditional scientific methodology: it seeks, through systematic, empirical means, the attainment of general, objective rules, or lawful relationships between predetermined variables, and it usually attempts to provide some rational, explanatory principles for its findings. It is therefore not coincidental that the eclectic movement takes for granted the realist doctrine, found among most scientists (e.g., J. Polkinghorne, 1989), that the knower can, in some instances, attain or at least approximate knowledge of an objective reality—that is, one which is independent of the knower's own constructing, languaging, theorizing (and so forth) processes (Held, 1990, 1991b, 1992, in press; Held & Pols, 1985a, 1985b; Pols, 1992a). Recall from our earlier discussion that the narrative therapy movement promotes an antirealism derived from its importation, from the humanistic disciplines, of certain postmodern (linguistic) philosophies and literary theories. Since the eclectic therapy movement adopts a traditional scientific realism, the eclectic and narrative therapy movements also occupy opposite sides of a science/humanities dichotomy.

Having seen that these two therapy movements can be classified by realist/ antirealist and science/humanities dichotomies in their efforts to preserve individuality in therapy, we are now in a position to understand how they can also be characterized by virtue of the modern/postmodern distinction we have just considered. Because it accepts the idea of progress by way of general, objective laws and truths achieved through science and rationality, and because it endorses the realist assertion of the determinacy of meaning in any text or event, the eclectic therapy movement may be said to exemplify a modern outlook. In contrast, the narrative therapy movement, because it rejects that idea of scientific progress and of general, objective laws and truths in favor of local, contextualized, subjective "truths," and because it endorses the antirealist assertion of the indeterminacy of meaning in any text or event, may be said to exemplify a postmodern outlook.

The eclectic therapy movement, then, by endorsing a modern scientific realism, provides a perfect example against which we may evaluate the narrative therapy movement's endorsement of a postmodern humanistic antirealism. What makes that comparison particularly useful, however, is not simply that the two movements constitute opposites, or that one, eclecticism, precedes the other in time, thereby supplying an historical context in which to situate the emergence of postmodern narrative therapy. Rather, the value of the comparison lies in the fact that both movements, in their different ways, are addressing the same problem that, as I claim, motivated their emergence—keeping the practice of therapy both individualized and systematic. As I demonstrate in Chapters 2, 3, and 4, the reader should be prepared to find that whereas one movement, narrative therapy, is in some (but not all) ways more successful in achieving an individualized therapy practice, the other, eclectic therapy, is more successful in achieving a systematic practice. The fact that these two movements have produced solutions that favor opposed sides of that problem suggests that a detailed comparison of them is necessary for a full understanding of the problem itself and of the implications of the various "solutions," modern or postmodern.

My own agenda, however, goes well beyond a mere exercise in comparing and contrasting. As I hinted at the outset, I hope to persuade the reader that at least some of my conclusions about the proper use of postmodern narrative therapy ideas are correct or true—and not in the postmodern sense of the term "truth." To accomplish that task, I provide, in my critical assessment of the postmodern narrative therapy movement, a philosophical basis for my claim that that movement, despite its self-proclaimed antirealism, is in reality at least *implicitly* adopting a modest realism, one which makes certain limited truth, or reality, claims. These claims, moreover, *transcend* the particularities of any one individual, situation, moment, or context. Thus, the claims are in no sense postmodern—that is, they are not merely local, contextualized, subjective "truths"/nonrealities. By using theoretical, philosophical, and logical (i.e., critical) analyses of the postmodern narrative therapy movement's own assertions about theory and practice, and by providing clinical illustrations of the practical implications of that movement's theory, I demonstrate how that movement undermines, or contradicts, its own self-proclaimed antirealism. Ironically, that self-contradiction is in some sense a good thing if that movement wants, as I think it does, to tell us something real or true about how therapy should and, moreover, *does* work.

AN OVERVIEW OF THE BOOK

In this chapter I have provided an introduction to the problem that I believe prompted the emergence of the postmodern narrative therapy movement. I have organized subsequent chapters in a way that, if successful, will lead the reader on a straight and secure path to my ultimate conclusions about the need for a modest realism in any theory of therapy that hopes to be taken seriously in its attempts to alleviate human pain and suffering. Of course, there are particular points along the path that require special attention if we are to achieve a full appreciation of its many twists and turns. In this final section of this introductory chapter, I therefore provide the reader with a glimpse of what is to come, so that he or she may anticipate the course that lies ahead.

In Chapter 2 I examine how the eclectic therapy movement has attempted, by adopting a modern scientific realism, to solve the problem of developing an approach to therapy practice that is both individualized and systematic. I concentrate on what has come to be known as "systematic" or "technical" eclecticism, and on the "matrix paradigm" that has come to define that type of eclecticism. (I also consider other eclectic formulations, such as "integrative eclecticism" and "pluralism.") In Chapter 2 I therefore assess the particular obstacles the matrix paradigm has faced in attempting to solve the problem of achieving an individualized yet systematic approach to therapy. In considering why the matrix paradigm has not solved the problem to the satisfaction of many therapists, including those who defend that paradigm in particular and the eclectic movement in general, Chapter 2 sets the stage for the emergence of an alternative solution, namely, that of the narrative therapy movement.

In Chapter 3 I set forth a generic model of therapy systems with three component parts: theories of problem causation (Component A), theories (with attendant methods) of problem resolution (Component B), and categories, or types, of clients or problems (Component C). I also consider the realism/antirealism distinction as it pertains to those three component parts. The primary purpose of this chapter is to show that the goal of keeping the practice of therapy individualized cannot be achieved by an appeal to the doctrine of antirealism, as postmodern narrative therapists seem to suppose. Rather, it can be achieved by a clearer understanding of (a) the nature and use of theoretical systems that guide the practice of therapy, in particular, whether or not they provide *all* three of the component parts listed above; and of (b) how the completeness of theoretical systems that guide practice determines the degree to which practice is rule-governed, or constrained, and therefore consistent or replicable (i.e., systematic) across cases. I demonstrate, by way of quotation, the equation, found within the postmodern narrative movement, between the client's presumed uniqueness and the doctrine of antirealism; I then explain why the postmodern narrative inclination to equate the client's unique, personal views of her life experiences with antirealism is a faulty premise. In fact, it is precisely that faulty premise that calls into question the attempt on the part of postmodern narrative therapists to keep their practice individualized by proclaiming the virtues of antirealism.

Chapter 4 provides a detailed overview of the narrative therapy movement. It constitutes my description of that movement's adoption of a postmodern humanistic, antirealist philosophy and literary theory, to solve the problem of formulating an approach to therapy that is both individualized and systematic. It is here, therefore, that I examine the current use of postmodern theory and philosophy as a theoretical foundation and a method for psychotherapy. I begin by quoting statements made by members of the postmodern narrative therapy movement. These statements reveal their commitment to the doctrine of antirealism in the act of knowing and thus their commitment to the view that therapy is nothing more than a linguistic, narrative, or storied enterprise—that is, one with no (knowable) independent, or extralinguistic, reality. I then distinguish two antirealist doctrines used widely by members of the narrative therapy movement, namely, constructivism (in which knowledge is relative to each knower), and social constructionism (in which knowledge is relative to each social/cultural/linguistic group of knowers). The theoretical system propounded by postmodern narrative therapists is set forth along the lines of the three component parts of my generic model of all therapy systems, which I describe in Chapter 3. To explain the literary aspects of the narrative therapy movement, I examine, with case examples, that movement's adoption of the client-as-text analogy. I then demonstrate how that analogy has paved the way for the recent use of (literary) deconstruction as a therapeutic method. The chapter concludes with a discussion of how the narrative therapy movement's insistence on viewing therapy as a postmodern literary enterprise is related to the problem of attaining an individualized yet systematic practice, and why that insistence also raises some serious ethical concerns.

In Chapter 5 I expose the hidden realism within the postmodern narrative therapy movement. I do so by revealing how, in its actual assertions about problem causation, problem resolution, and the nature of problems themselves, that movement oscillates between the realism it rejects and the antirealism it promotes. Chapter 5 therefore constitutes the critical core of the book. That criticism extends to the modest, or limited, realism inherent in the narrative movement's views about truth itself. In particular, I show how the pragmatic and antirealist philosophy that informs the postmodern narrative therapy movement—a philosophy that states that the only legitimate concern is the utility of a therapeutic intervention/formulation, and not its truth status—actually contains an unwitting but undeniable modest (or limited) realism within it. That modest realism is found in a clear equation between utility and truth. The equation between utility and truth is one that the narrative therapy movement overlooks but that nonetheless undermines, or contradicts, the narrative movement's own professed antirealism. Similarly, the hidden, modest realism behind the narrative therapy movement's adoption of a coherence theory of truth is exposed, again revealing that movement's oscillation between realism and antirealism. Given those oscillations/inconsistencies or—put more positively—signs of struggle in the narrative movement's fundamental philosophy, Chapter 5 concludes with a call for a more precise and consistent (i.e., an alternative) philosophy of knowing within narrative therapy, if it is to achieve internal coherence and its pragmatic goals.

In Chapter 6 I offer just such an alternative philosophy of knowing in the form of Pols's (1992a) concept of direct knowing. Here I review Pols's explanation of the current, pervasive confusion between the two functions of rationality defined by him—namely, direct rational awareness of an independent (of the knower) world, and a formative or constructive function that constitutes or constructs linguistic propositions (e.g., theories and narratives) and other artifacts (e.g., paintings and houses). Pols argues that this confusion has caused many philosophers, and now social scientists, including therapists, to believe erroneously that all knowing is based on the formative function of rationality. According to Pols, this belief has resulted in and explains the pervasive antirealism we have been observing in many postmodern humanities and now see in postmodern psychotherapy as well. I demonstrate how Pols's system—which permits (a) direct rational awareness or knowledge of some aspects of an independent reality, including, especially, constructed theories and narratives, and which also permits (b) indirect (or theory-mediated) knowledge of other aspects of an independent reality—provides a viable solution to the self-contradictory, oscillating antirealism found in the narrative therapy movement.

In Chapter 7 I offer my own solutions to the problem of keeping therapy both individualized and systematic, the problem which, I claim, has led to the use of postmodern theory in psychotherapy. These solutions take the form of my proposal of three modestly realist therapy systems. It is important to note that the three systems draw upon the contributions of the narrative and the eclectic therapy movements, and so retain both humanistic and scientific perspectives and properties. Each system has, in addition, a built-in program for empirical research. But most noteworthy is the fact that each proposed system retains an explicit modest/limited realism in its underlying philosophy/theory and in its practical manifestations. Therefore, none of the systems can, in its fundamental conceptualization, be considered postmodern in any sense of that term.

Chapter 8 is the most clinical or practice-oriented chapter of the book. It explores in some detail the clinical or practical, including ethical, implications of postmodern antirealist theories of therapy. In this exploration I do not merely discuss how such theories are now being used in therapy, but go on to question how they should and should not be used in the practice of therapy. In posing those questions, this chapter takes a decidedly ethical turn. In it I ask questions about what constitutes truth vs. lies, what constitutes help vs. harm, and what constitutes therapist expertise in antirealist views of therapy. These are questions that have received surprisingly little scrutiny, given the popularity of the postmodern, antirealist movement within psychotherapy. In this chapter I also take a new look at an old question: Should therapy be viewed as an art, and, if so, should a traditional or postmodern use of humanities prevail? Or should it be viewed as an applied science, and, if so, what model of science is appropriate for the therapeutic enterprise? I conclude with a final attempt to counteract the postmodern trends toward relativism and antirealism that now pervade psychotherapy, by calling for a modest realism in all psychotherapy theory and practice.

CHAPTER 2

The Eclectic Therapy Movement:
A Modern Scientific Realism

There can be no doubt that the eclectic therapy movement arose precisely because no one school or system of psychotherapy could accommodate the great variety of clients, problems, and therapists (Beutler, 1983; Garfield, 1980; Goldfried, 1982; Norcross, 1986; Prochaska & DiClemente, 1984). The eclectic therapy movement therefore sought to make good use of an expanding, scientific knowledge base about human problems and their solutions, without imposing on clients the theory and methods of any one school or system of psychotherapy. Of course, adherents of all psychotherapies try to avoid dogmatic practice by tailoring their systems to the unique aspects of each client. But because the eclectic movement does not confine itself to the views of any one school or system of therapy, greater possibilities for an individualized practice are open to its members.

Although historical accounts of eclecticism trace its origins to the 1930s, many agree that it did not begin to crystallize as a movement in its own right until the 1960s; in any event, it had a substantial presence by the 1970s (Goldfried & Newman, 1986). Before turning to the evolution of the distinct types within the eclectic therapy movement, let us first review a general definition of the movement and some reasons for its popularity. Norcross (1986) tells us in his editorial introduction to the *Handbook of Eclectic Psychotherapy* that "the term *eclectic* had been employed indiscriminately and inconsistently. A vague and nebulous term, its connotations range from 'a worn-out synonym for theoretical laziness' to the 'only means to a comprehensive psychotherapy' (Smith, 1982)" (Norcross, 1986, p. 5). Although Norcross admits that "there is some debate about whether eclecticism constitutes another theoretical orientation or simply the absence of one" (p. 5), he nonetheless claims that "what binds most eclectics together is a stated dislike for a single orientation, selection from two or more theories, and the belief that no present theory is adequate to explain or predict all . . . behavior (Garfield & Kurtz, 1977)" (p. 5). He then suggests that the most accurate definition of the term "eclecticism" is the one supplied by *Webster's Collegiate Dictionary*, namely, the "'method or practice of selecting what seems best from various systems'" (p. 5).

Why has a therapy movement that rejects allegiance to one school or system of therapy achieved such popularity now? In a survey conducted in the 1970s, Garfield and Kurtz (1977) reported that a large percentage of therapists considered themselves to be eclectics, despite what Norcross (1986) calls the pejorative connotation of that much-debated term. According to Norcross, at least as of 1986 that trend continued, for surveys at that time suggested that "one-third to one-half of present-day clinicians disavow any affiliation with a particular therapeutic school, preferring instead the label of 'eclectic'" (1986, p. 12). The arrival in the early 1980s and early 1990s of such journals as the *Journal of Integrative and Eclectic Psychotherapy* and the *Journal of Psychotherapy Integration*, respectively, gives further evidence of the health of that movement. Although it preceded the narrative therapy movement in time, it remains alive and well during a period when the narrative movement flourishes.

But what motivated the production of a movement as strong and sustained as the eclectic one? Norcross (1986) provides a succinct list of reasons most commentators agree with. According to him, "at least six interacting . . . factors have fostered the development of eclecticism in the past decade: 1. Proliferation of therapies, 2. Inadequacies of any one specific therapy, 3. Absence of differential effectiveness among therapies, 4. Growing recognition that patient characteristics and the helping relationship are the most efficacious components of successful treatment, 5. Resultant search for common components of effective treatment, [and] 6. External sociopolitical contingencies" (pp. 13–14).

Omer and London (1988) echoed these reasons for both (a) what they called the "end of the systems era"[1] — or the end of the reign of the separate, distinct schools of psychotherapy (such as psychoanalytic and behavioral), which exceeded a whopping 400 by one count (Karasu, 1986), and (b) the resulting move toward eclecticism, among other trends. According to Omer and London (1988), these reasons included the proliferation of new treatment techniques; equal effectiveness of all therapies according to comparative outcome studies; and the criticism of distinct schools from those who worked *within* the confines of the system they were criticizing, that is, the existence of widespread dissatisfaction with existing systems of therapy.

Moreover, the "end of the systems era" was hastened by the recognition that different systems of therapy shared common or nonspecific change factors. These common factors are the mechanisms responsible for therapeutic change that are thought to apply to all therapies, for instance, creating in the client an expectancy that change will and can occur (Strenger & Omer, 1992). In short, customers (in this case, practitioners) of therapy systems were dissatisfied with what the system they had "bought" could do for their diverse client loads. And when customers are dissatisfied, they shop around, making "intersystems dialogue" (Omer & London, 1988) inevitable.

THE EVOLUTION OF DISTINCT TYPES OF ECLECTICISM

As soon as the eclectic movement emerged as a distinct therapy movement, a major split appeared within its ranks. That split reflected disagreement about how to consider the role that theory should play within an eclectic therapy movement. More specifically, the disagreement centered around the question of whether an eclectic approach to therapy necessitated the use of some guiding "umbrella" theory—a theory that contained claims about what causes problems, pain, or psychopathology (i.e., problem causation) and about what causes the resolution or alleviation of problems, pain, or psychopathology (i.e., problem resolution). Such a theory could, of course, be used in each therapy case to guide the therapist in selecting methods or techniques from different therapy systems. Just how the term "theory" has been and should be used within the eclectic therapy movement continues to be a source of controversy and, in my opinion, much confusion. I therefore take up that question a little later. Just now I want to make the less debatable point that the question of the proper role of theory in therapy has spawned at least three different forms of eclecticism, namely, pluralism, theoretical integration, and technical/systematic eclecticism.[2] The emergence of these distinct types of eclecticism is also related to the problem of achieving a therapy practice that is both individualized and systematic. Let us therefore consider each of them in succession.

Pluralism

The pluralist argument is perhaps easiest to understand. Briefly, it consists in the conviction that many of the different schools or systems of psychotherapy have some validity or success—a belief certainly supported by therapy outcome research. Therefore, different schools should be permitted to coexist peacefully, side by side. This solution permits different therapists to decide what school or system of therapy fits them best. According to the pluralist position, then, each therapist must adopt the system of therapy she finds most satisfactory, both in terms of her own intellectual and personality characteristics, and in terms of her own personal experiences with client outcomes in therapy. Moreover, the writings about the few factors, common to all therapies, that are believed to enhance therapeutic change typically focus on this common view: that a therapist must have faith in the validity of his adopted therapy system and must then transmit that faith to his client in the form of hope, if his use of that system is to work its therapeutic or beneficial effects (cf. Cornsweet, 1983; Frank, 1973, 1987; Grencavage & Norcross, 1990; O'Connell, 1983; Omer & London, 1988, 1989; Omer & Strenger, 1992; Parloff, 1986a, 1986b; Strupp, 1973, 1986).

Given the fact that no one system of psychotherapy has yet to be judged most successful in alleviating problems in the accumulated therapy outcome research (e.g., Beutler, 1991; Luborsky, Singer, & Luborsky, 1975; Smith & Glass, 1977; Stiles, Shapiro, & Elliott, 1986), the pluralist position makes good sense. The now famous "Dodo Bird verdict," which Luborsky et al. (1975) appropriated from *Alice's Adventures in Wonderland*, namely, "*Everybody* has won, and all must have prizes," suggests that we should think twice before tampering with any of our theoretical systems in some spirit of integration. Thus, the first thing to notice about the pluralist position is that it is not an integrative one: it does not seek to take the "best" of each system of therapy in some grand effort to build a superior, more encompassing, unified "metatheory"—one that will be beneficial to all therapists and clients under all circumstances (see Omer, 1994). But that creates a problem: how does the therapist who, even in a pluralist spirit, adopts the one system of therapy that works best for her deal with the obvious fact that no one system is optimal for all therapists and for every type of problem or client? After all, every clinician has confronted at least one client who simply does not benefit from what she has to offer (cf. Lambert, 1989).

Omer and Strenger (1992), who have themselves adopted aspects of the narrative therapy view, suggest one solution to that problem when they state,

"Although the therapist's belief in his or her orientation is crucial, the pluralist position states that no metanarrative is or can be uniquely true, and none deserves absolute credence" [original is italicized] (pp. 259–260). Although they go on in this article to say they are not advocating relativism,[3] Omer and Strenger nonetheless imply that pluralist therapists must become relativists, or in some sense antirealists, by acknowledging that each "account is as right as possible from the *particular perspective* [italics added] through which the events are being viewed, but that other perspectives are possible as well" (p. 260).

In later chapters we shall encounter Omer and Strenger's contradictory suggestion again, but in the context of their own prescription for a flexible yet systematic pluralist practice. For now, it should be noted that it is not clear whether the problem of truth raised by the pluralist position requires a realist or an antirealist solution: in the realist case each therapist would believe—erroneously, of course—that her preferred system is the best, most accurate one; in the antirealist case each therapist would acknowledge her preferred system to be nothing more than that—a personal preference on her part. But in any case, the one certainty about the pluralist position as I have defined it is its answer to the problem of keeping the practice of therapy individualized and yet systematic. At the least, individuality is preserved by the mere existence of numerous systems of therapy, since this diversity of options ensures that the client, assuming he is educated in such matters, can pick and choose as he sees fit. Once the client has selected a particular type of therapy/therapist, however, the therapist must work within the constraints prescribed by her own self-selected system. At best, then, the therapist can do little more than try to tailor her therapeutic system to the particularities of any therapy case. For instance, a cognitive therapist can let the client determine the *particular* irrational beliefs/thoughts that are to be the object of discussion and change. But the same therapist would certainly not seriously consider using the transference relationship to make conscious any possible oedipal conflicts, as would a traditional (i.e., Freudian) psychoanalytic therapist. Note, then, that in the pluralist view described here the process of individualization does not occur at the level of each individual therapist, since each therapist applies the same system of therapy to all her clients. Thus, pluralism stands in stark contrast to those other eclectic approaches which individualize therapy by directing therapists to select different interventions from different therapy systems as a function of each particular client's particular problem situation.

Let us now turn our attention to the problem of how a pluralist effort can ensure a systematic approach to the practice of therapy. Put briefly, the pluralist attitude promotes systematic practice, since each distinct school of therapy retains its own theory, or systematic framework, including its own rules for clinical application. The interventions made by a particular therapist are therefore prescribed by that therapist's self-selected school or theoretical system of therapy. And, as I go on to demonstrate in Chapter 3, most systems of therapy contain some form of theory about problem causation and about problem resolution to guide practice in a systematic, or rule-governed, and therefore consistent, or replicable, way. Although therapists working within the constraints of different theoretical systems may practice quite differently from each other, those who work within one system should function in a relatively more similar way. But all therapists who are guided in practice by a theoretical system of some sort should produce a practice that is, to some extent, systematic. Both the individualization and systematization of practice, then, are ensured by the very existence and use of diverse systems of therapy. Still, given that diversity, the problem of the truth of the one system of therapy any particular therapist adopts remains unsolved from a pluralist position, and this has consequences for a therapist's faith in that system. I return to that problem in the last two chapters of this book.

Theoretical Integration (Synthetic Eclecticism)

Theoretical integration, or synthetic eclecticism, does precisely what pluralism does not: it attempts to capture the essence of the different therapy systems in an overarching umbrella theory, or what in the discipline is sometimes called a metatheory[4] — one that exists at a higher level of abstraction and so, in principle, can accommodate all varieties of clients, problems, and therapists. Unlike atheoretical and technical forms of eclecticism, integration attempts to achieve a unified conceptual or theoretical framework that synthesizes the many disparate theories of problem causation and problem resolution that are found in the various systems of therapy.[5] But, unlike the distinct systems from which it is synthesized, the metatheory is alleged to be broad and flexible enough to permit a highly individualized approach to therapy.

One of the best examples of an integrative metatheory, in my opinion, is Prochaska and DiClemente's (1982, 1984, 1986, 1992) "Transtheoretical Therapy." Prochaska and DiClemente drew the distinction between theories of problem causation and theories of problem resolution more explicitly than most psychotherapists. This allowed them to isolate and study the problem resolution components of 24 leading systems of psychotherapy (Prochaska, 1984), in an attempt to distill the most fundamental processes or methods of change, or problem resolution. Like Goldfried (1980), Prochaska and DiClemente said the concept of "process" represents a "middle level of abstraction between a complete theory or system of psychotherapy and the techniques proposed by the theory" (Prochaska & DiClemente, 1984, p. 33). They originally delineated five, and later ten, change processes: consciousness raising, self-reevaluation, self-liberation (belief in the ability to change and commitment to change behavior), counterconditioning (substituting positive behaviors for problematic ones), stimulus control (changing the environmental stimuli that elicit problematic behavior), reinforcement management (reinforcing positive behaviors), helping relationships (use of supportive relationships), dramatic relief (expressing feelings), environmental reevaluation (assessing the effect of the problem on the environment), and social liberation (societal interventions such as advocacy movements) (Prochaska, DiClemente, & Norcross, 1992, p. 1108; Prochaska, Rossi, & Wilcox, 1991, p. 104).

These change processes have been linked by Prochaska and his colleagues to distinct stages of change, namely, precontemplation, contemplation of the problem, preparation to take action, taking new action about the problem, and maintenance of the change. Prochaska and DiClemente (1982, 1984) also found five "levels," or factors, of problem causation within the same 24 systems—levels that reflected a "surface" to "depth" spectrum: symptom/situational factors, maladaptive cognitions, current interpersonal conflicts, family/systems conflicts, and intrapersonal (i.e., intrapsychic) conflicts.

According to Prochaska and DiClemente, the practice of therapy could be individualized by (a) considering the stage of change a client was in upon her entrance to therapy, (b) selecting the change process that, according to their empirical tests of their model, worked best at that stage of change, and then (c) focusing upon whatever problem-causation factors appeared to be operative for that particular client, for instance, inappropriate patterns/contingencies of reinforcement in the situation (i.e., a behavioral view), family conflicts (i.e., a family systems view), or underlying intrapsychic conflict (i.e., a psychoanalytic view). This is no unguided picking and choosing willy-nilly of whatever intervention seems right at the moment, that is, without benefit of some guiding theoretical framework, as we would expect to find in more atheoretical forms of eclecticism. Rather, Prochaska and DiClemente provide a carefully delineated metatheory, derived from many therapy systems, to guide the process of intervention selection. The resulting therapy practice itself is therefore both individualized and systematic.

Note that this therapy system constitutes nothing short of a modern scientific, realist position about what causes problems and what causes solutions. Thus, the five theories (i.e., levels) of problem causation (e.g., maladaptive cognitions or current interpersonal conflicts), the five stages of change,[6] and the ten processes of change are put forth as reflecting the problem-causation factors and the problem-resolution processes as they really exist, independently of the knower or the knower's theory. Accordingly, the change in the client's life produced by therapy really exists in an independent, extratheoretic reality—a reality external to the theory in use, including the linguistic constructions the theory comprises. On the basis of this realist position, we may rightly claim that family therapy can change patterns of interaction within a family as those patterns really exist apart from, or in addition to, the theoretical formulations about the family that the therapist adopts. We may also rightly claim that cognitive therapy changes the actual irrational thoughts a client may hold (e.g., that she is an incompetent person in all respects); that change, therefore, also occurs apart from the therapist's theory about those thoughts. Put differently, therapy helps clients solve their problems by changing something *more* than the stories or theories therapists and clients construct about those problems. But that last (deceptively simple) point is filled with subtle complexities, and so we shall take it up in considerable detail in Chapters 4 and 5. Indeed, it is itself central to the argument I make in this book about the problematic use of postmodern antirealism in therapy.

Although theoretical integration is perhaps the most widely embraced and fastest growing form of eclecticism,[7] it is not without its problems. Even those who advocate this approach admit that the task of creating a unified metatheory that does not sacrifice or trivialize the contributions of each of the component therapy systems is monumental, if not impossible. Then there is the problem of hubris: as Stiles et al. (1986) state,

> An implication of global encompassing resolutions is that therapists who subscribe to particular theories are operating with only fragmentary understanding and imposing unnecessary restrictions on their practice. This represents a rather condescending view of theories of personality and psychotherapy that have been the life work of some of the most respected thinkers in the field. (p. 174)

Strenger and Omer (1992, p. 118), Mahoney (1993, pp. 4–5), and Messer (1986, p. 385) all find fault with integration on the grounds that it creates the illusion that we can attain a common language—a "therapeutic Esperanto" of sorts—that "harmonizes" professional discussion:

From the proposed candidates for this role we can see how nearer we are to Babel than to Eden: the language of cognitive psychology, the language of research, the vernacular, a special artificial meta-language. But no descriptive language (including the vernacular) is ever neutral, all carry ontological and theoretical assumptions. The ideal of a neutral language, not only for psychotherapy but for any science, has been all but abandoned as one of the last dreams of the logical positivists. (Strenger & Omer, 1992, p. 118)

That last quotation has important implications for the workings of realism and antirealism within an integrative framework. Most of those who have, like Prochaska and DiClemente, worked to create an integrative metatheory have apparently done so with a belief in our ability to transcend the "language" problem. That transcendence of language is what allows us to attain some knowledge about the business of therapy that is real, or, put differently, that transcendence allows us to attain knowledge that is independent of the theory, or "language," used to describe the workings of therapy. But Strenger and Omer (1992), Messer (1986), and Mahoney (1993) seem to be suggesting something else, something that has decidedly antirealist consequences: that we can never get outside our language system to describe any event as it independently (or extralinguistically) exists. To quote Messer (1986), who appeals directly to Rorty's (1979) linguistic philosophy,

Whether we recognize it or not, as psychologists we are always viewing phenomena from one angle or another, none of which is ever free from theoretical bias. . . . what we perceive around us and how we perceive it are a function of the language we employ. . . . There is no immaculate perception! (pp. 385–386)

In that last quotation we clearly encounter the relativistic, or antirealist, claim that language *makes* the "reality" (or nonreality) we experience, rather than reflecting an independent (of the knower) reality. According to this antirealism, we cannot possibly combine the components of different theoretical systems—which are *themselves* merely different languages—to produce any metatheory that *makes sense or has meaning*, let alone one that works to produce extralinguistic or extratheoretic effects in therapy itself. Because in this view theoretical systems are themselves alleged to be nothing more than different languages, I adopt Pols's (1992a, p. 5) terminology for this theory-language relation, namely, "language-cum-theory." However, I have abbreviated Pols's terminology to produce the term "theory/language," which I use henceforth (see Chapter 6, Note 7 for elaboration). In any case, for Messer, as well as Strenger and Omer, those who work diligently to produce such an integrative system of therapy may indeed be hardworking, but they are nonetheless misguided in their realist assumption that "escape from that prison [of language] is possible" (Messer, 1986, p. 386). In fact, Messer (Lazarus & Messer, 1991) journeys even further into antirealist territory by applying the term "postmodern" to the activity of therapy integration. In so doing, he makes explicit that there is now a postmodern flavor within some portion of the integrative faction of the eclectic movement, perhaps as much as what we find in the narrative therapy movement. To quote Messer himself,

> If I have written any obituary it is not for empiricism or science, but for a positivistic and scientistic conception of psychology as a science. Such a conception "holds that only those things of which we are absolutely certain can be counted as knowledge" (Polkinghorne, 1983, p. 1). I am espousing a postpositivist or postmodernist conception that questions whether there is certain or objective truth or reality . . . . (p. 155)

It appears that, in at least some of its manifestations, even a therapy movement as rooted in the real as eclecticism is not immune to the postmodern/antirealist influence.

It should therefore come as no surprise that there now exists at least one integrative or metatheoretical system of therapy that has firm antirealist leanings; and, if that quotation of Messer is any indication, more are probably on the way. That antirealist system is called "Theoretically Progessive Integrationism" (TPI) (Neimeyer & Feixas, 1990), and it reflects an attempt to solve the language problem described above by appealing to antirealism. It makes that appeal by adopting as its metatheory the doctrine of constructivism. As I explain in Chapter 4, constructivism is a type of antirealist doctrine, and so it claims that all knowledge (of the world) is created, constituted, or constructed in language by the knower. Therefore, there can be no knowledge of an independent, extralinguistic reality according to constructivism. The proponents of TPI propose that those systems of therapy which, according to them, share a constructivist epistemology (e.g., personal construct theory, psychoanalysis, cognitive therapy, family systems therapy) are theoretically compatible, or share some common language. Therefore, those systems can allegedly contribute to the development of a constructivist (integrative) metatheory to guide the practice of therapy to be both individualized and systematic. Although I do not elaborate this antirealist integrative model here, in

Chapters 3, 4, and 5 I return to it again to illustrate how a therapy system that explicitly adopts an antirealist epistemology (in the attempt to individualize the practice of therapy) inevitably contradicts itself by oscillating between realist and antirealist propositions.

Although we are now finding attempts to attain an integrative system of therapy that can both individualize and systematize therapeutic practice, a widely accepted integrative model—one that unifies the field—is hardly imminent. There are simply too many competing ideas about how problems emerge and are resolved for the field to settle on any unified view. In fact, many integrationists believe that this diversity of opinion should not be sacrificed in the pursuit of unity.

Technical/Systematic Eclecticism

Technical, or systematic, eclecticism is believed by some to hold the greatest hope for producing an individualized and yet systematic approach to the practice of therapy. It may accomplish that feat by treating theory in a way that is different from what we have seen so far within the eclectic therapy movement. Technical/systematic eclecticism is just that: it is technical in the sense that it is technique rather than theory oriented, and it promotes a systematic practice in that techniques or interventions are not used in any unguided, or random, way. Technical eclectics (e.g., Beutler, 1983, 1989, 1991; Lazarus, 1967, 1986), then, concern themselves with determining what types of interventions (or techniques) have been empirically demonstrated to produce the best outcomes for distinct types or categories of clients/ problems. Technical eclectics try to make that determination without regard for the theoretical origins of those interventions—that is, without regard for the (theoretical) systems of therapy in which those interventions were developed, and from which those interventions were "borrowed." For instance, the technical eclectic therapist can combine behavior modification techniques quite compatibly with psychoanalytic interpretations, with no fear of contradiction, or theoretical incompatibility, since the theoretical origins of those interventions are of no concern. What matters is simply what intervention or combination of interventions works best for a given type of client. As Beutler (1989), an ardent proponent of this approach, defines it, "technical eclecticism seeks to extrapolate empirically derived dimensions from existent literature and to create an *objective* [italics added] theory of what changes can be expected under definable and controllable therapeutic conditions" (p. 17, Abstract).

Although this approach is not atheoretical, empirically proven results—that is, objective results—and not theory per se dominate its function. Technical eclecticism is therefore decidedly realist in its underlying epistemology. As Lazarus, another ardent advocate of technical eclecticism, put it,

> My worldview and its epistemological foundations are almost totally at odds with Messer's "hermeneutic" construction of knowledge and its derivatives. . . . Of course "there is no single truth out there to discover," but I would hope that some truths are not entirely colored by subjective inference. (Lazarus & Messer, 1991, p. 154)

There is, perhaps, some equivocation in the middle of that last quotation, but it is realist nonetheless.

We shall consider the way technical eclectics treat theory in just a moment. But for now it is important to notice that technical eclectics, in addition to emphasizing a systematic practice, are exquisitely attuned to the importance of individualizing therapy. We know this because their work has come to be titled the "matrix paradigm," and it is best defined by what is called the specificity question first proposed by Paul (1967): "*What* treatment, by *whom*, is most effective for *this* individual with *that* specific problem, and under *which* set of circumstances?" (Paul, 1967, p. 111). It is hard to be more specific or individual-oriented than this, especially in the context of a systematic approach to therapy. Thus, this "specificity" question helps define an ambitious research program centered around the problem of individuating or tailoring therapy to the individual case.

The cells of the matrix are defined by at least three primary variables, namely, types of clients/problems, types of treatments/interventions, and less often, types of therapists. It is worth mentioning that client/problem types are not limited to traditional diagnostic categories of psychopathology such as depression, schizophrenia, or phobia. In fact, Beutler (1986, 1989, 1991) has argued that clinical diagnosis may be the *least* effective way to define client/problem types, in that diagnosis may be too general for the individualized therapy being sought. As he put it,

> Clinical diagnoses are too broad and nonspecific to dictate the application of specific psychological treatments. While formal diagnoses have a role in the derivation of medical treatments . . . , psychological interventions must be tailored to more refined or specific qualities of patients' personalities, styles of coping [e.g., acting out, attention seeking, social withdrawal], and knowledge repertoires [e.g., skills] than clinical diagnoses allow. (Beutler, 1986, p. 101)

Beutler (1991, p. 227) listed many "potentially important patient variables" that include—in addition to diagnosis—defensiveness, subjective distress, dogmatism, dependency, treatment readiness, symptom type, life attitudes, goals, gender, ethnicity, and expectations, to name a few. Not one of these constitutes a clinical syndrome in our current list of mental disorders (i.e., *Diagnostic and Statistical Manual of Mental Disorders, Fourth Edition,* or *DSM-IV*).

Let us put the matrix paradigm and its resulting research program in historical perspective. Many believe the matrix quest was a reaction against the old "uniformity myth" (Kiesler, 1966). Therapists functioning under that myth were said to seek interventions that worked for *all* clients and therapists, regardless of individual circumstance. By contrast, proponents of the matrix paradigm, by seeking an *empirical* answer to Paul's (1967) specificity question, were clearly attending to the individuality problem while attempting to develop a system of therapy that would ensure a systematic or rule-governed practice: if the client had a certain type of problem or "patient quality," then the matrix would indicate what type of intervention to employ to achieve a desired outcome.[8] The relationships between problems, interventions, and outcomes would therefore be revealed by way of a systematic empirical research program, one that would eventually produce a highly particularized system of psychotherapy to guide a systematic practice.

It might be helpful to pause just here to consider the meaning of the term "system" as I have been using it. Recall that the term "theory" implies the term "system," at least insofar as a theory contains a systematic arrangement of ideas or principles (cf. Bok, 1989, p. 54); hence my use of the term "theoretical system." Of course, we cannot assume the converse—that a system is necessarily theoretical. For instance, a human being is a type of living system—complete with a hierarchy or organization of subsystems, such as organ systems. And although we may develop good theories about the way that the human system as a whole operates, any human system, as it really exists (i.e., independent of any theory about it), is certainly not *itself* a theory. Thus, a theory actually bears two relationships to the term "system": the theory is itself a system of thought or ideas, but those ideas usually refer to something real—that is, something extratheoretic, or something outside the theory, such as human biology or behavior. The theory therefore is both itself a system and may, if it is a good scientific theory, describe and explain other independently existing systems such as human beings—in particular, therapists and clients who, in their real interactions, create a real-life interpersonal system that is independent of any (psychological) theory in use.

I develop this notion of the relation between theoretical systems and extratheoretic entities/systems in Chapter 6. For now it is important to note that technical eclectics—unlike those who adopt an atheoretical eclecticism—do not see themselves to be operating without benefit of some guiding theory, or theoretical system of therapy/intervention selection—hence the alternative term "systematic eclecticism." (The use in practice of that theoretical system of course ensures that the practice itself will be to some extent rule-governed, or constrained, and therefore consistent or replicable—that is, systematic. I discuss this point in Chapter 3.) However, the technical eclectic system is not identical to the metatheory that integrationists seek. Let us therefore turn our attention to the question how technical eclectics employ theory in their work, since that question has some bearing on the problem of how to define categories for their matrix. These categories are central to the attainment of an individualized therapy practice—a pursuit that pertains directly to the arguments put forth in this book.

Technical eclectics place most of their emphasis on effective problem resolution—that is, on determining the proper selection of therapeutic interventions. Technical eclectics therefore tend, unlike integrationists, to deemphasize theories of problem causation or psychopathology—that is, theories about the origin or cause of the client's problem/difficulty (see Beutler, 1989, vs. Arkowitz, 1989, for a debate about this emphasis). For example, the technical eclectic is more concerned with the fact that an intervention like encouraging emotional expression works for a certain kind of client and less concerned with the reason for the client's problem to begin with. However, even technical eclectics cannot avoid positing reasons for the success of particular interventions in particular cases (see Lazarus & Messer, 1991, p. 147), and in so doing they suggest a theory of problem resolution. Lazarus (Lazarus & Messer, 1991) nonetheless puts his antitheoretical inclinations quite plainly when he states,

We need fewer theories and more facts. (p. 146)

Theories are essentially speculations that try to explain or account for various phenomena. . . . Observations simply reflect empirical data without offering explanations. (p. 147)

Physicians prescribe many effective remedies without fully understanding how and why they work. In essence, I am interested in what will yield the best results for the greatest number of people in the shortest period of time. *All the rest is intellectual fluff.* [italics added] (p. 155)

Lazarus is rather extreme in his antitheoretical stance, and so he is probably not representative of the majority of technical eclectics. Nonetheless, technical eclectics do tend to ignore theories of problem causation, to deemphasize *theories* of problem resolution, and to focus upon the most therapeutically effective use of methods of problem resolution, or interventions, themselves. In so doing they minimize the importance of the *connection* between interventions (e.g., encouraging emotional expression or realigning family relationships) and the theories of psychopathology and psychotherapy from which those interventions were imported (e.g., gestalt and family therapy, respectively). Thus, there has been within that movement relatively more concern with descriptive theory than explanatory theory (see Arkowitz, 1989). Whereas descriptive theory concerns itself with descriptions of data and the functional (i.e., empirical) relationships among events/variables, in this case, what intervention works best for what type of client, explanatory theories ask the additional question *why* that relationship obtains, that is, what is the mechanism of, or reason/explanation for, the observed treatment effect (Arkowitz, 1989, p. 10). Note from the quotation just above that Lazarus exemplifies the technical eclectic's preference for descriptive over explanatory theory.

But again, this difference between technical eclectics and integrationists may be diminishing: Beutler admitted, in 1991, that questions about "why the observed relationships [between clients/problems and interventions] exist" may be "important both to achieve a heuristic understanding of human behavior and to develop new techniques" (p. 231). Even Lazarus admits to his use of theory (of problem resolution) when he states,

> This technically eclectic maneuver [the use of a particular technique independent of its theoretical origins] was not atheoretical. It augmented and facilitated the behavioral shaping and retraining [i.e., the use of the *behavioral* theoretical system] that *guided* [italics added] my ministrations, but my use of it did not require me to adopt any of the theoretical assumptions that gave rise to it in *other* [italics added] quarters. (Lazarus & Messer, 1991, p. 147)

I consider Beutler's shift just below. But in general it is important to keep in mind that, traditionally, the theory employed by technical eclectics is the practical (descriptive) one about the empirical system of relationships between clients, treatments, and therapeutic outcomes.

Beutler's 1991 shift gives us a hint about how the term "theory" is employed and so how theory actually gets used within technical eclecticism. Because technical eclectics do not consider themselves to be atheoretical—that is, to be functioning without benefit of a theoretical system to guide intervention selection in the practical *doing* of therapy—they must admit to using some theory to guide their practice. From my reading, I can discern at least three ways in which theory operates in that approach, ways that, as I stated above, bear directly on the problem of individualizing the practice of therapy.

First, technical eclectics like Beutler and Lazarus state that the therapist is free to pick any umbrella, or superordinate, theory to focus the therapeutic discussion and guide intervention selection—so long as she remains aware of and open to the many possible interventions that have been demonstrated to help different types of clients. The umbrella theory, therefore, must be general and flexible enough to allow such diversity of practice. Beutler (1986) mentioned several such umbrella theories, namely, general learning theory, systems theory, cognitive theory, and, his own preference, (social) persuasion theory. It is beyond the scope of this chapter to discuss these umbrella theories. But suffice it to say that it is not clear to me how the adoption of such a theory to guide practice can be prevented from hampering or conflicting with the very point of the matrix paradigm: to use the intervention that works best for a type of client, without regard for the theoretical origin of that intervention. Put differently, the adoption of a *particular* umbrella theory, however general it may be, causes adherence to a school or system of therapy—the very adherence that sacrificed individuality in practice and so led to eclecticism in the first place.

Beutler himself freely admits that umbrella theories limit what can be seen as a legitimate intervention choice. He claims, for example, that although cognitive theory is a good choice for an umbrella theory because of its wide acceptance, "the disadvantage of this approach . . . may be in its ties to specific therapeutic frameworks and orientations (e.g., cognitive therapy). The theory may also place an unwarranted constraint on the number and type of therapeutic procedures considered appropriate" (1986, pp. 97–98). Use of a cognitive umbrella theory could preclude the use of such gestalt therapy techniques as the "two-chair" technique, a technique in which the client sits in different chairs to access and express different (perhaps conflicting) aspects of his emotional experience.

Thus, we find ourselves back in our original problem: how to use a theoretical system to guide a rule-governed, replicable (i.e., systematic) practice, without compromising the flexibility needed for the individualization of intervention selection. Ellis (1989), who wrote about deconstruction in literature, made a similar point by reminding us that the use of theory provides focus; it therefore must constrain or limit the way we understand our observations to make sense of things. One simply cannot use a theory without using the very constraints that, in the context of a therapy practice, limit both one's understandings/explanations of the client's problem and the interventions one selects to solve that problem. That constraining effect is what makes the practice of therapy systematic, but the particular constraints one applies may fit the individual characteristics of some clients better than they fit others. In the latter case, the effect on practice is deindividualizing.

There is another way to understand how technical eclectics use theory in their practice. That alternative use consists in viewing the empirical matrix itself—the system of empirically determined relationships between types of clients/problems, types of interventions/therapies, and types of outcomes—as the umbrella or superordinate theory that guides intervention choice in therapy. Thus, once the matrix is created, even though it is ever evolving, *it* becomes the *system* that guides therapeutic practice. Lazarus (1986), for instance, appeals to his well-known "BASIC ID" formulation of problem and intervention categories (i.e., behavior, affect, sensation, imagery, cognition, interpersonal relationships, and drugs/biology) to help define the client's problem area, and hence to guide intervention selection (Held, 1991a).

The discerning reader will notice that we are not out of the woods yet in our attempt to find a theoretical system of therapy that produces a therapeutic practice that is both systematic and individualized. For we have not yet addressed the question how the *categories* within the two most common variables of the matrix—namely, the types of clients/problems and the types of interventions—are themselves selected and defined. Put differently, what determines what constitutes the varieties of client problems, and so forth? What determines the composition of the cells in the matrix for which we investigate optimal outcomes, or the best client/problem-intervention relationships, in the first place?

It is here that Beutler (1991) can be seen to have made his shift concerning the role of theory in the matrix paradigm. For he now apparently believes that psychotherapy outcome research has been all too driven by the variables that are easily accessed or measured—that are convenient—rather than by the all-too-absent "organizing theoretical or empirical framework that predicted differential and interaction effects" (1991, p. 229). By the latter he means a conceptual framework (i.e., theory or system) that provides predictions about the kinds of interventions that are and are not likely to be helpful for different types of clients. Thus, Beutler believes clinical diagnosis (rather than, say, coping style) has been the basis for much matrix research, since diagnoses like depression "can be reliably diagnosed, not because there was some *theoretical* [italics added] reason to think that the [different] treatments [or therapy conditions used] might reveal their differences in this [clinical] population" (p. 229). Beutler goes on to make a similar argument about the selection of treatments or therapies themselves in outcome research. He again uses the National Institute of Mental Health collaborative study of psychotherapy, which compared the use of cognitive, interpersonal, antidepressant, and placebo interventions for a group of patients diagnosed with major depressive disorder (p. 229). Beutler states, "[These] therapies were selected because they had been manualized and could be taught reliably" (p. 229). According to him, they were not selected because of any compelling "theoretical rationale for expecting a differential effect among them when practiced on patients with major depressive disorder" (p. 229).

In short, to obtain a matrix of categories or dimensions that can be empirically tested and then applied systematically in therapy practice, we need some way to define the categories/cells in the matrix. For Beutler, the process of constructing the matrix must itself be systematic—that is, it must be guided by some combination of past (empirical) findings and future (theoretical) predictions about the differential effects of treatments. In other words, the matrix must be determined by some theoretical/empirical considerations, and not simply convenience in measuring variables. I refer here to both the theoretical and the empirical components of this process of matrix construction because all science advances by means of a cycling back and forth between theoretical prediction, on the one hand, and empirical tests of those predictions in direct experience, on the other. This cycling is what Pols (1992a) calls the "theoretic-empirical cycle"; I have more to say about it in Chapter 6. But most relevant to this discussion is that theory may be used in this third way in the matrix paradigm—that is, in the *selection* of matrix components. Nonetheless, the question still remains: is our problem of attaining a systematic and yet individualized therapy practice now solved? Does this final appeal by Beutler give us a (theoretical) system of therapy—an empirically evaluated matrix of client-treatment-outcome relationships—that guides practice so as to be truly individualized?

Let us assume for the moment the following: that with benefit of keen observational powers, we develop a taxonomy (i.e., categories) of client/ problem types that "gets it right," that is to say, a taxonomy that accurately reflects the types of clients/problems as they objectively exist independent of our taxonomic system and as they objectively pertain to the business of problem resolution. Put differently, the distinctions we make in our taxo-nomic system are the right ones and the only ones that must be made for the purposes of problem resolution/intervention selection. Not too few distinc-tions, not too many. For example, we may, speaking hypothetically, distin-guish between clients with avoidant vs. nonavoidant coping styles (cf. Beutler, 1991), because we know from our various theories and observations (i.e., from our theoretic-empirical cycling) that this distinction will make a differ-ence in the type of intervention that will be effective. Thus, the same interven-tion will not produce the same effects in clients with those two types of coping styles. But we do not need to distinguish, say (again hypothetically), between more educated avoidant types and less educated avoidant types, because the education dimension will make no difference. Let us also assume we accomplish the same feat with types of interventions, and even, perhaps, types of therapists.

Once these taxonomies are created and placed in a grid/matrix, one need only locate the appropriate client/problem cell in that grid to determine which intervention to apply to obtain the desired outcome. By adopting a systematic research program to fill in the cells of the matrix bit by bit, a progressive science of psychotherapy can be attained. Thus, the matrix para-digm, in a traditional, or modern, scientific spirit, holds great hope for making the practice of therapy systematic and yet tailoring it to each individual client.

Why, then, has this paradigm not solved the individuality/systematic prob-lem? Answers come from both inside and outside the ranks of those who defend the paradigm; we shall consider those answers in a moment. First I must point out that our hypothetical, correct, "got it right" matrix is still just that—hypothetical. We have, as Beutler (1991) asserts, yet to determine the relevant client dimensions and categories of the matrix. (Note here that a behavioral characteristic constitutes a continuum that can be segmented into discrete, mutually exclusive categories for the purpose of client classification. For example, clients can be placed at various points along an introversion-extraversion trait dimension, and these points each reflect more or less ex-treme degrees of either personality style. Hence, my use of the term "dimen-sions/categories.") Recall that we have no supreme authority to tell us when we have defined and delineated the dimensions/categories correctly. There is no authority other than the empirical workings of the "matrix in progress" we are employing at any given moment. Our only guide, then, is whether the matrix we have developed so far actually gives us its predicted effects. Since the matrix is itself based on our theoretical predictions about what interven-tions ought to have what effects on what types of clients (predictions which are themselves based on prior empirical observations), its production and use constitutes nothing less than a traditional scientific enterprise. And as we all know, good science works. So proponents of the matrix paradigm can claim that, despite its 25-or-so year history, it is still only a work in progress, and in the very early stages of scientific progress at that. Given our haphazard method of selecting client and intervention dimensions/categories (Beutler, 1991), this slow start is not surprising.

There are additional, if not quite so fundamental, reasons for the paradigm's failure to revolutionize therapy, or at least for its very slow progress. Beutler (1991, p. 227), whom we know by now to be a proponent of the matrix paradigm, acknowledges that the unwieldy number of dimensions/categories within each of the three primary variables (i.e., client/problem, intervention/therapy, and therapist type)[9] could ultimately produce a matrix with some 1.5 million cells. That is, to be sure, a daunting, if not empirically untestable, realization. Beutler argues that the problem can be solved not by abandoning the matrix paradigm but by reducing the number of dimensions/categories within each of the three primary variables to between three and 11, depending upon the variable. This effort would limit the number of cells in the matrix to under 1,000 — again, hardly a quick and easy research project, but certainly a manageable one given enough time.

This task of category reduction can be accomplished by reducing the conceptual redundancy found among the many dimensions/categories — for example, by determining their intercorrelations. Each new dimension/category would then constitute a higher, more general level of abstraction. In particular, Beutler (1986) argues that we should not use the large number of DSM diagnoses as distinct dimensions/categories to classify client types, since diagnoses may not always provide treatment-relevant information, and some diagnoses may share common treatment implications. Instead, he suggests that the three general dimensions of symptom complexity, coping style, and reactance level (each of which may have several categories or subtypes that constitute a continuum) can define most client types for the purpose of differentiating intervention selection.

Beutler (1986) defined coping style as the client's "method of avoiding anxiety and/or achieving interpersonal goals" (p. 102). He later (Beutler, Machado, Engle, & Mohr, 1993) refined this dimension to represent "a continuum from internalization (i.e., self-punishment, worry, restricted affect) to externalization (i.e., acting-out, control by environmental stimuli)" (p. 16). In 1993 he also offered another client type or dimension, namely, "resistance potential," which he said "represents, along a continuum, the likeli-

therapy cases, or moments in cases—that is, they are applied more or less generally. I return to that important point just below.

For now, let us consider one more example of the type of therapy research that, when applied clinically, should promote a therapeutic practice that is both individualized and systematic. Lambert (1989) provides just that example. Rather than asking what kinds of *interventions/therapies* work best for different kinds of clients (the traditional matrix question, which emphasizes the intervention/treatment variable), he asks what kinds of *therapists* (i.e., what therapist characteristics and behaviors) are successful and unsuccessful with distinct client types. The critical process of therapy for Lambert, then, is not technique, or intervention, bound; rather, it is therapist bound. He also advocates an inductive approach to theory construction, not unlike that in the events paradigm. But in Lambert's inductive approach we must empirically study the particular successes and failures of individual therapists to determine, ultimately, more general laws of therapy/change.

To support his argument, Lambert cites Ricks's (1974) finding that certain therapist behaviors and attitudes are correlated with positive vs. negative outcomes. In particular, two therapists who worked with disturbed adolescent boys produced quite different outcomes: whereas only 27% of Therapist A's more disturbed clients went on to become schizophrenic in adulthood, a full 84% of Therapist B's more disturbed clients had that negative outcome. When the behaviors of the two therapists were compared, it was found that Therapist A devoted more time to his most disturbed clients, whereas Therapist B devoted less time to these clients. Moreover, Therapist A used resources outside the therapy session, including the facilitation of everyday problem-solving, with those same clients; by comparison, Therapist B felt frightened by his more disturbed clients, withdrew from them, ignored the hopeful or positive elements of their lives, and emphasized the times when they seemed depressed (Lambert, 1989, pp. 472–473). Lambert indicates he also concurs with Luborsky, McLellan, Woody, O'Brien, and Auerbach's (1985) conclusion that "the outcomes of individual therapists could be reanalyzed and summarized to draw *general* [italics added] conclusions about therapist behaviors that were associated with positive and negative outcomes" (Lambert, 1989, p. 475). He cites Luborsky et al.'s (1985) finding that more helpful therapists could be discriminated from less helpful therapists on the basis of three general qualities: "(a) the therapist's adjustment, skill, and interest in helping patients; (b) the purity of the treatment they offered; and (c) the quality of the therapist/patient relationship"—which of course incorporates the client's as well as the therapist's characteristics (Lambert, 1989, p. 475).

In other words, more general rules—a *system* of psychotherapy—could be attained by relating individual therapists' behaviors, attitudes, and characteristics to the outcomes of their particular cases. Therefore—even in this highly individualized approach to therapy research—general, predetermined categories, or types, of therapist characteristics/behaviors, clients, and outcomes emerge. These categories are, of course, necessary to construct a rule-governed system of therapy that can be applied or generalized, however selectively, to all therapists and clients. Nevertheless, their very use compromises the attainment of a thoroughly individualized level of analysis.

THE ECLECTIC DILEMMA

Each of the alternatives to the traditional matrix paradigm that I have examined here attempts to individualize the practice of therapy. But however local, specific, momentary, and contextualized the categories within each alternative system of therapy may be, each system must ultimately assign individuals to categories. Recall that such classification/categorization is necessary to determine a *general* system of relationships among variables—a lawful system whose use makes the practice of therapy more consistent and so more predictable or systematic than it would otherwise be. From the postmodern viewpoint of the narrative therapy movement, this is a traditional scientific enterprise of the modern sort: rules—which must always contain *some* degree of generality—are accumulated in the interest of a progressive enterprise, one that aspires to *approach* or *approximate* an independent, objective reality. This, indeed, is the aspiration of all modern science, including the science (if not the philosophy) of quantum physics (see Pols, 1992a).

To be sure, the rules can always be refined to render them more and more precise, or particular, by specifying the conditions under which they are valid. For example, instead of asking whether gestalt therapy works better than client-centered therapy, we can ask whether a particular technique within gestalt therapy (e.g., the two-chairs technique) works better with clients who are struggling with a decisional conflict rather than a self-esteem problem. Moreover, supposing, hypothetically, we find for the former, we can then go on to refine our system of therapy by asking whether that same technique works better with some types of decisional conflicts than with others. The point in any event is this: the rules that constitute the therapy system can always be subjected to ever more specification (or particularization) and hence to more localization—that is, they can always become less generalized in their use or application. But they nonetheless must always have *some* degree of generality if they truly are rules—if, that is, they truly apply under the conditions in which they are claimed to be operative. No matter how much uniqueness any particular therapy client may be thought to have, that client must be seen to have *something* in common with (some) other clients within the therapeutic system (of rules) in use. The use of such a system, then, always requires that each client be placed in some general, predetermined problem category—however particular that category may be—for the purpose of intervention selection. No *system* of psychotherapy can exist without rules (for intervention selection) that embody some degree of generality. The question, then, is not whether there is generality in the rule-governed system, but *how much* generality.

That last claim means that postmodern narrative therapists should find it easy to argue that (technical/systematic) eclectic therapists do not practice therapy at the level of each unique, individual client. By virtue of using a rule-governed system of therapy to guide their practice, those eclectics simply cannot function in that way. The eclectic therapy movement therefore retains a systematic practice, but does it accomplish that feat at the expense of the individuality it wants to preserve? Is it reasonable to seek both an individualized and a systematic approach to therapy practice, or is a tradeoff inevitable?

Before answering that question, I must say that it seems to me odd that the eclectic movement, which was born in a spirit of pluralism and diversity, and which has attempted to design a theoretical system to maximize each client's individuality in therapy, is nonetheless unappealing to (most) adherents of a postmodern attitude that itself proclaims pluralism, diversity, and the sanctity of the local or individual perspective (Rosenau, 1992). The problem, of course, resides precisely in eclecticism's attempt to attain a systematic practice, for to do so it must construct (and use) rules based on the categorization of clients/problems, therapists, and treatments. And these rules—indeed, *any* rules—are by definition too global and unitary, too general, for the postmodern palate, however specific or particular those rules may be. Moreover, as I soon demonstrate, at least some degree of realism is behind the question, "What is the intervention that produces the best, most desired, outcome for a certain type (category) of client?" Thus, general truth, or reality, claims abound, or at least are pursued, within the eclectic therapy movement. And, recall that neither that which is real nor that which is general contributes to a postmodern outlook; when those two qualities are combined to produce realist generalities, the outlook becomes especially anti-postmodern—which is to say, it becomes a modern outlook. It is therefore precisely the fact that the eclectic therapy movement has tried to solve the problem of individuality in both a systematic, or generalized, and a realist way that is the cause of offense from the perspective of postmodernism.

In due course we shall consider how the narrative therapy movement has, in its adoption of a postmodern humanistic antirealism, tried to produce an individualized yet systematic approach to the practice of therapy. First, though, it will be helpful to examine in more explicit detail the components of any complete, or conventional (i.e., modern), system of therapy. That examination will give us a more precise understanding of how realism and antirealism operate within the postmodern narrative therapy movement.

CHAPTER 3

The Structure of
Therapy Systems and
the Realism-Antirealism Debate

A GENERIC MODEL OF
THERAPY SYSTEMS

Many therapists make a virtue of guiding their practice by a theoretical system that is well-organized, structured, coherent, and whole. I call the systems they design and use "complete theoretical systems of therapy," because they reflect attempts to give as complete an account as possible of the complex reality consisting of a therapeutic response, on the one hand, and the human conditions that require that response, on the other. In this chapter, I intend to establish the minimal internal structure a theoretical system of therapy must have in order to be complete.

Therapists who design or use such systems value them because they hope to find in them explicit rules for establishing a therapeutic practice that is itself rule-governed, or constrained, and therefore consistent or replicable—insofar as that is possible. They therefore see all aspects of their work—the construction of theory, the testing of it, and the application of it in practice—as nothing short of a systematic, scientific enterprise. Their systems are thus conventional—not in a pejorative sense, but in the sense that for a great part of the modern age science has worked successfully with a method that has certain well-established conventions. The designers and users of these theoretical systems of therapy, then, do not think of their work as postmodern, and so we should think of complete theoretical systems of therapy as modern rather than postmodern.

The generic model of complete therapy systems[1] I am about to propose is an ideal one; there are many systems of therapy that fall short of it. Some theoretical systems of therapy are more complete than others—more highly organized, structured, coherent, and whole—a fact that has implications for how rule-governed, or constrained, and therefore how consistent or replicable the actual practice of therapy can be under such systems. Systems of therapy that are, whether by design or inadvertence, less complete are by definition less organized, structured, coherent, and whole in their account of the reality they are intended to describe and explain than are complete therapy systems. The practice guided or, put more accurately, unguided by such incomplete systems must itself, then, be less rule-governed and so less consistent or replicable than those guided by complete therapy systems. The practice guided by incomplete systems is therefore somewhat unsystematic or even, in extreme cases, antisystematic.

Those therapists who prefer to design or use highly incomplete theoretical systems of therapy may rightfully be said to have antisystematic aspirations. By "antisystematic aspirations" I mean the deliberate attempt to reduce drastically the completeness of the theoretical system that "guides" therapeutic practice. Not surprisingly, those who have that aspiration do not view their therapeutic activity as a systematic, scientific enterprise—at least not in any conventional, or modern, sense of the term "science." Rather, they take themselves to be engaged in an art form or, perhaps, in some sort of unconventional, or postmodern, "science." I return to that view in Chapter 8.

The proponents of incomplete therapy systems are not my immediate concern in this section; they are dealt with later in this chapter and in the chapters to follow. Here I wish only to emphasize my claim that their antisystematic aspirations reflect an underlying attempt to fully individualize the practice of therapy, and that this goal must, as I argue again and again in this book, limit the extent to which therapy practice can also be systematic.

Determining which aspects of life a theoretical system of therapy must account for to be considered a complete system of therapy is not a value-free judgment. That determination derives, in my experience, from two factors: (a) the component parts of therapy systems as they have evolved by convention or use; and (b) my own judgment of what ought to be the most fundamental components of a discipline that has set as its goal the alleviation of psychological problems, pain, or suffering, and the promotion of psychological growth or well-being. Since my judgment is based on my own clinical experiences and training in a wide variety of therapy systems, factors "a" and "b" above are not independent of each other. Thus, the generic model of therapy systems I am about to propose defines the notion of the completeness of a system of therapy by way of those two overlapping factors. As I go on to explain in the pages to follow, that notion of completeness inherent in my generic model requires that the system contain three component parts; the degree to which those three component parts are distinct from each other will vary as a function of the particular therapy system in which they are located.

Complete, or conventional, therapy systems as I define them have two component parts whose importance is more or less constant — one or more predetermined theories of problem causation, and one or more predetermined theories of problem resolution (cf. Watzlawick, Weakland, & Fisch, 1974). Complete systems contain another component whose importance varies considerably from system to system — predetermined categories of clients/problems. I use the term "predetermined" to draw a distinction, used later in this chapter, between categories and theories that are derived from a system of therapy, and so are determined *prior* to their use in any particular therapy case, and categories and theories that each client brings to therapy as part of her unique, personal view of her problem. These unique, personal views have not been predetermined by the therapist's system of therapy; rather, they may be said to be client determined. This distinction gets to the heart of the problem of an individualized and yet systematic approach to therapy practice, which I discuss throughout this book. But here I must first elaborate the three components of what I am calling a complete therapy system.

Theories of problem causation — I call them Component A — form the basis of what therapists call the "content" of therapy: what gets discussed in the sessions, particularly as it relates to the theorized cause of the problem and the objective of the course of therapy (i.e., what needs to be changed to achieve that objective). Theories of problem resolution — I call them Component B — form the basis of what therapists call the "process" of therapy: the methods or procedures by which the desired change is thought to be produced, caused, or brought about.

Because a theory of problem resolution usually suggests a *way* of solving the problem, it must contain at least some implicit notion of a *method* of change. It should therefore guide the therapist in the actual practice of therapy by suggesting rules for effective therapeutic intervention. Because of the inevitable link between theories of problem resolution and therapeutic methods, I use the term "theory-cum-method." This term will be understood to mean: (a) that there is always at least an implicit method within a theory of problem resolution, and (b) that the use of the method can never in the actual practice of therapy be completely theory free — that is, there is always some rational explanation or reasoning behind its use.[2] Component B is also the most fundamental or important component in any system of therapy, since such systems are, above all, about solving problems.

Categories, or types, of clients/problems—I call them Component C— form the link between Component A and Component B. The linkage of these three components, then, constitutes the network of relations that make the therapy system a complete, rule-governed system in the sense discussed in Chapter 2. Obviously, Component C is very flexible, for the number and precision of categories or types of clients/problems may vary considerably, as Figure 3.1 suggests.

The reader will notice that the completeness of this generic model of therapy systems is compromised once we arrive at the point, at the far right of the continuum of Component C in Figure 3.1, where the system provides no (predetermined) client/problem types for use in the practice of therapy. In that case, Component C is for all practical purposes eliminated from the therapy system. Therapists who prefer that kind of system want to give each client the opportunity to supply her own definition or description of the problem; they therefore attempt to refrain from imposing on their clients any predetermined notions of what the problem may be. I believe they do so to maximize the individualization of their therapy practice. But in so doing, they also create and/or use a therapy system that is obviously less organized, structured, coherent and whole—that is, less complete—than systems that

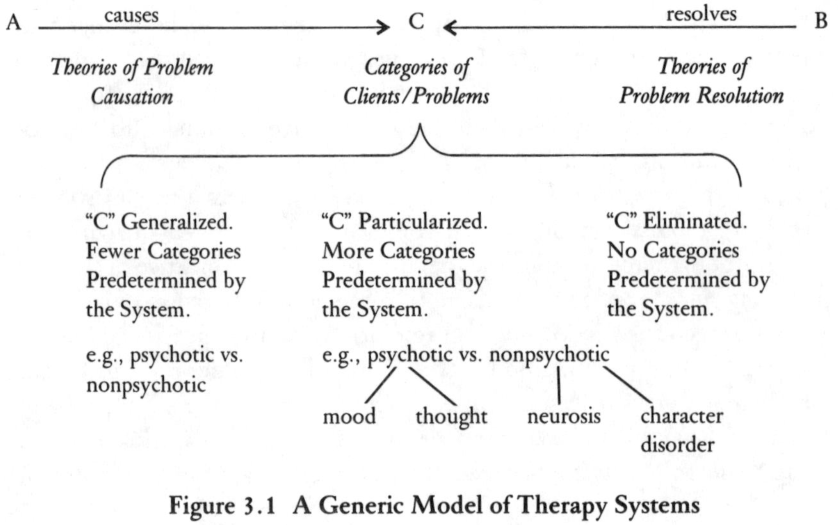

A ———— causes ————————→ C ←———————— resolves ———— B

Theories of Problem   *Categories of*   *Theories of*
Causation   *Clients/Problems*   *Problem Resolution*

"C" Generalized.   "C" Particularized.   "C" Eliminated.
Fewer Categories   More Categories   No Categories
Predetermined by   Predetermined by   Predetermined by
the System.   the System.   the System.

e.g., psychotic vs.   e.g., psychotic vs. nonpsychotic
nonpsychotic

                        mood   thought   neurosis   character
                                                         disorder

Figure 3.1 A Generic Model of Therapy Systems

include Component C. And, recall, the practice guided by a less complete system is less rule-governed/constrained, less consistent or replicable than practice guided by a more complete system. Therefore, the attempt to individualize therapy by using a less complete theoretical system to guide practice renders that practice less systematic. Complete erosion or elimination of Component C, then, brings us to those odd systems I mentioned: those whose proponents have aspirations that are antisystematic—thus antiscientific, or postmodern. As we shall see in Chapters 4 and 5, the proponents of those postmodern systems cannot articulate their antisystematic aspirations without retaining some vestigial version of a complete system of therapy.

Theories of Problem Causation

Theories of problem causation constitute theories about what caused the client to acquire his psychological or behavioral problem in the first place; consequently, they usually also incorporate theories about what might now be maintaining or perpetuating that problem.[3] Theories of problem causation therefore posit the existence of some obstacle that prevents the client from either achieving his goals or reducing his difficulties in life. Not all psychological difficulties are represented by DSM-IV categories of mental illness/"psychopathology"; for instance, a parent's difficulty in getting his child to comply with his rules can hardly be considered a form of mental illness in itself. I therefore prefer the term "behavioral or psychological problem," which is certainly a broader, more neutral term than the term "mental illness" or "disorder." But I could just as easily define theories of problem causation as theories about the causes of psychopathology.

It is most important for the purposes of our discussion, however, to understand that theories of problem causation form the basis for the "content" of therapy, that is, what gets discussed in the sessions themselves. This usually has something to do with the reasons for the client's problem/difficulty, distress, or failure to achieve her goals. Put differently, the content of therapy constitutes the object, or "target," of what must be changed to solve problems, alleviate distress, or achieve goals. (That change is of course accomplished through the use of some therapeutic method, with whatever theoretical explanation—or theory of problem resolution—surrounds *its* use.) Theories of problem causation, then, may be regarded as theories about the behavior or aspect of experience that is thought by therapists to bear some causal relationship to the problem or distress and so is made the focus of therapeutic intervention. I provide examples below of how theories of problem causation form the content of the therapeutic discussion and so become the target for the therapeutic intervention process.

Theories of problem causation include biological factors (e.g., neurotransmitter imbalances in the case of schizophrenia and depression), intrapsychic factors (e.g., unconscious mental conflicts in psychodynamic theories; irrational thoughts in cognitive theories), current interpersonal factors (e.g., problematic peer or family relationships in interpersonal and family/systemic theories), and sociopolitical factors (e.g., poverty, unemployment, and discrimination in community psychology or psychosocial theories), to name only a few. These factors form the content of the actual therapy sessions— *what* gets attended to in the intervention process.

Theories of Problem Resolution

Theories of problem resolution constitute theories of psychotherapeutic change, that is, theories about what causes the alleviation of behavioral or psychological problems. It is important to note that many, but not all, systems of psychotherapy posit something explicit about what originally caused or now maintains problems; that is, they contain explicit theories of problem causation, or Component A. By contrast, *all* systems of psychotherapy must always, by definition, posit something explicit about how to resolve, or at least minimize, problems. Thus, any system of therapy must be explicit about the problem resolution process if it is to be a true system of therapy and not merely a theory about the cause of problems or psychopathology (see Held, 1991a, and Prochaska & DiClemente, 1982, 1984, for elaboration of this distinction between Components A and B).

To put all this differently, theories of problem causation tell us *what* (content) needs to be changed in therapy (e.g., irrational thoughts), and they give explanations as to why that is the case. By contrast, theories of problem resolution tell us *how*, by what methods, actually to produce or cause that change (e.g., challenge irrational thoughts), and why those methods should prove helpful. Theories of problem resolution therefore explain the *process* of therapy, or problem resolution. Recall that theories of problem resolution at least imply some method in their description and explanation of the therapeutic process; hence my use of the term "theory-cum-method" to emphasize that relation. However, some therapy systems are more precise than others about how in practice the therapist is to translate a general theory-cum-method of problem resolution (e.g., challenge irrational thoughts) into more particular interventions (e.g., ask the client many questions to illustrate the logical inconsistency of those thoughts). In any case, the therapist's actions—what she *does* to promote problem resolution—is usually guided by some theoretical, or explanatory, principles about the nature of therapeutic change itself.

Prochaska and DiClemente (1982) make this (process/content) distinction in the following statement:

> The processes of change are the contributions unique to a theory of therapy. The content that is to be changed in any particular therapy is largely a carryover from that system's theory of personality and psychopathology. Many books supposedly focusing on therapy frequently confuse content and process and end up describing primarily the content of therapy with little explanation about the processes of therapy. As a result, they are really books on theories of personality rather than theories of therapy.
>
> Those systems of therapy that do not contain theories of personality . . . are primarily process theories and have few *predetermined* [italics added] concepts about what will be the content of therapy. (p. 282)

As clear as that distinction may sound, in actuality theories of problem causation and problem resolution are not completely distinct. That is because one cannot define a general process of problem resolution, or even a more particular intervention, without pointing, at least implicitly, to a general focus (or content) for intervention. To demonstrate this point, let us consider the ten processes of change—e.g., dramatic relief, self-liberation, stimulus control, and so forth—that were defined by Prochaska and DiClemente and that we reviewed in Chapter 2. Each of these change processes points to some very general focus or target of intervention. For instance, to use dramatic relief as a method/process of change is to target the expression or release of emotions or feelings to resolve problems; to use stimulus control is to target the aspects of the environment that elicit negative responses as the focus of change, and so forth. Thus, one cannot explain how to resolve problems without giving some minimal, implicit view of the causes of those problems. Put differently, one cannot define an intervention process without implicitly defining some general content area in which to intervene.

Note, then, that theories of problem resolution have their counterpart in or in some way incorporate theories of problem causation. That is no accident: a *theory* of problem resolution must explain *why* a therapeutic method should work for any, or even all, problems. In providing that explanation, it cannot avoid implicating those factors that are theorized to cause or maintain the problem. Moreover, to the extent that one's theory (cum-method) of problem resolution points, as it always must, to some object of therapeutic intervention, it at least implicitly tells us something—however general—about problem causation. In short, problem resolution cannot be completely distinct from problem causation.

Let us consider other examples to make this important point clearer. If a therapist believes that an intervention designed to restructure the interactions between members of a family (e.g., who interacts with whom around what issues) will resolve a problem (e.g., a mother's/wife's depression), she is at least implicitly suggesting that the problem is caused and/or maintained by problematic family interactions, and not, say, a biochemical imbalance. Conversely, if a therapist believes that an intervention designed to alter a neurotransmitter function (e.g., an antidepressant drug) will resolve the same problem, he is at least implicitly suggesting that the problem is caused by a biochemical imbalance, in which case it would be foolish to use only interpersonal interventions. It is not that the use of treatment interventions associated with different theories of problem resolution are mutually exclusive; a therapist with a depressed client could certainly use a drug treatment intervention (e.g., an antidepressant to target a neurotransmitter imbalance) in conjunction with a psychological treatment intervention (e.g., cognitive therapy to target possible irrational ideas behind the depression). But, in the case of the last example, that combination of interventions would be determined by a belief that both biological and psychological factors play some causal role in the problem.

Client/Problem Categories

Let us now turn our attention to the specifics of the client/problem category (Component C) of our diagram. Notice that in Figure 3.1 the client/problem categories (or problem descriptions, as I sometimes refer to them) can be represented as more generalized or more particularized. In the former case, the categories are defined more abstractly or generally, and so they can subsume a larger number of clients, with a broader range of differences among them. For example, the more general category of psychosis may be particularized to distinguish psychosis with thought disorder from psychosis with mood disorder. Similarly, the more general category of nonpsychosis may be particularized to distinguish neurotic disorders from character, or personality, disorders. Of course, we can particularize these more particularized categories even further—for instance, we can distinguish between phobic and obsessive subtypes of neurotic disorders. In any case, the degree of particularity of our (predetermined) categories should always be guided by the attempt to attain a theoretical system that will ensure that the practice of therapy guided by it will be as individualized and yet as systematic as possible. There again is that daunting problem.

The point to notice is this: as long as each client/problem category is truly a category—that is, as long as it has, no matter how particular it is, a sufficient degree of abstraction, or generality, to allow the inclusion of many clients—a rule-governed system of therapy may be developed. That is, these client/ problem categories (C) may then be "embedded" within the problem causation (A) problem resolution (B) linkage, as Figure 3.1 illustrates. This linkage constitutes the rule-governed system of therapy that specifies what methods or interventions (B) to use with what kinds of client/problem types (C).

Needless to say, if clients can no longer be assigned to predetermined client/problem categories—that is, if Component C is eliminated from the therapy system because each unique client occupies his own unique "cell" or "noncategory," then a system composed of relationships between predetermined component parts is no longer possible. If each unique client determines his own unique problem, then general client/problem types or categories cannot be predetermined (i.e., determined prior to any particular therapy case) and used to guide the practice of therapy. In that case, the content of therapy practice becomes highly, indeed maximally, individualized—there are no general, predetermined descriptions of problems to constrain whatever therapeutic content emerges in the course of any given case or session.

That is precisely the situation that confronts postmodern/narrative therapists. They believe that there can be no general, predetermined categories of clients/problems, because each client's problem (description) is indeed *uniquely* his own, with unique causes or explanations that cannot be captured by any general, predetermined theory of problem causation (A) (see, e.g., Anderson & Goolishian, 1988, 1992; de Shazer, 1991; Gergen & Kaye, 1992).

Let us consider the logical implications of that move. If each client's problem is uniquely his own, Component C is—for all theoretical and practical purposes—eliminated from the system of therapy, and with that elimination the linkage between Component A and Component B is broken. I return to that point in a moment. For now, note that by removing Component C from one's system of therapy, Component A is also in effect eliminated: how can there be (fixed) causes of nonexistent entities? Thus, if one's system of therapy no longer contains Components A and C, then one has no general, predetermined content to guide one's practice. Here we catch a glimpse, to be elaborated later, of the strong connection between Components A and C, and their mutually supportive role in determining the content of therapy. But in any case, only one component part remains in one's theoretical system, namely, Component B, or therapeutic process. And, recall, one component part cannot, by itself, constitute a system,[4] which by definition requires a set of interrelated component parts.

Needless to say, the effect of all this is nothing less than the erosion of the network of relationships that constituted the (rule-governed) system of therapy to begin with. The resulting "system" is then less organized or structured, less coherent and whole—less complete—than what we find in more conventional therapy systems; and its use produces a practice that is less systematic, or even antisystematic, to use my terminology. In Chapter 4 I examine in more detail the nature of the postmodern narrative therapy "system," including how the antisystematic aspirations of its proponents cannot be fully realized. I also consider how the controversy about realism and antirealism pertains to that system.

FLESHING OUT THE MODEL: ILLUSTRATIONS FROM SOME CONVENTIONAL SYSTEMS AND THE INDIVIDUALITY/SYSTEMATIC TENSION

To appreciate fully the antisystematic aspirations of the postmodern narrative therapy movement as they pertain to the individualization of therapy practice, let us consider how a complete, conventional system of therapy works to constrain, and so systematize, the content and process of therapy.

Those therapy systems that are most conventional are also most explicit in their formulations of Components A, B, and C. They are therefore more complete, and so their use produces a practice that is more systematic but less individualized relative to less conventional, or more incomplete, therapy systems, although they may vary considerably in that effect. Let us use one such conventional system of therapy to illustrate these claims, namely, Freudian or classical psychoanalytic therapy. A cursory review must suffice to illustrate my point.

In classical psychoanalytic therapy, we find a general description of problems (C) and a general theory of problem causation (A)—ones that apply to all clients: unconscious mental conflict (C), which is expressed as symptoms of varying sorts, is caused by the traumatic clash between instinctive drives and societal constraints in early childhood (A). The more common symptoms include neuroses such as obsessions, hysterias, and phobias; less common are

psychoses such as schizophrenia. Note that problem/client types (C), although particularized by types of mental symptoms, are all *subsumed* by the
more generalized notion of mental conflict (C), which itself is always caused
by the traumatic clash of instincts and reality (A).[5] There is, in addition, a
general theory of problem resolution (B)—a theory-cum-method that also
applies to all clients, regardless of symptom type: the therapist must help the
client achieve conscious awareness of the underlying mental conflict and its
causes to free her of her symptoms; this constitutes the theory of problem
resolution. The therapist accomplishes this goal by (a) providing what ana-
lysts call a transference relationship, in which the client can reexperience and
so rework the (childhood) source of the conflict, and by (b) utilizing the
method of free association to access all relevant unconscious thoughts and
affects. This constitutes the therapeutic process or method that is applied in
practice universally.

Note here the correspondence between the theory of problem causation
(A) and the theory-cum-method of problem resolution (B), and their linkage
by way of descriptive categories of problems, in this case mental conflict that
is expressed as symptoms (C). To be sure, the therapist must always, in the
practical application of this theoretical system, tailor her problem description
(C), problem causation explanations (A), and problem resolution explanations and interventions (B) to the unique particulars of the client's situation.
In that sense this complete therapy system can be individualized, especially
with regard to the content of therapy, or Components A and C, since this
system's process of problem resolution (B) is supposed to be applied more
consistently across cases than is its content (A and C). Nonetheless, in this
most conventional of therapy systems, we find clear A, B, and C components
that guide or constrain the content as well as the process of therapy. Because
of its use of a complete theoretical system to guide its practice, then, the
practice of psychoanalytic therapy itself may be highly systematic, but at the
expense of its individualization.[6]

The inability of conventional, complete therapy systems to solve the problem of individuality in practice motivated the emergence of the integrative/
eclectic therapy movement in the 1970s. In hindsight, that movement constitutes a clear compromise between the completeness of the conventional A B
C systems, which guided practice that was systematic enough but not fully
individualized, and the incompleteness of the yet-to-be-created, unconventional postmodern narrative therapy "system," which guides practice to be
more individualized but antisystematic. This compromise consists in the elimination of any one, general theory of problem causation (A), theory-cum-

method of problem resolution (B), and description of problems (C) that applies universally to *all* clients. Instead, we find within the eclectic therapy movement the selective or systematic use of different, more particularized theories of problem causation (A) and theories-cum-methods of problem resolution (B) for different client/problem types (C). We therefore find the abandonment of universals, a move that surely constituted that movement's quest to individualize the practice of therapy. The attempt to organize or systematize the therapist's selection of different interventions for different client/problem types produced the matrix paradigm of the technical/systematic eclectic therapy movement.[7] Figure 3.2 depicts a generic matrix system of therapy in terms of my generic model of therapy systems.

Two points about this generic matrix system must be made explicit. First, note the elimination of Component A. The result is a system that is less complete than the psychoanalytic system we just considered, a system containing all three A B C components. It is nevertheless more complete than what we shall find in the narrative therapy "system," which aspires to eliminate both Components A and C. Recall from Chapter 2 that technical/systematic eclectics, such as Beutler and Lazarus, seek systems that eliminate predetermined theories of problem causation (A) and want instead to provide only the empirical relations that obtain between client/problem categories (C) and interventions (B). That aspiration raises a question: how can a therapist aspire to a systematic practice and yet remove from his theoretical system one of the three components of my generic model — Component A? Recall that Lazarus (Lazarus & Messer, 1991) dismissed such underlying theories as "intellectual fluff." Surely the elimination of Component A makes the eclectic therapy system incomplete, just as the elimination of Components A and C makes the narrative therapy system incomplete. This is an important point for my comparative analysis; let us therefore consider it more carefully before returning to the generic matrix system.

C	B
Client/Problem Type	*Theory of Problem Resolution* *"Theory-cum-Method"*
1.	1.
2.	2.
3.	3.
4.	4.
infinity	infinity

Figure 3.2 A Generic Model of Matrix Therapy Systems

Beutler's client/problem categories—e.g., coping style, resistance potential—in effect combine the type of client/problem relevant to intervention selection with the cause of the problem. Thus, Components A and C are compressed into one component (C), which constitutes the predetermined content of therapy for the matrix system. There is potential confusion in that argument, since clients rarely seek therapy because of a coping style or resistance potential. Instead, they seek therapy because of some more particular, concrete problem in their lives—e.g., an inability to keep friends or make an important life decision. Therapists like Beutler must implicitly recognize this, for they evidently believe such particular problems may be caused by more general factors, for instance, an externalizing or acting-out coping style in the case of the friend problem, and an internalizing or ruminative coping style in the case of the decisional problem. Thus, to say *explicitly* that coping style defines or describes the client/problem category (C) for the purpose of intervention selection is at once to speak *implicitly* of the cause (A) of the client's more particular, presenting problem.

Another way to make my point is to say that there is some confusion within psychotherapy theory about how to define problems themselves (C) as distinct from their causes (A); hence my view that Components A and C, to the extent that they are indeed inseparable within a theoretical system, determine together the content of therapy guided in practice by that system. However, it is beyond the scope of this book to try to disentangle that conflation in any thoroughgoing way.[8]

My first point about a generic matrix (paradigm) system, then, is this: unlike the postmodern narrative system of therapy, which explicitly contains only Component B, the technical/systematic eclectic system of therapy explicitly contains Components B and C. Thus, there is a true system of interrelated component parts in the latter case, but not in the former. Put differently, the technical/systematic eclectic therapy system is more organized or structured, coherent and whole—more complete—than its narrative therapy counterpart, even though it is less complete than a conventional A B C system. Nonetheless, the greater completeness of the eclectic system relative to the narrative system means that therapy practice itself can be more rule-governed/constrained and so more consistent/replicable (i.e., more systematic) than any practice found in the narrative therapy movement, which uses therapy systems that are very incomplete according to my generic model. I elaborate this important point in a moment.

Let us now turn to my second point about the matrix paradigm. Technical/systematic eclectics, such as Beutler and Lazarus, work with a theoretical system of therapy that is more particularized than most—their systems have more categories or types of clients/problems (C), more methods of problem resolution (B), and thus more linkages between those two components, than do most complete or conventional (A B C) systems. Of course, the more particularized the system is, the more individualized the practice of therapy guided by that system can in principle be. To make that fact apparent, and to illustrate what I mean by a more particularized system, let us compare the following two examples of matrix (B C) systems.

In the matrix system of Figure 3.3, note that all clients fall into one client/problem category or the other—hence the categories are mutually exclusive. The assignment of a client to a distinct client/problem category then determines the selection of (in this case, one of two) distinct interventions or methods of problem resolution. It should be readily apparent that this system is more individuated than one in which the *same* theory of problem causation (A), the *same* theory-cum-method of problem resolution (B), and the *same* description of problems (C) are applied universally, that is, applied to *all* clients, regardless of their individual circumstances. By contrast, no category of problems (C) or intervention/method (B) is applied universally in the matrix system—a fact that individualizes the therapy practice of those who are guided by such a therapy system.

In the example of Figure 3.3, the matrix system contains two mutually exclusive categories of problems (C) and methods/interventions (B). How would the individualization of the practice of therapy be affected if it were guided by a system that contained four mutually exclusive categories of problems and interventions instead of two? To illustrate my point, let us contrast the matrix system of Figure 3.3 with that of Figure 3.4.

In Figure 3.4 I have simply particularized my list of types of problems (C) and methods (B) further, to produce categories that are themselves less general or abstract. Thus, notice that each category of problems and methods applies to, or subsumes, fewer clients. For that reason the therapy practice guided by that system can be more individualized, just as the system itself is

C	B
Client/Problem Type	*Theory of Problem Resolution*
	"Theory-cum-Method"
1. Psychotic	1. Method 1
2. Nonpsychotic	2. Method 2

Figure 3.3 A Less Particularized Matrix System of Therapy

C	B
Client/Problem Type	*Theory of Problem Resolution*
	"Theory-cum-Method"
1. Schizophrenia	1. Method 1
2. Psychotic depression	2. Method 2
3. Neurotic disorder	3. Method 3
4. Character disorder	4. Method 4

Figure 3.4 A More Particularized Matrix System of Therapy

more individuated or particularized by virtue of the number of its own internal distinctions. Put differently, there is less generality in the system of Figure 3.4 then in the system of Figure 3.3. (I should add that my number of problems and methods is purely arbitrary; e.g., some combination of two methods could prove empirically to be sufficient for all problem types.)

Beutler has himself proposed a different type of matrix system, as we saw in Chapter 2. He understands that too many categories, too much particularization of the B and C components, creates a matrix that is too unwieldy to test: recall his estimate of 1.5 million cells! Too much particularization, then, can produce a system that is unusable by virtue of its size, and so its use produces a practice that is as antisystematic as a practice guided by a more incomplete system (e.g., one containing only Component B), such as a postmodern system. Beutler also believes that types of mental disorders, which are for the most part mutually exclusive categories (i.e., each client cannot fit all of them simultaneously), are not the best way to predict response to (predetermined) intervention categories/treatment methods. He therefore propounds the use of three or four *dimensions* (e.g., coping style or resistance potential) that apply to *all* clients. Each client, then, fits one end *or* the other of each dimension, and *those* mutually exclusive categories determine the differential use of distinct methods of problem resolution (Component B). Figure 3.5 illustrates my interpretation of Beutler's vision of a proper matrix system.

Note that Beutler particularizes, by virtue of his C categories (which in this case are dimensions), those aspects of behavior (common to all clients) that are relevant to the selection of distinct interventions. But also note that clients are then individuated *within* those dimensions, by means in this case of the two mutually exclusive categories that constitute each dimension, categories that determine the differential use of those distinct interventions.

Whatever version of technical/systematic eclecticism prevails, that type of

C	B
Client/Problem Type	*Theory of Problem Resolution*
	"Theory-cum-Method"

1. Coping Style: 1. Type of Therapy:
   a. Internal   a. Insight
   b. External   b. Skill-building
2. Resistance Potential: 2. Therapist Style:
   a. High   a. Nondirective
   b. Low   b. Directive

Figure 3.5 A Matrix System of Therapy Based on Beutler et al. (1993)

matrix system (C B) is still more complete than the postmodern narrative therapy system (B). The matrix system is also less complete than conventional therapy systems (A B C), which, owing to their completeness, permit a more systematic practice than do either the matrix or narrative therapy systems. An inverse trend obtains when we consider the *individualization* of therapy practice. Because it applies general, predetermined categories of problems (C) to clients, the matrix system produces a practice that is less individualized than does the postmodern narrative therapy system, which aspires to eliminate Component C. However, practice guided by the matrix system is also more individualized than practice guided by a complete, conventional (A B C) system: the matrix system fits particular clients to distinct problem categories (C), which then determine the use of distinct interventions (B). Thus, the matrix system, unlike complete, conventional systems, does not apply to all clients the *same* deindividualizing A B C universals.

Table 3.1 summarizes these comparisons of the three types of systems— Conventional "A B C" systems, Matrix "B C" systems, and Postmodern "B" systems—as they pertain to the individualization of therapy practice. Note that the extent to which practice is individualized by the use of any given therapy system is further differentiated by the distinction between therapeutic content and process. Also notice that in regard to the dimensions of degree of completeness and individualization of therapeutic content in practice (Components A and C), the technical eclectic movement is midway between the complete A B C system of classical psychoanalytic therapy and the incomplete system of postmodern therapy. But something different happens when we consider the individualization of therapeutic process (B), as Table 3.1 indicates. I return to a full discussion of that important problem in Chapter 4, in which I set forth in detail the components of the postmodern narrative system of therapy.

Table 3.1 The Relationship between the Completeness of a Theoretical System
and the Individualization of the Process and Content of Therapy Practice

Theoretical System	Completeness of System (Components A, B, C)	Individualization of Therapeutic Content (Components A & C)	Individualization of Therapeutic Process (Component B)
1. Complete, conventional (e.g., classical psychoanalysis)	1. High (A, B, C)	1. Low, same general A and C used in all cases	1. Low, same general B used in all cases
2. Matrix	2. Moderate (C, B) (C and B are particularized)	2. Moderate, different Cs used for different clients (No one, general C applied universally)	2. High, different Bs used for different clients (No one, general B applied universally)
3. Narrative	3. Low (B)	3. High, no predetermined constraints on content. Each client determines his own unique, personal content	3. Low, same general B used in all cases

REALISM AND ANTIREALISM IN COMPLETE AND INCOMPLETE THERAPY SYSTEMS

Complete or conventional therapy systems—those with all three Components A, B, and C—are usually put forth in a realist way. That is, it is usually taken for granted that the three component parts—alone and together— tell us something that is true independent of the theory—something that is extratheoretically true. Thus, the theories of problem causation and resolution that are put forth in conventional therapies are usually assumed to make objective claims about the real causes of problems and of solutions. Similarly, the client/problem categories put forth in conventional therapy systems are assumed to provide the true, or extratheoretic, nature of problems as they exist in an independent reality.

I use the word "assumed" above because one can in principle construct a complete or conventional (A B C) system of therapy from an antirealist position. Although that seems odd, that is in fact what (postmodern) linguistic philosophers (like Rorty) advocate in their philosophy of science. In that philosophy, scientific theories can be highly complete and yet always give us only an antirealist story, one that can never in principle say anything true about an extralinguistic reality. I, of course, do not adopt that antirealist philosophy of science myself; but the social constructionism of the postmodern narrative therapy movement may be used in just that way—namely, to produce an antirealist system of therapy, however complete or incomplete that system may be.

I consider social constructionism and how it pertains to the individuality/systematic tension in therapy in Chapters 4 and 5. Just here, I emphasize my point that the *completeness of a theoretical system has no necessary bearing on the realism or antirealism of that system.* (Nevertheless, it does relate to the individuality/systematic question—see Table 3.1; I shall have more to say about that latter relation in due course.) Thus, a less complete system—such as the postmodern narrative system of therapy, which is extremely incomplete—may be put forth in a perfectly realist way. In short, the completeness or incompleteness of a theoretical system and its alleged realism or antirealism—that is, whether it is said to attain an extratheoretic reality—are quite independent features of systems.

But what about the realism of a moderately complete therapy system, such as technical/systematic eclecticism, which retains two (B C) of the three components of our generic model? Here the same reasoning applies. The diminished completeness of that system of therapy in no way determines the epistemological preferences of its proponents, although they happen in my experience to be realists. Technical eclectics, such as Beutler and Lazarus, operate with a realist view of the components of their systems (C B), no less than do the proponents of more complete, conventional (A B C) systems, such as classical psychoanalytic therapists. To the extent that Component A is implicitly contained within Component C in technical eclecticism, it, along with Components C and B, is taken seriously as a real, extralinguistic factor in the client's life. [9]

REALISM AND ANTIREALISM IN CLIENT/PROBLEM TYPES (C) AND THEORIES OF PROBLEM CAUSATION (A): A CLOSER LOOK

To appreciate how the realism/antirealism distinction has been used in therapy systems, whether complete or incomplete, we must take a closer look at clients/problems (C) and theories of problem causation (A). That is because the postmodern narrative therapy movement is most explicitly antirealist about those two components of therapy systems, components which, recall, predetermine the content of therapy and which postmodern narrative therapists therefore aspire to eliminate. It is also my claim that what that movement *takes* to be an act of *antirealism* is in reality only its *antisystematic* attempt to eliminate those two components from its "system," and to replace them with whatever unique, personal (i.e., nonpredetermined) problems or "problems"[10] each client brings to therapy. (Just below I discuss the problematic equation within narrative therapy of the unique/personal on the one hand, and subjectivity/antirealism on the other.)

Let us begin with two assertions: (a) despite the narrative therapy movement's attempts to eliminate Components A and C, there are realist vestiges of both components in its "system," as I demonstrate in Chapters 4 and 5; and (b) the realism the narrative therapy movement tries to deny nonetheless reveals itself most clearly in its theory of problem resolution (B). That component (B), which is the only *acknowledged* (predetermined) component of the narrative therapy "system," is nothing less than a fully realist component of the "system," even though that system's designers fail to recognize it.

Within the "system" proposed by postmodern narrative therapists, then, we find unwitting realism. That realism pervades its unacknowledged, predetermined theory of problem causation (A), its unacknowledged, predetermined description or view of problems themselves (C), and its acknowledged, predetermined theory of problem resolution (B). But before we can fully appreciate how realism and antirealism apply to the components of the narrative therapy system, we must first be clear about my use of the term "personal theory."[11]

Therapists who rely on Components A and C of a complete therapy system to provide a description of problems and a theory of problem causation to guide their practice are of course applying to their clients the components that have been predetermined within that therapy system. These components therefore must have some degree of generality, that is, they must apply to more than one client. Conventional or modern therapists tend to use such general, predetermined[12] components to guide the diagnosis, or description, and explanation of the client's difficulties; their use therefore guides or constrains the content of therapy in a consistent way.

By contrast, therapists—such as postmodern narrative ones—who try to eliminate Components A and C from their system accomplish two things: (a) they render their system less complete in their antisystematic attempt to retain only Component B; and (b) they also try not to predetermine (i.e., not to employ any generalizations about) the content of therapy—what gets discussed in practice in terms of the description of the problem (C), its causes (A), and hence, ultimately, the client's goals or objectives. Instead, they must look elsewhere for their source of content. That search must lead them to each unique client's unique life experiences and, more important for the postmodern narrative therapy movement, each unique client's unique views or narrative of her life experience. Those unique views may, if they incorporate some causal assumptions about the "problem" (as they usually do), constitute a (client's) personal theory of problem causation, or simply a personal theory.

The question of realism and antirealism arises when postmodern narrative therapists assume that the client's unique, personal description of and causal theory about his problem are subjective by nature; on that assumption, they allege that no reality claim can be attached to it. That epistemological view should not be surprising, since the postmodern narrative therapy movement adopts the antirealist epistemology of postmodernism in general; it therefore does not believe that the general, predetermined categories of client/problem types (C) and theories of problem causation (A) of (complete) systems of therapy can give us any independent, extratheoretic reality. Postmodernism, then, extends its antirealism to even the most complete scientific theories, which are alleged to be nothing more than local, contextualized, consensually validated stories or narratives—that is, social/linguistic constructions that are *always* antirealist. [13] So there is, from the postmodern perspective, no truth to be lost by trying, in the pursuit of an individualized therapy practice, to eliminate from practice the use of general, predetermined categories and (causal) laws (i.e., Components A and C).

That move makes the practice of postmodern narrative therapy less rule-governed/systematic than is practice based on more complete, conventional therapy systems, in which the objective truth of the predetermined categories of clients/problems (C) and of the predetermined theories of problem causation (A) is simply taken for granted. Conventional, or modern, therapists can therefore use those categories and theories in a systematic way to enhance the process of problem resolution. But that systematic employment of general, predetermined categories and causal theories is always at the expense of some individualization in therapy practice—a cost perhaps made more acceptable to modern therapists by the expectation that the use of these generalities increases their ability to attain truth, and with it the real resolution of real problems. There again is that tension between the individualized and the systematic, for that which is systematic requires the deindividualizing use of generalities.

Realism and Antirealism in the Client's
Personal Problem Description (C) and
Theory about Its Causes (A)

In narrative therapy the description of the problem and the theory about its causes are supposed to be determined by each unique client's unique narrative of her unique life experience, and so they are not supposed to be predetermined by Components A and C of some complete therapy system. Nevertheless, that does not automatically make the client's personal view an antirealist one. Indeed, one can just as readily assume that the client, in defining his problem and giving his views of its causes and effects (i.e., its implications and meanings), is also giving the therapist some truth about his life as it exists independent of his theory or narrative. Still, some qualification would be helpful here.

Conventional or modern therapists tend to believe that clients' own descriptions of their problems (C) and theories about their causes (A) have less realism in them than do the general, predetermined categories and causal theories of whatever system of therapy a therapist uses. Established systems of therapy are, after all, usually seen as more complete and scientific than any particular formulation the client may offer. And for many modernists at least, science is supposed to give us the best available purchase on the many aspects of the real to which we have no direct access. [14] Nonetheless, there is no reason for any therapist to think that the client's personal view is fully antirealist, unless that client is believed to be psychotic in *all* respects. Yet, I know of no therapist—modern or postmodern—who believes her clients cannot know and relate—in more or less correct approximation to their extralinguistic reality—at least the temporospatial events that have taken place in their lives (e.g., the fact that a family member got married, or committed suicide).

Knowledge of events/happenings is surely more directly accessible than knowledge of the causes (and effects) [15] of those events. This is true whether that causal knowledge is a product of some scientific theory or of a particular client's unique, personal theory. I use the distinction between knowledge of events and knowledge of their causes (i.e., the distinction between descriptions and explanations of events) to make an epistemological point in Chapter 6. But here I would insist that a personal theory does not necessarily require an antirealist interpretation, at least not in its entirety. Rather, a modest, or limited, realism may reasonably be applied to such a personal view of one's life. And I believe it is precisely because the (postmodern) antirealist view of personal—indeed of all—theories is unsustainable, that we find an oscillation between realism and antirealism within the postmodern narrative therapy movement.

Postmodern narrative therapists of course give all theories/narratives/ views/stories an equally antirealist interpretation, regardless of whether they make claims about life in general or about a particular individual's utterly unique, personal experience.[16] Despite that interpretation, there are two ways that some degree of realism appears in narrative therapists' theory and practice, especially regarding therapeutic content. First, their theoretical system of therapy contains a predetermined theory of problem causation (A), although it is so highly general that it places no *practical* constraints on the doing of therapy. It is therefore easily disregarded, denied, or ignored. Still, that predetermined component is put forth as nothing short of realist. Second, in practice, they *treat* the client—no less than does the modern therapist—as if his personal views referred more or less adequately to some extralinguistic reality. Thus, there is some contradiction (caused by the unintended use of realism) both *within* the antirealist theory postmodern therapists propound and *between* that antirealist theory and the way those therapists actually practice therapy.

Although I elaborate and support these claims in Chapters 4 and 5, here I call attention to one point: the source of theory for the content of practice— whether it is predetermined by some complete therapy system or is determined solely by the client's unique, personal views—does not automatically determine a realist or antirealist interpretation of that theory. Thus, (general, predetermined) components of therapy systems, indeed, entire therapy systems themselves, can be interpreted in either a realist or an antirealist way. Similarly, a client's personal theory about her life experience, which may apply only to that one person, can be considered to be either realist or antirealist. Recall that it is simply the use itself of some system of therapy— and not whether that system is put forth as realist or antirealist—that diminishes the individualization (as it increases the systematization) of practice.

This last point is important; let me therefore drive it home: the *degree* to which the practice of therapy is individualized (vs. systematic) is—contrary to what postmodern therapists may believe—in no way a function of the realism or antirealism of the theoretical system used to guide practice, but is rather a function of the *completeness* of that system, in terms of the three (A B C) component parts. To use the client's unique, personal theory in a realist way, with minimal use or imposition of general, predetermined theory, makes the practice of therapy just as individualized, but just as antisystematic, as using the client's personal theory in an antirealist way. The adoption of realism, therefore, does not prevent the attainment of individuality in the practice of therapy. Conversely, to use or impose predetermined theory in an antirealist way is to make the practice of therapy just as deindividualized, but just as systematic, as using such theory in a realist way. The adoption of antirealism, therefore, does not insure the attainment of individuality in the practice of therapy; rather, it is actually irrelevant to that pursuit.

This argument prompts a question: why would the members of the postmodern narrative therapy movement cling to an antirealism that (a) they cannot adhere to consistently in either their theory or their practice, and that (b) in any case is not necessary to achieve an individualized approach to the practice of therapy? I address those questions again in Chapters 4 and 5, along with the problems the narrative therapy movement encounters when it fails to see that, despite its best intentions, it does indeed have a predetermined theory of problem causation (A) within its system. Because that theory is so highly generalized, abstract, or nonspecific, it may at best seem only implicit — a fact which may explain why its very existence seems to be overlooked, or at least unacknowledged. But that theory really exists; moreover, it contains a claim about human existence that is fully realist.

Using Predetermined Theory vs. the Client's Personal Theory in the Practice of Therapy: A Question of Balance in Therapeutic Content

It is important to note the ever-present distinction between a theory about how therapy should work, and the actual practice of the therapy that is guided by that theory.[17] That distinction is especially relevant to this discussion, since I know of no therapist — modern or postmodern — who works exclusively with content that has been predetermined by a system of therapy or that is determined by each unique client. Even though the postmodern narrative therapy movement tries to individualize its practice by eliminating from its system Components A and C, the fact that it cannot fully attain that goal is, in my view, a good thing: it forces its therapy practice to be more systematic (with regard to content) than it would otherwise be. By contrast, even though the technical/systematic eclectic therapy movement tries to use its matrix of predetermined categories to select the best possible intervention (B) for a type of client/problem (C), the fact that it cannot in its practice ignore the client's unique, personal understandings of her experience is also a good thing: it makes its therapy practice more individualized than it would otherwise be. Indeed, to ignore the client's personal view of her problem/experience is to do bad therapy—whatever one's epistemological preference may be, for then the therapist loses sight of the individual. Thus, even fully complete, conventional (A B C) therapy systems (such as classical psychoanalysis) must always, when used in practice, leave room for what is uniquely personal.

In short, to be systematic, all good therapy practice both needs and uses content that is predetermined by a therapy system; to be individualized, all good practice both needs and uses content that is determined by each unique client. All good therapy practice, then, must have some degree of both types of content in its composition; no therapy, in its actual practice, can work exclusively with content predetermined by a therapy system or by the client's personal views. It is, rather, a question of balance—the relative weight put on the use of general, predetermined theory vs. unique, nonpredetermined theory in selecting the content of therapy. Of course, modern therapists who work with more complete systems place relatively more emphasis on the former; postmodern therapists on the latter.

We therefore find that the content predetermined by a therapy system is never, in the actual practice of good therapy, unmodified by the unique circumstance, including the personal theory, of the client to which it is applied. Rather, it is always in the act of therapy *tailored* to fit the nuances of any individual case, thereby rendering that content more specific, or particularized. This is usually done by means of a collaborative process of understanding between therapist and client. For instance, unconscious mental conflict, which constitutes a general, predetermined understanding of problems in psychoanalysis, must always have its particular nature determined, and hence affected, by the specifics of each client's unique case (see Figure 3.6).

Conversely, the content obtained from the client's unique, personal theory or view is never, in the actual practice of good therapy, unmodified by whatever predetermined content the therapist is using.[18] Thus, the client's personal theory is always *reformulated* in the act of therapy to fit the constraints, or concepts, of the therapy system in use, concepts which usually give some shape to the client's personal theory. For instance, a client's ideas about the cause of her depression at the personal-theory level—that it is the result of some recent negative life experience—will probably be reformulated in terms of unconscious mental conflict in psychoanalysis, a current pattern of interpersonal interaction in systemic family therapy, or an irrational cognition in cognitive therapy (see Figure 3.6).

To summarize, in the actual practice of therapy, general, predetermined theory must be tailored to fit the specifics of the client's unique, personal experiences and views; conversely, clients' unique, personal views must be

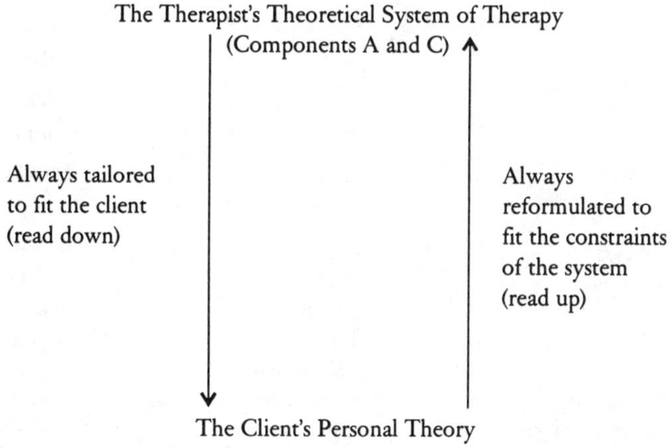

The Therapist's Theoretical System of Therapy
(Components A and C) ↑

Always tailored
to fit the client
(read down)

Always
reformulated to
fit the constraints
of the system
(read up)

The Client's Personal Theory

Figure 3.6 The Practical Interaction between the Therapist's (General, Predetermined) System of Therapy and the Client's Personal Theory

reformulated to fit the constraints of whatever general, predetermined theory is in use. This is a perfectly general claim about the practice of all therapy as it pertains to therapeutic content (Components A and C).

For the purpose of this critique, it is important to note that the second part of that last claim is called into question in one unconventional circumstance. To understand the conditions under which the claim does not hold, we must first understand more precisely the relation between the nature of therapeutic generalities and the individualization of therapy practice. The most important point is this: if one varies the *degree of generality* of a theory of problem causation (and definition of problems themselves) that is applied *indiscriminately*, or without exception, to all clients (an act that stands in sharp contrast to what occurs in the matrix paradigm),[19] one can potentially affect the degree of individualization attained in practice. That relation obtains because more general theories place fewer constraints on the way the therapist uses the client's unique, personal theory than do more specific, particular, or precisely formulated theories that are applied indiscriminately to all clients. To clarify this difficult relation, let us consider an example of how varying the degree of generality of the one problem causation component of three (equally complete, A B C) therapy systems affects the degree of individualization obtained in practice (see Figure 3.7). I hope to demonstrate that this effect on individualization is caused by the degree of constraint placed on the way personal theory gets used in practice.

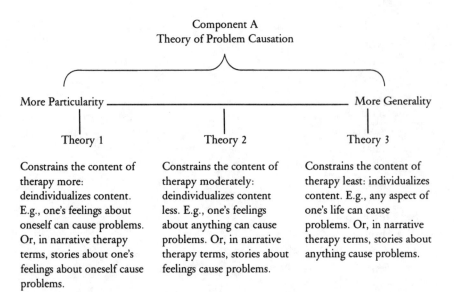

Figure 3.7 **How the Degree of Generality of the Theory of Problem Causation Affects the Individualization of the Content of Therapy**

Let us assign to each of the complete systems I use to illustrate this relation the three component parts of the generic model: one theory of problem causation (A), one description or notion of what constitutes problems (C), and one theory of problem resolution (B). But let us allow Component A to vary in its generality. In the least generalized, or most specific/particular, version—I'll call it Theory 1—let us assume that Component A states that feelings about the self cause (the experience of) problems. In the middle, more generalized, or less specific/particular, version—I'll call it Theory 2—let us assume that feelings in general—that is, feelings of no particular sort—are the cause of (the experience of) problems. Notice that in Theory 2 the generality, or nonspecificity/nonparticularity, of the claim means that any and all feelings a client experiences can become the focus or content of therapy, without any predetermined specifications or constraints placed on the particular types of feelings to consider. By contrast, in Theory 1 the higher specificity, or particularity, of the claim means that the therapist will always, that is, in all his cases, attend to feelings of a more particular sort— namely, feelings about the self. Thus, if the client's experiences and personal narrative of those experiences do not readily fit that Theory 1 specification, they will have to be reformulated by any therapist who wants to use Theory

1 to guide his practice. For instance, a client who describes his problem as distress owing to his wife's negative feelings about him may have that particular content reformulated by being asked (by a therapist using Theory 1) to consider how his wife's feelings about him may affect the way he feels about himself.

Now let us consider Theory 3, which constitutes the most general, nonspecific, or nonparticular theory of problem causation of all—namely, that the way one narrates, or finds meaning in, one's life causes "problems." Notice that now we need not concern ourselves with the particularity or nonparticularity of feelings at all. Instead, *whatever* personal ideas/meanings/theories/stories/views/understandings (and so forth) the client brings into therapy constitutes its content, with no need for a *particular* type of reformulation (i.e., with no need for a predetermined reformulation)—not ever! Therefore, the usual constraint on the content of therapy practice caused by the use of Component A is here, for all practical purposes, nonexistent.

This last example (Theory 3) exemplifies the claims about both problem causation and problem resolution found within the postmodern narrative therapy movement. Because this one theory of problem causation within the postmodern narrative system of therapy is so very general, nonspecific, nonparticular, or imprecisely formulated, two effects obtain: (a) that theory of problem causation escapes the attention of even those who constructed and/or use it; and (b) that theory places, for all practical purposes, no real constraints on the content of therapy—that is, on the direction in which the client's views, or personal theory, should be taken. (Therefore, in Chapters 4 and 5, I refer to this component of the narrative therapy system as a "vestigial" component.)

To summarize, the unconditional, or indiscriminate, use of the *same* theory of problem causation for *all* cases—that is, regardless of each client's unique circumstances—is usually deindividualizing. However, the extreme generality, nonspecificity, nonparticularity, or imprecise formulation of this one (and only) theory of problem causation of the postmodern narrative therapy movement is such that it can accommodate—without reformulation—any personal content supplied by a client. In this one case, then, the client's personal theory can indeed, whatever its content, play a completely unmodified role in determining the content of therapy (at least initially), as the members of the narrative movement rightly (in my opinion) claim. This affords great individualization in the practice of such therapy. But that individualization always comes at the expense of those constraints that make that practice rule-governed and, therefore, systematic—in this case, in regard to its content.

A RECENT EMPHASIS ON PERSONAL PROBLEM DESCRIPTION AND PERSONAL THEORY OF PROBLEM CAUSATION IN CONVENTIONAL (COMPLETE) THERAPY SYSTEMS

There is currently a trend among a good many conventional or complete psychotherapy systems to put more explicit emphasis on the client's unique, personal description of her problem and unique, personal theory about its causation, and to deemphasize general, predetermined categories of problems (C) and general, predetermined theories of problem causation (A). Those systems therefore reflect the antisystematic aspiration to eliminate the use of predetermined content in therapy. We find this trend even though theories of problem causation are not—indeed cannot—be completely eliminated from any system that calls itself a therapeutic one. (All therapy systems must contain some theory-cum-method of problem resolution (B), and that type of theory always points, at least implicitly, to the target of the intervention—a target that is perceived to be connected to the problem in some causal way.) In any event, this tendency to emphasize unique, personal theory, and to deemphasize general, predetermined theory, is noteworthy because the therapies that reflect it began as conventional or complete—i.e., non-postmodern—ones. Thus, they did not evolve expressly to incorporate the antirealist and the antisystematic tendencies we find within postmodern thought.

Rather, postmodern ideology has apparently influenced some conventional or complete, and widely used, therapy systems. In so doing it has established itself and broadened its impact, to the point that we may now indeed speak with authority of a postmodern narrative therapy movement. This infiltration is most pronounced in psychoanalytic therapies, cognitive therapies, family therapies, and even integrative/eclectic therapies—although it is by no means limited to them. These therapies all began with more complete theoretical systems and so contained general, predetermined understandings of problems and their causes—understandings that were also typically put forth as realist.

In those therapies we now find an increasing preoccupation with the application to therapy of postmodern antirealist, and sometimes antisystematic, philosophy and literary theory. Regarding the antisystematic trend, there is an attempt to use the client's unique, personal theory, narrative, understanding, or views about his problem as the exclusive (content) focus for therapeutic intervention. We therefore sometimes find the antisystematic aspiration to eliminate Components A and C from those (heretofore more complete) systems of therapy. Regarding the antirealist trend, the client's unique, personal view is usually taken to be antirealist (although again there is no good reason to make that equation). In this way, the antisystematic aspiration to create therapy systems that are incomplete becomes linked with the adoption of antirealism in postmodern therapy. The examples that follow illustrate attempts to make therapy systems both (a) more incomplete, leading to a less systematic, or an antisystematic, practice, and (b) fully antirealist. Note that in the following examples I use as many direct quotations as possible, and that I sometimes place some of my own commentary within brackets internal to those quotations.

Not long ago family/systemic therapies were dominated by talk about how dysfunctional interpersonal/family patterns of interaction caused pathology/problems (this is, needless to say, a realist theory of problem causation). Now, however, there is considerable talk of how the unique, personal and subjective, or antirealist, meanings of each family member's "experience" define and cause "problems" that supposedly exist only in language. Anderson and Goolishian (1988), for example, discuss the increasing dissatisfaction with the view that therapists should know the optimal condition for clients and therefore can, from an independent or objective position, both diagnose pathology and "fix" that pathology (p. 376). According to Anderson and Goolishian, this objectivity is to be eschewed. They argue instead that "there are no 'facts' to be known, no systems to be 'understood' [i.e., no real, extralinguistic dysfunctions/problems and their causes], and no patterns and regularities [i.e., no consistent categories or generalities that lend themselves to systematic study and intervention] to be 'discovered'" (p. 378). Thus, for them,

> Problems and the [interpersonal] systems organized by them are not fixed entities existing over time until they are resolved or repaired. Problems and problem-organizing systems are changed and reinterpreted just as often, and just as rapidly, as the other narratives around which we organize meaning and social exchange. . . . Problems are in the *intersubjective* [italics added] minds of all who are in active communicative exchange and, as such, are themselves always changing. (p. 380)

Note in this one broad stroke both the *antirealist* elimination of any (knowable) extralinguistic reality, and the *antisystematic* elimination of any generalities—that is, any enduring entities, or systems—within that reality. Instead, there are only antirealist stories about unique, now-you-see-them-now-you-don't "problems"—such stories can therefore never be fixed or predetermined, and so they cannot be used to systematize the practice of therapy.

Other family/systemic therapists, such as Epstein and Loos (1989), reiterate this position when they state,

> We view the process of problem definition as a collaborative venture in which the therapist acts as a coconspirator with the client(s) in the creation of a therapeutic reality [note the postmodern antirealist idea that reality is made, or created, and not discovered]. The therapist is not a passive investigator of "facts" nor merely a mirror for the client's self-representation. In addition, the therapist is not a diagnostic expert. This means that the definition of the problem or diagnosis must be developed together and can no longer be based on "objective" notions of health or psychopathology. (p. 414)
>
> Therapy is not a process of searching for and treating the "correct" problem definition [note the use of quotation marks around the words "facts," "objective," and "correct" to undermine the existence of independent, true facts]. . . . We can only evaluate the utility [note the emphasis on the pragmatic question] of a particular problem definition locally through conversation [note the complete nongeneralizability, the extreme locality, of problems, which contributes to an antisystematic thrust]. (p. 415)
>
> Diagnoses are creations [within therapeutic conversations] . . . that may either limit or expand the context for generating new ideas. (pp. 414–415)

In these quotations we again find the elimination of extralinguistic, objective truth or reality and of general, enduring entities, or systems, within that reality. Such entities, or systems, would presumably, within a modern (realist) epistemological context, prompt the development of (complete) theoretical systems to study and understand them. Instead, because this is a postmodern (antirealist) framework, nothing exists outside or independent of the evanescent ebb and flow of language/conversation.

We find a similar trend within cognitive therapy, which has traditionally sought to define the types of irrational, unrealistic, or incorrect beliefs and ideas—including the "inaccurate attributions of causality for negative events" (Neimeyer & Feixas, 1990, p. 10)—that cause problems/pathology. As Neimeyer and Feixas (1990) put it, the traditional goals of cognitive therapy

> presuppose the existence of an absolute truth, which can be accessed through the proper use of logic or the direct testing of our belief systems against external reality. . . . [In place of this, Neimeyer and Feixas endorse Wessler

and Wessler's (1986)] Cognitive Appraisal Therapy, [which] attempts to bring into awareness those implicit "personal rules for living" [PRL's] that guide a client's self-appraisal and decision making [rules that, consistent with the anti-realism being promoted, presumably need not reflect extralinguistic reality to be "viable"]. . . . [I]t is the viability [note again the pragmatic thrust], and not the rationality of these "PRL's" that is crucial. . . . A further point of departure from objectivist cognitive-behavioral theories is their [Wessler & Wessler's] relatively greater attention to reconstructing a phenomenological developmental narrative that helps a client make sense of his or her *personal* [italics added] history. Again, this corresponds to the growing emphasis on narrative or story-telling psychologies . . . . (Neimeyer & Feixas, 1990, pp. 10–11)

Mahoney, who is an important figure within the cognitive-behavioral therapy movement, now speaks of the personal subjectivity of all therapy, indeed of all knowing itself: "there is an increasing recognition that the knower/observer cannot be removed from either the process or the product of knowing" (Mahoney, 1989, p. 1374). A clearer statement of (a postmodern) antirealism cannot be found, and that antirealism dominates much of Mahoney's recent writings (e.g., Mahoney, 1993), including his book *Human Change Processes* (1991).

The same trend occurs in psychoanalytic therapies, which have, incidentally, always placed considerable emphasis on the unique, personal meanings clients construct from their experiences. These meanings are often taken to be highly subjective in these therapies, and so we find in them the previously discussed equation between the unique/personal on the one hand, and subjectivity on the other. But that emphasis on unique/personal, and allegedly subjective, meaning was always, traditionally at least, understood within the context of general and allegedly objective claims about the true cause of real, objective problems/pathologies. For example, within psychoanalytic therapy systems there are (reality) claims about how the conflict between internal drives (e.g., for pleasure) and the constraints of external reality, or society, causes symptoms. According to Neimeyer and Feixas (1990, p. 9), "some [psychoanalytic] theorists have distanced themselves even more forcefully from metapsychology [i.e., claims about how internal, instinctual drives and forces determine symptom formation], by focusing on concrete clinical heuristics tied directly to the analytic encounter. For example, Peterfreund (1983) enjoins the therapist to '*discuss unique personal meanings*'" [italics added] (Neimeyer & Feixas, 1990, p. 9). Note here the antisystematic focus on individuality, by means of discussing unique, personal theory or meanings, rather than discussing any general, predetermined ones in therapy.

Schafer (1992), in his book *Retelling a Life: Narration and Dialogue in Psychoanalysis*, expresses a similar idea. Consider, for instance, the following statements:

> Subjective experience itself is viewed as a construction of human agency. Experience is not simply "there in the mind" waiting to be found and retrieved by objective introspection. Different people tend to construct experiences of the same event differently, each for reasons of his or her *own* [italics added].[20] (pp. xiii–xiv)

> It is especially important to emphasize that narrative is not an alternative to truth or reality; rather, it is the mode in which, inevitably, truth and reality are presented. We have only *versions* [italics added] of the true and the real. Narratively unmediated, definitive access to truth and reality cannot be demonstrated [note that, true to antirealism, theory/language *always* gets between, mediates, the particular knower and the known in such a way that it can always be counted on to alter in experience the true nature of that reality]. In this respect, therefore, there can be no absolute foundation on which any observer or thinker stands; *each* [italics added] must choose his or her narrative version [again, note the emphasis on the unique, personal quality of each subjective, or antirealist, *version* of "truth" and "reality"]. (pp. xiv–xv)

> To agree that analysts interpret interpenetrated or cohabited texts is to accord to constructivism and its corollary, perspectivism, an essential place in psychoanalysis and to put into permanent question the traditional psychoanalytic claim to the status of an empirical, inductive, objectively observational science. (p. 177)

> This [traditional] image [of the analyst as an "objective and independent clinician who simply observes what analysands set forth and draws the inevitable conclusions" (p. 179)] is, however, merely one of a number of possible images of the analyst, and to some analysts it has already become a joke. (p. 179)

It is noteworthy that the proliferation of this rhetoric about unique, personal, and allegedly subjective, or antirealist, narrative/meaning is now appearing within some factions of the integrative/eclectic therapy movement itself (see Chapter 2). That is surprising, because that movement has, in its pursuit of individuality, worked to hold to a systematic, scientific—and implicitly realist—approach to the theory and practice of therapy. Nonetheless, such antirealists as Neimeyer and Feixas (1990) are not lesser members of the integrative/eclectic therapy movement because of their antirealism. But they are still atypical within that movement because they attempt to integrate various psychotherapy movements by explicitly claiming they share a common constructivist, or antirealist, metatheory, which they call Theoretically Progressive Integrationism (see Chapter 2). Consider these remarks made by them:

> Human knowledge is ultimately (inter)*personal* [italics added] . . . and evolutionary . . . , with no simple prospect of validation against and [*sic*] objective reality beyond our constructions. (p. 6)

> From this *personal* construct [italics added] view, it follows that therapy is more a *creative* than a *corrective* enterprise . . . . Rather than directly challenging the validity of the client's existing constructions, the therapist helps the client *invent* [italics added] new, and perhaps more viable alternatives. (p. 9)

> Effective psychotherapy requires a subtle appreciation of the nature of a client's *personal* [italics added] system [of constructs/meanings], . . . because its content determines the locus of intervention . . . (Neimeyer & Harter, 1988). (p. 13)

Note here that the client's unique, personal theory or view of her problem is supposed to supply the content of therapy, or object of problem resolution.

In a more recent article, Neimeyer (1993, p. 225) states (in a table) that the "target of intervention" consists in the "personal narratives" of clients, and that the "interpretation of client's meanings" is "metaphoric, idiosyncratic." Again, we see an antisystematic attempt to eliminate from their theoretical system any general, predetermined content. Moreover, as the quotations indicate, Neimeyer and Feixas always take these personal meanings/narratives to be subjective, or antirealist—there is that equation between the uniquely personal on the one hand and antirealism on the other. Hence we find in these authors both the antisystematic and antirealist aspirations that characterize postmodernism itself. The antirealism notwithstanding, the effect of their antisystematic aspiration is a therapy practice that is, to be sure, more individualized. But that practice is also, unavoidably, less systematic.

Others within the integrative therapy movement have made similar observations. Messer, for instance, has put forth an approach called "Evolutionary or Assimilative Integration" (Lazarus & Messer, 1991). In promoting that approach he argues,

> We do not simply discover what is inherent in nature, but we *invent our theories and categories, and view nature through them* [all italics added]. [Note here the antirealist doctrine that there is no reality available to the knower that is

independent of the knower or the knower's theory/language, or categories.]
In this view, multiple interpretations of experience are considered legitimate,
desirable, and in any case, unavoidable. . . . [T]here is no single truth out there
to discover. (p. 150)

In place of what he calls the "unitary/discovery" model of knowledge, Messer
offers "creative diversity," which bears striking resemblance to the local, personal, and allegedly subjective "truths" of postmodernism. Another quotation
of Messer makes the postmodern reference explicit: "I am espousing a post-
positivist or postmodernist conception that questions whether there is certain
or objective truth or reality" (p. 155).

Solovey and Duncan (1992) have made contributions to both the family/
systemic and the integrative/eclectic therapy movements. They nonetheless
reveal their antisystematic and antirealist inclinations by preferring the use of
theory that is unique to each client (or personal) and subjective (or antirealist)
and so by rejecting the use of theory that is general (or predetermined) and
objective (or realist):

> Constructivism [an antirealist doctrine which they endorse] elevates the client's
> view of reality, particularly the client's meaning system regarding the presenting
> problem, to paramount importance in the therapeutic process. The application
> of constructivism to therapy makes the client's meaning system hierarchically
> superior to the therapist's theoretical orientation and/or personal beliefs. Con-
> structivism, therefore, provides a strong rationale for respecting the preemi-
> nence of the client's world view. In practical terms, it emphasizes the client's
> idiosyncratic meaning system as the impetus for therapy. (p. 55)

Note here that constructivism, a form of antirealism I discuss in some detail
in Chapter 4, is equated with the client's "idiosyncratic," or personal, views,
which are thus always seen as subjective, or antirealist. Hence we again see
that equation between the unique or personal, on the one hand, and antirealism, on the other. I must therefore again emphasize that the uniquely personal
experience or view of experience need not of necessity be equated with
subjectivity, or antirealism—certainly not any more than the generalized (or
nonunique) experience or view of experience need be equated with objectivity, or realism. Indeed, perfectly generalized views (those held by many) are
sometimes taken to be fully antirealist views, for instance, within the doctrine
of social constructionism, which I also discuss in Chapter 4. [21]

In these many heretofore complete therapy systems, then, there is a common postmodern trend—the attempt to rid each therapy's theoretical system, and therefore the practice guided by that system, of two elements: (a) general, predetermined and allegedly realist, or objective, categories of problems (C); and (b) general, predetermined and allegedly realist, or objective, theories of problem causation (A). (Note again the presumed pairing of generality and realism by postmodern therapists.) There is also the attempt to replace those so-called objective generalities with what, according to postmodernists, is the client's unique, personal and subjective, or antirealist, story about his problem experience. (Note again the presumed pairing of uniqueness, or ultimate particularity, and antirealism by postmodern therapists.) In short, the aspirations being expressed are at once both antisystematic and antirealist. This broad convergence of thinking is what constitutes the emergence of the postmodern narrative therapy movement as a distinct movement in itself—a movement that may be characterized by its emphasis on the unique individuality of each client's (antirealist) "problem." But that individualization of the content of therapy can be accomplished only by sacrificing the completeness of the theory that guides practice, a move which necessarily makes that practice less systematic than it might otherwise be.

I must once more remind the reader that there are two fundamental problems with those attempts to be antisystematic and antirealist in the pursuit of a truly individualized approach to therapy practice. First, it is the *use itself* of general, predetermined categories of problems (C) and general, predetermined theories about their causes (A), and not the realist or antirealist nature of those categories and theories, that determines the extent to which the content of therapy can be truly individualized. Thus, the realism or antirealism of one's theoretical system is irrelevant to the pursuit of individuality; only the use of (predetermined) generalities—that is, only the completeness of the therapy system—matters in that regard. Second, not all objective or truth claims—that is, not all objective generalities—about the nature of problems and problem causation have been successfully removed from the postmodern narrative system of therapy. Rather, those claims have merely, perhaps by virtue of their *extreme* generality or their more implicit expression, managed to escape the attention of the members of that movement.

But postmodern narrative therapists have nonetheless *explicitly* propounded an objective, or realist, generality. That generality consists in an explicit, universally applied theoretical claim about the process of problem resolution. Thus, postmodern narrative therapists retain in their system one component (B) without equivocation. Let us now turn our attention to that component.

REALISM AND ANTIREALISM IN
THEORIES OF PROBLEM RESOLUTION

The philosophical/theoretical picture is much simpler when we turn to theories of problem resolution. That is because that component of therapy must be made explicit within any system of therapy that aspires to be in any sense a true system of therapy, however complete or incomplete it may be. That component is therefore essential.

Theories of problem resolution, then, constitute a necessary component of all therapy systems. Thus, in formulating a system of therapy, one cannot strive to eliminate all predetermined generalities about the process of problem resolution and still have a system—in any sense of that term—of therapy. Recall from our earlier discussions that systems of therapy can exist (although incompletely) without explicitly providing (general, predetermined) categories of problems (C) and theories of problem causation (A). But as Prochaska and DiClemente (1982, 1984) argued, a system of therapy must explicate some theory about the problem resolution, or therapeutic, process—a theory-cum-method, in my terminology—if it is to be in any sense a system of *psychotherapy* itself. Thus, a theory-cum-method of problem resolution—of how the therapeutic change process itself works—is more at the core of, more essential to, the very articulation of a theoretical system of therapy than is a taxonomy of problem categories (C) and their theorized causes (A). After all, those categories and causal theories, which supply or predetermine the content of therapy, do not necessarily tell us how the fundamental process of therapy itself should operate. We saw evidence of this last assertion in Beutler's attempt, in his technical/systematic eclecticism, to emphasize theories of problem resolution and to deemphasize theories of problem causation. Also recall the quotation of Prochaska and DiClemente that made that assertion explicitly.

The postmodern narrative therapy movement, then, makes—as it must (i.e., however unwittingly) and as it *should*—thoroughly general claims about the process of problem resolution. These claims are therefore much more explicit than are its unacknowledged, and so usually more implicit, claims about what constitutes problems and problem causation. Thus, just as that movement denounces and therefore deemphasizes general, predetermined categories of problems and their general, predetermined causes, so it pronounces and emphasizes a general, predetermined theory of problem resolution.

That general, predetermined theory of problem resolution is, moreover, always put forth as realist in postmodern therapies—certainly no less so than in more complete, conventional (i.e., modern) therapy systems. That is true even if the realism of that claim about problem resolution is, in the service of loyalty to antirealism, not acknowledged. Recall that according to the doctrine of realism, the knower can attain or at least approximate knowledge of reality as it really (or objectively) exists, independent of the knower's cognitive operations and the theoretical, linguistic, or narrative constructions produced by those operations. Thus, the knower can obtain knowledge of reality without necessarily imposing a theory, language, narrative, or construct that *alters* the true nature of that object in experience. To apply that doctrine to theories of problem resolution is to make the claim that we can know something about what really, or objectively, helps clients *resolve* their problems (or "problems"), even if (as I believe is the case) we cannot always know what really, or objectively, *caused* those problems to begin with.

The existence of some modest, or limited, degree of realism about the problem-resolution process is therefore undeniable in all therapy systems. Nonetheless, the postmodern narrative therapy movement professes a pervasive antirealism, one that denies our ability to know any true, objective, real, or independent (of the knower) reality—including the reality of problem causation and of problem resolution. Yet, that same therapy movement, *no less than any modern therapy movement*, promotes the use of a theory-cum-method that is treated as a true, objective, real, or independent (of the knower) cause of problem resolution. In Chapter 5 I support this assertion by using statements made by members of that movement.

For now, let us consider a brief example or two. When Beutler argues, based on his research, that skill-building interventions are more effective in resolving the problems of clients who have an externalizing/acting-out coping style, he is making an explicit reality claim about problem resolution (skill-building interventions *cause* solutions in certain cases). He is also making an implicit reality claim about problem causation (externalizing/acting-out coping styles, which by definition involve skill deficits, *cause* problems in life). But when the proponents of the narrative therapy movement say, as we just saw in the quotations of the last section, that the therapist and client must together "co-create" a new, unique, personal narrative to resolve the client's (allegedly linguistic) "problem," they too are unwittingly making a reality claim about how to cause problem resolution. This claim holds for those "problems" that are alleged by postmodernists to reside only within language itself—language that supposedly bears no relationship to any extralinguistic reality.

Just here the point to emphasize is this: claims about what processes (i.e., therapeutic methods or interventions) really, truly, or objectively cause problem resolution—resolution that manifests itself in real, observable (linguistic and extralinguistic) changes in the client's life—are made by postmodern and modern therapists alike. They are made by all therapists because they are inescapable. Indeed, without those claims there would be no competing systems of psychotherapy with their competing theories about the processes or causes of problem resolution, including what constitutes real therapist expertise.[22]

In conclusion, no system of therapy that is to be taken seriously can explicitly adopt the *antirealist* position that we cannot know anything objective or real about how to help people solve their problems (or "problems"). Nor can it take the *antisystematic* position that all general, predetermined knowledge is irrelevant to the process of problem resolution, since it is precisely the explication of that general knowledge of problem resolution that constitutes systems of psychotherapy in the first place. Recall that these systems are, above all, designed to alleviate real distress. Whereas a theory of problem causation need not be made explicit for a system of therapy to be constituted (although its absence of course makes the system less complete), the same cannot be said of a theory-cum-method of problem resolution. Such theory is *necessary*, but perhaps not sufficient, for the very existence of a system of therapy (Prochaska & DiClemente, 1982, 1984). Thus, a general, predetermined theory of problem resolution is always put forth explicitly in any true system of therapy, however antisystematic the proponents of that system aspire to be in their practice. Moreover, that theory must always reflect at least some minimal or modest degree of extratheoretic reality—it must be modestly realist—if the system of therapy that contains it claims to effect real change in real lives, as all therapy systems so claim. That modest realism inheres even if reference to the real is unacknowledged or denied, as is the case in the professed antirealism of the postmodern narrative therapy movement. Let us, therefore, finally turn our full attention to it.

CHAPTER 4

The Narrative Therapy Movement: A Postmodern Humanistic Antirealism

INTRODUCTION TO THE CLAIMS MADE BY THE NARRATIVE THERAPY MOVEMENT

In Chapter 1 I stated that within the postmodern narrative therapy movement therapy is defined as a narrative, linguistic, or storied enterprise—one that, moreover, eliminates objective truth or knowledge of an independent reality. In Chapter 3 we examined some statements that demonstrated that position. These statements reflect the attempt to move therapy away from the business of defining problems and their causes with some degree of objectivity and generality, and into the business of defining "problems" and their "causes" with complete subjectivity and nongenerality or unique particularity.[1] These moves reflect nothing less than the emergence of the postmodern narrative therapy movement itself—an emergence that, I argue, is intended to individualize the practice of therapy.

In this chapter I explore in more precise detail what it means to say that therapy is a narrative, linguistic, or storied enterprise. To structure that exploration, I use the three components of the generic model of therapy systems I put forth in Chapter 3—namely, client/problem categories (C), theories of problem causation (A), and theories-cum-methods of problem resolution (B). I also develop a clearer distinction between two antirealist epistemological doctrines—constructivism and social constructionism—as they have been used within the narrative therapy movement. In order to explain the literary aspects of the narrative therapy movement, I examine the "client-as-text analogy" adopted by many proponents of the narrative therapy movement; I give particular attention to how that analogy paves the way for the recent endorsement of the use of (literary) "deconstruction" as a fundamental therapeutic method.

THERAPY AS A NARRATIVE, LINGUISTIC, OR STORIED ENTERPRISE

The narrative therapy movement has called upon the linguistic philosophy of Rorty (1979) and Wittgenstein (1953), and the poststructural literary theory and philosophy of such writers as Foucault, Derrida, and de Man, to characterize therapy as a linguistic enterprise. To clarify what this means, let us begin with an examination of two particular postmodern narrative therapists, Anderson and Goolishian (1988), who have promoted this narrative/ linguistic paradigm vigorously and who therefore illustrate the position of many who share that paradigm.

Anderson and Goolishian (1988) have interpreted Rorty's (postmodern) call to "keep the conversation going rather than to find objective truth" (Rorty, 1979, p. 377) to mean that therapy should function only with local, unique, personal (i.e., nongeneralized) theory (of problem definition and problem causation). Recall that for postmodernists such theory is always seen as thoroughly subjective, or antirealist. Before turning to the antirealism behind their position, let us consider one example of a statement that makes explicit reference to Rorty:

> Using Rorty's [1979] metaphor of the mirror, the therapist is not simply a mirror reflecting more accurate representations of reality for the clients' [*sic*] benefit. Therapy is not a process of mirror polishing whereby the therapist inspects, repairs, and polishes defective mirrors so that the client can attain more accurate representations of the "real" psychological world.
>   The therapist is [instead] a master conversational artist, an architect of dialogue . . . . (Anderson & Goolishian, 1988, p. 384)

Within the narrative therapy movement the frequent reference to Rorty— with his emphasis on ongoing conversation and his repudiation of (seeking) objective truth—reveals two related emphases: (a) the attention given to language or conversation that is therapeutic, and (b) the adoption of an antirealist epistemology. Antirealism, recall, is the epistemological doctrine that theory/language always mediates between the knower and the known in a way that of necessity alters or distorts in experience the reality to be known.

Therefore, the knower must always create, in language, the (non)reality—or the linguistically altered reality—she experiences. Therefore, the adoption of antirealism has built into it an acute and pervasive attention to language itself. That attention to language, not surprisingly, surfaces in the rhetoric of the postmodern narrative therapy movement, which has of course adopted the antirealist doctrine. Hence, the postmodern narrative therapy movement emphasizes how language itself, especially the language of therapy, works to create new "realities" (i.e., nonrealities). In keeping with the antirealist agenda, however, many within that movement argue that language, including the language of therapy, does not reflect, represent, correspond to, or give us any (extralinguistic) reality that is independent of the knower, or the knower's theory/language/narrative/story (e.g., Anderson & Goolishian, 1988; de Shazer, 1991, 1993; Epstein & Loos, 1989; Gergen & Kaye, 1992; Hoffman, 1990; Lax, 1992; Neimeyer, 1993; Parry, 1991; White, 1993; White & Epston, 1990). It is my claim that the members of that movement do not, indeed cannot, adhere consistently to the antirealism of that argument—hence the oscillation between realism and antirealism that is central to the argument of this book.

Before we turn to evidence of that oscillation, let us examine some statements made by narrative therapists that demonstrate that they have indeed adopted an antirealist position. In reviewing these quotations, it is important to keep in mind the following three components of the antirealist doctrine: (a) there is no access to an independent (of the knower) reality; (b) theory/language always mediates between the knower and the known in a way that of necessity alters in experience the true nature of the object (or reality) to be known; (c) theory/language may therefore be said to make, construct, constitute (and so forth) the "reality," or nonreality, that is experienced. In short, reality is neither discovered nor reflected by language.

That last statement is important. Many postmodern narrative therapists do not suppose that real experiences—real physical happenings—form or affect the nature of the client's story, a story which then reflects those experiences (the realist position). Rather, those within the narrative therapy movement who adopt an extreme linguistic relativism presume, borrowing from (postmodern) linguistic philosophy and literary theory, that the narrative, story, theory, language, or proposition one holds about something makes, creates, constitutes, or determines one's experience of that something, including one's interactions with others in one's social context (e.g., Anderson & Goolishian, 1988, 1992; de Shazer, 1991, 1993; Epstein & Loos, 1989; Gergen & Kaye, 1992; Neimeyer, 1993; Parry, 1991; Polkinghorne, 1992; White, 1993;

White & Epston, 1990). Recall here the quotation of McNamee and Gergen from Chapter 1:

> Our formulations of what is the case are guided by and limited to the systems of language in which we live. What can be said about the world—including self and others—is an outgrowth of shared conventions of discourse. Thus, . . . one cannot describe the history of a country or oneself on the basis of "what actually happened;" rather, one has available a repertoire of story-telling devices or narrative forms and these devices are imposed on the past. (1992, p. 4)

For emphasis, we may add to that the following remark by Lax (1992): "The client, in essence, does not have a singular 'true' story independent of a 'reader' to whom she is telling that particular story" (p. 73).[2]

It is also important to recall that this view stands in stark contrast to the realist view of those technical/systematic eclectics who advocate a matrix paradigm. In the narrative therapy movement there are no distinct, predetermined, and objective categories of problems and their causes to which clients are assigned for the purpose of determining the proper intervention, as one finds in the matrix paradigm. Therefore, individuality can be maximized within the narrative approach. Again, that is because the discourse that determines the content of the therapeutic narrative (the problem description and its theory of causation) is kept at a local or personal level, unique to each client. Omer and Strenger (1992), who promote the narrative approach, demonstrate this position when they state, "The belief that psychotherapy works by unearthing or undoing the *real* [italics added] origins of pathology is gradually vanishing from the field. . . . [P]sychotherapy works by transforming a person's self-narrative and the self-concept embodied in the narrative. . . . Our self-narratives become our lives" (p. 253, Abstract). Alternatively, *"the way a life is told determines how it is lived"* (p. 254).

With these considerations in mind, let us now examine several quotations that document the adoption of antirealism among members of the narrative therapy movement. Some of these were supplied in Chapter 1, but it will do no harm to review them again:

1. "A common theme of the postmodern epistemology is that linguistic systems stand between reality and experience (Rorty, 1989[a]). Each language system has its own particular way of distorting, filtering and constructing experience" (Polkinghorne, 1992, pp. 149–150). "Our experience is always filtered through interpretive schemes" (p. 149).

2. "Since we cannot know objective reality, all knowing requires an act of interpretation" (White & Epston, 1990, p. 2). Note again the claim that interpretation/language mediates between knower and known, and in so doing allegedly prevents knowledge of any independent (of the knower) reality.

3. "Constructivism[3] asserts that we do not discover reality, we invent it (Watzlawick, 1984). Our experience does not directly reflect what is out there but is a selecting, ordering, and organizing of it. . . . Thus, our understanding of reality is a representation, not an exact replica, of what is out there. Representations of reality are shared meanings that derive from shared language, history, and culture" (Hare-Mustin & Marecek, 1990a, p. 27). Note that language is said always to mediate between knower and known, thus preventing direct awareness of "what is out there." Incidentally, here we catch a glimpse of the social constructionist idea that shared or generalized views of reality (i.e., theories or languages) can be as antirealist as unique, personal ones. "Postmodernism creates distance from the seemingly fixed language of established meanings and fosters skepticism about the fixed nature of reality" (p. 56). Once again there is an emphasis on language and a reference to postmodernism, with its unfixed, unstable "reality," or nonreality.

4. "The epistemology to which we subscribe departs from the traditional 'paradigm of objectivity'" (Efran et al., 1990, p. xiv). "The new epistemology acknowledges that our lives take place mainly in a world of meanings—in 'conversation'" (p. xv). Note the implicit claim that meanings/conversation, that is, language, gives the knower no objective standpoint.

5. "Post-structuralists, in fact, question the opposition of the subject and the object upon which the possibility of objectivity depends" (de Shazer, 1991, p. 50). Note that, for poststructuralists/postmodernists, the subject is not independent of the object to be known, and so cannot achieve objective knowledge.

6. "Constructivists challenge the traditional separation between the knower and the known, arguing that processes inherent in the organism largely determine what is taken to be 'the real'" (McNamee & Gergen, 1992, p. 3). See comment for Number 5 above. "In effect, what we take to be 'the real and the good' are largely products of textual histories" (p. 4). Note that language—the textual—is said to determine what is "real." Note too that questions about the good are also merely linguistic creations: in Chapter 8 I address the consequences of this claim for ethics in therapy.

7. "Therapists can undermine the idea that they have privileged access to the truth by consistently encouraging persons to assist them in the quest for understanding. . . . Therapists can challenge the idea that they have an expert view. . . . The therapist can call into question the idea that s/he possesses an objective and unbiased account of reality" (White, 1993, p. 57). Note how the antirealism of the narrative therapy movement calls into question the existence of the therapist's expertise—a question raised later in this chapter, in the next chapter, and again in Chapter 8. "These knowledges [e.g., client's stories] are not about discoveries regarding the 'nature' of persons and of relationships, but are constructed knowledges that are specifying of a *particular strain* [italics added] of personhood and of relationship" (p. 38). Note that constructed knowledges/stories do not reflect the discovery of any generalities or any independent, objective truths. Rather, they give us only local, specific, particular, contextualized discourses—i.e., individualized discourses, which are in this quotation equated with subjectivity/antirealism.

8. "The complete adoption of a narrative paradigm for therapy is proposed . . . , especially for life in a post-modern world that lacks any objective frame of reference" (Parry, 1991, p. 37, Abstract). "The narrative therapist seeks no deeper truth or meta-level according to which to compare or understand someone's story of her experiences. Each person's experience is explicitly responded to as her *unique perspective* [italics added] on a given situation" (p. 44). Note again that unique, personal stories cannot give us any general or objective truths about human nature, nor need they do so. We can therefore see in these quotations how in therapy individuality is emphasized and equated with subjectivity.

9. "There are no wet beds, no voices without people, no depressions. There is only *talk* about wet beds, *talk* about voices without people, *talk* about depression [all italics in original]. There are no family systems, no family structures, no psyches: just talk about systems, structures, and psyches. . . . *[T]here is nothing outside of the therapy session that can help us understand what is going on in the session* [italics added]. Even in our follow-up studies we are only having a conversation about the results: We never *have* results, only depictions of results. As Wittgenstein says . . . , 'You've got what you've got and that's all there is'" (de Shazer, 1993, p. 89). Note the emphatic insistence that not only is there no *extralinguistic* reality, but also no (relevant) *extratherapy* reality, which is, presumably, the same thing.

10. "This view of human interconnectedness does not rely on a definition of perception and cognition that requires a representational or objective view

of reality. . . . [Instead, this view contains] the belief that reality is a social construction. We live and take action in a world that we define through our descriptive language in social intercourse with others" (Anderson & Goolishian, 1988, p. 377). "Within this framework, there are no 'real' external entities, only communicating and languaging human individuals. There is only the process of the constantly evolving reality of language use. Thus, there are no 'facts' to be known, no systems to be 'understood,' and no patterns and regularities to be 'discovered.' This position demands that we give up the view of humankind as the 'knowers' of the essences of nature. In its place is substituted a view of humankind in continuing conversation" (p. 378). Note the attempt to eliminate any extralinguistic reality, the resulting emphasis on language itself, and the implicit reference to Rorty's (1979) call to "keep the conversation going."

11. "All therapy takes the form of conversations between people and . . . the findings of these conversations have no other 'reality' than that bestowed by mutual consent" (Hoffman, 1990, p. 4). Again, there is no extralinguistic, and, moreover, no extratherapy reality. There is only the antireality, or nonreality, of some linguistic consensus,[4] in this case, the consensus called social constructionism (see Note 3).

12. "In contemporary post-structuralist thought, our world—our social, interactional context—is seen as created by language, by words. . . . [L]anguage constitutes 'the human world and the human world constitutes the whole world' (Harland, 1987, p. 141)" (de Shazer & Berg, 1992, p. 73). "For post-structuralists in general, signs, words, and concepts are seen to float or slide: A sign or a word simply means (or refers to) another sign or word rather than to a structurally linked referent" (p. 78). Note again that there is no extralinguistic reality; rather, language, which is itself alleged to be unstable, creates or constitutes our (human) world, which is supposedly the only world.

13. "(1) 'Realities' are constructed *locally* [italics added] by persons in conversation. (2) Problems occur 'in language.' (3) Therapy is first and foremost the 'management of conversation.' (4) Therapists and clients create a therapeutic reality (meaning system) through *languaging*" (Epstein & Loos, 1989, p. 407). Notice again that language creates reality, including problems, and it does so only at the local, or nongeneral, level; hence the pairing of that which is antirealist with that which is unique, personal, or individualistic. "Language . . . is not merely the representation of reality through symbols.

Rather, the act of 'naming' objects (making distinctions) creates the reality experienced by the observer" (p. 409). Notice again that language creates rather than reflects reality. "We acknowledge the importance of one's *personal* [italics added] construction of reality. We see the world as composed of a 'multiverse' of realities. We believe that reality is continuously invented and reinvented, not 'discovered.' Furthermore, reality is constructed through language" (p. 412). Again, antirealism is identified or paired with that which is personal, or individualized.

14. "Human knowledge is ultimately (inter)personal . . . and evolutionary . . . , with no simple prospect of validation against an objective reality beyond people's constructions" (Neimeyer, 1993, p. 222). Note the antirealist position that there is no way to get outside of our linguistic constructions to determine their relation to any extralinguistic reality. "Like the broader postmodern zeitgeist from which it derives, constructivist psychotherapy is founded on a conceptual critique of objectivist epistemology. In particular, it offers an alternative conception of psychotherapy as the quest for a more viable *personal knowledge* [italics added], in a world that lacks the fixed referents provided by a directly knowable external reality" (p. 230). Note again the pairing of the unique/personal with antirealism, which is here explicitly tied to postmodernism.

15. "Our social world is constituted in and through a network of multiple stories or narratives (the 'story' that our social world is constructed in or through multiple stories or narratives being one of them). . . . From this perspective, language is not representational; what we call *'reality'* resides and is expressed in one's descriptions of events, people, ideas, feelings, and experiences" (Sluzki, 1992, pp. 218–219). Again, no extralinguistic reality exists or is available to the knower. However, this author is clever enough to see that this claim can only be yet another antirealist "story," or nonreality.[5]

16. "It was once accepted that psychotherapy worked by digging into the unconscious . . . and curing symptoms by exposing truth. Conflicting therapies disagreed about the meanings or factors behind symptoms, but all believed that only dealing with these 'real things' in their 'real places' could really cure. These metaphors are no longer valid. Meanings are not objectively *there* to be found, but are *constructions* of therapists' and clients' minds. The story of clients' lives, which develops in therapy, is not the real history, archeologically reconstructed, but is one possible *narrative*: perhaps more orderly, detailed, and coherent than the pretherapeutic one, but not necessarily more true

(Spence, 1982). The process of therapy cannot, therefore, be described as one of discovering life stories, but rather as one of *transforming* them (Strenger & Omer, 1992)" (Omer & Strenger, 1992, p. 253). "Meanings are not given but created. . . . Wittgenstein (1958) . . . arrived at the same conclusion that man cannot escape the social construction of the world through language games: We are always amidst meanings, and these are not determined by nature, but are our *own productions*" [italics added] (p. 255). Notice again the idea that there is no extralinguistic, external-to-therapy reality to which clients' stories/constructions/narratives/meanings refer. Therapists and clients supposedly do not—indeed cannot—discover independent truth. They merely transform one antirealist story, or nonreality, into another equally antirealist story, or nonreality, by virtue of their own meanings, which are themselves unstable.

17. "Everything is constructed. This requires a new epistemology. . . . The patient and therapist are then conceived as engaged in a duet for two voices, in which meaning is translated and constructed, and is no longer expected to be self evident. . . . Truth is constructed rather than revealed" (Bouchard & Guérette, 1991, p. 386). Notice the antirealist assertion that linguistic constructions (e.g., theories) do not reveal any self-evident or independent reality.

* * *

The antirealism expressed in these quotations is unmistakable. If nothing else, the strategic use by these authors of quotation marks to indicate dubious usage of such terms as "objectivity," "truth," and "reality" clearly reveals that antirealism. Also unmistakable in some quotations is the attention to the local, specific, unique, personal (i.e., nongeneral) construction of some antirealist story in therapy. Thus, we see a clear linkage between antirealism, on the one hand, and that which is local, unique, or personal, on the other. However, we also preview in some other quotations a more generalized form of antirealism which is known as social constructionism. I return to that doctrine just below.

Now a question emerges: if each knower constructs his own unique, personal view of reality—a view that is of necessity antirealist—then how does the narrative therapy movement deal with the fact that we sometimes manage to communicate and, more important, agree with each other, especially about how best to go about the business of doing therapy? For instance, how can the members of the narrative therapy movement understand and agree with each other about the virtue, *in general*, of a narrative approach to therapy? How can there be agreement about any approach to the practice of therapy, let alone a systematic one? The answer to that question is lurking in some of the above quotations, as we can see from the references to interpersonal, or generalized, rather than to purely unique, or personalized, constructions of "reality." That reference implies a distinction between that which is particular, individual, or personal, on the one hand, and that which is general, social, or interpersonal, on the other hand. Let us now turn our attention to that distinction.

CONSTRUCTIVISM VS.
SOCIAL CONSTRUCTIONISM

All of the above quotations claim that we invent or construct multiple "realities" in language rather than discovering any one, true, independent, extralinguistic reality. Yet there is some debate about whether that constructed "reality," or nonreality, is completely unique to each individual, or has some commonality with the constructed "realities" of others within a particular discursive/linguistic/cultural context. The term "constructivism" originally seemed to reflect the former view, and "social constructionism" the latter view. However, both terms now appear to be used interchangeably in psychotherapy literature to reflect the latter view: that "reality" (i.e., nonreality) is socially constructed in language[6] (for more commentary, see Cade, 1986; Coyne, 1985; Efran, Lukens, & Lukens, 1988; Gergen, 1985; Mahoney, 1991; Speed, 1984, 1991; von Foerster, 1984; von Glasersfeld, 1984; Watzlawick, 1984).

This equivocation—this wanting to have it both ways so that constructions of "reality" are both personal, or individualized, and yet social, or generalized—is most explicitly reflected in the above quotation of Neimeyer (1993) when he places the prefix "inter" in parentheses: "Knowledge is (inter)personal." The equivocation produces this difficulty: the moment we make the construction of "reality" a social/consensual rather than an individual phenomenon, we can come to agreement about the general character of whatever "reality" we have socially constructed. But we then lose that emphasis on the uniquely personal that played no small part in motivating the emergence of the postmodern narrative therapy movement in the first place.

Notice that such generalized, linguistically constructed "realities" are as fully antirealist as the personalized, linguistically constructed "realities" we have been considering. That is because these generalized views are alleged to be limited or constrained not by independent reality itself but rather by nothing other than the nature of the (agreed-upon) linguistic system, context, or conventions in which those constructions arise.[7] And recall that according to antirealists one's linguistic context, or language, always insinuates itself between one's act of knowing and the object of one's knowing—an insinuation that always, for antirealists, alters in experience the true, independent of the knower (or knower's language) reality.

Thus, those who share some "linguistic context" (and therefore share some linguistic conventions or constraints) should, given the antirealism of social constructionism, construct overlapping, or generalized, social nonrealities. The following formal definition of social constructionism reinforces my point:

> In contrast to logical positivism, social constructionism takes the position that reality as an *individual or group* [italics added] experiences it is, to a substantial degree, conceptually constructed rather than sensorily discovered by that group. Objective knowledge about the world is significantly limited because "facts" and "raw data" can only be known within a particular, pre-empirically established cultural, social, and linguistic context. (Fishman & Franks, 1992, p. 177)

Again, we see in this quotation that oscillation between the individual and the social, or group, construction of "reality." We also see the linking of the linguistic with the social/cultural.

Social constructionism, then, clearly allows the generation of a more generalized, consensual—albeit antirealist—understanding or theory of the workings of the world, including the world of human behavior. That understanding must transcend each individual's unique, personal experience. But that unique, personal experience must itself—according to that antirealist epistemological doctrine—always be filtered through—and so altered by—the shared conceptual or linguistic system or context to produce that consensual understanding. Put differently, within a social constructionist framework, experience comes to each of us in a way predetermined by the cultural/linguistic context in which we function together.[8] This is what is meant by the expression, often used in the postmodern (narrative therapy) literature, "Language structures, makes, or constitutes reality." It therefore should come as no surprise that all views/understandings/theories/narratives of the world would of necessity be shared within a linguistic context. (There is, of course, a Kantian flavor to this line of thinking.[9]) But because social constructionism is unquestionably antirealist, or relativistic, the resulting theory, view, or understanding of the world cannot tell us anything about the real workings of an independent, extratheoretic, or extralinguistic reality. This is the case no matter how organized or structured, coherent and whole—how complete—that theory, view, or understanding may turn out to be. Thus, the completeness of a theoretical system and its epistemological status may be quite independent of each other. But most important for my purpose is the claim that the cultural/linguistic context ensures that we can communicate our (linguistically mediated/altered) experiences, and so we can reach some consensus about our experiences or constructions of some nonreality. This antirealist game, in short, is rigged in favor of achieving such consensus.

All of this can be summarized by saying that one can, within the confines of a social constructionist epistemology, posit general "laws," that is, a predetermined (i.e., determined prior to any particular case) theoretical system that transcends the uniquely individual, and yet still manages to be fully antirealist. The antirealism of that system obtains because it is supposedly *merely* a shared linguistic construction—one with no relationship to any extralinguistic reality. But the point I want to make now pertains specifically to therapy: the use of that antirealist theoretical system may, if it is complete enough, ensure a highly rule-governed, or constrained, and therefore systematic approach to the practice of therapy. However, it sacrifices, no less than an equally complete but realist theoretical system of therapy, the individualization of practice that motivated the postmodern narrative therapy movement in the first place. This point was made in Chapter 3, when I stated that the degree to which the practice of therapy is individualized vs. systematic is not a function of the realism or antirealism of the theoretical system used by the therapist to guide her practice. Rather, it is a function of the degree to which the theoretical system in use is complete: the completeness of the theoretical system of therapy in use refers to whether the process (Component B) and content (Components A and C) of any therapy case are (a) *predetermined* by the generalities (the components) of the theoretical system or (b) *determined* by each client's unique experiences and views of those experiences. Recall that the client's unique views cannot be known prior to any particular therapy case and so cannot be part of a theoretical system.

This identical sacrifice of individuality in practice that occurs when a therapist uses an antirealist system of therapy that is as complete (and as particularized) as a realist one obtains for the following reason: when a therapist uses general, predetermined, antirealist categories of problems (C), their general, predetermined, antirealist causes (A), and their general, predetermined, antirealist solutions (B), there is indeed subjectivity, or antirealism.

But that subjectivity is not then determined by each unique client's unique, idiosyncratic, or subjective language or experience. Rather, that subjectivity is defined by, or relative to, many subjects—that is, to the entire pertinent social/cultural/discursive context that permits shared, consensual (i.e., generalized), though antirealist, meanings and understandings within that context. That discursive context could in fact be as broad as the entire human species, if we assume universal discursive practices—a position that, it seems to me, is too general or global, and so too decontextualized and deindividualizing, for any postmodernist attitude that I have investigated. [10]

But regardless of the broadness of the discursive context in question, social constructionism implies that within any particular discursive context there can be no *completely* unique or individualized antirealist stories. Hence, individuality is always compromised if one adopts social constructionism—a point I return to in due course. However, the application to all one's clients of a general, predetermined theoretical system of therapy—even an antirealist one—increases the likelihood of achieving a rule-governed and hence a consistent or replicable—that is, systematic—approach to one's therapeutic practice. There again is that tradeoff between the individualized and the systematic. Later in this chapter and again in Chapter 5 I provide examples of this more generalized, or less individualized, subjectivity of social constructionism as it manifests itself within the postmodern narrative therapy movement. I also, in Chapter 5, reveal the hidden, modest realism that subverts that subjectivity. For now, let us examine the component parts of the (antirealist) system of therapy propounded by postmodern narrative therapists.

THE SYSTEM PROPOUNDED
BY POSTMODERN
NARRATIVE THERAPISTS

Most postmodern narrative therapists have adopted the antirealism of social constructionism, a doctrine that permits shared understandings within some linguistic, or discursive, context. They can, therefore, prior to any particular therapy case, predetermine a shared or generalized (but antirealist) system of psychotherapy—that is, one with predetermined component parts (i.e., A, B, C) that apply to therapists and clients in general. Despite the consensual nature of social constructionism, that system of therapy emphasizes the unique story of each unique client and so explicitly strives to avoid imposing on the client predetermined content about problems (C) and their causes (A). But narrative therapy must nonetheless be systematic in at least some minimal sense, since it unavoidably puts forth, in the very act of articulating a system of therapy, general, predetermined systemic components that apply to all therapists and clients. Thus, even in the act of articulating their highly individualized, antisystematic aspirations, narrative therapists cannot avoid compromising the degree to which a complete individualization of their therapy practice can be attained.

With this in mind, let us now consider how the three components of our generic model of therapy systems—namely, client/problem categories (C), theories of problem causation (A), and theories-cum-methods of problem resolution (B)—play a role even in the narrative therapy movement. Let us also keep in mind what consequences this has for the movement's goal of making the practice of therapy as individualized as possible.

Problem/Client Categories

As the quotations in Chapter 3 and above demonstrate, in the narrative therapy movement there are no categories of clients/problems that are predetermined by the system of therapy in use and that help to determine the selection of proper interventions, that is, interventions also predetermined by the system. For postmodern narrative therapists, then, each client's unique, nonpredetermined story—whatever its content may be—*is* the problem, and thus each unique story is the functional equivalent of a client/problem category, although only in some vestigial form. I use the expression "vestigial form" to emphasize that because the content of problem description (C) is not predetermined by the narrative therapy system, there are, for all *practical* purposes, no constraints on that aspect of therapeutic content. Thus, the narrative therapy system may be considered to be a less complete system in regard to therapeutic content. The equation between the client's unique, personal story and her "problem" is made because, as we saw, the extreme linguistic relativists within the narrative therapy movement claim that there is no extralinguistic or extratherapy reality, including the reality of problems, to which anyone's story refers (e.g., Anderson & Goolishian, 1988, 1992; de Shazer, 1991, 1993; de Shazer & Berg, 1992; Gergen & Kaye, 1992). Rather, the client's personal narrative or story about her life determines her perceived options and actions in life—including, sometimes, her perception or experience of a lack of options.

Since the linguistic construction, story, or narrative of a unique "problem" experience *is itself* what requires therapy, that same story or narrative determines the unique, or nonpredetermined, solutions or options *within language* available to the narrator/client.[11] Lax (1992, p. 69), for instance, states that "psychotherapy is the process of shifting the client's current 'problematic' discourse to another discourse that is more fluid and allows for a broader range of possible interactions." Notice here that the problem exists only in the client's "'problematic' discourse," or language, and so, not surprisingly, does the solution. White and Epston (1990) also reflect this same sentiment when they say that "although Jerome Bruner's [1986] comments on narrative relate to the structure of texts of literary merit, we believe that persons generally ascribe meaning to their lives by plotting their experience into stories, and that these stories shape their lives and relationships" (p. 79). Here we catch a glimpse of the "client-as-text" analogy to be discussed in a moment.

Another way to put this is to say that despite the adoption by narrative therapists of *social* constructionism—that is, one concerned with an interpersonal or generalized consensus about how to understand life—narrative therapists claim that problems (and their causes) consist in unique, personal languages/stories/narratives that are, in effect, personal *theories*. Here again we begin to see that oscillation between the individualized (or personal) and the generalized (or social) I mentioned earlier. In any case, let us consider a few statements made by members of the narrative therapy movement that make this emphasis on the unique, or personal, apparent.

In his article entitled "An Appraisal of Constructivist Psychotherapies," Neimeyer (1993) states that constructivist therapists "characteristically inquire closely into the *personal* meanings that form the subtext of the client's explicit statements (Kelly, 1955). . . . It follows that therapist interventions are more likely to be reflective, elaborative, and *intensely personal*, rather than persuasive, analytical, and technically instructive [all italics added]" (p. 224). A bit earlier in the same article he says that "constructivist approaches are quintessentially postmodern, promoting the elaboration of the client's narrative without the convenience of simple criteria for determining what constitutes an acceptable story" (p. 224). If we substitute the term "general, predetermined problem categories and causes" for the term "simple criteria" in the last sentence, my point about the postmodern avoidance of the general is strengthened.

We may, to appreciate this point, recall the previous quotation of Anderson and Goolishian's (1988, p. 378), namely, "there are no 'facts' to be known, no systems to be 'understood,' and no patterns and regularities to be 'discovered'." We can take this quotation to mean that there are no general, predetermined categories of problems (C) and their regular, patterned, lawful causes (A) (and solutions [B]) to be discovered and then used in some systematic, or generalized, way in therapy practice. We may, in addition, consider White's (1993, p. 38) statement that "life is constituted through an ongoing storying and re-storying of experience."

Thus, whatever experience is—and this is never clearly or consistently explained within the narrative therapy movement—it is the *storying* of experience that defines or determines life, including problems in life. "With repetition, stories harden into reality, sometimes trapping the storytellers within the boundaries that the storytellers themselves have helped to create (Bruner, 1986)" (Efran et al., 1990, p. 80). Note here again that it is stories—and not extralinguistic events—that trap the teller and so are *themselves* the problem.

Nonetheless, there is an obvious conflict within this movement: on the one hand, there is the desired emphasis on the social/cultural/consensual domain—on that which works to produce general, predetermined discourses. On the other hand, there is the desired emphasis on the individual/personal/ unique domain—on that which works to produce the uniquely particular, or nonpredetermined, discourse. Thus, if, as social constructionism alleges, clients' and therapists' experiences of reality are always filtered through, altered by, their cultural/linguistic/discursive contexts, then their narratives or stories about their experiences must always reflect whatever cultural discourses they share. In that case, those stories are not—*indeed cannot*—ever be completely unique to any one individual client—or therapist—who shares a cultural/ discursive context with others. [12]

According to social constructionism, then, whether the therapist (a) explicitly adopts some general, predetermined therapy system, (b) creates her own, unique system to generalize across clients, or (c) does neither and so functions in a highly antisystematic, case-by-case way, the therapist—like the client— has experiences of reality that are always filtered through or altered by (and so are limited or constrained by) her social/linguistic/discursive context. Ultimately, within this epistemological framework, any concepts a therapist or client uses to make sense of experience—including the experience of therapy—must be predetermined by that discursive context. In short, the content of therapy can never in principle (i.e., according to the linguistic antirealism of social constructionism) be completely unique to an individual who exists within some shared linguistic/discursive context.

Some feminist postmodern therapists seem to be aware of the problem of seeking the attainment of unique, personal discourses in therapy within the context of a social constructionist doctrine. Hare-Mustin (1994) seems particularly sensitive to this problem, when she states:

The therapeutic conversation is also not idiosyncratic. Both the process and content in the mirrored room are limited by the discourses that are brought into the room [hence, the room can only mirror or reflect what has been brought into it to begin with]. Thus, there is "predetermined content" to therapy—that provided by dominant discourses. Conversation can be oppressive, not so much by what it includes as by what it excludes. Therapists who do not recognize this will fail to do more than render existing norms a little less onerous for those most disadvantaged by them. (pp. 32–33)

Note, incidentally, the postmodern reference to discourse analysis, including the postmodern idea that dominant discourses (which are—like all discourses—antirealist) always oppress. Also note that for Hare-Mustin the processes, or methods, of therapy, no less than the content of therapy, are predetermined by the dominant discourses of the social/linguistic context.

Postmodern narrative therapists stand in sharp contrast to modern therapists.[13] According to their critics in the postmodern narrative therapy movement, modern therapists "impose" on the client, in the name of truth, some general, predetermined, and allegedly objective, problem type (e.g., that the client has unresolved oedipal struggles if the therapist is a Freudian psychoanalyst). By contrast, some postmodern narrative therapists work expressly to locate in the client's story any elements of just such a predetermined, or "oppressive," dominant-discourse story, whatever its source. According to those narrative therapists, all therapists must replace general, predetermined, dominant discourses with a story that is ever more personalized and unique to each client. The new story should therefore not be predetermined—either by the cultural/discursive context at large, or by any theoretical system of psychotherapy that exists within that larger context. With that accomplished, clients are said by these narrative therapists to be liberated from the oppression of the dominant discourse or theory. White (1993) and White and Epston (1990), who promote this view, call this liberation process the attempt to produce "unique outcomes" in the client's life by means of some new, unique, personalized, nonpredetermined, nondominant story or theory. Here we see the growing influence on narrative therapists of Foucault's postmodern ideas about the relation between dominant discourses, on the one hand, and power and oppression, on the other.

Theory of Problem Causation

The narrative therapy movement is claiming something more sweeping than the claim that the client's unique, personal (nonpredetermined) story of her unique experience *is* the (linguistic) "problem." It is also saying, though often implicitly and so without much apparent awareness, that the client's story is the *cause* of the "problem." Hence, the predetermined theory of problem causation (Component A) within the narrative therapy system is highly abstract and general in its formulation. That component of the narrative therapy system is, in all its generality and simplicity, this: stories, or narratives, of experience, *whatever* their content, cause the experience of "problems," which are themselves nothing more than (antirealist) linguistic constructions. Thus, there are no predetermined theories of problem causation other than this very abstract and general one which, in a deindividualizing move, is applied to all clients without discrimination. There is thus only one general client/problem category (C)—the client's personal story, and only one general theory of problem causation (A)—again, the client's personal story. Put differently, Components A and C are completely client-determined within the narrative therapy system.

Oddly enough, this one theory of problem causation is—despite its client-determined status—predetermined within the narrative therapy system no less than is any theory of problem causation within any therapy system, realist or antirealist. That is, this theory of problem causation exists prior to any particular client and is applied in advance to all. But because its generality is so extreme (it is determined only by *whatever* views the client herself brings to therapy), it places no constraints on the way any *particular* client's personal theory/story/narrative about her problem gets used in therapy, and so it allows the client's unique, personal (and allegedly subjective) theory/story/narrative to determine fully the content of therapy. It can therefore accommodate any client's personal theory without producing a need for the therapist to reformulate that personal theory to fit the constraints of the theoretical system's component parts (see Chapter 3, Figure 3.6). That is not surprising, *since all therapy takes place within narrative to begin with*; therefore, using clients' unique, personal narratives as the *only* causal explanation for problems in living constrains nothing in the way of therapeutic content. But that lack of constraint means Component A, like Component C, exists only in some unconventional or vestigial form in the narrative therapy system—a condition which renders that system in some sense less whole or complete than conventional therapy systems. And recall that when the practice of therapy is guided by an incomplete theoretical system, that practice is then itself less rule-governed/constrained and so less systematic. Of course, such therapy practice can be highly individualized. But that is the point of the narrative therapy movement, in my opinion.

Theory of Problem Resolution

The correlative of this very general, unconstraining theory of problem causation is an equally general theory of problem resolution or, rather, theory-cum-method of problem resolution. It too is predetermined generally within the postmodern narrative therapy movement's system of therapy, for it also applies in advance, without discrimination, to all clients. It is this: therapists must help clients co-create, co-construct, or co-narrate a new narrative/story—a new meaning—of their experience, or more precisely, of their experience of a "problem." That makes sense because if an old story—any old story—is constitutive and causative of the "problem," then a new story must surely be necessary to solve, eliminate, or "dis-solve in language" (Anderson & Goolishian, 1988) the "problem." Equally important, the content of the new story is supposedly no less uniquely personal (or nonpredetermined), and so is allegedly no less subjective (or antirealist), than the content of the original problematic story that required therapeutic "rewriting" in the first place. The narrative therapy system's one general, predetermined proposition or rule about problem resolution is that new stories about life experiences can help to provide (the experience of) new options or solutions in the client's life, and so can pave the way for new life experiences themselves.

The idea here is that the therapeutic intervention consists in *changing* the client's unique, personal, and allegedly subjective, or antirealist, story about her "problem" to *another* unique, personal, and allegedly subjective, or antirealist, story—but one that is in principle less constricting, more liberating, than the original one (see White & Epston, 1990, above). Moreover, the professed antirealism of the narrative therapy movement is allegedly kept intact because, as we saw in the above quotations, it is supposed that neither story—old or new—gives us any knowledge of reality that is extralinguistic (or independent of the knower and of the knower's constructed story).

Nonetheless, in contrast to its one generalized, unconstraining theory of problem causation (the content of which is always completely client determined), the narrative therapy movement attempts to specify or particularize the methods by which a new narrative of the "problem" can be constructed. These methods are not determined by each client, as is therapeutic content; rather, they constitute the *therapist's* expertise in the narrative therapy movement. Hence, that movement indeed provides a theory-cum-method of problem resolution that, by virtue of its explicit delineation of distinct therapeutic methods, constrains the practice of therapy (but only in regard to process). That makes sense since, recall, there can be a system of therapy—but not a complete one—with no explicit specification, or predetermination, of types

(C) or causes (A) of problems (i.e., content). But there cannot be a system of therapy without some specification, or predetermination, of just how (by what process) to go about solving problems in ways that produce real effects (B). In due course, I discuss the problems that last observation presents for the narrative therapy movement.

To summarize, within the postmodern narrative therapy movement we find a therapeutic system that can be seen to conform to our generic model of therapy systems: it contains the three components of that generic system — namely, a theory of problem causation (A), a description of what constitutes problems (C), and a theory-cum-method of problem resolution (B). But there are two factors that make that system different from the conventional complete system: (a) The first two components — A and C — are defined with such generality that the client's own personal view of his life (whatever its content) can fully determine the content of therapy, with none of the usual theoretical constraints that result in some degree of (predetermined) content reformulation in practice. This allows the (content of) therapy to be fully individualized, but it also makes Components A and C of that system func-tionally nonexistent — or vestigial, in my terminology — for all *practical* pur-poses. The resulting theoretical system is therefore, when used in practice, incomplete, and so its use produces a more antisystematic practice in regard to the content of therapy. (b) All three components are allegedly antirealist ones; they supposedly do not refer to or reflect any independent, extralinguis-tic reality. Before considering the problem with that second factor, let us first explore in more detail the nature of the therapeutic intervention or problem resolution process (B) itself — in particular, how it has led many narrative therapists to adopt postmodern literary theory and (e.g., deconstructionist) methods as their theory-cum-method of problem resolution. That move re-flects the idea that the client's "problem" is analogous to a literary text to which such literary methods can appropriately be applied for the purpose of "restorying" her narrative.

THE CLIENT-AS-TEXT ANALOGY: POSTMODERN LITERARY THEORY AND METHODS IN PSYCHOTHERAPY

It is probably best to begin our understanding of how postmodern literary theory and methods have been adopted within psychotherapy by considering what it means to say there is a "client-as-text" analogy. One way to do that is to notice that within the postmodern narrative therapy movement some theorists have explicitly blurred the distinction between the individual/self as a real individual being and the "text" of her narrative, or story, about her life. If we recall the discussion in Chapter 1 of the pervasive dissolution within postmodern theory, including postmodern psychological theory (see, e.g., Gergen, 1991a), of the ontological status of the self/individual with a consistent identity, then that analogy makes more sense. Thus, in postmodern theory the true self with an independent, consistent existence and identity is replaced with antirealist stories about the self that fluctuate from one interpersonal/discursive context or moment to the next.

The self, then, is, according to postmodernists, constituted solely in language and so is itself indistinguishable from the (words in the) text that constitutes it (cf. Bruner, 1986; de Shazer & Berg, 1992; Frank, 1987; Gergen, 1991a; Hare-Mustin & Marecek, 1990a; Hoffman, 1990; Lax, 1992; Omer & Strenger, 1992; Shotter & Gergen, 1989; White & Epston, 1990). Glass (1993), who is himself critical of that analogy, best illustrates that position when he refers to (a) the postmodernist notion (attributed by Alford, 1991, p. 12, to Amelie Rorty) of "'the person as rhetorical strategy'" (p. xii), (b) Foucault's view of "the self as consciousness in language" (p. xi), and (c) his own reiteration of "the postmodern assertion that the self is constituted by language" (p. 25). I myself assess the "client-as-text" analogy critically. But to understand that assessment we must first review a bit of literary theory and method, and then consider some statements made by members of the postmodern narrative therapy movement that make the literary/text analogy explicit.

One cannot speak of the client, or any individual/self, as a text without also speaking simultaneously of the therapeutic application of the literary method of deconstruction to that "text." In order to understand the text analogy and the deconstructive methods of therapy derived from that analogy, we must first grasp what it means to use the term "deconstruction" to define a distinct therapeutic method.

As the quotations to follow reveal about the intent of narrative therapy, to deconstruct the client's text/narrative of his life/experience—i.e., to deconstruct the client's understanding of his self or identity (since the client's self is analogous to a text)—is to question and challenge the client's story about his life/experience. In particular, therapeutic deconstruction questions and challenges underlying or implicit presumptions and expectations about the self and others. This is done in the hope that such a process will produce a new, less constricting—and so less "problematic"—story or understanding of his experience.

As more than one postmodern narrative therapist (e.g., Hare-Mustin & Marecek, 1990a, p. 48; Parry, 1991, p. 42) has noted, most conventional (i.e., realist) therapies also question and challenge the client's ideas and presumptions about his problem, in order to help reshape or reformulate his view of things. But unlike postmodern narrative therapies, those conventional therapies assume the ideas and views put forth by the theoretical system in use provide some extralinguistic reality, or truth. Parry (1991), for instance, thinks that that extralinguistic reference is a bad thing because it constricts the client in ways that caused her problem in the first place—namely, the imposition of general, predetermined (i.e., "dominant" or "normative") ideas/stories/discourses/narratives, including, especially, the established theories of therapy systems. Nonetheless, Parry does not see narrative therapy as making a complete break with more conventional therapeutic method:

> The only thing a narrative paradigm would eliminate is the gratuitous attempt to explain the meaning of a person's story with regard to a normative structure concerning what makes individuals, families, or systems in general tick [i.e., with regard to what I take to be some general, predetermined and allegedly realist, or objective, causal principles]. By embracing the belief that the power to change is in the story and need not be looked for anywhere else [note that there presumably is, once again, no extralinguistic, extratherapy reality], the inventive capacity inherent in stories can be released. (p. 42)

Note that the adoption of a postmodern antirealist narrative approach to therapy, with its full employment of poststructuralist/deconstructionist literary theory and method, is justified by virtue of the "inventiveness" concerning the solutions it promises. Put differently, the adoption of such an approach focuses therapeutic attention on the nuances of the client's individuality by eliminating the oppressive, constraining, deindividualizing, anti-inventive effect of "imposing" on clients (general) predetermined categories of, and causal explanations about, behavior. The term "inventive" also suggests that the therapeutic process can be more creative when we adopt a postmodern doctrine, which does not predetermine the stories that can in principle liberate clients from their "problems." But the unanswered question of course remains: whether a therapy that is so dedicated to inventiveness can still be systematic/rule-governed, in practice. There once again is that core problem—the trade-off between the unique (the individualized) and the general (the systematized).

But what of the definition of the term "deconstruction" as it has been used within the (postmodern/poststructuralist) literary movement to which postmodern narrative therapists have excitedly turned? To consider that body of literature would be a monumental undertaking, since volumes have been written on the subject. [14] Nonetheless, there are, within literary theory and criticism circles, critiques and summaries of deconstruction theory and method to which we can turn to give us a summary understanding. We shall therefore begin there, and then quickly turn our attention to the way deconstruction is actually used in narrative therapy, since that application is most fundamental to the critique I offer in this book.

Ellis (1989), in his excellent criticism of deconstruction, manages "to abstract [or generalize] from all of this [collection of particular arguments and doctrines in deconstructive thought] a particular strategy, a kind of deconstructive logic of inquiry or, as advocates themselves put it, a *performance* of a distinctive kind" (p. 137). Ellis (1989, p. 139) lists four basic positions that represent the deconstructive doctrine:

(a) "Words do not refer to things in the real world but only signify other words." Note the inherent antirealism of this statement.

(b) "Authors do not create the meaning of their texts by composing them, but instead readers, by reading them." This idea, which reflects the popular poststructuralist trend called "reader-response criticism" (e.g., Suleiman & Crosman, 1980; Tompkins, 1980), seems to have influenced such narrative therapy proponents as White and Gergen. True to social constructionism, they argue that the interpersonal/social context in which an observer/reader is located determines the meaning of any text/event, including the "text" of selves, or identities (recall the postmodern equation between texts and events described in Chapter 1, p. 10). This view is evident in a quotation of Lax we have already considered (1992, p. 73): "The client, in essence, does not have a singular 'true' story independent of a 'reader' to whom she is telling that particular story."

(c) "Texts do not have a particular meaning that can be investigated but are limitless in their meaning because of the free play of signs." Note here the poststructuralist idea of the indeterminacy of meaning. This idea makes an appearance within narrative therapy when its proponents advocate the (postmodern) embracing of ever-changing and hence "multiple views or narratives of reality."

(d) "A careful reading does not give knowledge of a text, because all readings are misreadings; whatever the obvious meaning of a literary text is

taken to be, one must stand that meaning on its head." This idea is again seen
clearly in the work of White, who speaks of challenging in therapy the
meanings that reflect the dominant discourse, or cultural consensus, that the
client accepts, and allegedly suffers from. Recall that White, among others,
therefore encourages the use of more private, unique, personalized meanings
in the construction of a new life narrative. De Shazer (1991, pp. 50–51)
speaks explicitly of all readings or understandings of clients/texts/events/lives
as being "misreadings."

Ellis (1989, p. 140) perhaps best summarizes literary deconstruction when
he states, "There is a heavy emphasis on moral terminology in deconstructive
writings. Deconstruction is 'disturbing,' 'disruptive,' it 'unmasks,' 'subverts,'
'dismantles,' 'exposes,' 'challenges,' and, a favorite word, it is a 'scandal.'" He
also reports the deconstructionist's (inconsistent) avoidance of the general and
attraction to the unique and the particular (p. 147). As we shall see in the
quotations that follow, both the "moral" terms listed by Ellis, and the attention to the uniquely particular rather than to the shared, or general, are found
in the writings of postmodern narrative therapists. Let us therefore now turn
to them, noting that they describe both the client-as-text analogy and the
methods for deconstructing and reconstructing that "text."

1. "If we assume that there is an identity between the structure of texts and
the structure of the stories or narratives that persons live by, and if we take as
our interest the constitution of lives through stories, we might then consider
the details of how persons live their lives . . . " (White, 1993, p. 37). Note
that lives are constituted by stories/texts. "Deconstruction has to do with
procedures that subvert taken-for-granted realities and practices: those so-
called 'truths' that are split off from the conditions and the context of their
production; those disembodied ways of speaking that hide their biases and
prejudices; and those familiar practices of self and of relationship that are
subjugating of persons' lives. Many of the methods of deconstruction render
strange these familiar and everyday taken-for-granted realities and practices by
objectifying them. In this sense, the methods of deconstruction are methods
that 'exoticize the domestic'" (pp. 34–35). Note the subversion of dominant
meanings which are seen as oppressive (see Foucault), and the antirealism, or
relativism, that lies behind that subversion. "Perhaps the approach that I have
described here on the deconstruction of the stories and knowledges that
persons live by is not entirely dissimilar to Derrida's work on the deconstruction of texts (1981). Derrida's intention was to subvert texts and challenge

the privileging of specific knowledges with methods that 'deconstruct the opposition . . . to overturn the hierarchy at a given moment.' He achieved this by developing deconstructive methods that: (a) brought forth the hidden contradictions in texts, rendering visible the repressed meanings—the 'absent but implied' meanings, (b) gave prominence to those knowledges 'on the other side,' those considered to be secondary, derivative, and worthless" (pp. 49–50). "As persons separate from the dominant or 'totalizing' stories that are constitutive of their lives, it becomes more possible for them to orient themselves to [and so express by words and actions] aspects of their experience that contradict these knowledges" (pp. 39–40).

The method of therapeutic intervention proposed by White is elaborated upon and illustrated just below. Here I draw the reader's attention to the general claim that predetermined, privileged, or dominant meanings (including psychological theories) create "problems," and so must be challenged or subverted to alleviate those "problems." Also, note that White thinks—contrary to Derrida's own deconstruction theory—that he himself can know Derrida's true authorial intent.

2. White and Epston (1990, p. 6), in a "Table of Analogies," expand the "text analogy" by stating that within it "social organization [is] constructed as . . . behavioral text," that "problems [are] constructed as . . . performance of oppressive, dominant story or knowledge," and that "solution [is] constructed in terms of . . . opening space for the authoring of alternative stories." They go on to argue that "social scientists became interested in the text analogy following observations that, although a piece of behavior occurs in time in such a way that it no longer exists in the present by the time it is attended to, the meaning that is ascribed to the behavior survives across time. It was this ascription of meaning that drew their attention, and in their attempts to understand this they began to invoke the text analogy. *This enabled the interaction of persons to be considered as the interaction of readers around particular texts. This analogy also made it possible to conceive of the evolution of lives and relationships in terms of the reading and writing of texts, insofar as every new reading of a text is a new interpretation of it, and thus a different writing of it* [italics added]" (p. 9). The meaning of this quotation is clear and consistent with what I have been attributing to the narrative therapy movement. It is nonetheless noteworthy that White and Epston claim that (a) *behavior* worthy of attention is itself not consistent or enduring (a basis, presumably, for the postmodern elimination of a stable, real identity/self), but that (b) *meanings* ascribed to behavior are supposedly stable. The stability, or survival over time, of

meanings, and presumably of the narratives that contain them, is an important point (with some modest realism intrinsic to it). This point is one I return to in Chapter 6, where I offer a realist alternative to the antirealist philosophy now advocated by postmodern narrative therapists.

White and Epston also reveal their preference for the unique and the particular over the universal and the general when they compare the "logico-scientific" with the "narrative" mode of thought. Regarding the former, they quote Bruner (1986): The "logico-scientific mode of thought ' . . . attempts to fulfill the ideal of formal, mathematical system of description and explanation. It employs categorization or conceptualization and the operations by which categories are established, instantiated, idealized, and related one to the other to form a system. . . . [It] deals in general causes . . . and makes use of procedures to assure verifiable reference to test for empirical truth'" (pp. 12–13, cited by White & Epston, 1990, p.78). By contrast, "the narrative mode of thought . . . is characterized by good stories that gain credence through their lifelikeness. They are not concerned with procedures and conventions for the generation of abstract and general theories but with the particulars of experience. They do not establish universal truth conditions . . . " (p. 78). The attention to individuality is unmistakable in the narrative approach as it is expressed in this quotation; accordingly, the problem of achieving a general, systematic approach to therapy is not solved.

3. Hare-Mustin and Marecek (1990a) make the text analogy as clear as any when they state, "The therapist's task of listening and responding to the client's narrative is akin to a deconstructive reading of a text. Both seek subtexts and multiple levels of meaning. Just as deconstructive readings disrupt the frame of reference that organizes conventional [read dominant] meanings of a text, so a therapist's interventions disrupt the frame of reference within which the client customarily sees the world. Such disruptions enable new meanings to emerge (Watzlawick et al., 1974). As a multiplicity of meanings becomes apparent through such therapist actions as questioning, explaining, interpreting, and disregarding, more possibilities for change emerge. The deconstructive process is most apparent in psychoanalysis, but, indeed, all therapy involves changing meaning as part of changing behavior" (p. 48). Note the use of the term "disrupt" to characterize the deconstructive therapeutic process; it is the kind of "morally loaded" term that Ellis (1989) spoke of. More important, note that, like Parry (1991), Hare-Mustin and Marecek realize that postmodern therapy is similar to most modern therapies, which explicitly propound the need to change the client's understanding of his

problem. But unlike modern therapies, postmodern therapy rejoices in a multiplicity of contextualized (read, relative or nonobjective) meaning to do the job—that is, antirealism prevails.

4. De Shazer (1991, pp. 50–51) is even more explicit about the psychotherapeutic use of post-structural literary theory—especially reader-response criticism—in his references to the deconstructionist work of Jacques Derrida (1978) and Paul de Man (1979). De Shazer uses Anderson and Goolishian's definition of deconstruction (1989, p. 11): "to deconstruct simply means to take apart the interpretive assumptions of the system of meaning that you are examining, to challenge the interpretive system in such a manner that you reveal the assumptions on which the model is based. At the same time . . . , you open the space for . . . alternative understanding." Note again the emphasis on challenging the client's hidden assumptions to create room for something new.

De Shazer's emphasis on the "reader"/listener, rather than on the "text"/ event itself or the "author" of the "text"/event, is clearly apparent in the following quotation: "The reader brings to the task of reading all of his previous experiences, all previous uses of the words and concepts, which *contaminate* [italics added] what he reads. For this, the deconstructivists use the term 'misreading': Seen in this way, one cannot read, one can only misread. . . . 'There can never be "objective" interpretation—only more or less vital readings' (Leitch, 1983)" (1991, pp. 50–51). De Shazer continues, "Furthermore, the reader can never know what the author might have meant because he cannot know what the author brought to the meaning of what he wrote. Similarly, the author himself cannot read what he wrote; he too can only misread. Misreading is not a problem to be solved, just a fact to be lived with (De Man, 1979)" (p. 51).

That last quotation of de Shazer is extremely important. It shows, without qualification, the explicit influence on psychotherapy not only of deconstruction itself, but also of the popular poststructural reader-response theory and criticism. In that approach it is generally denied that the text/event has a structure independent of the reader/observer. Rather, in that approach there is an emphasis on the psychology of reading, rather than on the independent (of the reader) meaning of the text. In that type of literary theory, where the psychology of reading is paramount, there is therefore typically a strong psychoanalytic or psychological component, and (notions or theories of) the mind/self (including psychoanalysis) are not distinguishable from (notions or theories of) language/literature/text (e.g., see Brooks, 1992; Culler, 1980; Fish, 1980; Gerrig, 1993; Krieger, 1987; Suleiman, 1980; Tompkins, 1980).

This viewpoint has been taken to its extreme by such poststructural writers as S. Fish, who have merged the notions of text and self even further by claiming that the act of reading creates or writes the text/self. It is worth our while to take a short digression here to consider Tompkins's (1980, pp. xvi–xvii, xxii–xxiii) account of Fish's (and Culler's) theory, since that account gives us language very similar to that used within the postmodern narrative therapy movement: "There is no preexistent text to which the reader responds, nor is there 'reading' in the traditional sense. Texts are written by readers, not read, since, the argument now states, the formal features of the text, the authorial intentions they are normally taken to represent, and the reader's interpretive strategies are mutually interdependent" (p. xxii). "[I]nstead of claiming that one's interpretations of literature are a response to what the author meant, or to what is there on the page, one must acknowledge that they are the result of the *interpretive strategies one possesses* [italics added]" (p. xxiii). "[T]he self that his [Fish's] theory posits is one constituted by its own interpretive categories, which are *public and shared* [italics added]. In that case, the self as an independent entity vanishes and, in Culler's words, 'its functions are taken up by a variety of interpersonal systems that operate through it.' . . . Thus, the powerful arguments these critics launch against the objectivity of the text make the nature of the interpreter's self into a problematic issue. As meaning comes to be defined more and more as a function of the reader's consciousness, the powers and limitations of that consciousness become an object of critical debate" (p. xxiii). Note here the (highly confusing) expressions of the interdependence of text and self, and the absence of objectivity. But most important is that whatever "self" exists, it is constituted solely in language—that is, in interpretive categories that are a function of some public, shared, consensual, interpersonal (discursive) context. This is precisely the argument we have seen in the social constructionism of many postmodern narrative therapy writers, most notably, White, de Shazer, and Gergen. [15]

One final quotation of Tompkins more or less sums all this up: "The later reader-response critics deny that criticism has such an objective basis because they deny the existence of objective texts and indeed the possibility of objectivity altogether. Relocating meaning first in the reader's self and then in the interpretive strategies that constitute it, they assert that meaning is a consequence of being in a particular situation in the world" (p. xxv). Note the postmodern emphasis on the particular and the unique—that is, on the specific context that relativizes all observation/reading and, ultimately, relativizes the self as well. This is an emphasis clearly found in postmodern narrative therapy. But again, because "interpretive strategies," or categories, are shared within that linguistic context, there can be no truly unique (that is, unique to any one individual) meanings or narratives, at least not as unique as the narrative therapy movement would, in my opinion, like to have it.

We see this interdependence of text and self surfacing in postmodern narrative therapy when Lax states, "The client, in essence, does not have a singular 'true' story independent of a 'reader' to whom she is telling that particular story" (1992, p. 73). De Shazer also seems to be reaching for this kind of reader-response position when he argues that neither readers nor authors can ever know just what it is they are reading and writing. They can only interpret subjectively (i.e., antirealistically) what they read or write, and so, presumably, what they allegedly can *become*. There is never some assurance that any one interpretation gets at some independent reality—reality which is, for de Shazer, nonexistent, or at least unattainable. (Recall that in his function as a therapist there is only the reality of language in therapy.) Also of note is de Shazer's wish to obtain more "vital" readings, as opposed to true ones, as a shared goal of both literature and therapy. I examine this goal in Chapter 5.

5. To continue on with Lax (1992), who elaborates the text analogy in proposing a deconstructive method for therapy, we find similar arguments. Lax invokes the deconstructionist distinction between the meanings and ideas that are *absent* ("the not-said") as opposed to those that are *present* ("the said") in any text, in order to broaden the range of possible interpretations or understandings of the text. He calls these potential alternative meanings "traces" that are always waiting to be "called forth" by the reader: "Following the 'reader-response' perspective (see Culler, 1982), these new distinctions are not like artifacts, waiting to be discovered, but different views available to each reader based on that person's perspective within which she views the text" (p. 72). Lax appears to endorse the self/text equation, or text analogy, described above. As he states, "This *narrative or sense of self* [italics added] arises not only through discourse with others, but *is* our discourse with others. There is no hidden self to be interpreted" (p. 71). However, to his credit, he also expresses justifiable discomfort with the text analogy: " . . . the text analogy from literary criticism is limited in its application to human systems" (p. 69); "Clients are not passively inscribed texts waiting to be interpreted by a reader, even if the interpretation is not a fixed, right, or privileged view. Each reading is different, given the interaction between the client and therapist. . . . The interaction itself is where the text exists and where the new narrative of one's life emerges" (p. 73). Given the quotations

of the reader-response (literary) theorists cited above, Lax appears, despite his apparent misgivings, to be closer to that literary theory than he may think.

6. Frank (1987), who also adopts the text analogy explicitly in a section entitled "Psychotherapy and Hermeneutics—The Patient as a Text" (p. 297), shares some of Lax's concerns about the fit of that analogy. According to him, "Unlike a written text the patient continually modifies his or her apologia in response to the demand character of the treatment situation . . ." (p. 297). He nonetheless goes on to provide "examples of [how] the therapeutic power of reinterpretations of the patient's 'text' abound. [For instance], a powerful way of enhancing the patient's self-confidence is by convincing the patient that his or her symptoms are not as ominous as the patient has feared" (p. 297). Of course, as Parry (1991) and Hare-Mustin and Marecek (1990a) have pointed out, reinterpreting patients' experiences is nothing new in psychotherapy. It is only the claim that those interpretations and experiences bear no relation to any extralinguistic reality that is new, and, as I go on to argue, is problematic for therapy, if not for actual (i.e., literal) literary texts and their readers.

7. I conclude this collection of quotations about the text analogy and deconstructive method of therapy with Parry, who makes some particularly clear statements. "The post-modern treatment of a story as simply a story [which I take to mean as having no extralinguistic reference or constraints], hence something endlessly inventive, offers the narrative therapist a tool for enabling clients to shake off constraining beliefs so that they can live their stories henceforth as they choose" (pp. 42–43). Note that the antirealism of postmodernism works in the service of endless inventiveness, the elimination of constraints, and thus, ultimately, the enhancement of uniqueness and individuality in therapy. To continue that emphasis on individuality: "Therapy is a process of encouraging people to re-story their experiences, past and present, according to their *own* [italics added] experience" (p. 45). "The goal of therapy . . . [is] to facilitate a process in which a person finds her own voice to tell a story of *her* descriptions of *her* experiences" (p. 44). "When a person finds her own voice, she takes charge of her own story" (p. 44).

Regarding the deconstruction process itself, Parry states, "The deconstruction of a life story involves an introduction to the realization that each person's story is inescapably connected to the stories of others as well as to many larger stories" (p. 45).[16] Note the reference here to the inescapable effects of an interpersonal, or shared, linguistic (discursive) context on the formulation of life experiences/stories; Parry evidently is aware of the problem of pursuing the uniquely personal in the context of a social constructionist epistemology, which connects individuals by way of stories that are themselves merely shared linguistic experiences/understandings (of the world). Thus, in elaborating a deconstructionist approach to therapy, Parry emphasizes the importance of asking clients questions about the roles they may be expected to enact in the stories of others, including their willingness to enact those roles: "The process of therapy is one of questioning and challenging the unacknowledged assumptions and beliefs [e.g., role expectations of self and others] of persons held in the grip of life problems" (p. 51). Again, note that this process of therapy, or theory-cum-method of problem resolution, need not be an antirealist one.

There is one last point about the text analogy that I find curious and so must comment upon. It seems noteworthy that psychotherapy is turning to (postmodern) literary theory to make sense of itself just when (postmodern) literary theorists, especially reader-response theorists, are emphasizing the psychology of reading rather than the true meaning of the text itself, which is allegedly unknowable from a postmodern position. (How these postmodern literary theorists can presume to know the truth about the psychology of reading presents the familiar problem of making a truth claim in the context of adopting an antirealist doctrine. That action is no less contradictory than the one confronting postmodern narrative therapists who presume to know the truth about the workings of therapy, as well as the nature of knowing itself.) It therefore seems that each discipline is turning to the other to make sense of itself. As a colleague of mine who is a classicist put it, it is as if two mirrors are facing and so reflecting each other, with nothing between them but a very large void (Boyd, 1991). But that is a story for another book.

In conclusion, the widespread adoption of the text analogy as a therapeutic theory that supports literary deconstruction as a therapeutic method (i.e., a theory-cum-method) eliminates any doubt about the prevalence of an antirealist (social-constructionist) epistemology in the narrative therapy movement. I have demonstrated how the adoption of that epistemology reflects an attempt to preserve in therapy the individuality that conventional, realist therapies allegedly subvert by offering the client a new narrative, but one that is more "dominant," or predetermined by a complete theoretical system, and so is allegedly more "oppressive." In due course I discuss the problems with this text analogy and its attendant method, both in theory (its inevitable production of an oscillation between realism and antirealism) and in practice (the ethics of an antirealist approach to therapy). But first we must consider an

example or two of how this theory-cum-method of problem resolution works
in the practice of postmodern narrative therapy. These examples should help
reveal how the actual practice of that therapy may not be all that different
from what so-called conventional, realist therapists do in their practice.

EXAMPLES OF THE NARRATIVE/
TEXTUAL APPROACH TO THERAPY

White (White, 1993; White & Epston, 1990), Anderson and Goolishian
(1988), and McNamee and Gergen (1992), among others, provide some
specific suggestions about how to go about deconstructing and reconstructing
clients' narratives. Let us therefore consider some of their methods, so we can
be clear about just what they recommend.

White and Epston (1990) ground their narrative approach in what they
call "externalizing the problem." By this they mean "an approach to therapy
that encourages persons to objectify and, at times, to personify the problems
that they experience as oppressive. In this process, the problem becomes a
separate entity and thus external to the person or relationship that was
ascribed as the problem. Those problems that are considered to be inherent,
as well as those relatively fixed qualities that are attributed to persons and
to relationships, are rendered less fixed and less restricting" (p. 38). "The
externalizing of the problem enables persons to separate from the dominant
stories that have been shaping of their lives and relationships" (pp. 40–41).
Each person is then free to create a new, more uniquely personal story about
her life, a story that in theory allows each to live her actual life differently,
free from the constraints of the oppressive, dominant story. White and Epston
(1990) refer to this last idea as the performance of "alternative stories," or
sometimes the "performance of meaning around unique[17] outcomes," rather
than the performance of the same old (dominant) story. I interpret them to
mean that when the client notices a desirable, new (i.e., unique for her) life
experience/event and then constructs a narrative that incorporates that new
experience/event, the narrative itself works to solidify the change and so
ensure that other desirable, new experiences/events continue to happen. As
Omer (1993, p. 62) put it, "Clients are encouraged to 'perform meaning'
around these unique outcomes, that is, to re-narrate life-events in this competing frame, and to experiment with *behaviors* [italics added] that are allowed
for by the new, but not the old, narrative." Narrative therapy may therefore
be said to affect two aspects of the client's life: the linguistic aspect (what the
client says—her narrative) and the extralinguistic aspect (what the client

does—how she lives). As I demonstrate in Chapters 5 and 6, this approach can easily be incorporated within a modestly realist doctrine, rather than the antirealist one White and Epston (among others) propound.

For example, White and Epston (1990, pp. 56–57) provide an exemplary case of a 26-year-old woman named Katherine who, having seriously injured her back at age 13, suffered from severe chronic pain and disability, anxiety, depression, and isolation from contact with strangers, all of which limited her range of potential relationships. Katherine and her mother came to the first session. White separated the problem—in this case, pain and resulting social isolation—from the client's own self. He did this by asking the client, as he usually does, to map the "problem's" influence on her, and her influence on the "problem." In this case, he asked Katherine "if she could recall a time when she could have let pain [and anxiety] prevent her from having personal contact with another person but refused to submit to its demands" [note how the problem is rendered external to the client's own self here] (p. 57). Katherine reported one such (unique) instance in which she nodded "hello" to a stranger who passed her on the street. White then explains how the client (and her mother) were encouraged to "perform meaning around [i.e., construct a story/narrative about] this event," by answering such questions as: "How did Katherine cope with her anxiety as the stranger approached? How did she stop it [the externalized pain/anxiety] from turning her back? What had she done to prepare herself for this?" (p. 57). As White reports it, "The identification of this historically located unique outcome constituted a turning point" (p. 57), and paved the way for the inspection of other instances of the mother's "refusal to participate in 'pain journalism'" (p. 57). Both Katherine and her mother reportedly went on to lead more satisfactory lives.

Now, there can be no doubt that this case is an example of some very good therapy. In fact, I have found, as a clinician myself, that many of the case reports of those within the postmodern narrative therapy movement are nothing short of exemplary. These include case reports by de Shazer, an ardent postmodernist/antirealist. His method of finding exceptions to the problem situation—i.e., those occasions when the problem does not occur or does not occur in the same old way, but rather when something new happens—seems compatible with what White and Epston have described in this and other cases.

But the question I am always left with is this: is the case we have just considered an example of antirealist epistemology put into actual *practice*? Does the case require an antirealist epistemology to *explain* its actual workings in some theoretical, or systematic, way? Instead, isn't it perfectly reasonable to assume that (a) the client's reports/narrative of her own unique experiences, (b) her co-construction (with the therapist) of new meanings about those experiences to produce a new narrative, and (c) whatever *behavioral enactments* result from those new meanings/narrative, all actually refer—to some extent—to some extralinguistic, or real, events, including those behavioral enactments? For instance, that Katherine suffered from an injury, that she said hello to a stranger on the street, and that the therapist's questions *caused* her to think and then behave differently all constitute events that are not *merely* linguistic constructions, even for postmodern therapists. (Note, however, that the third event in that sequence involves a causal claim that is itself not directly knowable; I return to it later.)

To put the matter another way, the client's unique, personal story about her life, and the therapist's general, predetermined story, or causal claim, about the good effects of rewriting the client's story (i.e., the therapist's predetermined theory-cum-method of problem resolution), are not of necessity antirealist stories. It therefore seems reasonable to assume that at least a modest, or limited, realism—and so more conventional theoretical systems of therapy—could account for that method of therapeutic practice in general, and the success of this therapy case in particular. For example, traditional cognitive therapists "restructure" clients' views/understandings of their experiences as they are expressed in narratives, but this is done within the confines of a modern scientific realism and not a postmodern humanistic antirealism. That is, those therapists seek to bring clients' understandings into better conformity with reality, to solve their problems.

White (1993) provides a catalogue of—that is, he specifies or particularizes—the kinds of questions that help clients "externalize" and "restory" their problems. He does this by, as he puts it, separating clients' problems from the "dominant or 'totalizing' stories that are constitutive of their lives . . . [thus allowing them] to orient themselves to [unique] aspects of their experience that contradict these knowledges" (pp. 39–40). We saw an example of these questions in the case illustration provided just above. These questions include:

(a) "Landscape-of-action questions," which ask about the performance of unique (new) outcomes. For example, "How did you get yourself ready to take this step?", " . . . [D]id you nearly turn back? If so, how did you stop yourself from doing so?", "What did you tell yourself that pulled you through on this occasion?" (p. 41).

(b) "Landscape-of-consciousness questions," which "encourage the articulation and the performance of . . . alternative preferences, desires, personal and relationship qualities, and intentional states and beliefs" (p. 44). For example, "Let's reflect for a moment on these recent developments. What new conclusions might you reach about your tastes?", "What do these discoveries tell you about what you want for your life?", " . . . [W]hat suits you as a person?" (p. 44).

(c) "Experience-of-experience questions," which "encourage persons to provide an account of what they believe or imagine to be another person's experience of them"—imaginings "that are constitutive of alternative experiences of themselves" (p. 45). For instance, "If I had been a spectator to your life when you were younger, what do you think I might have witnessed you doing then that might help me to understand how you were able to achieve what you have recently achieved?" or "Of all those persons who have known you, who would be least surprised that you have been able to take this step in challenging the problem's influence in your life?" (p. 46).

Although these are excellent questions to ask in therapy—they call attention to, elaborate, and so solidify whatever gains a client starts to make—I must once more ask the recurrent question: what about any of them requires an underlying antirealism? To ask a client about her *perceptions* of, and *personal (causal/explanatory) theories* about, (a) how she kept from turning back, (b) her alternative preferences and desires in life, and (c) her imaginings of others, is to ask about her true perceptions and theories. That is, we hope the client tells us the truth about what those perceptions and theories really are— regardless of how accurately or inaccurately they may reflect any extralinguistic reality. We shall return to that important point in a moment.

Turning now to Anderson and Goolishian (1988), we find eight distinct positions that therapists are encouraged to take to attain a "therapeutic conversation"—one that *causes* new options to open. These positions, as with White's distinct questions, constitute the more particularized theory-cum-method of problem resolution we find in the narrative therapy movement relative to its nonparticularized theory of problem causation. According to Anderson and Goolishian, the therapist (a) allows the client to determine the parameters of inquiry about the problem and moves outside of those parameters very slowly, (b) simultaneously considers many, even contradictory, ideas, (c) selects language that is cooperative, to be respectful rather than judgmental, (d) uses the client's language, which is seen as a metaphor for the client's life experience, (e) listens respectfully and strives not to understand the client "too quickly," (f) asks the kind of questions that elicit more questions rather than answers to hypotheses or the discovery of information, (g) assumes responsibility for creating a context that allows the problem definition to emerge in a mutual, collaborative way, rather than in a predetermined, authoritative way, and (h) engages in a continual conversation or dialogue with himself or herself, so as to stay open to new ideas (pp. 382–383). All of these constitute Anderson and Goolishian's (1992) "not knowing" position, a position in which they avoid the holding, testing, and especially, imposing of any general, predetermined, or, as they say, "pre-held theoretical narratives" (p. 28). But in taking the client's unique, personal meanings, understandings, theory, or narrative/story "seriously" (p. 30), Anderson and Goolishian may be using personal theory in a more realist way than they realize or care to admit. They are also, like White and Epston, adhering to some degree of realism about the therapy (i.e., problem resolution) process, as we shall soon see.

Finally, Gergen and Kaye (1992) recommend that therapists consider the therapeutic effects that can be obtained "by the exploration of experience from multiple perspectives, by sensitizing another to the relational context in which behavior is situated, and by a thorough *relativizing* of experience" (p. 183). Gergen (1991b) and Gergen and Kaye (1992) are explicit about the need to teach clients to be antirealists/relativists when they encourage "acceptance of unbounded relativity of meaning" to allow (i.e., to *cause*) the "freeing of experience" (Gergen & Kaye, p. 183). (I discuss the ethical implications for therapy of that point of view in Chapter 8.) For them, clients can, for instance, be encouraged

> to find exceptions to their predominating experience; to view themselves as prisoners of a culturally inculcated story they did not create; to imagine how they might relate their experience to different people in their lives; . . . to consider how they would experience their lives if they operated from different assumptions—how they might act, . . . what new solutions might emerge. (p. 183)

Again, as is true for all postmodern therapists, unique, personal theory is emphasized. But there is every reason to suppose that when that theory is used in the actual practice of therapy, it makes implicit reference to an extralinguistic reality and, moreover, that its use can produce solutions. There is therefore a realist claim lurking in this approach to problem resolution. Let us now turn our attention to it.

THE NARRATIVE THERAPY SOLUTION TO THE INDIVIDUALITY/ SYSTEMATIC PROBLEM

All these examples of the therapeutic method that accompanies the client-as-text analogy (i.e., the theory-cum-method of problem resolution) have at least one thing in common: the claim that the client's unique linguistic "problem" can be solved only if a new story is constructed and acted upon, or "performed." That new liberating story—like the old oppressive one—is not supposed to reflect any extralinguistic truth according to the narrative therapy movement. But that movement nonetheless applies to all clients, without discrimination, one overarching "metatheory" (Omer & Strenger, 1992) of problem resolution: therapists must help clients "co-create" new meanings/narratives of their problem experience, to achieve problem resolution. As we have seen in the examples of this chapter, this is typically done by questioning and challenging the client's previous view or narrative of his problem—that is, by challenging his personal theory (which allegedly contains the oppressive elements of some "dominant discourse") and by encouraging the client to imagine a new (even more uniquely personal) view or narrative of his experience. The challenges and imaginings refer at least to real imaginings and to real, extralinguistic events in the client's life (e.g., saying "hello" to a stranger on the street). These imaginings and events therefore call into question the viability (the truth) of the old narrative.

Before I turn to the epistemological problem this unacknowledged nod to reality poses for the narrative therapy movement, I return my focus to the two competing goals within that movement: its attempt in practice to emphasize the unique, personal aspects of each client's experience (its attempt to individualize), but to do so by employing one, universal, or general, theory-cum-method of problem resolution (its attempt to systematize). That attempt indeed constitutes two contradictory goals. The former, of course, is in the interest of preserving a practice that is individualized; the latter of ensuring a practice that is, by virtue of the use of a generality, rule-governed and so systematic. Recall, however, that the attempt to attain both goals is made by way of the explicit adoption of antirealism.

On Preserving Individuality vs. Rule-Governed Practice

The narrative therapy movement abandoned the assignment of clients to general, predetermined categories of problems (Component C) and their causal explanations (Component A). I have argued that this was motivated by an attempt to preserve in therapy practice the individuality of each unique client—individuality compromised by the matrix paradigm, and indeed by all conventional, complete therapy systems (with their general, predetermined client/problem categories [C] and theories of problem causation [A]). That individuality could in principle be preserved within the narrative therapy movement by letting each client at each moment occupy a unique "cell" or problem situation in that person's own unique narrative. As we saw above, Anderson and Goolishian (1992) call this "letting the client be the expert" about his problem/narrative.

Let us now ask the obvious question how a therapy movement that applies to all clients the same theory-cum-method of problem resolution (B), namely, co-creation of new narratives, can be truly individualized, especially when compared to a movement, such as the matrix paradigm of technical/systematic eclecticism, which advocates the flexible selection of interventions (B) as a function of client/problem type (C).[18] Omer and Strenger (1992), who promote the narrative approach, seem to be aware of this problem when they state, "A pluralistic [i.e., postmodern] era is precisely the one to eschew such a unifying view, but, surprisingly, a pluralistic metamodel seems to be emerging: that of man as the self-narrating species" (p. 254). If we take the postmodernism of Foucault and Lyotard seriously, Omer and Strenger are right to worry about the adoption of any metamodel in that intellectual context: as Glass (1993, p. 2) aptly puts it, "For him [Lyotard], these metanarratives exercise a debilitating influence on action and perception; they *confine* thought and *impose* meaning; therefore, the function of metanarrative is to assure obedience, acquiescence to systems of value and power which dominate and alienate consciousness" [all italics added]. In other words, all metanarratives, including, presumably, those of the narrative therapy movement, constitute the "dominant discourses" that allegedly oppress or alienate one from one's (unique) self. (Of course, according to postmodernism, that unique self allegedly changes as *its* true creator—language *itself*—changes!)

That "unifying view" to which Omer and Strenger refer nonetheless has individuality built into it. Thus, we can say with some assurance that the narrative movement would defend itself on two grounds against charges of a uniformly or generally applied—and thus, ironically, deindividualizing (but, predictably, systematizing)—"metatheory" of problem resolution. The first defense is that the privileging of the client's unique, personal narrative ensures individuality at the level of the content of therapy—that is, the definition of the problem (C) and its theory of causation (A). The content of the new, less problematic, less "oppressive," story/narrative must therefore also be similarly unique. That individualization is possible because, recall, the predetermined description of problems and theory of their causation in the narrative therapy system (namely, narratives themselves both *constitute* [C] and *cause* [A] "problems") are so very general that they place (for all practical purposes) *no* constraints on the way clients' unique, personal views are to be used in therapy. Put differently, clients' stories require no reformulation whatever to fit the narrative therapy system's general definition of problems and theory of their causes; the content of therapy is therefore always—insofar as it is possible—completely client determined (see Figure 3.7 in Chapter 3).

Clearly, though, the universal use of its one theory-cum-method of problem resolution, of its "unifying view," causes the practice of therapy to be rule-governed, or constrained, and so consistent or replicable in regard to therapeutic process (Component B). However, the degree of constraint placed on process is again a function of how much the theory-cum-method of problem resolution is specified, or particularized. Thus, the specification, or particularization, of rules for reconstructing new narratives will insure a more systematic intervention process than will the highly general mandate to "restory" the "problem" in *any* way possible. I return to that problem in Chapter 7.

The narrative therapy solution to the individuality/systematic problem, then, is this: the content of therapy (Components A and C) is not, for all practical purposes, predetermined by the system—it is client determined and so it constitutes the individualization factor. The (one) process of therapy (Component B) is fully predetermined by the system and, moreover, is universally, or unconditionally, applied—it is not client determined and so it constitutes the systematic, rule-governed, or replication factor. Put differently, the narrative theoretical system allows a practice that is fully individualized with regard to therapeutic content, but not with regard to therapeutic process. That same system allows a practice that is systematic with regard to process, but not with regard to content. But the narrative therapy system is in any event an incomplete system. Components A and C are so general they add nothing to what the client herself brings to therapy in the way of content; in that sense they are merely vestigial—they place no constraints on the content of practice. That system, then, retains, for all practical purposes, only one component, namely, Component B.

The narrative therapy movement's second line of defense against the charge of a deindividualizing metatheory of problem resolution is based on the adoption of antirealism. According to the extreme linguistic relativism (i.e., antirealism) of many members of the postmodern narrative movement, all interventions constitute changing nothing more (or less) than those option-limiting, "problem"-causing narratives. Therefore, there is no sacrifice of a diversity of problem-resolution methods within that movement. That is, according to the narrative movement, all interventions from all schools of therapy (e.g., recovery of the unconscious in psychoanalysis, or the realignment of relationships in family therapy, or the reworking of irrational cognitions into rational ones in traditional cognitive therapy) work only on—and so exist only in—the domain of language/narrative itself. My point here is perhaps too abstract; an example may help: according to the narrative view, psychoanalysis works because in actuality it alters *only* the client's narrative about her problem by providing a more compelling, coherent, and consistent story about her experience, and not because it necessarily makes conscious some real underlying truth about the client's past or unconscious (cf. Spence, 1982, pp. 27–28).

That last point raises what is for me a serious concern about the narrative therapy movement's professed antirealism. Although I consider the ethical implications of an antirealist approach to therapy in more detail in Chapter 8, just now I must make one point: that to see or treat people's actions, including their utterances, as literary texts to be deconstructed is to apply a metaphor that brings with it some danger that the therapist will be tempted to ignore or minimize the importance of the (extralinguistic) reality of the real person sitting before the therapist, with all her real life experiences. These include real psychological, social, and economic circumstances, for instance, poverty, oppression, abuse, and even, contrary to the narrative view, real mental illness, such as schizophrenia or depression.[19] For if all we need to do to solve the client's problem is change her (antirealist) narrative/view of it, then we need not put any efforts and resources into trying to change the real circumstances of that extralinguistic reality. For instance, in that case we need not work to change the way real money does or does not get allocated for the legal and physical protection of victims of battering and sexual abuses. Another way to state the inappropriateness of the client-as-text analogy is that texts, unlike clients, are not themselves in pain, nor are they paying therapists money to alleviate that pain—that is, to "rewrite" them.

In her review of Glass's book, *Shattered Selves: Multiple Personality in a Postmodern World*, Ayoub (1993) quotes Glass (1993, p. 139) as saying, "Human beings suffer; letters do not," and as the review in the *Chronicle of Higher Education* continues, "That, argues James M. Glass, is what such postmodernists as Jean Baudrillard and Gilles Deleuze appear to forget when they celebrate the indeterminacy of a self as they do the indeterminacy of a text." Glass himself has some other noteworthy comments along these lines, for instance, (a) "Real selves that live out the psychological imperatives of multiplicity have nothing in common with selves deconstructed in texts" (p. 14), (b) "What happens inside a text and what happens inside the self are often radically different forms of being and becoming. . . . The 'deconstructing' of identity is what happens in psychosis" (p. 12), and (c) "For postmodernists to dismiss all forms of psychological suffering and psychoanalytic interpretation as consequences of perverse knowledge/power epistemes is to ignore the fact that individuals do actually suffer from conditions such as multiple personality disorder and schizophrenia" (p. 26). I consider the ethics of the text analogy further in Chapter 8.

Ironically, proponents of the postmodern narrative therapy movement accuse conventional, modern, realist therapists of that same failing—of not taking the client's story seriously—because they are said to impose on their clients deindividuating, or "dominant," "discourses," the generalized use of which is justified by an erroneous appeal to their objectivity, realism, or truth. According to postmodernists, these are the very same theories, or discourses, that are alleged to have caused the client's problems to begin with, by devaluing or undermining the client's unique, personal experiences/views/story (see Anderson & Goolishian, 1992, p. 30; Hare-Mustin, 1994, p. 20; Parry, 1991; White & Epston, 1990). As Hare-Mustin (1994, p. 20) states, "Indeed, therapy has been described as *inflicting* [italics added] on patients the same dominant discourses by which they have previously been harmed (Cushman, 1990)." Note the very general claim about problem causation in that last statement. (It is important here to recall yet again that it is the completeness of a predetermined theoretical system of therapy and not the realism or antirealism of that system that determines the individualization and systematization of therapy practice guided by that system.)

Fortunately, the narrative therapy movement does not seem to take its own antirealism completely seriously, either in its theory or in the applications of its theory in practice. I refer here to its (unwitting) oscillation between realism and antirealism. It therefore is not likely to ignore the client's extralinguistic circumstances, certainly not as much as it might if it were indeed consistent about its antirealism. In any case, I must reinforce one important point regarding this disagreement between realists and antirealists about taking the client's personal experiences or views of life events seriously: paying attention to the client's unique, personal story and remaining open to alternative explanations/interpretations/theories/stories about her life experiences do not require the adoption of an antirealist epistemology. Indeed, such openness is characteristic of the traditional, realist scientific enterprise as it has been pursued over the ages. That is, in good science, rival or competing theories and hypotheses are always entertained and tested as we try to approximate the real nature of some extratheoretic reality. And attention to the client's individual views of his unique circumstances has never been denied or ignored in more conventional, realist therapy systems: as we saw in Chapter 3 (see Figure 3.6), therapists who use those systems always tailor their general, predetermined theoretical formulations to the unique nuances of each case.

Thus, the attention to uniqueness and the openness to alternative explanations are perfectly compatible with the modest realism I propose. That realism permits direct (objective) rational awareness of some—but not all—temporospatial entities and events. That realism also permits varying degrees of access to explanations—or causal accounts (which are themselves not directly observable)—of those directly observed events.

CHAPTER 5

Epistemological Oscillation in Narrative Therapy: A Critique and a Hope

OSCILLATION BETWEEN REALISM AND ANTIREALISM

The oscillation between the antirealism it propounds and the realism it unwittingly expresses is the primary target of my critique of the postmodern narrative movement's system of therapy, for this oscillation undermines the logic, coherence, and internal consistency of the theory that supposedly guides that movement's practice. Nonetheless, the *practice* of narrative therapy, as it has been put forth in some case examples, is one I often find to be in accord with sound, effective, realist approaches to therapy—that is, the practice of narrative therapy does not reflect the pervasive antirealism of its alleged theory. There are, therefore, discrepancies to be found both *within* the narrative movement's theoretical system of therapy and *between* that theoretical system and the practice it is meant to guide. In this chapter I demonstrate the hidden, implicit realism within the narrative therapy movement's system of therapy, and the consequent oscillation between that implicit realism and the movement's explicit antirealism. This demonstration leads ultimately to the call for that movement to develop a more consistent and precise philosophy of knowing.

Let us begin with the narrative therapy movement's theory of problem causation (A), and more important, its theory-cum-method of problem resolution (B). I say the theory-cum-method of problem resolution is more important because it is in the fleshing out or specification of that component of the narrative therapy system that we find the preponderance of its unacknowledged reality claims about therapy, that is, its realism. (That makes sense since, recall, that is the only component of that system that does not exist in so highly general a form that it becomes virtually nonexistent—i.e., fully client determined or vestigial.) Here, simply put, are the narrative therapy movement's thoroughly general, predetermined claims about problem causation and resolution, respectively: (a) A personal and subjective—i.e., antirealist—narrative, or story, of some (nonpredetermined) aspect of the client's life has caused the experience of a (linguistic) "problem" (A). (b) Therapists must therefore use certain (predetermined) methods to help each client co-create a new personal and equally subjective—i.e., antirealist—narrative, or story, to cause the experience of a (linguistic) solution—that is, to solve the "problem" (B).

Note that these claims transcend the unique, particular, and supposedly subjective, or antirealist, content of any individual client's narrative. Thus, they are indeed perfectly general claims—that is, they apply to all clients, and so they give us some assurance of a systematic/rule-governed, and therefore consistent or replicable (yet still allegedly antirealist), approach to the process (but not the content) of therapy. But those claims also contain some modest degree of unacknowledged realism, even if that realism is confined to linguistic productions themselves. This is a subtle but important point I shall explain in some detail in Chapter 6.

But first let us consider the additional and even more problematic central claim of the narrative therapy movement: that the way one narrates, or constructs in language, the experiences/events of one's life affects not only the perception/experience of problems and of solutions/options, but ultimately also the *behaviors*, or *actions* (especially, interpersonal interactions), one performs.[1] It is in this last claim that we find reference to an extralinguistic, independent reality.

We therefore find an oscillation between realism and antirealism in the theoretical system of the postmodern narrative therapy movement. The realism consists in the fundamental proposition, or truth/reality claim, just mentioned: one's narrative about one's life determines, or causes, one's (experience of) problems, options/solutions, and, most important to my argument, one's real (i.e., knower independent) *actions* in life. These actions are themselves events that can be directly (and so objectively) observed or known,[2] according to even some of those who most ardently promote the antirealism of the narrative view (for elaboration see Spence, 1982, pp. 290–292, especially his discussion on p. 292 of Gergen, 1981). As Lax (1992, p. 74), for example, has stated, "Real events do happen in our lives, but we then develop a narrative around them that sometimes freezes them." Presumably we can know the extralinguistic (real) events themselves directly (and so objectively) enough to create a narrative about them, even if the explanations of the events contained in our narratives, or theories, do not provide an accurate account of the real, extralinguistic, causes and effects of those events.

But whether the problem and solution narratives exist only in language, with no extralinguistic referent whatever (as many members of that movement also claim), or whether those narratives indeed refer to an extralinguistic, behavioral/situational reality is at best a highly problematic question within the narrative therapy movement's theory. The theory opts for the former—that narratives give us no extralinguistic reality. But it then goes on to assert unequivocally that the nature of discourse/narrative really, truly, or objectively affects/causes not only the perception/experience of problems, options, and solutions but ultimately also the behavior the client enacts or, to use the preferred term, "performs"[3] (see Omer, 1993, p. 62). This behavior, like the events Lax speaks of, constitutes real (extralinguistic) events that can be known directly as such, even by postmodern narrative therapists. Indeed, it is knowledge of these extralinguistic events that provides (some of) the content of narratives. In short, discourse, or narrative, or stories, both (a) employ as content, and more important, (b) causally affect real events, that is, affect (extralinguistic) reality. Hence, the oscillation between realism and antirealism within the narrative therapy movement begins to reveal itself.

Since my last point is an important but difficult one, let us consider it again. There are two ways in which (often unwitting) reference to an extralinguistic reality occurs in the narrative therapy movement's theory. The first is that real events occur and can be known (directly) as such. These events form the objective data for the *descriptive* part of the narrative content, even though the *explanations*—the causal accounts—of those data may be incorrect. In that latter case, we have a bad or wrong theory about the client, a theory that is not all that different from a scientific theory that simply gets it wrong. For example, a client observes that her husband yells at her whenever things do not go well at his work. She therefore, in her therapeutic discussion, posits the personal theory that feelings of inadequacy about his work performance cause him to yell at her. The fact that he yells at her, and only when he has a bad day at work, are the events that are directly observable and thus objectively real or true; they constitute the descriptive part of her narrative. The causal claim, or explanation, for the yelling is not directly observable; it is inferred, and so may or may not reflect the true, extralinguistic, extratheoretic cause of the husband's yelling. That causal claim constitutes the explanatory part of her narrative.

The client's narrative, then, can in principle get the directly observable events right. (This is what Spence, 1982, p. 291, calls observation language or plain narrative, which is dependent on historical truth.) But, like a scientific theory, the way the narrative explains the events or links them in some causally meaningful way may not get it right in terms of the true, extralinguistic linkages.[4] (This is what Spence calls causal language or significant narrative, which, he says, is dependent on narrative truth—the coherence and consistency of the story.) As Spence, quoting Walsh (1958), states, "The validity of a *significant* narrative (its narrative truth) cannot be checked by making an appeal to the known facts because 'the connections between events are not open to inspection in the way the events themselves are. . . . Causal language is of a different logical order from observation language . . .' (p. 483)" (Spence, 1982, p. 291). We shall consider this distinction in more detail in Chapter 6, as it applies both to science in general and to therapy in particular.

The second way narrative therapy makes reference to an extralinguistic reality in its theory, and the one I emphasize, is in its claim that narratives, once formed, can affect extralinguistic behavior. This claim is independent of the question whether narratives are (extralinguistically) correct in their explanatory, or significant, narrative content (and even in their event, or plain, narrative content). Thus, even a bad or wrong theory/story can have profound effects on extralinguistic behavior, as many narrative therapists have pointed out, sometimes by using a discourse analysis based on Foucault. Indeed, were it not for the pervasive postmodern belief that discourse in general, and dominant discourses in particular, can affect (extralinguistic) reality by bestowing power on some and by oppressing others, there would be little reason for postmodern theorists of any sort to concern themselves with the "analysis" of discourse in the first place.

Within the postmodern narrative therapy movement we therefore find a general causal claim: narrative/discourse *itself*—that is, whether or not any particular manifestation of it is extralinguistically true—affects extralinguistic behavior or events. In the example cited above, the client's belief/story/ theory that her husband yells at her because he feels inadequate at work could lead to a very different behavioral response (e.g., feeling sorry for him and so trying to cheer him up about his job performance), from that elicited by a belief/story/theory that he yells at her because he feels she deserves that sort of treatment (in which case she might simply feel free to yell back, assuming her sense of self and agency is reasonably intact, so that she does not share his opinion of her). Again, this claim about the effects of narrative/discourse on extralinguistic behavior is perfectly general precisely because it transcends the unique, particular content of any individual client's narrative; indeed, it is the adoption of this sort of general, predetermined claim that entitles narrative therapy to call itself a *system* of therapy. Thus, the fact that the problem and solution narratives—whatever their particular content—may not, according to the postmodern narrative system of therapy, accurately reflect any independent, extralinguistic reality does not diminish the realism behind its claim that narrative/discourse *itself* affects behavior that is external to—independent of—the language/narrative in use.

Let me now drive home the point that the narrative metatheory of problem resolution (i.e., that the co-creation of new narratives is the way to solve "problems") retains an underlying realism that is denied but that nonetheless permeates the very tissue of its argument. I first review, by means of the three components of the generic model of therapy systems, the causal claims the narrative therapy movement actually puts forth. I then consider statements that explicate the belief, held by members of the narrative therapy movement, that changing narratives (in therapy) affects behavior that is indeed external to the narrative, that is, affects extralinguistic behavior.

Problem Categories (C)

Here we find no causal claim but merely a definition: that narratives/stories of life events are themselves (linguistic) "problems." These "problems" allegedly exist only within narrative, or language (and hence the use of the pejorative quotation marks). This definition was illustrated in the quotations provided in Chapter 4.

Problem Causation (A)

The narrative/story the client brings to therapy not only *is* the "problem," but also *causes* (the experience, or perception, of) that "problem." Note so far that we are still, according to the narrative therapy movement, solely within the domain of narrative/language[5]—that is, no reference to an extralinguistic reality is explicitly made, at least not yet. Nonetheless, the discerning reader will find a subtle note of implicit realism in that last claim: to say that stories can cause the perception, or experience, of a linguistic "problem" is to say that stories (really) cause perceptions, or experiences. Put differently, the perception, or experience, of a "problem," even one that supposedly exists only in language, is nonetheless a perception, or experience, that in a particular sense really exists—exists in much the same way that a client who is called upon by a narrative therapist to imagine other ways of being may be said to have real imaginings of those other ways of being.[6] This is a difficult point to make; I explain the (modest) realism of a linguistically defined experience more fully in Chapter 6.

Problem Resolution (B)

Here three causal claims are made. The first two do not make explicit reference to an extralinguistic reality—although they make that reference implicitly; the third one does make such explicit reference. The three claims are: (a) The therapist's interventions, which consist in such methods as "deconstructing"—or challenging and questioning—the client's old, problematic narrative, cause the production of a new narrative/story. That is, such interventions cause a new linguistic production to materialize. The truth, or reality, of this claim can be determined by comparing the client's old, problematic narrative with the new, co-constructed one, to see whether it is indeed different. Thus, although the claim tries to confine itself to the workings of language (with the exception of whatever extralinguistic behavior the therapist exhibits in the therapeutic interchanges[7]), there nonetheless is some realism in that claim. That realism derives from the fact that we can know directly the real nature of narrative propositions, or (linguistic) statements, which have their own independent existence. Thus, we can know whether two propositions or narratives are themselves the same or different, quite apart from the question of whether they make a correct or incorrect reference to some extralinguistic reality. We shall consider the truth and workings of those last two sentences in Chapter 6.

(b) The new narrative/story, or new linguistic production, causes the perception/experience of new options or solutions for the old "problem." Note that the perception/experience of new options or solutions also, allegedly, occurs solely in the domain of language. But like the perception, or experience, of "problems," it is again a real perception, or experience. Moreover, like the comparison of the old and new narrative/story about some life event, those new options and solutions can be compared directly to the perception, or experience, of the old options and solutions—the ones that attended the old problematic story, to see if they too have really changed, even if that change has occurred only in language. Thus there is again some realism in that claim, as I explain further in Chapter 6.

(c) The new narrative/story, with its attendant new options and solutions, causes the *enactment* or *performance* of new behavior. Here, finally, we can clearly see the explicit reference to extralinguistic reality in the causal claim. The claim can be tested by observing directly the behavior that accompanies the new narrative/story, and comparing it to the behavior that accompanied the old narrative/story. This behavior can occur within the therapy session itself (in which case the therapist need not rely on the client's report), or it can occur outside of therapy (in which case the therapist must rely on the client's report of that extralinguistic behavior, as in the White and Epston case of the woman with the injured back who approached a stranger on the street). But in that latter case, note that the client's report/story/narrative refers to the extralinguistic reality of the client's life events.

Before turning to quotations that make these claims explicit, let us first consider an example to both illustrate them and show how they may be tested. A client may enter therapy complaining of persistent shyness and an inability to assert her limits or speak her mind. She believes that these personal, enduring qualities have caused her repeatedly to take on the tasks and obligations of others, obligations which themselves cause her discomfort and which she does not want to accept—e.g., her doing the tedious job that rightly belongs to a co-worker. According to the narrative therapy movement, the client's unique, personal narrative (or linguistic construction) of this unique aspect of her unique life—namely, how her shyness and lack of assertiveness cause her to take on obligations she does not want to assume—both *is* her problem and, moreover, *causes* her (perception/experience of a) "problem"—that is, her narrative causes her perception, or experience, of discomfort or unhappiness of some unspecified sort.

Notice that according to narrative therapy the experience of a "problem" (i.e., discomfort about some life circumstance) occurs whether or not the particular content of the client's narrative is true—that is, whether or not the client's narrative gives a valid causal account of her struggles as they exist extralinguistically, or in reality. Of course, the extralinguistic truth of that—or any—causal account constitutes knowledge which cannot, according to the antirealism of the narrative therapy movement, ever be attained. Thus, although the narrative movement claims that all narratives/stories/theories/causal accounts are by definition antirealist—that is, they can never give us any independent, extralinguistic reality—it is equally possible that the client has gotten it right: in this instance, her lack of assertiveness may indeed be behind her propensity to take on the work of others, and therefore may be the true cause of her experience of a "problem" or discomfort.

In any case, by challenging the client's narrative—the belief that she is stuck with those enduring qualities that have caused such situations as the one with her co-worker—the therapist helps the client create a new narrative. This new narrative could, for instance, be that there have actually been some times in her life when this client has spoken her mind and asserted her limits, and so she can't really be as shy and unassertive as she thinks. (Notice we can compare this new narrative to the original one, and so we can see that it is different. Notice also that both the old and the new narrative [unwittingly] reflect or refer to extralinguistic events in the client's life—the times when she did or did not assert her limits. These are events which the therapist has every reason to believe occurred in reality.) Based on this new narrative, the client comes to perceive ways to handle her co-worker's requests other than simple compliance. She therefore now perceives new options or solutions, for instance, expressing to her co-worker her sincere wish to help but pointing out the existence of her own heavy workload, and perhaps even asking the co-worker to help *her*.

It is here that we arrive at my key point. Because this client now perceives herself as having had, on occasion, the ability to act assertively (i.e., because she now has a different *view or image* of herself, or a new "self narrative," to use the preferred jargon[8]), and because she now can perceive alternative ways to solve her problem that are consistent with that new self-image, the client—predictably—begins to assert herself at work. She simply refuses to do jobs that are not rightfully hers. Contrary to the antirealism of narrative therapy theory, the therapist probably accepts the truth of this change in the client's extralinguistic reality/behavior on the basis of the client's *report*, or narrative, of that same extralinguistic reality/behavior. (Here we catch a glimpse of how the practice of narrative therapy subverts the antirealism of the theory used to guide it.) But in any event, I submit that that therapist truly believes that it really was the new, co-constructed narrative of the client's life that *caused* the change in the client's extralinguistic, extratherapy behavior, as well as her report of that behavior. It is that belief, after all, that entitles the narrative therapist to claim real results as a function of his real expertise, and so to take real payment for his real efforts in the first place. And it is precisely that (theoretical) causal claim that constitutes the realism I find within narrative therapy theory itself—realism that is so vehemently denied by the proponents of that theory.

Let us now consider some quotations of members of the narrative therapy movement that clearly illustrate that last causal claim, with its explicit reference to (extralinguistic) reality/behavior itself. In some cases these quotations illustrate some of the other reality claims as well. Again, we have previously considered some of these quotations.

1. "Psychotherapy works by transforming a person's self-narrative and the self-concept embodied in the narrative. . . . Our self-narratives become our lives" (Omer & Strenger, 1992, p. 253, Abstract). Alternatively, *"the way a life is told determines how it is lived"* (p. 254). Note that the therapist's intervention consists in changing the life narrative, and that that narrative of one's life determines/causes the actual (extralinguistic) living of that life.

2. "These are but a few examples of means by which people can be enabled to construct things from different viewpoints, thus liberating them from the oppression of limiting narrative beliefs and relieving the resulting pain" (Gergen & Kaye, 1992, p. 183). Note that viewpoints can be more or less limiting. Hence, narrative beliefs can either *cause* oppression and pain—that is, cause the problem—or can *cause* liberation from the problem. In this quotation, moreover, "oppression," "liberation," and "resulting pain" do not appear themselves to be *merely* linguistic. To elaborate, "A story is not simply a story. It is also a situated action in itself, a performance with illocutionary effects. It acts so as to create, sustain, or alter worlds of social relationship" (p. 178). Note that stories both create and alter relationships. Also note that the use of the term "worlds" here is ambiguous—are they worlds of stories about actual relationships or worlds of actual relationships? In either case, there is a reference to an extralinguistic reality. Gergen and Kaye, incidentally, propose that we go beyond the mere altering of narrative in therapy by teaching clients how to "relativize" their (realist) stance toward experience (including meaning) itself (p. 183). In other words, they propose the more radical view (radical even for the narrative therapy movement) that to be effective, therapists must turn *clients* into ardent antirealists, rather than just giving them a new narrative about their life. For them, the danger of the latter is that clients could then mistakenly take that new narrative in a realist way, which, according to Gergen and Kaye, would be limiting and oppressive. I consider the ethics of that theory-cum-method of problem resolution in Chapter 8.

3. "In regard to family therapy—which has been our area of special interest—the interpretive method, rather than proposing that some underlying structure or dysfunction in the family determines the behavior and interactions of family members, would propose that it is the meaning that members

attribute to events that determines their behavior" (White & Epston, 1990, p. 3). Note that meanings—which is another way of speaking of narratives or stories—cause or affect, without qualification, behavior itself. White makes this more explicit in the following quotation.

4. "Externalizing conversations are initiated by encouraging persons to provide an account of the effects of the problem on their lives. This can include its effects on their emotional states, familial and peer relationships, social and work spheres, etc., with a special emphasis on how it has affected their 'view' of themselves and of their relationships" (White, 1993, p. 39). Note that the narrative about the problem presumably gives us a true account of the real effects of the problem on extralinguistic lives, including real emotions and relationships, in addition to its effects on views of self and relationships. Notice that the *views* of the self and relationships are distinguished from the actual emotions and relationships the client encounters and is asked to give an account of in the first part of the quotation. "As persons become engaged in these externalizing conversations, their private stories cease to speak to them of their identity and of the truth of their relationships—these private stories are no longer transfixing of persons' lives. Persons experience a separation from . . . these stories. In the space established by this separation, persons are free to explore alternative preferred knowledges of who they might be, alternative and preferred knowledges into which they might enter their lives" (p. 39). Notice that stories transfix, have a real constraining effect on, real lives, including one's identity and relationships. The therapeutic intervention of challenging the old stories—by means of externalizing conversations—really allows room for new views or narratives of the self to emerge. These new views/narratives evidently affect the options perceived by the client and, ultimately, the actual living of actual lives.

5. "All psychotherapies depend on the *fact* [italics added] that human thinking, feeling, and behavior are guided largely by the person's assumptions about reality, that is, the meanings that he or she attributes to events and experiences, rather than their objective properties" (Frank, 1987, p. 293). Note that meanings affect thoughts, feelings, and, most relevant for my purposes, behavior. Frank goes on to say, "The power of an interpretation to carry conviction to the patient depends on many factors, among them, . . . and, perhaps most important, its fruitfulness—the beneficial consequences of the interpretation for the patient's ability to function and sense of well being" (p. 297). Note that the ability to function and sense of well-being may be taken to have a real, or extralinguistic, reference.

6. "Through therapeutic conversation, fixed meanings and behaviors (the sense people make of things and their actions) are given room, broadened, shifted, and changed" (Anderson & Goolishian, 1988, p. 381). Note that conversation/narrative has the power both to change ideas or narratives themselves (the sense people make of things) and to change behaviors or actions that are not qualified in any way and so may be fairly taken as extralinguistic events.

7. "Any meaningful change in the dominant stories . . . will affect the way problems are conceived, perceived, described, explained, judged, and enacted" (Sluzki, 1992, p. 220). Note that changing stories/narratives again has causal consequences for the client's ideas, perceptions, or experiences of the problem (and hence his options). In the final word of that quotation, we find that changing stories also has causal consequences for the way the client behaves, or enacts, those problems. Again, the reference to an extralinguistic reality is unmistakable.

8. "As a multiplicity of meanings becomes apparent through such therapist actions as questioning, explaining, interpreting, and disregarding, more possibilities for change emerge. The deconstructive process is most apparent in psychoanalysis, but, indeed, all therapy involves changing meaning as part of changing behavior" (Hare-Mustin & Marecek, 1990a, p. 48). Again, the therapist's intervention, which consists in questioning, challenging, etc., changes stories/narratives/meanings. This change in meaning, ultimately, plays at least some causal part in changing behavior itself.

9. "An interpretation, then, may bring about a positive effect not because it corresponds to a specific piece of the past but because it appears to relate the known to the unknown, to provide explanation in place of uncertainty" (Spence, 1982, p. 290). Note the claim here about how therapeutic interpretation, which, true to antirealism, may not reflect the truth about the past, nonetheless, in violation of antirealism, really or objectively works to produce real positive effects: interpretation works, in reality, by providing explanations that reduce uncertainty.[9] "We have come to see that certain kinds of pragmatic statements can produce changes in behavior simply by virtue of being stated" (p. 290). Again, statements/narratives/stories can, in themselves and independently of their truth status, cause change in behavior itself.

10. "Beliefs are embedded in the story; change the story and old beliefs are *shattered*" (Parry, 1991, p. 43). Again, note that changing stories really

changes the ideas, views, or beliefs the client has about the problem (and hence his options for solving that problem). Although this quotation does not discuss behavior, according to narrative therapists these beliefs are distinct from, but causally related to, the behavior that results from those beliefs.

The realism within these quotations should by now speak for itself. Nonetheless, I remind the reader of two facts about the claims these quotations contain. The first fact is this: therapeutic narrative interventions (e.g., questioning and challenging the client's story about her life/problem) work to affect the client's extralinguistic behavior itself, as well as the client's linguistic productions—her narratives—about that behavior. Put differently, therapy really helps people change real aspects of being (aspects that are independent of the knower)—their thoughts, feelings, and actions, as well as changing what people say or narrate, however correctly or incorrectly, about those aspects of their being.

The second fact pertains to the individuality/systematic problem. It is this: because the narrative therapists just quoted make (general, predetermined) claims about what causes and resolves *all* problems (system components A and B respectively), they also impose a general approach to therapy practice no less than do therapists who work with *comparable* so-called realist claims. To be sure, in many cases these postmodern narrative therapy claims are just as realist as are the claims made by many so-called modern, realist therapies. In any event, it is important to recall just here that the one claim about problem causation (A) in narrative therapy is uncommonly general in its formulation: stories (of any sort) can cause "problems." Therefore, each client's unique, personal theory, story, or narrative about his life can determine—with no *particular* type of reformulation required—the content of therapy to be targeted for narrative therapy intervention. This means that the practice of narrative therapy can be fully individualized, or antisystematic, with regard to *content*, even though the same theory-cum-method of problem resolution (B)—deconstruct old narratives and co-construct new narratives— is used universally. That means the *process* of narrative therapy can be highly systematic to the extent that the theory-cum-method of problem resolution is clearly specified, so that precise rules for therapeutic intervention can be derived from it. But in any event the process of narrative therapy cannot be individualized qua process if it is applied universally, that is, applied in the same way to all clients, without discrimination, which is now the case.

THE MODEST REALISM
INHERENT IN NARRATIVE THERAPY'S
VIEWS ABOUT TRUTH

By now it should be apparent to the reader that the narrative therapy movement has, in its own theoretical assertions, oscillated between the antirealism it propounds and the realism it unwittingly expresses. To complete our assessment of that movement's internal contradictions, we must examine its own theory of "truth" more precisely—theory which it uses to support its own "truth" claims without, it supposes, the burden of the contradictions I have exposed.

Typically, the narrative therapy movement appeals to either a utility/pragmatic theory of truth, or a coherence/congruence theory of truth, or some combination of the two (since both invoke the notion of social consensus). This appeal is made to support that movement's claims about therapy within the confines of an antirealist doctrine. That is, it has used these two doctrines about "truth" to allow itself to say, on the one hand, that there is no independent reality available to the knower, but that, on the other hand, "not just anything goes" (see, e.g., Efran & Clarfield, 1992; Epstein & Loos, 1989; Howard, 1991; Omer & Strenger, 1992). Let us therefore now consider those two doctrines about "truth" as they have been expressed and used within the narrative therapy movement. In particular, I hope to demonstrate that even behind those doctrines there is a modest, or limited, realism.

The Utility/Pragmatic Theory of Truth

According to this doctrine, the (extralinguistic) truth of an assertion—be it a scientific proposition or a therapeutic interpretation—can never be known. Instead, we can only know whether the assertion, in the case of science, gives a good prediction of our observations or, in the case of therapy, produces some desired outcome, consequences, or effect. Since we can allegedly agree about the occurrence of an observation or effect in some particular context, the concept of social consensus becomes relevant to pragmatism. Thus, when postmodern narrative therapists claim, as they often do, that it is not the objective truth of any therapeutic interpretation, or narrative, that is of concern, but rather its effect on, or consequences for, a particular client in a particular context, they may be said to be adopting a pragmatic, or utility, theory of truth.

Strenger and Omer (1992) distinguish two types of pragmatic value that

are relevant to therapy: (a) "a construct's [or narrative's] helpfulness in facili-
tating treatment (internal [to the therapy] value)" (p. 125), for instance, the
reduction of resistance to and enhancement of cooperation with the therapist's
ideas and suggestions; (b) "a construct's [or narrative's] helpfulness . . . in
promoting symptomatic and functional improvement (external [to the ther-
apy] value)" (p. 125), for instance, the reduction in the symptom or problem.

The pragmatic doctrine is held to be antirealist for two related reasons.
One has to do with the particularity of any effect—that is, an effect of an
intervention may hold for one client/moment/context, but not for the next,
thereby precluding the attainment of claims that hold any degree of generality. As Epstein and Loos (1989), whom I quoted above, make clear,

> A dialogical constructivist position implies that every person's reality has valid-
> ity within his or her own domain of existence. The measure of validity, or
> utility, is ultimately a matter of values, and not a matter of truth or correctness.
> . . . [O]ne's reality has utility for a particular purpose in a particular context. A
> crucial part of the therapist's task, then, is to understand the "rightness" of the
> client's position within his or her own unique perspective. (p. 417)

Note here again the narrative movement's typical—but unnecessary—pairing
of the unique/particular with antirealism. Thus, we find an emphasis on the
utility of a narrative, or linguistic construction of one's experience, for a
particular purpose; we are then asked to conclude that because that purpose
was a particular, or nongeneral, one, the effect or utility of the narrative, or
construction, was solely a function of the knower, and not of any independent (of the knower) reality. Spence (1982) also makes the specificity of the
effect apparent when he states,

> In defining an interpretation as either a pragmatic statement or an artistic
> creation, we are emphasizing the fact that its truth value is contingent. By
> definition, therefore, an interpretation can no longer be evaluated in its singular
> propositional form but must be considered with respect to the conditions under
> which it was expressed (created) and the outcome it produced. (pp. 276–277)

The second reason the pragmatic position is held to be an antirealist one is
that the independent, or objective, truth of an interpretation or proposition is
alleged to be unnecessary for the interpretation to produce its intended or
desired effect in any particular context. Accordingly, it is the instrumental
function of a statement, claim, or interpretation that is of interest, and not its

truth status. Spence (1982, p. 271) makes this clear when he cites Singer's definition of a pragmatic statement:

"When someone makes a statement, which he wants to induce himself or others to believe, but which he does not at the time know to be true or could not possibly know to be true, *in order to bring about its truth*, I shall say that he is using language pragmatically, and that the statement in question is a pragmatic statement" (Singer, 1971, p. 27).

Spence continues,

He [a politician who states "he is going to win next Tuesday"] makes the statement, not because he *knows* the outcome, but because he wishes to *influence* the outcome. . . . Now it seems that an interpretation can be described in the same way. It is, first of all, a means to an end, uttered in the expectation that it will lead to additional, clarifying clinical material. (p. 271)

The interpretation, then, can be defined by a claim to a *belief* in the proposition and nothing more [by "nothing more" I take Spence to mean the proposition's referent or its historical truth] . . . . (p. 273)

The analyst . . . commits himself to a belief in his hypothesis and is inclined to use it in a pragmatic fashion, as a way of making something happen. (p. 275)

Neimeyer (1993) also links the narrative therapy movement with a pragmatic theory of truth when he states,

These constructivist therapies are united in their rejection of a correspondence theory of truth. . . . Instead, they hold that the viability of any given construction is a function of its consequences for the individual or group that provisionally adopts it (cf. von Glasersfeld, 1984), as well as its overall coherence with the larger system of personally or socially held beliefs in which it is incorporated (R. A. Neimeyer & Harter, 1988). (p. 222)

There are two problems with connecting this line of thinking with antirealism, both of which point to a form of modest realism. The first problem has to do with the general/particular distinction made above. To say an effect occurred in any particular instance is to claim to have observed the effect in that instance—that is, really, truly, or actually to have observed it, even if the effect never happens again. Thus, when a therapist gets a particular client to co-construct a unique narrative about his unique life experience in a new way, and then observes that the client behaves differently, or at least talks about—reports—behaving differently, the therapist is observing something real, something that is not merely her own linguistic creation. The fact that the observed sequence of events may have occurred just once does not make its occurrence—including the therapist's inference that her narrative helped cause the change in the client—any less real. And even narrative therapists like to report that an observed change, or effect, in any particular client's life has *some* consistency over time and across situations in that client's life. In making that claim, they establish the generality of the effects of their interventions *within* each client's life. The fact that the change, or effect, observed in a particular client (following the use of a particular therapeutic narrative) fails to generalize to *other* clients may mean that that particular narrative cannot reach the status of a scientific proposition; such propositions, recall, require *some* degree of consistency, or generality, under specified conditions. But that failure to generalize sufficiently does not preclude the fact that the observation is an observation of a real sequence of events—namely, a new narrative is constructed and the client then behaves differently. *That* observation is perfectly real, even if the therapist's *causal inference* about those events turns out not to be true; that is, it is always possible that the client changed for reasons other than the therapist's efforts to help him produce a new life narrative. But in any case, the real observation of a unique event in therapy is not unlike—not any more antireal than—observing a rare bird fly by once in a lifetime. Here is an instance of the modest realism I will speak of in the next chapter.

The second problem with pairing the unique with antirealism in narrative therapy has to do with the relation between the truth status of (the particular content of) a therapeutic proposition/interpretation/narrative and its utilitarian, or pragmatic, value/effect. To say an interpretation/narrative need not be true to produce some effect—some influence—or to make something happen, to use Spence's terms, does not eliminate any independent, or objective, truth claims. It merely removes them from the *content* of the therapy—the *particular* narrative constructions about the causes and effects of each client's unique problem—and deposits them in the *process* of therapy—the *general* act itself of deconstructing/challenging old narratives and co-constructing new narratives to solve the problem. (That act or therapeutic process is, of course, defined in narrative therapy independently of the particular content of any narrative.) Thus, a therapist can believe he is (a) helping the client discover the correct meaning and history (the true causes) of her problem experience (the realist/conventional view of therapy) or, alternatively, (b) helping the client co-create some new meaning that allegedly makes no such reality reference but that nonetheless serves to liberate her from the real effects of a (languaged) "problem" (the antirealist/narrative view of therapy). It makes no difference. For in principle the therapist is, in either case, causally affecting the client's perception or experience of a problem and, ultimately, if therapy works as it should, the client's (extralinguistic) behavior/life.

The fact that the new narrative may not give us a true causal account of the client's life does not—according to the narrative therapy claims quoted above—undermine the reality of the presumed *effect* of that narrative on the client's life. That effect includes the way the client actually behaves/interacts (the extralinguistic effects) and now speaks of those behaviors/interactions (the linguistic or narrative effects). For instance, the client with the back pain described in White and Epston (1990) both greeted a stranger on the street and then reported or spoke of that new behavior. My point is this: to profess the view that it is more useful to the pursuit of opening new options and, ultimately, new behaviors when we allow many new meanings to evolve, without imposing predetermined constraints on the content of therapy, is to make an irrefutable (and, incidentally, general) reality claim about what makes therapy more effective. That claim has appeared repeatedly in the narrative therapy literature and, moreover, cannot be circumvented by even the most ardent antirealist. In short, the question whether a given narrative in particular, and new narrative in general, is useful for the purpose of therapy/ problem resolution is also the question whether they are *truly* useful. Truth and utility are not at odds with each other, at least in that sense.

We can state all this differently by asking the narrative therapist the question, "Can we know whether an effect or change has occurred in the client's life, including the way the client talks about/narrates her life?" To be sure, the narrative therapist must answer with a resounding "yes." In answer to the question, "Can we know whether a new narrative has proven useful to the client, that is, has actually caused that effect or change?" the narrative therapist must—given the indirect or inferential nature of causal knowledge— answer with a resounding "I think or hope so."

The narrative therapist makes these determinations by directly observing the client's in-therapy behavior and report/narrative of her extratherapy behavior. The client's report may even include the client's own assessment about whether and how the new story she has co-created with the therapist has been useful to her. Again, the therapist is usually inclined to accept these reports or narratives as reasonably accurate, unless the client behaves in a way that gives the therapist reason to doubt the veracity of those reports. In any case, my point here is that the therapist, based on his direct observation of the client's in-therapy behavior and reports of her extratherapy behavior, can make a determination about the existence of an effect, difference, or change in the client's life. And in all probability he will be inclined to believe that effect was, at least in part, a function of his therapeutic interventions.

The determination of the existence of an effect, difference, or change raises a question about the causes of the observed effect, difference, or change. Answering that question requires a conclusion about causality that cannot be reached by direct observation; rather it must be inferred, that is, reached by the use of indirect knowledge. We shall consider the distinction between direct and indirect knowing in the next chapter. Here I emphasize the fact that the narrative therapist can, and often does, give affirmative answers (with varying degrees of assurance) to the above questions about the existence of change and its causes—a fact that puts some degree of realism in the narrative therapy movement. That realism must be modest, or limited: we simply cannot have access to all causal knowledge about all those events we can directly observe. But it is realism nonetheless. That realism also makes it ethical for the narrative therapist to claim real expertise, and so to collect real payment for her efforts—matters I consider in Chapter 8.

The generality of these claims about the beneficial effects of narrative therapy is as important as their truth, or realism. To say, as do narrative therapists in a demonstration of social consensus, that (a) a narrative, of any (unspecified) sort, can cause the perception or experience of a "problem," and that (b) the act of challenging old, problematic narratives and co-constructing new ones can cause the perception or experience of options/solutions and so, ultimately, can cause new thoughts, feelings, and actions, is to make thoroughly general claims about the process (Component B) of therapy. That process, therefore, is not confined to the particularities of any one client, moment, or context—that is, it is independent of any particular case content, and so that therapeutic process may, to the extent that it is clearly specified, be used systematically to produce a rule-governed and hence consistent or replicable practice. That practice, however, can never be as systematic as practice that is guided by a more complete theoretical system of therapy— that is, a system that provides predetermined content (one in which Components A and C actually constrain content) as well as predetermined process (Component B). I therefore conclude that the pragmatic argument behind narrative therapy—that narratives, whether they themselves are true or not, can be truly useful—is not any more nongeneral than it is antirealist. That is to say, it is both a general argument and a realist one.

The Coherence/Congruence Theory of Truth

The coherence or congruence theory of truth, as used in narrative therapy, actually has two components: (a) The *internal* coherence or consistency of the narrative itself, that is, the extent to which the components of the narrative — e.g., the sequencing of its events — form a consistent, organized, aesthetic whole (see Spence, 1982, for elaboration). According to Strenger and Omer (1992), "coherence refers to the goodness of fit between a construct and other data or constructs [within the narrative of a given case]. A good construct has to take into account all the pertinent therapeutic data [within a case], be consistent with them, and explain them as well as possible. This can be called the desideratum of *internal coherence*" (pp. 123–124). (b) *External* coherence refers to the "external congruence [of the narrative's constructs] with what is accepted as knowledge" (Omer & Strenger, 1992, p. 260). In my reading of these two authors, this concerns the extent to which the therapeutic or case narrative shows some correspondence not with any extra-linguistic/extratheoretic (i.e., independent or objective) reality (what Spence calls historical truth), but with what an appropriate discipline considers agreed-upon or consensually validated discourse: the knowledge base of that discipline, or its "linguistic net," to use linguistic philosophy terminology. As Strenger and Omer (1992, p. 124) put it, "the construct [used by the therapist] must also fit with accepted extratherapeutic [i.e., external to that case within some broader psychotherapeutic discourse or "normative narrative line" (p. 124)] data and theories. This is the demand for *external coherence*."

A coherence theory of truth, then, is surely consistent with social constructionism, in which a general, predetermined theory is put forth and achieves a degree of social consensus, but with an antirealist flavor: the predetermined theory is alleged merely to fit into the (linguistic) consensus itself; it allegedly gives us no extraconsensual, extratheoretic reality.

The coherence/congruence theory of truth as it has generally been expressed is not distinct from pragmatism, which in philosophical circles propounds the doctrine that truth constitutes nothing more or less than "communally accepted belief" or "socially certified agreement" (McGinn, 1993, p. 27). There is no concern for the relation of the object (content) of the social consensus to any extralinguistic, extraconsensual reality, since that reality is supposed to be unattainable.

But the problem, once again, is the hidden, modest realism within this theory of truth as well. For it assumes that we can know what the component parts of a narrative are, whether they are internally consistent, and whether others see them as such. Regarding external congruence, this doctrine assumes we can know what the consensually agreed-upon theories—or dominant discourses—of any discipline or social/linguistic context actually are, so that we may compare the extent to which our particular narrative/discourse is congruent with them. Thus, in answer to the questions of whether we can know what any individual's particular narrative actually is, what any relevant broader discourse actually is, whether that broader discourse is dominant or marginalized, and whether the particular narrative is or is not congruent with that broader dominant or marginalized discourse, the narrative therapist in particular—as well as the social constructionist in general—must once again answer with a resounding "yes." That is because the narrative therapist directly observes the individual's narrative and directly observes—reads or hears—the broader discourses that comprise the socially constructed theories that permeate the discipline. If she is particularly astute, she may even have some knowledge of the discourses that constitute her cultural/linguistic/discursive context as they exist beyond—and so may affect—her particular discipline. She may then infer, or have indirect knowledge of, which discourses are dominant or marginalized based upon her direct observations of (a) the numbers who participate in one or another discourse/theory, (b) the conclusions of others about a discourse's dominance, (c) her own experiences with others when she tries to promote a particular discourse/theory, and so forth. She can also theorize about the meaning, especially the causal effects, of those discourses for the world, including the world of human behavior. This theorizing can occur in much the same way that narrative therapists and their clients theorize about—narrate—the meaning of events in a client's life: in particular, how those meanings and the narratives that organize/comprise them have causally affected and will affect—both positively and negatively— the actual life of the client. Those discourses/meanings/narratives are real (linguistic) entities no less than people, trees, rocks, and houses. That is, they have an existence independent of the knower, an existence that is sometimes a highly stable, consistent, and hence change-resistant one (cf. V. Fish, 1993, p. 232 and Chapter 4, Note 12). These linguistic entities can therefore be known directly, as I explain in the next chapter.

For now we must ask a question that seems almost too simplistic—too silly, perhaps—even to formulate: how, given the pervasive, extreme antirealism of the narrative therapy movement—an antirealism that precludes our ability to know *any* independent (of the knower) reality, can we know what the social consensus or dominant discourse (or any other discourse) about any domain really *is*, let alone whether our discourse (including our discourse about therapy) has any causal effect on human lives, including the lives of clients? On the one hand, the social constructionism of postmodern narrative therapy is supposed to give us general, consensually validated theories/languages/discourses that, because they are allegedly only antirealist (linguistic) stories, cannot give us knowledge of any extratheoretic, extradiscursive, or extralinguistic, reality. But, on the other hand, the proponents of postmodernism fail to see that that same antirealist doctrine also precludes our knowledge of real theories/languages/discourses *themselves*; that is, it precludes direct knowledge of theories/discourses *as* theories/languages/discourses, independent of the extralinguistic truth of their content.[10] Therefore, postmodern narrative therapists cannot in principle know the statements/narratives their clients (and they) are really constructing and co-constructing, or even that a real client who is uttering those statements, one who is not merely their own linguistic construction, is actually sitting before them. If they cannot know even those fundamental things, they certainly cannot know—even indirectly—whether narratives actually cause the perception/experience of new options and solutions, which in turn cause the enactment of new behaviors themselves. Yet they seem to rely on that very ability to know—especially the ability to know the linguistic propositions put before them—to make their case for the monolithic antirealism of the social constructionism they so enthusiastically propound.

This point is important; let me therefore try to restate it. The narrative therapy movement says that our narratives do not give us any extralinguistic reality, since we can never get outside of language (e.g., our clients' reports/stories of their lives and our reports/stories of their reports) to know that reality as it really is, independent of the knower's language. However, that movement also assumes—at least implicitly—that we can know what narratives really exist in the social community to which we turn to legitimate our linguistic constructions/narratives, including our scientific theories, the stories our clients tell us, and the stories we tell ourselves, our clients, and each other. These are stories which we presumably can know directly as stories. This *implicit* assumption is of course even more fundamental to that movement than its core *explicit* assumption about the causal effect of therapeutic (narrative) interventions on clients' linguistic productions—that is, on their new, option-enhancing stories, which in turn affect their actual (extralinguistic) lives.

More troubling is what sometimes happens when such a reality/truth claim is pointed out to members of the postmodern narrative therapy movement. They have been known to say that the statement referred to was no such thing, but only an instance of a "preference" or an "opinion," which, they indicate, is all we can ever hope to have (see, e.g., Efran & Clarfield, 1992, p. 201). Rorty (1989b, p. 11, cited in Glass, 1993, p. 4) makes this postmodern preference for preference over truth explicit when he states, "We are making the purely *negative* point that we would be better off without the traditional distinctions between knowledge and opinion." But postmodernists in general, and postmodern narrative therapists in particular, in that case do not tell us how—given their uncompromising antirealism—we can know what anyone's preference really is, let alone how we can distinguish between preference, on the one hand, and truth/knowledge—especially about the workings of narrative therapy—on the other. It seems the narrative therapy movement is in need of a more precise philosophy of knowing if it is to be itself internally consistent.

SIGNS OF STRUGGLE: A HOPE FOR A MODEST REALISM

By stating that members of the narrative movement subvert their own antirealism by making implicit and explicit references to (knowledge of) reality, I do not mean to suggest that they do so to be contrary, recalcitrant, or duplicitous. Nor do I suggest that they seek to rejoice in the confusions caused by the (sometimes deliberate) contradiction so lauded by some post-structuralist literary theorists and philosophers (see Ellis, 1989, for examples). Rather, I believe this oscillation reflects a serious struggle to come to terms with an eternally defiant problem—the nature of knowing. The difficulty of that problem is compounded by its application to the difficulties of the therapeutic enterprise and by the proliferation of postmodern antirealism in many disciplines that now affect that enterprise.

Some therapists sympathetic to the narrative/constructivist viewpoint have argued that they really do allow for realism in their theory (e.g., Guterman, 1991; Oz, 1991), and that I have simply failed to notice that fact because I have misinterpreted them. In those cases, perhaps, we find therapists who never meant to sound as extreme and monolithic in their antirealism as the statements we reviewed above appear to be. But those statements nonetheless do promote an unqualified antirealism—one that really does not permit access to any independent or extralinguistic reality. In particular, those statements do not make the important (epistemological) distinction between knowledge of (a) temporospatial (i.e., nonlinguistic) entities and events themselves (e.g., a bird flying from tree to tree), and of (b) narratives/theories/discourses about those entities and events. Those narratives/theories/discourses of course give causal accounts of those events and entities, accounts that are, from a traditional modern scientific perspective, to be assessed for their degree of (extralinguistic) truth value. But the monolithic antirealist claim that we have no access to any independent, objective reality precludes making those distinctions for epistemological purposes. Thus, postmodern narrative therapists fail to see that if they are right about their antirealism, not only can we never know whether our theories or narratives are valid—that is, whether they give us indirect knowledge of some aspect of reality as it exists independent of our theory/language—but also we can never know the reality of the theories or narratives themselves *as* theories or narratives. Nor can we know the reality of the temporospatial entities and events themselves that those theories or narratives try to explain.

It should therefore come as no surprise that, in addition to the unwitting, implicit, or unintentional references to extralinguistic or independent reality made by narrative therapy proponents, we also find here and there explicit and apparently intentional references to an independent reality. Although the latter references are simply unavoidable in the context of the articulation of a discipline, they are perhaps intentionally made because postmodern narrative therapists, struggling to make their epistemology more consistent, recognize the (nihilistic) problems associated with adopting an unlimited, unbridled, antirealism. Their awareness of those problems, in my opinion, moves them to adopt a social constructionism that constrains what can be called legitimate knowledge rather than a solipsistic constructivism with no such constraints. In my view, it would be better to let reality itself serve as that constraint, as I argue again and again in this book.

In any event, when either an antirealist or a realist doctrine is qualified— that is, when limitations or constraints are placed upon it—the qualification must be done in a way that is not self-contradictory. For instance, we cannot say on the one hand that there is no extralinguistic reality available to the knower but on the other hand certain events that impinge dramatically and unacceptably on the observer are real and knowable as such. Yet no postmodern therapist that I know of would wish to deprive the battering of women, for instance, of its patent reality status. That is but one example of a class of vivid, concrete, and unacceptable events that most postmodern therapists would be unwilling to call merely linguistic constructions. Since we must surely include in this majority the many postmodern feminist therapists who share the social constructionism/antirealism of narrative therapists (e.g., Goldner, 1993; Hare-Mustin & Marecek, 1990a, 1990b), their stance, at least, undermines their antirealist position. Fortunately, we can distinguish, as

I have already begun to do, between things we can and cannot know directly, and so we can at least qualify our epistemology in that way. But as I argue in Chapter 6, once we do that, we have left the realm of antirealism and entered one of a modest, or limited, realism.

Let me now illustrate the existence within the narrative therapy movement of a modest realism—one that permits direct, theoretically unmediated, knowledge of some aspects of an independent reality and indirect, theoretically mediated, knowledge of some other aspects of an independent reality. My illustration consists of statements made by narrative therapy proponents that indicate the signs of epistemological struggle that I find within the narrative therapy movement. In the next chapter we shall see how those struggles can be incorporated into a more precise and consistent philosophy of knowing—one that is potentially more appropriate for the narrative therapy movement. In considering these quotations, note the attempt to distinguish different types of knowledge about an independent reality; these distinctions are drawn along the lines I suggested just above and are developed fully in Chapter 6.

1. "Real events do happen in our lives, but we then develop a narrative around them that sometimes freezes them. As we develop a new perspective about the event . . . we change our narrative about it. From this perspective, insight can be considered merely a new understanding which makes sense to the person at that moment in time: it is not the discovery of some truth about one's existence, it is the development of a new story that one can utilize for the future until a new insight emerges" (Lax, 1992, p. 74). Note that, as is typical of postmodern narrative therapy, events, which are real and are presumably knowable *as* events (i.e., they exist extralinguistically), are distinguished from the stories we tell about them. These stories are not themselves supposed to be extralinguistically true. But they can nonetheless become frozen and, if unfrozen, can be utilized (note the pragmatic thrust here) for the future, which I take to mean they can have some extralinguistic effects on the client's life. Also note that we can presumably know (a) the client's stories as stories—both before and after they were frozen, (b) whether or not the stories are frozen, and (c) that the stories are unique to a particular person at a particular moment in time—that is, they are highly individuated with regard to both person and time.

2. "To be sure, unless the patient is psychotic, the reports are constrained to some extent by reality; in Spence's (1982) terms, narrative truth is not

totally unrelated to historical truth. Nevertheless, all self-reports contain irreversible margins of uncertainty created by at least three major sources. . . . [e.g.] patients' memories may be strongly influenced by their mood at the time the memories are elicited. . . . [and] patients' reports may be distorted by their perception of what the therapist expects" (Frank, 1987, p. 299). Note that the reports of psychotic patients are distinguished from the reports of those who are not psychotic; reports of nonpsychotic patients apparently are at least somewhat constrained by an extralinguistic reality. Note also that those latter reports, which here can give us some modest degree of independent historical truth of events that have actually taken place, are knowable as reports. Note also that perfectly general scientific claims about the potential sources of error in reports—namely, mood and expectations—are made. In Chapter 6 I go on to consider how the postmodern narrative therapy movement has relied upon the findings of conventional, realist science to support its antirealist assertions—a paradoxical situation at best.

3. "The stories that persons live by are rarely, if ever, 'radically' constructed—it is not a matter of their being made up, 'out of the blue,' so to speak. Our culturally available and appropriate stories about personhood and about relationship have been historically constructed and negotiated in communities of persons and within the context of social structures and institutions. Inevitably, there is a canonical dimension to the stories that persons live by. Thus, these stories are inevitably framed by our dominant cultural knowledges. These knowledges are not about discoveries regarding the 'nature' of persons and of relationships . . . " (White, 1993, pp. 37–38). Note again that "reality" constrains the stories that in turn affect/constrain the way people live their (extralinguistic) lives. Note also, however, that, truer to social constructionism than the previous quotation, the constraining reality is not extralinguistic; rather, it is the discursive context in which people (have allegedly learned to) narrate their experience. But the author here presumes we can know what those culturally available stories/dominant discourses really are, even if they give us no extralinguistic truth, including the truth of how they really came to be constructed.

4. "It may be helpful at this point to introduce the distinction between *plain* and *significant* narrative, which was first proposed by Walsh (1958). The first is a 'description of the facts restricted to a straightforward statement of what occurred.' The second is an account of the facts 'which brought out their connections' (p. 480). The *plain* narrative is clearly dependent on historical truth and the *significant* narrative on narrative truth. Walsh makes clear

that the validity of a *significant* narrative (its narrative truth) cannot be checked by making an appeal to the known facts because 'the connections between events are not open to inspection in the way the events themselves are. . . . Causal language is of a different logical order from observation language . . . ' (p. 483)" (Spence, 1982, p. 291).

By drawing the distinction between narrative and historical truth, Spence tells us that *events* that actually occurred historically can be directly known as such—at least in principle. By contrast, the causal *connections* between, or meanings/interpretations/implications of, those events cannot be known directly. Causal connections cannot therefore belong to the same type or be held to the same standard of truth as (some) events themselves. Although I do not agree with the degree of antirealism Spence holds for things that cannot be known directly—for instance, causal connections or inferences that form the core of scientific theories, including theories of how narrative therapy works—his distinction here is important: it shows us he does not dismiss access to *all* aspects of an independent reality. We have seen that access dismissed by the same narrative therapists who invoke Spence's name to support the explicit expression of their far more extreme—less nuanced—antirealism. They proclaim their more extreme antirealism even as they make explicit claims about the causes (or explanations) of problems and solutions, causes that we cannot, according to their own doctrine, know. (See Spence, 1982, p. 31, for a definition of narrative truth.)

To solidify his important distinction between plain and significant narrative, Spence goes on to say, "To a significant degree, the narrative that emerges from the analytic work can be regarded as a kind of theory [in my terminology, a personal one], and to an important extent, theories remain independent of facts" (Spence, 1982, p. 292). This quotation is indeed important; it tells us that facts are not created in theory/language, as antirealists would have it. Rather, theory, even the unique, personal theory of a therapy client, can give us independent facts/events, if not the meaning of, or connections between, those events. Interestingly, Spence summarizes the most extreme antirealist of all those within the narrative therapy movement to make his distinction: "A recent discussion by Gergen (1981) makes the point very clearly. He points out that a theory represents an interpretation of a particular meaning of an action, and that this meaning cannot be observed per se. 'The symbolic meaning of observables is . . . not open to objective verification or falsification. There is no observable referent to which the investigator can reliably point. The meaning of human action is dependent on the observer's system of interpretation. The observer must bring to the event a conceptual system through which behavioral observations may be rendered meaningful. There is no means of verifying or falsifying a "mode of interpretation"' (p. 335)" (Spence, 1982, p. 292). But what Spence does not seem to notice in that last quotation is the subtle shift from his own idea of access to historical truth—i.e., the independence of facts from theories—to Gergen's more radical antirealist position that the knower's "conceptual system" or theory/language always gets between the knower and the known, or is always "brought to the event," so that the knower cannot in principle have access even to objective knowledge of the event itself, that is, to historical truth.

In concluding this chapter, I emphasize the possibility that most postmodern narrative therapists do not, according to their own writings, wish to advocate an antirealism as extreme as the one they explicitly promote. However, they express that extreme explicitly when they speak of epistemology (and not of therapy), and then withdraw from that extreme when they speak of their theory and practice of therapy (and not of epistemology). Evidently, they are caught between a realization that there are many things in life, especially life in therapy, that we either cannot know directly or cannot know at all—not even indirectly—and the wish to insist that nevertheless there is some knowledge of reality about the workings of therapy. (And I expect them to tell me if this interpretation of their writings does not reflect their true authorial intentions, thereby revealing that interpretations/theories can at least sometimes be tested.) There is, however, a solution to the tension between that realization and that wish. That tension, incidentally, is not unrelated to the tension between the attainment of an individualized and yet systematic approach to therapy practice. In Chapter 7 I offer some solutions to that latter tension. But first, in Chapter 6, I offer a solution to the epistemological oscillation that follows from that former tension—a solution that takes the form of an alternative philosophy of knowing. Let us therefore now turn our attention to that.

CHAPTER 6

An Alternative Philosophy
of Knowing

In Chapters 4 and 5 I discussed how members of the postmodern narrative therapy movement have attempted to eliminate general, predetermined components within their therapy "system," and to rely instead only on each unique client's unique, personal views. I explained that this is not necessarily an antirealist endeavor, as members of that movement appear to think, but is, rather, only an antisystematic endeavor. Indeed, the oscillation between realism and antirealism that we saw in the many quotations of postmodern narrative therapists in Chapter 5 reveals that these therapists cannot adhere consistently to their own antirealist preferences. To the extent that they retain *any* general, predetermined components of a therapy system to guide their practice, neither can they adhere to their own antisystematic aspirations.

These problems have led me to conclude that if postmodern narrative therapy has something substantial to contribute to the individuality/systematic dilemma—and I think it clearly does—then it needs a more precise and consistent philosophy of knowing, or epistemology, to strengthen that contribution. The fundamental question of concern in this book, then, may be put in this way: is there a way to keep the practice of therapy both individualized and systematic, and moreover to do so within a consistent epistemological framework? In this chapter I address the epistemology question by providing an alternative philosophy of knowing. In the following chapter I examine, using that alternative philosophy, some emerging trends within the narrative therapy movement that suggest possible solutions to the individuality/systematic problem.

Let us begin by reconsidering the narrative therapy movement's epistemological oscillation. Recall that the narrative therapy movement says, in accord with its professed antirealism, that our narratives, stories, or theories do not give us any extralinguistic reality: the knower supposedly can never get outside of language or a "discursive context" to know that reality as it exists independent of the knower (e.g., Anderson & Goolishian, 1988; de Shazer, 1993; Gergen & Kaye, 1992; White & Epston, 1990). Instead, according to the social constructionism of that therapy movement, the knower's theory/ language/discourse always mediates—intervenes—between the knower and the known in a way that must *of necessity* alter or distort in experience (the true, independent nature of) any object of knowing.[1]

Having said that, the narrative therapy movement then goes on to claim— and here is the contradiction—that we can know what narratives/theories/ discourses really (i.e., independently of the knower) exist in the social community, or discursive/cultural context, to which we turn to legitimate our linguistic constructions or narratives, including our scientific theories, the stories our clients tell us, and the stories we tell ourselves, our clients, and each other. Moreover, even though these theories/stories/narratives are not themselves supposed to give us any extralinguistic reality, they nonetheless are alleged to affect both the linguistic productions (in the form of new, transformed stories) and the extralinguistic behaviors/lives of those who construct and listen to, or live by, them.

In short, the central claim of the postmodern narrative therapy movement, and indeed of most versions of postmodernism, is that stories/discourses are important—and so must be analyzed—*precisely because* they causally affect the very extralinguistic reality to which we are not, in principle, supposed to have any access. Here of course is that truth claim—a clear metaphysical statement about the workings of the world[2]—that subverts the antirealism, or social constructionism, of the postmodern movement in general. What can we do about that problem?

DIRECT KNOWING

The philosopher Edward Pols (1992a), in his latest book, *Radical Realism: Direct Knowing in Science and Philosophy*, makes several distinctions that help provide an answer to this problem as it has manifested itself within psychotherapy. He claims that all knowing is based on the *active* nature of the faculty he calls rationality. That faculty comprises two distinct but cooperating functions: (direct) rational awareness of reality independent of the knower, and a formative function (see Table 6.1 for a summary of these functions). To take the second function first, the *formative function* of rationality creates, makes,

Table 6.1 A Summary of Pols's (1992a) System of Direct Knowing

The Two Distinct Functions of Rationality

Rational awareness	Formative function
Direct knowing of an independent, real world. There are two types of (direct) rational awareness: 1. *Primary rational awareness:* Direct awareness of temporospatial entities like trees, rocks, and people (which are not made by rationality's formative function), and temporospatial entities like houses and paintings (which are made by rationality's formative function). 2. *Secondary rational awareness:* Direct awareness of nontemporospatial entities, in particular, linguistic items like theories/propositions/narratives (which are made by rationality's formative function). These linguistic items can in many cases give us *indirect* knowledge of things we cannot know directly, like subatomic (very small) or cosmological (very large) events.	Makes or creates things that can then be known by way of rational awareness, including linguistic ones like propositions, theories, and narratives, and temporospatial artifacts like houses and paintings.

constitutes, or constructs things like art, houses, music, and, most relevant for my purpose, (linguistic) propositions—or theories/stories/narratives—about life and about the world in general.

The first function of rationality, *rational awareness*, has direct and nontheoretical (i.e., not theoretically mediated) access to two things: (a) things in whose production the formative function has played no role, and (b) things in which the formative function has played a significant role. The first group (a) includes such natural temporospatial entities as people, trees, birds, and rocks, together with the events in which such entities interact with one another—such events as a bird flying from one tree to another. These entities and events are in no sense formed, constructed, or constituted by the formative function. The second group (b) includes two sorts of products of the formative function: on the one hand, temporospatial artifacts such as houses, machines, paintings, and sculptures; on the other hand, nontemporospatial entities such as propositions in general, theories (which are expressed in propositions), and narratives—entities, in short, that are in the broadest sense linguistic. Our rational awareness of items in both groups, (a) and (b), may find expression in language: we may say, "Look at the cardinal flying towards the sugar maple," or "That's my house just behind that spruce tree." But the language does not then form or constitute the items in question, as antirealists claim. Of course, some of the items in the second group *are* linguistic items, and this raises some subtle questions I will take up a little later. For the moment, it is enough to note that they are *formed to be* linguistic items, and that when we attend to them, we become rationally aware of them as having just the nature we have given them. Put differently: the fact that we can form or constitute linguistic items does not mean that being rationally aware of linguistic items is itself a formative or constitutive act.[3] Table 6.1 summarizes these distinctions.

As Table 6.1 indicates, Pols calls direct awareness of all temporospatial things in our size range[4] *primary rational awareness*, and direct awareness of linguistic propositions/theories/narratives, which are clearly not temporo-spatial entities, *secondary rational awareness*. Pols argues that both kinds of rational awareness are direct: their objects are not known by way of theory or by way of other linguistic entities that are attended to by the knower. Put differently, knowledge, though expressed in language, is not always, as postmodernists think, mediated by theory. Recall that for postmodernists, theory/language not only *always* mediates between knower and known but also *always* does so in a way that distorts or alters in experience the true, independent (i.e., extratheoretic or extralinguistic) nature of the thing known.

In addition to being direct, rational awareness is an active process or engagement with the real; it is worth our while to digress for a moment and consider that point. To say that Pols endorses the idea of an active knower is to say (obviously) that he does not subscribe to the notion of the passive, "spectator" knower. This is a notion that, according to many antirealists, characterizes the position of all realists; it is sometimes called naive realism. When Pols speaks of rational awareness as an active knowing process he means just that: the knower brings *universal* cognitive, or knowing, functions to his active engagement with whatever particular reality he is at any moment experiencing. It is beyond the scope of this book to provide Pols's arguments in any complete detail. But let me say here that the knowing process is one of active, directed *attention*, in which the knower engages the real and attains it in a sense that can only be called *active knowing*. It includes two components united in one act of the knower. The first component, which Pols calls the experiential pole of knowing, is her experience in the here and now, experi-ence which is always concerned with the *particulars* of whatever here and now she is experiencing (e.g., the fact that a particular object, a bird for instance, is moving in a particular way, in this case flying). The second, which Pols calls the rational pole of knowing, is her conceptual understanding of that here and now experience—understanding that entails all the generality/ universality that the conceptual bestows upon any particular act of knowing.[5]

It is of prime importance that the two poles are inextricably fused in the act of knowing; to use Pols's own words,

> Knowing is, before all other things, an activity, function, state, or condition of the knower that completes itself in the independently real. All knowing has both a rational and an empirical, or experiential, pole; but in direct knowing— that is, rational awareness—the two poles are inseparably fused and in mutual support, even though each is distinguishable and partly characterizable. . . . [T]he term 'awareness' [in "rational awareness"] is not meant to call attention to a mode of experience that functions at a subrational level, nor is the term 'rational' [in "rational awareness"] meant to call attention to some purely conceptual or propositional way of functioning. Rational awareness is *reason experiencing* rather than reason responding to experience. (p. 155)

> The fusion of the rational and the experiential poles in direct knowing means that the awareness [experiential component] supports and justifies the articulation, while the articulation [rational component] focuses, intensifies, and stabilizes the awareness. Direct knowing can focus on the common sense world (or some part of it) or on a body of scientific theory (or some part of it); . . . we called these two focuses respectively primary rational engagement and secondary rational engagement.
>
> The rational pole is a universal, symbol-generating transcendence of the here and now, but its functioning depends on the presence of the experiential pole—and the latter is unfailingly present, even in our most formal intellectual exercises. . . . [T]he fusion of the two poles must be taken seriously: although the rational pole plays the governing and active role in our cognitive access to the real, it does so only under the constraint of the experiential pole. The experiential pole, on the other hand, is our sense-based receptivity to the real by way of the particularity of the here and now, but only under the governance of the rational pole; so the receptivity is not merely an openness to particularity but rather an openness to reality by way of particularity. (p. 156)

There is more information in that quotation than I can hope to explain here. But my interest in it, in relation to the active and direct nature of knowing, concerns Pols's use of the conceptual (or linguistic) in that process. It is not that language plays no role in the act of direct knowing; rather, language—the conceptual—helps govern and stabilize our direct experience of the (particular) real. Thus, unlike the antirealist view of the *mediating* role of language in all knowing—a role that for them always alters or distorts in experience the true, independent nature of what is known—here language neither makes nor alters/distorts the reality that is experienced, or attended to, directly. The reality that is attended to directly, of course, is the reality that we can attend to without having to attend to something *else* to get at it, that something else being a theory/language/discourse for antirealists.[6] Instead, for Pols, language *helps* us attain direct knowledge of the independently real: this idea is surely a radical one for antirealists and is no doubt in part behind his adoption of the term "radical realism" to describe his philosophy.

Pols's argument is important but unique; let me therefore try to restate it a bit differently. To say that language plays a role in the active, direct knowing process is not automatically to accept the antirealist claim (of most postmodernists and linguistic philosophers) that language, or theory,[7] makes or constitutes some nonreality, rather than calling attention to a true reality.[8] Indeed, it is Pols's position that theory expressed in linguistic propositions is necessary for the attainment of indirect knowledge of much, but certainly not all, that is extralinguistically or extratheoretically real. I believe it is this last point that is a source of much confusion about realism and antirealism both within and beyond the narrative therapy movement. For that reason, I return to it just below in my discussion of the role of theory in indirect knowing.

Let us return now from our digression about active knowing to the idea of direct knowing of two sorts, primary and secondary rational awareness. Let us begin with secondary rational awareness—(direct) awareness of nontemporospatial (linguistic) entities. Pols argues that we know the proposition or narrative before us *as a proposition or narrative* just as directly—i.e., without mediating theory and so without any *risk* of theoretical distortion—as we know that there is a person conversing with us in our therapy room. To know that a person is talking is of course itself an instance of primary rational awareness (i.e., direct awareness of a temporospatial entity), quite apart from the linguistic content of the speech. The existence of *secondary* rational awareness solves the problem of how narrative therapists, or anyone, can know *what* words the client is actually producing at any given moment; that is, it gives us direct cognitive access to that which is linguistic, including the discourses that do or do not prevail in any given context. The existence of *primary* rational awareness solves the problem of how narrative therapists can know that there is actually a client in the same room who is in the *act* of sitting, standing, speaking, or not speaking.

But neither type of rational awareness—primary or secondary—can provide us direct knowing of things we cannot hear or see directly—for instance, what motivates the person to say what he has been saying, what he wishes to convey by his utterance, what is going on inside his nervous system at any given moment and how it relates to his overt behavior. And, to turn to the physics of very small (subatomic) events or the very large events studied in cosmology, neither primary nor secondary rational awareness can provide us direct knowing of things outside of our own scale or size range. We therefore need another kind of knowing that indeed employs mediating theory (but not the kind that of necessity alters or distorts) to get at that level of reality. Pols calls that other kind of knowing *indirect* knowing, and we shall now consider it in relation to the realism/antirealism controversy in therapy, and in science as a whole.

INDIRECT KNOWING AND THE CLAIMS
OF NARRATIVE THERAPY AND SCIENCE

We know the proposition or narrative before us directly *as* a proposition or narrative by means of secondary rational awareness. But that proposition itself often makes reference to some other (nonpropositional) aspect of reality that—because it is not in our size range, or is, like motivation, otherwise inaccessible—we cannot know directly, either in that moment when we are knowing the proposition, or in any foreseeable future point in time. When the proposition purports to tell us something about reality that we cannot know directly, it may then be said to give us *indirect* knowledge of reality— provided that the knowledge in the final analysis turns out to be an accurate description or representation of the (independent) reality under investigation. Indirect knowing of something occurs when we know that something by attending directly to something *else* that describes or represents it—usually a theory or proposition about it. Direct knowing, by contrast, occurs when we attend directly to something and not to something else—a theory or proposition—that describes or represents it.[9]

Propositional complexes that are intended to give us a correct account of extratheoretic reality in a more formalized or systematic way are usually called scientific theories or hypotheses. Many such theories or hypotheses about the nature of the world in general are of course made by physicists, chemists, biologists, geologists, and so forth. Those that apply to the workings of the human part of the world are made by, among others, psychologists, anthropologists, linguists, sociologists, historians, economists, and, most important for my purpose, therapists, including postmodern narrative therapists.

The latter theories—those that belong to what are often called the human sciences—have been the object of much more (postmodern) scrutiny and therefore controversy than those of the physical sciences. Accordingly, postmodernism has made greater "inroads" in the social sciences, as Rosenau (1992) calls them, than in the physical sciences.

A crucial point in Pols's realist argument is this: it is precisely and only because we have direct rational awareness of some things (i.e., things in our size range) that we can construct theories that give us indirect knowledge of other things that we cannot know directly (i.e., things not within our size range, or otherwise inaccessible). Our direct knowledge of an independent reality, then, is needed in two ways: (a) in the *construction* of the theory itself—we cannot create or construct a theory about some aspect of reality without having observed at least some things within that reality directly, and (b) in the *testing* of the theory—we cannot make observations that test the theory without observing something directly (e.g., the numbers on some technical equipment if one is a physicist, or certain behavior if one is a psychologist). The making, or constructing, and the testing of theories thus employ pieces of the real that are directly known; that is why those theories can in principle give us indirect knowledge of other aspects of that same reality that are not directly accessible. My point here is perhaps a bit abstract; let us consider some examples that may help.

In the propositions that follow note that instances of direct knowledge are made use of both in constructing/making the proposition itself and in determining whether the proposition is true/adequate.

1. The snow outside the window is white.

2. John is depressed.

3. Depression is caused by holding the story that one cannot control events in one's life.

4. Depression can be relieved by holding a new story that one can actually control events in one's life.

5. The universe began with a big bang.

Let us begin our analysis of these propositions by noting the use of direct knowlege in the *construction* of each one: (1) We have (direct) rational (i.e., theoretically unmediated) awareness of the existence of the snow and its whiteness. [10] (2) We have (direct) rational awareness of the existence of John but not of the depression itself. (3) We have (direct) rational awareness of the behaviors we consider to be indicative of depression (e.g., not getting out of bed all day in the absence of physical illness, or getting a high score on a depression inventory) but not of depression itself, which we know only indirectly by attending directly to the behaviors we consider to be indicative of depression. We also have (direct) rational awareness of a certain story *as* a story and of a particular person's holding that story (the person has perhaps told us so). (4) We have (direct) rational awareness of the behaviors we consider to be indicative of the reduction of depression (e.g., getting out of bed in the morning, or getting a lower score on a depression inventory). But, like depression itself, we do not have (direct) rational awareness of the reduction, or alleviation itself, of the depression. That can be known only indirectly, by attending directly to the relevant behaviors. We also, as in Number 3, have (direct) rational awareness of a certain story *as* a story and of a particular person's now holding a story different from the one she held previously. (5) We have (direct) rational awareness of some aspects of the universe within our size range (but not of the universe itself in all its totality) and of certain events (e.g., numbers that appear on an instrument) that we take to be evidence of a distant big bang, which of course is itself not directly knowable.

Let us also note that as we proceed from Proposition 1 to Proposition 5, it becomes increasingly more difficult to *test* the claim. That is, more indirect knowledge is required to assess the claim's validity, even though some (direct) rational awareness is always needed to test a theory empirically.[11] Thus, to test Proposition 1 we might only need go to the window to know directly whether the snow on the ground is or is not white. To test Proposition 2 we need to observe whether John gets a high score on a depression inventory (which we can know directly) or gets out of bed (which we may or may not experience directly—we may have to rely on his or someone else's report of that fact). We may then infer, or know indirectly, whether, based on our (operational) definition of depression, he is depressed or not. Again, however, we do not see the depression itself directly; we only see the behavior or scores we take to be indicative of the existence of depression. To test Proposition 3 we must know the stories that people who meet the criteria for depression tell us (stories which we can know directly *as* stories). But we then must *infer* whether those stories are actually *causing* or *motivating* the behaviors we believe reflect the depression we cannot know directly. We cannot observe the causation itself directly, a point that, recall, Spence (1982) made when he distinguished between observable events and their causal connections.

Incidentally, it is important to note that even though we can know the story directly as a story for everyday purposes—that is, know both its words and its usual, stable meanings—we might need some way to tell us with greater-than-usual precision whether the particular issue of scientific interest (in this case, of control) is located in it. After all, the word "control" might not be used explicitly in any particular story. But a formal content analysis, or sorting of the story into predetermined content or thematic categories, may reveal that there is indeed a control issue or theme of some general sort in the story—a theme that most or all readers of the story can agree upon reliably, that is, with some consistency and so some objectivity (cf. Ryan & Wild, 1993). That the story needs some atypically formal and explicit framework in order to interpret it more consistently for unusually precise or scientific purposes, rather than for everyday/commonsense purposes, does not automatically mean that the story itself and/or its meaning is completely unknowable, indeterminate, reader-determined, context-determined (and so forth). Nor is its scientific interpretation necessarily at odds with the one we get when we are not seeking scientific reliability. The fact that we may need such a formal system to help us interpret the meaning of stories more reliably for scientific purposes poses no problem for (direct) rational awareness: the system of meanings itself, as well as the stories, is directly knowable by way of secondary rational awareness. That is, that system of meanings also has words with stable uses and meanings that are directly knowable as such. [12]

Finally, to test Proposition 5, we must directly observe *something* that allows us to infer that the universe as whole, which itself cannot in all its intricacies—both large and small—be observed directly, began with, or was caused by, a big bang. That something we know directly might be the numbers on some instrument—numbers which, we then go on to infer, give us an indication (e.g., of the background radiation in space) that the universe is expanding at some rate predicted by the big bang theory. The fact that we must, to test the scientific theory, *interpret* the numbers we know directly in terms of the phenomenon they are supposed to be measuring does not, once again, mean that the numbers *themselves* (and/or their usual meaning as numbers) cannot be known directly. Surely they, the numbers, are not constituted/constructed and reconstituted/reconstructed in each and every act or instance of knowing/reading them; certainly not any more than is the existence of the snow outside the window. But however extreme that last suggestion sounds, it is the very suggestion that lies behind much of the postmodern/poststructural/antirealist theory to which many psychotherapists have been attracted in recent years. I therefore return to a fuller consideration of that suggestion later in this chapter.

What applies to all the illustrative propositions, then, is the fact that, contrary to antirealism, no theory intervenes between the knower and that which she can observe *directly* to test some theory (e.g., the particular numbers on the instrument or John's report that he still has days when he does not get out of bed). Therefore, in consideration of real, independent linguistic entities, I emphasize that most of us can have some reasonably stable understanding of what particular numbers and words are before us, and what they can possibly mean or give reference to, at least for usual, everyday purposes. Moreover, most of us can get some stable grasp of what they mean for some scientific or more specialized purpose, especially if we are given enough information about that special purpose. But again, that more precise, specialized, or scientific meaning need not negate or oppose the commonsense meaning of that linguistic entity, which is directly known. After all, no matter what the particular "interpretive context"[13] — that is, the social/linguistic context which, for some postmodernists or poststructuralists, is constituted by and in each and every instance of knowing — a number or word that is intelligible to its knower cannot mean just anything. (The additional fact that some words really do have a greater range of meanings than others does not alter the truth of that last sentence.) And many postmodern narrative therapists have, fortunately, shown themselves to be cognizant of that stability of meaning in language — a point I illustrate at the end of this chapter. In any case, to return to my direct/indirect distinction here, the scientific theory or proposition itself, which we can know directly *as* a theory, can give us only indirect, theory-mediated knowledge of that which we cannot know directly.

According to the realist doctrine, constructed propositions/theories such as these, *because* they are based on what can be known directly, can in principle give us indirect knowledge of an independent reality that cannot be known directly. Thus, Propositions 3 and 4, which reflect causal claims of the narrative therapy movement, operate in a way that is perfectly typical of all traditional science. (Incidentally, I was challenged by an astute audience at a liberal arts college on the grounds that Propositions like 3 and 4 probably require more indirect knowledge — and so are more remote from direct rational awareness — than Proposition 5. Evidently, they have more faith in the ability of physics to get at the real than in that of psychology — a sentiment shared by many linguistic (antirealist) philosophers!) We can therefore go back to Chapter 5 to the more general claims found within narrative therapy — that old stories cause the experience of a problem, that therapist interventions such as challenging old stories cause the co-construction of a new story, that new stories cause the experience of new options and solutions, and hence, ultimately, new extralinguistic behaviors—and subject these claims to the same sort of analysis that we conducted on our five exemplary propositions.

Here I draw the reader's attention to what I consider to be a point of fundamental importance in understanding the confusion generated by the postmodern emphasis on the linguistic, and the postmodern linking of linguistic entities (including theories/propositions/stories/narratives/discourses) with antirealism. It is this: **All theories are constructions.** [14] Put differently, constructing theories is the business of science, of **all** science, including the science of narrative therapy, however antisystematic that science may strive to be. But that fact does not, contrary to postmodern opinion, automatically make all scientists antirealists. Moreover, those participating in the realism/ antirealism debate take it for granted that all theories are constructions—a fact that does not automatically assign anyone to one or the other side of the controversy (Held, 1991b). Thus, to say that knowledge of (some aspects of) reality involves social/linguistic construction because it involves the use of constructed theories is like making the discovery that we speak prose. Scientists have known the former, and most of us the latter, all along. But then to say, as social constructionists/postmodernists say, that those constructed theories are the *only* reality we have—that is, that reality itself, or knowable reality itself, *is only* a "social construction" (because we supposedly have no direct, theoretically unmediated access or even an indirect, theoretically mediated access to any reality that is independent of the knower/ knower's theory)—is to confuse two things: (a) the linguistic status of the theory itself with (b) the (extralinguistic or extratheoretic) reality that that theory is attempting to approximate indirectly.

That confusion is distinct from the problem of how postmodernists can claim to know what that theory, or nonreality, that has been socially constructed actually itself *is*, as it exists (as a theory) independent of the knower. That second problem occurs because, according to postmodern antirealism, *some*—perhaps some *other*—theory/language/discourse must *always* mediate between the knower and *any* object of knowing, even such linguistic objects of knowing as propositions. The problem of course lies in their claim that *all* objects of knowing are altered or distorted by that inescapable theoretic/ linguistic mediation (the so-called "interpretive context") in the act of knowing. Recall that Pols avoids that problem by arguing that we know the linguistic construction directly—without having to attend to something *else* to know it—by means of secondary rational awareness. This is true whether or not that theory/construction gives us an accurate, unaltered, or undistorted account of the aspect of reality it addresses.

I believe the culprit behind much of this confusion is the word "construct" (noun or verb), and by extension the word "construction." These words— especially the verb "construct"—imply an active knowing process on the part of the knower, an idea that I, Pols, and many cognitive scientists endorse. It may help if I again point out that just because we *actively* construct (in language) theories about a reality we cannot know directly does not automatically mean that the reality under investigation is a mere linguistic construction (a nonreality, according to postmodernists), either as it exists itself or as it is known to the investigator. Thus, the idea of an *active* rather than *passive* knower is falsely assumed to imply antirealism. Pols himself attributes the confusion to a failure to distinguish between the two functions of rationality (the function of rational awareness and the formative function); I return to his argument in a moment. Just here, I think it necessary to provide the reader with evidence that scientists themselves, as opposed to many philosophers of science, take a decidedly realist view of their own endeavors.

For example, the physicist John Polkinghorne states,

> Philosophically, physicists are realists. To them the history of high-energy physics in the period 1950–80 is that of a tightening grasp of an actual reality. We have found out something about the constitution of the physical world that we did not know before.
>
> Most physicists are bewildered by having any other proposition put to them. How otherwise could one explain the success of science? (1989, p. 161)[15]

And in their new book, *Higher Superstition: The Academic Left and its Quarrels with Science*, Gross and Levitt (1994), two scientists, have this to say about realism and science:

> Science is, above all else, a reality-driven enterprise. Every active investigator is inescapably aware of this. . . . Reality is the overseer at one's shoulder, ready to rap one's knuckles or to spring the trap into which one has been led by overconfidence. . . . Science succeeds precisely because it has accepted a bargain in which even the boldest imagination stands hostage to reality. Reality is the unrelenting angel with whom scientists have agreed to wrestle. (p. 234)

Here again I remind the reader that the fact that theories (which give us indirect knowledge) change over time does not make the scientific enterprise an antirealist one. Polkinghorne makes this point explicit in his book about high-energy physics. Science is supposed to change its accounts as we achieve successive approximations of the really real.

HOW THE CONFUSION BETWEEN THE RATIONAL AWARENESS AND THE FORMATIVE FUNCTIONS OF RATIONALITY FUELS THE ANTIREALIST AGENDA

It is Pols's claim that the culprit behind the popular antirealist/social constructionist/postmodern belief that *all* knowing is a product of rationality's formative function is a pervasive confusion or conflation—a failure to distinguish—between the two functions of rationality defined by him: (a) (direct) rational awareness of an independent (of the knower) world, and (b) a formative or constructive function that constitutes or constructs linguistic propositions (e.g., theories and narratives) and other artifacts (e.g., paintings and houses). According to Pols, it is precisely the belief that all knowing is a product of the formative function of rationality, with the attendant failure to distinguish the rational awareness component of rationality, that has resulted in and explains the pervasive antirealism we have been observing in many postmodern humanities, and now see in postmodern narrative therapy as well.

That confusion may again be stated in this way: because we construct or form or constitute *some* things in language (i.e., nontemporospatial entities such as theories or narratives), we have therefore constructed or formed or constituted *all* (known) things in language—that is, we have constructed or constituted the nonreality we know in its entirety. To put this differently, rational awareness, or attending to something directly, is for postmodernists/antirealists identical to constructing or constituting that something in language.[16] We therefore, according to that view, cannot attend to (be rationally aware of) something without altering, distorting, (re)constituting, (re)constructing that something in the very act of knowing/attending. That is, that something cannot be known as it is distinct from—independent of—the act of rational awareness.

According to Pols, this confusion leads all those who are subject to it, and so hold that belief, to fail to see that we have direct rational awareness of such nontemporospatial constructed things as the very theories and narratives we have constructed *from* the things we *can* know directly, things which include *both* temporospatial entities (e.g., a person's overt behavior) and *other* nontemporospatial entities—that is, *other* theories or narratives that we know directly as such and that we use to construct a *new* theory or narrative. For instance, the narrative therapist must know the client directly *as* an individual (by way of primary rational awareness), and must have direct knowledge of the client's personal linguistic account (i.e., theory or narrative) of his life experiences *as* a linguistic construction (by way of secondary rational awareness), in order to help the client co-construct a new theory/narrative/story/account (by means of the formative function of rationality). Note the two distinct functions of rationality in that last example. That the postmodernist simply takes for granted that she has these directly known linguistic and nonlinguistic entities at her disposal for the purpose of constructing a new linguistic entity (theory/story/narrative) does not make their independent existence, or her direct knowledge of them, any less real. The realist nature of her knowledge obtains no matter how much her direct knowledge of that independent reality—and the dependence of her formative function on that direct knowledge of that independent reality—escapes her attention.

The fact that we have direct rational awareness of such (linguistic) things as constructed theories and narratives is precisely the reason we are able to make arguments in language that others can read or hear, understand or not understand, follow or not follow, and agree or disagree with in the first place. But the fact that the theory itself is a linguistic construction made by the formative function of rationality, and that we can—by way of the (secondary) rational awareness function of rationality—know that theory itself directly as a linguistic construction (i.e., as it independently exists), does not answer the additional, more familiar question fundamental to the distinction between realists and antirealists: does that theoretical/linguistic construction give us any (indirect) knowledge of the extratheoretic, independent reality—the really real—to which the theory refers? Realists of course answer "yes" and antirealists "no."

Indeed, it is the very fact that the mind/rationality produces or forms constructions (i.e., theories) about that aspect of reality that we cannot know directly—a fact about which both realists and antirealists agree—that leads antirealists, who have conflated the formative and rational awareness functions of rationality, to an automatic and erroneous assumption: that reality itself, or at least all knowledge of reality, is nothing more than a mere construction in language produced by that formative function. For antirealists, then, linguistic (e.g., theoretical) constructions supposedly give us nothing that is extralinguistically or extratheoretically true. Again, they hold that belief because for them rational awareness, knowing, or attending is *itself* indistinguishable from—conflated with—linguistic constructing, forming, or constituting (i.e., the formative function). It is precisely because they fail to realize that this constructive or formative process *always* relies on direct rational awareness of (independent) temporospatial and propositional entities to supply the reality/stuff from which to construct a theory or narrative (as well as to test it), that they suppose the act of knowing itself always, of necessity, alters, distorts, reconstitutes, or reconstructs in experience the true nature of the known.

For antirealists, then, there can be no "knowing/awareness/attending without altering" (in language) the independent nature of what is known; for them there can therefore be no truth that transcends the *particular* theory/language that has supposedly constituted it. Thus all "truths"—or nonrealities—must always be relative, or local/nonuniversal/nongeneral, since linguistic or "interpretive" contexts are said by postmodernists to vary across person, place, and time. (I return to their contradictory claim that linguistic contexts themselves are real and at least somewhat stable later in this chapter.) Ironically, all this—as Pols points out—adds up to nothing less than a claim about the reality of knowing that subverts the very antirealism it is meant to support. Put differently, the postmodern/social constructionist/antirealist claim about knowing is put forth as a universal truth that is exempt from the relativism, or postmodern knower-dependency/contextualization, that qualifies all other claims about reality.

That postmodern position of course poses a problem for the modern scientific enterprise itself. Modern science has traditionally held that constructed theories (which provide indirect knowledge of an independent reality) can be tested precisely because the observations made to test them are in no sense a product of the theory being held and tested. That is, the observations made to test a theory are in no sense a product of any formative function of rationality. If the postmodern position were the case, there could be no independent, external-to-the-theory empirical test of the theory, which is precisely the position that antirealist philosophers of science take. Put differently, the test of any theory would then be only *another* instance of forming, constituting, or constructing some nonreality, as is supposedly the act of constructing the theory itself.

But the theoretical-empirical cycle so central to the scientific enterprise (see Chapter 2) does not, according to Pols and most if not all scientists, including J. Polkinghorne, the physicist I quoted just above, work in that postmodern/antirealist way. For them and us, the observations (instances of direct knowing) a scientist makes to test some theory—e.g., the numbers she reads off a technical instrument, or a score on some psychological measure, or some directly observable behavior such as whether someone gets out of bed in the morning—are not determined/mediated/altered/constituted by the theory being held and tested. We therefore know those observations directly (by way of primary or secondary rational awareness, depending on their temporospatial status), just as we know the theory directly by way of secondary rational awareness. Thus, scientific knowledge of the real can actually progress—a notion that is acceptable to modernists, but not postmodernists, as we discussed in Chapter 1.

Perhaps an example will make all of this clearer. To use an earlier one, let us assume we hold a theory that depression (operationally defined in some particular way, whether a score on an inventory or getting out of bed) is caused only by clients' holding a distinct kind of story about control over their lives. We can then make observations to see whether holding such a story correlates with (or, better still, in an experimental manipulation, increases) people's scores on some measure of depression or the enactment of certain behaviors. In any case, the observations of the stories or of the scores on the measure are not *themselves* determined/mediated/altered/constructed by the theory being tested.

Moreover, even if the story is first subjected to the use of some predetermined content categories to attain a highly reliable assessment of the presence of control themes within it, the system of content categories (or "interpretive context"), as well as the story, is still directly known by way of secondary rational awareness: the system must be so known if the content coder/rater is to determine what content categories apply to what stories. (Put differently, if the coder constituted and reconstituted the system of predetermined coding categories and the stories to be coded in each and every act of knowing, the reliability of the assessments of each story would decrease rather than increase when such a coding system was used.) Indeed, an observer with no knowledge whatever of the theory being tested could—if he is given sufficient information about the dial from which he should read numbers or the way sentences in a story should be coded for content categories—make or report those same observations reliably. Raters or coders who are ignorant of the hypotheses/theory being tested and/or of the psychological status of the subject being assessed are often used for just that purpose in scientific (especially psychological) experiments, where the risk of experimenter bias is always a consideration.

Ironically, many antirealists, including postmodernists/social constructionists, have relied upon the findings of conventional, realist science to support their antirealist arguments; this is a paradoxical situation at best (e.g., Blum, 1978; Gergen, 1985; Held & Pols, 1987a, 1987b; Howard, 1991; von Foerster, 1984; von Glasersfeld, 1984). That they can make that move is attributable to their failure to distinguish (a) the rational awareness and formative functions of rationality, and (b) the primary and secondary modes of direct rational awareness. To begin with the simplest example, von Foerster has repeatedly argued that "the nervous system is organized (or organizes itself) so that it computes a stable reality" (1984, p. 58), or alternatively, "our nervous system computes invariants on perpetually changing stimuli" (1985, p. 520). Note that the (extralinguistic) reality being computed/constructed is itself (i.e., independent of the knower's perception of it) unstable, or perpetually changing, an alleged fact we can presumably know by way of primary rational awareness. Also note that according to von Foerster we can know how the knower himself is really constituted in terms of his real nervous system, and how the knower's nervous system really operates upon/constructs the real world; this is knowledge that was probably obtained indirectly by means of both primary and secondary rational awarenesses, which are both used in the theoretic-empirical cycle described above.

Gergen (1985) appears much more aware than von Foerster of the contradiction that comes with the claims to knowledge von Foerster feels comfortable making. He therefore denies that social constructionist inquiry can tell us anything about how a theory-independent or mind-independent (i.e., objective) reality works, including the reality of the mind itself. Instead, he argues that social constructionist inquiry must focus on how (scientific, among other) understandings/accounts of the world are the product not of any theory-independent, or direct, empirical observations, but rather of "historically situated interchanges among people" (p. 267). These interchanges or social processes themselves, for example, "communication, negotiation, conflict, rhetoric" (p. 268), cause a form of understanding to prevail or not to prevail. Gergen therefore requests that we turn our attention to *these* processes by (a) asking such questions as "Are there generic rules governing accounts of human action from which common conventions are derived?" (p. 268) and "whether the folk models of mind within a culture necessarily determine or constrain the conclusions reached within the profession" (p. 268), and by (b) developing a "general theory for the negotiation of reality" (p. 268), that is, by "rendering accounts of human meaning systems" (p. 270).

In my opinion, Gergen does a better job than von Foerster of avoiding the trap of claims about how the mind/cognition itself really works.[17] Still, he fails to notice that in asking about the nature of the social negotiation processes that cause linguistic accounts of the world—even antirealist accounts that give us no extralinguistic reality—we must have some awareness of (a) the social processes themselves (which, to the extent that he agrees that there really are people conversing/negotiating, requires his use of primary rational awareness/empirical observation), and of (b) the linguistic accounts that those processes produce (which, to the extent that he agrees that there really are stable, intelligible linguistic/theoretical antirealist accounts, requires his use of secondary rational awareness/empirical observation). Thus, while eschewing the use of the "empiricist account of scientific knowledge" (p. 271), Gergen evidently fails to notice that he must make certain empirical observations—at least of real linguistic propositions that have really been socially constructed—to make his case for antirealism/social constructionism. That is, he fails to notice his own reliance on (direct) empirical observation.

Moreover, in saying that these historically and culturally located (i.e., nonuniversal) social processes cause the formation of particular theoretical accounts/linguistic products, Gergen makes a clear causal claim that sounds realist enough; in any case, that claim requires the traditional scientific method of indirect knowing (i.e., the theoretic-empirical cycle) to get at, test, its causal component. This causal claim is evident when, in citing the kind of research we should be doing, he concludes, "Such changes in conception [e.g., of the child, romantic love, mother's love, self, emotion] do not appear to reflect alterations in the objects or entities of concern but seem lodged in historically contingent factors" (p. 267)—these are factors that Gergen, at least, apparently thinks we can know.

Although Gergen does not reference Blum's (1978) article, "On Changes in Psychiatric Diagnosis over Time," Blum, who like Gergen endorses Foucault's views of the historical/contextual nature of all knowledge, provides a perfect illustration of the kind of research I believe Gergen would endorse. He also, quite conveniently, illustrates my own argument. Blum found that the use by mental health professionals of distinct mental diagnoses changes as a function of historical context or era. In particular, they covary both with treatments that are available at any given time (e.g., the rise in the schizophrenic diagnosis as antipsychotic drugs became available, the rise in depression as antidepressants became available, and the decrease in neuroses as psychoanalysis declined) and with the way the physician has *interpreted* existing behavioral symptoms. For example, Blum charts a tendency to *perceive* anxiety as the primary symptom in the 1950s, when psychoanalysis was available to treat neurosis but when antidepressants were not, and a tendency to see depression as the primary symptom in the 1970s, when antidepressants became widely available and psychoanalysis declined. Moreover, he reports that the tendency to label any given symptom as primary (an act forming the basis for diagnosis) was not proportionate to the actual *prevalence* of that symptom in the population studied. Rather, the rate at which a symptom was labeled as primary was clearly correlated with the availability of means to treat that symptom.

Blum therefore concludes that mental illness categories do not reflect real, extratheoretic mental entities or structures. Rather, they are for Blum, as for Gergen, merely relativistic, antirealist social constructions. But again like Gergen, Blum fails to notice that in reporting these trends, he must, to make his case, observe reports of the actual diagnostic categories and treatments that were used in any era, and reports of the prevalence of certain behaviors/symptoms as opposed to their status regarding their perceived primacy. To be sure, all of these linguistic things are known directly by way of secondary rational awareness. But that secondary rational awareness appears to give Blum at least some indirect knowledge of (extralinguistic) behaviors/symptoms and treatments that really existed at different points in time; Blum at least appears to take them in that realist way. In any case, both Blum and Gergen must rely on some real empirical observations to make their respective arguments—even if those observations are confined to linguistic entities; and so there is realism in their (postmodern) work, even if it is of a modest or limited sort. That is, there is nothing subjective about Blum's investigation; his own knowing process is not altering or distorting the reality about the relation between diagnosis and historical/treatment era he investigates and reports.

Gergen (1985), however, goes well beyond the claim that social/linguistic interactions cause the construction of knowledge or theories, a claim that is a counterpart to the postmodern narrative therapy claim that the social exchange between therapist and client causes the production of a new narrative. Gergen, like most of the postmodern narrative therapists reviewed in Chapters 4 and 5, claims that it is important to understand the process of theory construction because our theories constrain or affect our other (extralinguistic) actions/events:

> Descriptions and explanations of the world themselves constitute forms of social action. As such they are intertwined with the full range of *other* [italics added] activities.[18] The opening, "Hello, how are you?" is typically accompa-

nied by a range of facial expressions, bodily postures, and movements without which the expression could seem artificial, if not aberrant. In the same way, descriptions and explanations form integral parts of various social patterns. They thus serve to sustain and support certain patterns to the exclusion of others. To alter description and explanation is thus to threaten certain *actions* [italics added] and invite others. To construct persons in such a way that they possess inherent sin is to invite certain lines of action and not others. Or to treat depression, anxiety, or fear as emotions from which people involuntarily suffer is to have far different implications than to treat them as chosen, selected, or played out as on a stage. (1985, p. 268)

Gergen later states, "To the extent that psychological theory (and related practices) enter into the life of the culture, sustaining certain patterns of *conduct* [italics added] and destroying others, such work must be evaluated in terms of good and ill" (1985, p. 273). Of course, this presumed extratheoretic effect of narrative/discourse—that discourse affects (actions and conduct in) reality—is the reason why postmodernists, including postmodern narrative therapists, find the understanding of narrative to be important in the first place. That is what makes the social constructionist enterprise worthy of our attention.

Let us return now to narrative therapy itself. I stated above that narrative therapists appear, in their avid endorsement of antirealism, to miss the point that we all have direct rational awareness of the very theories and narratives we or others have constructed from the things—both temporospatial and linguistic—we know directly. Indeed, that direct rational awareness of theories and narratives is why we can make arguments that others can know directly and so can agree or disagree with, follow or not follow, etc. This includes the arguments made by members of the narrative therapy movement. Put differently, once someone forms or constructs a theory or narrative in language by virtue of rationality's formative function (with its deployment of direct rational awareness for that very purpose), and once we commit that theory or narrative to paper, tape, or even memory, it—the theory or narrative—then takes on an existence that is independent of the knower (and its creator). That existence is, moreover, a stable existence not unlike that of a house or painting—i.e., a temporospatial object—also created by the formative function of rationality. Therefore, it (the words or equations the theory is composed of) is not *itself* (re)constructed or (re)constituted (by the formative function of rationality) differently—altered or distorted in the act of knowing by the deployment of some *other* theory/language/discourse—each time we encounter it. That our *understanding* of the theory may change—but not, given the constraints of the language in which it is written, in an unbounded way [19]—with repeated exposure to it, to education, and so forth (i.e., with a change in the so-called "interpretive context") does not change this point: that the theory itself remains stable and known as a stable theory, that is, with some objectivity or some degree of stable meaning that can be agreed upon, at least until someone comes along to alter it. That someone who comes along to alter the theory could well be none other than the (narrative) therapist who deliberately works to alter the client's theory/narrative about his life/problem by changing the very words and hence meanings in the client's story.

To put all this somewhat differently, the fact that a theory is a product of rationality's formative function does not mean it cannot, once made, stand on its own and be rationally attended to objectively, without alteration, much like a house, painting, or any other temporospatial artifact. In fact, to the extent that the theory is known by way of words on a page or computer screen, it *is*, in that sense, a temporospatial artifact.

There is a reason I emphasize the stability of linguistic propositions, which are produced by the formative function of rationality but then known directly by the (secondary) rational awareness function. The reason is this: stability of some sort and degree is fundamental to an entity's ontological existence as an (independent) entity. But I also emphasize that stability because the members of the narrative therapy movement themselves, as well as others who call themselves postmodernists, seem on some (but not other) occasions to accept that very stability of discourses/stories/narratives/theories in language. In so doing they give stories a real, ontological status, and hence make them available to (direct) rational awareness. Ironically, that occasional acceptance of the stability of narratives or discourses is a subversion of some postmodern theory which, at other times, says that there is no such stability, because what we know is reconstituted in each and every act of knowing/attending. To quote White and Epston again, "*every* [italics added] new reading of a text is a new interpretation of it, and thus a different writing of it" (1990, p. 9). [20]

Before providing particulars, let me here make a general point along these lines: that the stability of theory/narrative/story in language is taken for granted within narrative therapy can be argued by pointing out that narrative therapists must believe their clients' life narratives are stable, committed, or intractable in the telling and retelling of them; otherwise, people wouldn't need narrative therapists to challenge and so help destabilize or change clients' stuck/stable narratives in the first place. Moreover, clients wouldn't "resist" (to use a forbidden term in narrative therapy) that attempt at destabilization—the process of therapy itself—if their narratives were unstable to begin with.

To get more specific, recall Lax's earlier remark about how narratives become "frozen" and in so doing limit options in life; "frozen" narratives is surely a concept connected to the stability of the narrative over person, place, and time, and to its effect on the stability of options/solutions and actions, as we discussed in Chapter 4. Neimeyer (1993) addresses the stability of narratives directly when he states,

> Because these belief systems and personal accounts [i.e., personal narratives] are seen as having a substantial continuity over time, therapy is more likely to examine the developmental dimensions of the client's psychopathology . . . , paying particular attention to the primary attachment relationships that shaped the client's most fundamental assumptions about self and world. (p. 224)

Presumably, for Neimeyer, not only are narratives about the self and world real and stable, but so also are the extralinguistic relationships that brought them into being—co-constructed them—in some extratherapeutic context.

White and Epston (1990) make explicit the stable existence of narrative constructions in stating,

> Social scientists became interested in the text analogy following observations that, although a piece of behavior occurs in time in such a way that it no longer exists in the present by the time it is attended to, the *meaning* [italics added] that is ascribed to the behavior survives across time. It was this ascription of meaning that drew their attention, and in their attempts to understand this they began to invoke the text analogy. This enabled the interaction of persons to be considered as the interaction of readers around particular texts. This analogy also made it possible to conceive of the evolution of lives and relationships in terms of the reading and writing of texts, insofar as every new reading of a text is a new interpretation of it, and thus a different writing of it. (p. 9)

Although White and Epston, true to reader-response criticism/poststructural literary theory, try in that last sentence to rescind the stability of the "text" they explicitly proclaim in the first sentence ("the meaning that is ascribed to the behavior survives across time"), that proclamation is there nonetheless. Note, incidentally, that behavior, which I take to be extralinguistic behavior, is supposedly no longer existent by the time it is attended to (that point is not necessarily true—I can attend directly to your act of talking to me *while* you are still talking). But behavior nonetheless can, according to this quotation, be attended to, thereby conferring upon it the (temporospatial) reality of some extralinguistic existence.

Hare-Mustin (1992b), who is very vocal about her endorsement of a postmodern feminism, as we saw earlier in quotations from her work, alludes more indirectly than those just cited to the stability of language/narrative/discourse. As she states,

> [M]eanings are not simple. One is hard pressed to select a word that has one true meaning as the authors attempt. Furthermore, conversation is an imperfect art. On the one hand, we never know precisely what meaning something has for another person. On the other hand, we are constrained by the meanings available in our language community. (p. 309)

The phrase "we are constrained by the meanings available in our language community" is a tricky one. It suggests to me that there really are available meanings, and that they are generalized and so somewhat stable in their use within a "language community." But note that the "language community" itself also, apparently, has a real, stable existence, even if "language community" is used here in a more circumscribed way than simply the language—e.g., English—in use in any setting. If the "language community" is a particular group of people who (a) interact with each other and in so doing (b) talk in particular ways—that is, adopt certain discourses or ideas within any given language—then we can presumably know that community by way of both primary (point "a" just above) and secondary (point "b" just above) (direct) rational awareness.

The actual language in use in any location (e.g., English) surely has stability as a linguistic system; it therefore can be known directly as such and constrains the meaning of anything said within it. Hare-Mustin's phrase "we are constrained by the meanings available in our language community" also suggests to me that those stable meanings allegedly "constrain" either (a) the way we can actually *be* in extralinguistic terms, or (b) the way we can understand any experience (which must always be filtered through the supposedly distorting lens of some "theory/language," or some discourse). In either case, this is simply the typical antirealist/social constructionist argument that theory/language/discourse constitutes reality, reality which we allegedly cannot know.

Here again I emphasize that this line of thinking suggests that we can know, by way of secondary rational awareness, what the "dominant discourse" in any context or "language community" really *is*. As Hare-Mustin (1992b) herself goes on to say,

> [T]he therapist and client are not a self-contained linguistic system. The therapeutic conversation is not free to invent anything. The meanings available are those that reflect the norms and beliefs in the dominant discourses of the society. These discourses provide the metaphors, the shared meanings and predetermined content of therapy. If the participants are unaware of marginalized meanings and discourses, such meanings remain outside the therapy room. (pp. 309–310)

Presumably, both dominant and marginalized discourses have a real and stable existence and can in principle be known as such, again, according to Pols, by way of secondary (direct) rational awareness.

The next quotation is a more complete version of one I have also used previously (see Chapter 4, Note 12). I nonetheless restate it here again because its author, a therapist who endorses a type of postmodern mindset, speaks directly to the question of the stability of the (linguistic) productions of the formative function of rationality—including the meanings and hence interpretations of those productions:

> Derrida has criticized Western philosophy since Plato for its "logocentrism:" the treatment of "the word" as conveying, in itself, fixed meaning—"the truth." In deconstructing logocentrism, however, Derrida does not suggest that there are no meanings, nor that interpretive contexts are necessarily unstable. On the contrary, a task of deconstruction is to investigate the relative stability of given interpretive contexts (Derrida, 1988, pp. 143–150). (V. Fish, 1993, p. 232)

The stability of the interpretive context in that quotation is relative, to be sure, but it is stability nonetheless.

Gergen also speaks to this stability when he states,

> Constructionism offers no foundational rules of warrant and in this sense is relativistic. However, this does not mean that "anything goes." Because of the inherent dependency of knowledge systems on communities of shared intelligibility [again, is this the system of language in use—e.g., English?—or is it some more limited discursive context?], scientific activity will always be governed in large measure by normative rules. However, constructionism does invite the practitioners to view these rules as historically and culturally situ-

ated—thus subject to critique and transformation. There is stability of under-standing without the stultification of foundationalism. (1985, p. 273)

The problem, of course, is that Gergen, like most postmodernists, wants it both ways: stability is there to ground knowledge when *that* is desired ("not just anything goes"). But that stability must be just unstable enough to under-mine that grounding, because any such grounding runs the risk of providing the foundation for knowledge that postmodernists/antirealists want to avoid.

To conclude, I have in this section given evidence of the belief, within narrative therapy, in the stable, independent (of the knower) existence of narratives—both their words and their meanings. I did that because the social constructionist position narrative therapists adopt presents a problem they have failed to resolve. On the one hand, they may cry "foul" in response to my argument, exclaiming that social constructionism permits knowledge of our socially constructed antirealist representations, or stories, of our *experience* of the world, but not of the world itself. But, on the other hand, they have failed to notice that once formed by rationality's formative function, those stories have a real, independent (of any particular knower), consistent exis-tence *as* stories, or linguistic entities. That is, the stories themselves become part of knowable reality, and a directly knowable reality at that. Indeed, dominant discourses would not oppress and so would not be the object of so much postmodern concern if they did not persist—both in their composite parts and in their meanings—over persons, place, and time. They also could not be the object of systematic postmodern study (e.g., Blum's research about diagnosis) if they themselves—realist or antirealist—were not directly knowable *as* discourses.

Social constructionists, then, take for granted direct knowledge of their linguistic constructions—however antirealist those constructions may be. In so doing they do not recognize their own modest realism. That realism is modest only in the sense that at the very least they take it for granted that they know the actual stable discourses in the actual stable "discursive/linguis-tic contexts or communities" that, they claim, actually dominate/affect their own thinking and behavior. To be sure, in that very last thought we see a slippage into the extralinguistic world of behavior once again. That slippage makes the realism of social constructionists somewhat less modest than it would be if it were confined only to knowledge of linguistic propositions, constructions, or entities—that is, confined only to secondary rational aware-ness. Put differently, if we can know constructed stories directly, as they really or independently (of any particular knower) exist, then surely we can know other knower-independent entities directly—either entities we have constructed with the help of rationality's formative function (e.g., houses) or those we have not so constructed (e.g., rocks, trees, birds). As Pols has explained, this direct knowledge is surely the basis for the indirect knowledge that scientific theories, for instance, give us. It is the same direct knowledge that postmodernists use all the time in formulating *their* narratives.

CONCLUDING COMMENTS: THE REALITY OF PROPOSITIONS AND WHAT THEY REFER TO

Pols's philosophy, with its clear distinction between the two forms (primary and secondary) of rational awareness, on the one hand, and the formative function of rationality, on the other, is unquestionably in opposition to the fashionable linguistic (i.e., antirealist) philosophies that have dominated the English-speaking world for the past half century or so. It also, relatedly, stands in opposition to the more extreme postmodern/poststructural reader-oriented literary theories of criticism, in which it is claimed that each reader quite literally creates and recreates the "text" through each act of reading (see, e.g., S. Fish, 1980). These theories deny any stable, independent (of the reader) existence of a text itself; a text therefore allegedly cannot have even a possibility of some stable meaning that readers can hope to converge upon with objectivity, that is, in common. Thus, Pols's philosophy stands in opposition to the very two humanistic trends that have been imported by postmodern narrative therapists to make sense of therapy—a fact which makes my appeal to his philosophy an unlikely cause for celebration within that therapy movement.

Regardless of the reception his philosophy receives, the distinctions Pols makes provide us with a way to explain just how it is we can know what the client's story is at any point in time, even a story we are in the ongoing process of co-constructing with our client. They also explain how we can know what the dominant discourses of the day are, including the arguments or propositions that the narrative, or any other, therapy movement hopes to persuade us to believe, to accept as true. Those distinctions, moreover, explain why we can feel free to believe that the theoretical propositions of science, including the antisystematic science of narrative therapy, can in principle give us some degree of truth about—some approximation of—the extratheoretic reality they are attempting to describe and explain indirectly. For instance, we can feel perfectly free to accept—with no guilt whatever—the possibility that the narrative therapy claim that holding stories can cause the experience of problems, or negatively valued (extralinguistic) events, and also cause the experience of solutions, or positively valued (extralinguistic) events, is, in reality, a correct claim. That is, it may be shown by means of various systematic/scientific investigations—or theoretic-empirical cycling—to warrant some confidence in its extratheoretic truth.

With this alternative philosophy of both direct and indirect knowing, then, we have a philosophy that restores our purchase on the really real. But it does so without minimizing the importance of language itself both (a) in knowing (directly and indirectly) the real and (b) as an object of some real part—the propositional/linguistic part—of the reality to be known. Thus, we can say with assurance that once propositions/theories/narratives gain admittance to the realm of the really real along with people, trees, rocks, and houses—i.e., once they are seen to have an independent, stable existence that can be known directly—we can begin to talk about using *them* in a realistic way and, perhaps, also a systematic way in therapy. We then can surely avoid the epistemological contradiction and antisystematic quality that now plague the narrative therapy movement's efforts.

Let us now turn to my own alternative—and thus more realist—use of the narrative therapy movement's contributions to the theory and practice of therapy. In particular, I emphasize how those contributions pertain to relieving at least some of the tension between an individualized and yet systematic approach to the practice of therapy.

CHAPTER 7

Three Proposed Modestly Realist Therapy Systems

THE REALITY OF THERAPY SYSTEMS AS THEORETICAL SYSTEMS/ LINGUISTIC ENTITIES

In Chapter 6 I argued that—once constructed by the formative function of rationality—propositions, theories, stories, and narratives are real and so have a stable existence with stability of meaning independent of any particular reader or listener. I also argued that linguistic propositions, theories (and so forth) can be known directly *as* propositions by means of secondary rational awareness. Whether those propositions give us any (indirect) knowledge of the independent, or extralinguistic, reality to which they refer is a question that determines one's position in the realism/antirealism controversy. Recall that those who answer "yes" to that question are realists, those who answer "no" are antirealists. But even antirealists must know that question directly *as* a question (by secondary rational awareness) to be able to answer "no" to it, and so they are realists in at least that modest sense.

The present chapter is based on the assumption that there is much that is good—indeed indispensable—for therapy in the linguistic focus of the narrative therapy movement, but that the antirealist assumptions and antisystematic aspirations of *postmodern* narrative therapy diminish the systematic translation of that focus into actual practice. Moreover, those assumptions and aspirations may seduce some therapists into a neglect of the empirical outcomes of their therapeutic interventions. The success of narrative therapy, therefore, it seems to me, depends on a systematic, empirical—hence realistic—approach to the nature and efficacy of narrative therapy interventions. If

I am right about this, we may be in a position to develop, on the basis of a modified narrative therapy system of the right sort, a real, stable system of therapy that attends more directly (and so more systematically) to language use than do most conventional, realist therapies. That exercise makes sense because—as narrative therapists are quick to point out—psychotherapy takes place in and makes use of language/narrative in the pursuit of problem resolution, or change.

In this chapter I therefore propose three alternative systems of therapy with a narrative focus. Each system entails both empirical assumptions and a built-in empirical research program on a realist basis. The built-in research program makes it possible for each of the three systems to be improved in practice. I provide considerable detail about each of these three proposed systems, including a scholarly context for each, in later sections; however, let me summarize them briefly here:

1. A *generic narrative system*, in which we determine therapeutic narrative structures that affect the behavior[1] of the generic client; it therefore directs us to determine laws for narrative intervention (Component B) that should be applied universally, or indiscriminately, across clients.

2. A *linguistic/narrative matrix paradigm*, in which we determine distinct therapeutic narrative-intervention types (Component B) that affect the behavior of clients with distinct narrative types (Component C). Unlike the first proposed system, it does not involve the attainment and use of universal laws but instead categorizes clients in advance in accordance with the kinds of narratives in which they express what they perceive to be their problems.

3. A *traditional matrix paradigm with a linguistic twist*, in which we determine distinct therapeutic intervention types (Component B) that affect the behavior of clients with distinct problem types (Component C). Unlike the second proposed system, it does not limit its intervention and client categories to linguistic ones but instead relies on a classification scheme determined by both traditional matrix criteria and strictly linguistic criteria.

Note that the components of the three proposed systems are described in terms of the A B C components of the generic model of therapy systems that I provided in Chapter 3.

Before going into detail about these three proposed systems and their built-in research programs, I must make three important points and then discuss some of the questions they raise. First, the client/problem and intervention categories that appear in these three systems are put forth as tentative and subject to revision, depending upon their empirical success or lack of it. Second, in proposing these three systems, I do not mean to suggest that a narrative focus in therapy should supplant the establishment of a general theory of human nature as a foundation for all therapy systems. I mean only to suggest that if we are going to attend to language use in therapy, then we should do so more seriously than is typical within the narrative therapy literature. I discuss what I mean by this just below. Finally, I want to be very clear about the fact that the postmodern narrative therapy movement, even as it exists today in its unreformed state, already involves a modest, or limited, realism. That realism is found (a) with respect to secondary rational awareness both of theories about narrative and of narratives themselves, and (b) with respect to the implicit reliance on primary rational awareness to make such general claims as the fundamental ones within narrative therapy, namely, that the way one narrates one's life affects the perception of options in life, and that this perception in turn affects the way life actually gets lived. These claims bring with them the realist imperative that we understand how language or narrative, as a *system*, itself works to produce maximum impact on clients' understanding and behavior.

To put these points another way, I suspect there is some truth or reality in the narrative therapy movement's claims, despite the antirealist interpretation narrative therapists give their claims. Those claims should therefore be taken more seriously. By this I mean they should (a) be given an unequivocally realist interpretation, (b) be tested more systematically or scientifically, and (c) be applied more rigorously or systematically in the actual practice of therapy.

The point of the three-part exercise just described is the attainment of that elusive goal that has organized my thinking in this book: how to attain a theoretical system of therapy that is complete enough (i.e., organized or structured, coherent and whole) to guide a practice that is systematic, rule-governed, or replicable, and yet is individualized. The way the narrative therapy movement now attends to language does not help achieve that goal: although the incompleteness of its theoretical system (the erosion of Components A and C) ensures individuality in therapeutic content, it does so only at the expense of a systematic practice. Moreover, narrative therapy oscillates between realism and antirealism in its formulations.

Again I remind the reader that just because each therapy case is unique and individual in *some* ways does not mean it is unique and individual in *all* ways: if that were true it would indeed legitimate the antisystematic attempt to eliminate the use of a predetermined system of any sort to guide therapeutic practice. Surely there are enough similarities across cases—general truths about human nature itself—to warrant the search for systems of therapy that when put into practice manage the tension between the individualized and the systematic more successfully. Even narrative therapists, who proclaim the uniqueness of each case, use the same theory-cum-method of problem resolution (Component B), namely, co-construct new narratives, across all clients.

A Very Modest Realism for Systematic Practice

The three alternative systems of therapy I propose in this chapter attend differently to the problem of attaining an individualized yet systematic approach to therapy practice. Although each proposed theoretical system stresses the focus on language, or narrative, that has constituted the narrative therapy movement's attempts to individualize therapy, I again stress that each proposed system is nonetheless realist in at least one modest sense: that we can know the propositions in the theoretical system directly as propositions, and that these propositions themselves contain real, stable meanings that also can be known directly. We therefore can know the theoretical system itself directly as a real, stable theoretical system, a fact that is distinct from the question whether the theoretical system gives us any independent, extratheoretic reality. Thus, all theoretical systems—even if they are the antirealist ones that social constructionists, including postmodern narrative therapists, claim to construct—are modestly realist in that we know them directly by way of secondary rational awareness. Simply put, we do not invent and reinvent *them* in each and every act of knowing. Again, we may refine our understanding of the system and its propositions as we use it, become more educated, and so forth. But its composition as a theoretical system (its component propositional parts) and its possible meanings are by no means indeterminate.

Why is that last point so important? Because to miss that point is to dismiss the possibility of an approach to therapy practice that is at all rule-governed or systematic. Recall that even the practice of narrative therapy, which for all practical purposes provides no predetermined types (Component C) or causes (Component A) of problems, is minimally systematic insofar as it is guided in all cases by a universally applied theory-cum-method of problem resolution (Component B). Thus, if we are going to be at all systematic or consistent in practice, we must be able to *know* directly some real (independent), stable plan or theoretical system of therapy that does not suffer a change in *its* meaning and constitution in each and every act of knowing/attending to it, and in each and every act of using/applying it. This is true even though we may choose, in a particular therapy session, to modify the way that system gets used to maximize individuality (see Chapter 3). Therefore, to be systematic in one's practice requires some modest realism in that modest (i.e., [direct] secondary rational awareness) sense. (To the extent that you know you have a client in your office with whom you are engaged in conversation, you also are of course employing [direct] primary rational awareness.)

But my realism is not just a modest one. As I demonstrated in Chapters 4 and 5, a system of therapy that deals more explicitly with language use itself, including the incomplete system of the postmodern narrative therapy movement, nonetheless must incorporate the real effects of language use not only on the client's linguistic productions, but on the client's extralinguistic behavior/life as well. Again, theory/language (see Note 7, Chapter 6) or narrative is important in therapy precisely because, as narrative therapy explicitly claims, it affects the way lives are actually lived. Put differently, if postmodern narrative therapists did not believe that language—in the form of theories/narratives/stories/understandings—affects the *reality* of our lives, in all its many manifestations, they would not be so concerned with its supposedly oppressive or liberating effects on real lives. That, after all, is the whole point of the postmodern narrative therapy movement.

Thus, if we grant that narratives—once formed by clients, therapists, or expert theoreticians—have a real, stable existence that can be known directly as narratives (i.e., without alteration in each and every act of knowing/attending), we are then in a position to determine what really makes certain (directly knowable) narrative "moves," forms, or structures more useful to the therapeutic pursuit of opening new options and solutions, and so to the pursuit of problem resolution/change itself. Questions about how real, stable, or enduring narrative structures really, or truly, create their effects on human linguistic productions and extralinguistic behavior already, therefore, imply that these structures transcend each unique therapy situation or moment. That is, there is some generality in the way these structures are constituted and then work their real effects on the reader/listener. That generality allows us all to understand the therapeutic (change-inducing) use of language as a system itself, a system that can be used to guide us in a therapy practice that is more systematic, rule-governed, or replicable than what we have typically found in the postmodern narrative therapy movement.

A less modest realism than that inherent in the use of secondary rational awareness (of linguistic entities) is nonetheless implicit in all that I have just said. The reader will recall that the question of whether a therapeutic narrative (or narrative move, form, component, or structure) is useful in problem resolution is also the question whether it is *truly* useful. Contrary to antirealism/social constructionism, truth and utility are not at odds with each other, at least not in this sense. But I suspect that the reason narratives have extralinguistic effects (e.g., on overt behavior)—the reason narratives are truly useful—in the first place is because they make at least some minimal contact with the extralinguistically real. Put differently, narratives that make no contact with any independent reality are less persuasive, as I argue below.

To summarize: if narrative is a real phenomenon that—once constructed by an author, theorist, therapist or client—has an existence independent of any particular knower/listener, then we can systematically study how *it*—narrative and its component parts—really or truly works its therapeutic, or antitherapeutic, effects on human behavior/life, in the broadest sense of that term. That question incorporates the question of whether the narrative must reflect an extralinguistic reality more or less adequately to affect the listener (see Spence, 1982). This is no poststructuralist/postmodern stance, for I am suggesting that both authors of narratives and their narrative creations—however co-created and evolving those creations may be—are real and enjoy an existence independent of any particular knower/listener who at some point in time becomes rationally aware of them.

Thus, to say (a) that interpretations, understandings, theories, stories, or narratives of life events can cause the experience of problems and solutions, and so can affect the way life itself gets lived, and (b) that they may themselves be altered (in therapy) by "narrative" interventions is not to say that the events the narratives refer to, as well as the narratives themselves, cannot be known directly as events and narratives. Rather, all this suggests is that the causal connections between events—the very stuff that gives events their meanings or implications and that therefore makes for the stuff of narrative—cannot be known directly (see Spence, 1982, p. 291, who distinguishes between events, which can in principle be known/reported directly, and their causal connections, which cannot). Because those causal connections can be known only indirectly, by means of inference, we must construct theories, stories, interpretations, narratives to give us that indirect, inferential understanding. Some of those constructs will, as in science itself, fit the (directly) observable facts or events at hand better than others. That is why rival theories exist in science, and in life.

It is the therapist's job to help the client arrive at an understanding that helps him experience his life/problem in a new way. This new understanding supposedly helps him see new options that he could not see within his old understanding, and so ultimately helps him live his life (i.e., think, feel, and act) differently. It is precisely those causal connections (between events) that cannot be directly known, the theorized causes and effects of events, that give the events their meaning. Those *theorized* causal connections, according to narrative therapists, should therefore *themselves* be the object of reformulation for the purpose of therapeutic change. And as in science, the therapist can help the client reformulate her meanings and understandings by "testing" the client's "theories" about the causal connections in her life. To be sure, this "testing" is accomplished in therapy by some more informal, less systematic version of the theoretical-empirical cycling that constitutes the scientific enterprise itself. For example, a college student may complain that he cannot get good grades in a crucial course because the professor does not like him; the therapist can then advise him to test that causal claim by studying more effectively, to see if that factor has any consequences for his performance. This is, in fact, perfectly consistent with the methods of traditional cognitive or cognitive-behavioral therapists, who work within the confines of a modern scientific framework that is fully realist. Thus, unlike postmodern narrative therapists, they have no problem admitting that they strive to replace the client's erroneous assumptions with true or correct ones.

Even narrative therapists eschew creating causal understandings, or meanings, that violate what they find in their observations of their clients, including the real life events that their clients report; recall that for them "not just anything goes." Thus, even for them, the challenging or deconstructing of old narratives requires an appeal to empirical observations—events in reality—that render the client's (antitherapeutic) narrative less tenable. In that sense, they too (much like traditional cognitive therapists) are "testing" the client's theory or understanding in light of an empirical reality, and replacing it with a more adequate one. Whether that new understanding works better for therapeutic purposes if it does indeed give realistic knowledge is of course an empirical question, although it should be clear by now where my choice lies.

To restate the question at hand: if theories/stories/narratives/understandings about one's life (events) affect or cause one's perception of problems, options, and solutions, which in turn affect the way one's life is actually lived/enacted, then how can we structure therapeutic narratives to produce beneficial change? What real, stable, enduring narrative types, forms, moves, or structures do we have at our disposal for the purpose of altering clients' understandings in some systematic way?

I have taken it for granted that the reader has some very general, perhaps even vague, understanding of such terms as narrative types, moves, forms, or structures. And I shall in due course discuss the meanings of these terms with a degree of precision I think appropriate, given the mission of this book. But first I must raise a question about the stability or instability of language—in particular, the stability or instability of the meanings of words and the narratives in which they are used. The question is this: why are narrative therapists so attracted to the postmodern conviction that language, meanings, narratives (i.e., linguistic entities) are free-floating, that is, characterized by instability? I believe the answer to that question is to be found in the whole point of therapy in the first place: to achieve change of some beneficial sort. And the notion of change, no matter how precisely and stably we define it, is ultimately *about* the instability of something. Therapy is, above all else, dedicated to the idea that the therapist can really help the patient get unstuck, or *destabilized*, about something—preferably something undesirable. If meanings or understandings play a key role in that endeavor (as I, along with narrative therapists, believe they do), then the degree to which the meanings or understandings held by the client can be changed affects the degree to which we can reasonably hope for a change of some sort in the client's behavior/life. Thus, if meanings or understandings float freely as a function of ever-changing linguistic and extralinguistic contexts,[2] as the postmodernists like to claim, and if the client's problem is *merely* linguistic, then the possibility of change is maximized. On the other hand, change is then so easy that there cannot be the resistance to change (i.e., "stuckness") that is said to require narrative therapy intervention in the first place.

But that supposed instability of meaning, that supposed easiness of therapeutic change, then makes the whole therapeutic enterprise itself less consistent or stable. That is because whatever theoretical system guides practice cannot *itself* have any stable meaning or existence that we can call upon with regularity, and so the practice of therapy becomes extremely antisystematic. A very modest realism is therefore necessary for any systematic approach to therapy practice: even if the theoretical system in use is alleged to be antirealist—i.e., alleged to give us no extralinguistic reality, it must itself, *as* a linguistic entity, have a reality that can be known directly as such by way of secondary rational awareness.[3] Thus, even if, as social constructionists, we profess to use an antirealist theoretical system to guide our practice, we can make that practice systematic as a result of that use only if: (a) there is a stable theoretical system with a stable meaning that *exists* independent of any particular knower, and (b) the therapist/knower can *know* that theoretical system directly as it really, independently exists. Yet the theoretical system cannot *have* that stability, that independent reality, if the therapist/knower reconstitutes or alters it in every act of knowing. In applying postmodern doctrine to their own endeavors, I am of course arguing that postmodern narrative therapists do in fact rely upon a direct knowledge of *their* theoretical system to make their case for its merits.

In any case, now let us return to the question of efficacy in therapy. I am suggesting that behind the postmodern, antirealist claim that all is constituted and reconstituted in each and every act of knowing, and that accordingly there can be no real, stable existence of anything known, including meanings and doctrines themselves, there lies an optimistic attitude about the possibilities for change of some therapeutic/beneficial sort. Thus, if the thing needing change (the meanings or understandings held by clients) is highly unstable, then it is more easily or readily changed. Indeed, the quotations assembled in Chapters 4 and 5 suggest a very hopeful, optimistic attitude on the part of postmodern narrative therapists about the possibility for change in all therapy cases.[4] Frank (1973, 1987), who himself has narrative therapy leanings, is one of many to have discussed the importance of therapists having faith in their (supposedly antirealist) systems of therapy. He claims that such faith allows therapists to create hope, optimism, and the expectation for positive change in their clients. This attitude has been called by many a "common factor" or key component of beneficial change in all therapies; one does not want to destroy it, if it is indeed necessary to solve problems or produce change (e.g., Grencavage & Norcross, 1990; Stiles et al., 1986). But postmodern pluralism dictates that therapists should not believe that their own system of therapy can give them any independent reality or truth. Therefore, they either should not give their particular system too much "credence" (Omer & Strenger, 1992, pp. 259–260), or they should "forget" any system once they have learned it (Sluzki, 1992, p. 229), because the consistent use in practice of any predetermined therapy system is too constraining and hence deindividualizing. This mandate creates a conflict for those therapists who also take Frank's claim seriously.

Contrary to that postmodern position, what could be more hopeful than the knowledge that we can attain at least some independent knowledge of the real? And since I am arguing that that (knowable) reality, both in its linguistic and extralinguistic manifestations, has some stability within *it*, it can in principle give us the kind of stable knowledge we need to develop stable theoretical systems that allow us to work systematically or consistently enough to attain beneficial change in therapy practice. Notice that the manifestations of change are also real and directly knowable: recall that the therapist can compare at different points in the course of therapy the client's reports of his behavior and experience outside of therapy, or compare at different points the behavior that can be observed directly in therapy. Therapeutic change itself is, moreover, potentially—but not necessarily—stable across situations and time: therapists, including postmodern narrative therapists, must hope that the effects of their interventions are not limited to one, unique, now-you-see-it-now-you-don't instance of knowing. Again, the reality of that stability, including the reality of the stable or enduring effects of the use in practice of certain therapy systems, is precisely what allows therapists, including narrative therapists, to make the claims they make about the *enduring* benefits of therapy. Conversely, what could be more discouraging than the idea that everything in each and every act of knowing is of the knower's invention, that all such acts can never give, even twice, the same antirealist, or knower-dependent, "version" of what is being attended to/known.

Let us now turn to the three systems that I propose in order to make our therapeutic narratives more useful (i.e., truly useful) for the purposes of problem resolution or change. Again, each consists in a (potential) way to conceptualize a theoretical system of therapy, and so each has applied/practical therapeutic implications, as well as research implications. Note that two of them (Proposed Systems 1 and 2) draw upon the contributions and (reality) claims of the narrative therapy movement, including the disciplines to which that movement turns, such as literary theory and rhetoric, whereas one of them (Proposed System 3) does not. Also note that two of them (Proposed Systems 2 and 3) draw upon the structure of the matrix paradigm of the eclectic therapy movement, whereas one of them (Proposed System 1) does not. All three systems, however, pertain to the attempt to keep the practice of therapy systematic and yet individualized, but in different ways. Finally, again note that each system has some modest degree of realism within it, which I make explicit. I therefore make one more proposal: that regardless of which, if any, of the three therapy systems makes the most sense to any particular reader, she should notice the modest realism that of necessity lies behind *any* system of therapy, including systems that make use of so-called postmodern ideas. Put differently, the importation of concepts from literary theory, even postmodern theory, to build a system of therapy is an activity that is properly taken as realist. That activity, moreover, always produces a system of therapy that contains within it some degree of realism, a fact which must be made explicit. Only then can the existence of that realism be openly acknowledged for what it is.

PROPOSED SYSTEM 1: HOW TO
CONSTRUCT THERAPEUTIC
NARRATIVE TO AFFECT THE BEHAVIOR
OF THE GENERIC CLIENT

Here we are not concerned with the selection of particular narrative interventions for clients with particular types of narratives. Rather, we are concerned with two questions: (a) How does narrative or language *in general*
operate, and so (b) how may narratives be constructed to be maximally
persuasive or therapeutically effective, regardless of the particularities of the
client?

There is, to be sure, some structuralism lurking in those questions. The
first (a) asks how language itself works as an internal system which, like all
systems, must by definition have component parts and relations among them.
Eagleton (1983, pp. 103–104) said that structuralism created a "new literary
science"—namely, narratology—which has to do with the way (the rules by
which) the component parts of language or narrative may be combined to
create meaning (see also Groden & Kreiswirth, 1994). To the extent that
structuralists believe the workings of language are universal/ahistorical and
also reflect the universal workings of mind—that is, the way mind organizes
or structures reality to create meaning—they are indeed also talking about
real, universal mental functions (see Gerrig, 1993, for elaboration of those
functions).

That point about universality, which the poststructuralists rejected when
they challenged the workings of language itself as an *independent* system, is
well beyond the scope of this book (see Eagleton, 1983). More relevant to
my purpose is the poststructuralist emphasis on the *psychology* of reading, an
emphasis which insists that there are no stable, independent (of the reader)
systems of language with universal rules for generating meaning. Rather, they
claim that each and every act of reading "rewrites" the text, that is, creates its
own meaning. This emphasis implies a different definition of "narratology"
from the one generated by structuralism, a definition that relates to the
second (b) question in the paragraph above—namely, how can language be
used to create maximum impact on the reader/listener, either particular types
of readers, or all readers in general?

This question has much to do with the movement within literary theory
and criticism, called reader-response criticism, which we discussed in Chapter
4 in relation to the postmodern narrative therapy movement. Eagleton's
(1983, p. 114) suggestion that, for critics of structuralism, meaning has to do

with the intended *effects* or *consequences* of one's language use is perfectly compatible with the therapist's—any therapist's—agenda: to say things to the patient, and to encourage the patient to say things, that have real consequences for her life. Recall that this was what Freud called a "talking cure." To be more precise, Eagleton, in his discussion and critique of structuralism, said that to ask about one's intentions is not to ask about one's internal mental processes; rather, to ask the question

> 'What do you mean?' is really to ask what effects my language is trying to bring about . . . . Understanding my intention is grasping my speech and behaviour in relation to a significant context. . . . It is to see language as a practice rather than as an object; and there are of course no practices without human subjects. . . . [This] shift away from structuralism has been in part . . . a move from 'language' to 'discourse.' 'Language' is speech or writing viewed 'objectively,' as a chain of signs without a subject. 'Discourse' means language grasped as *utterance*, as involving speaking and writing subjects and therefore also, at least potentially, readers or listeners. (pp. 114–115)

Quotations like the one above, when seized upon by therapists, make the "psychology of reading" or listening as legitimate for them as for the literary theorists who invented that concept for their own purposes. Moreover, according to postmodernists, there is nothing stable, consistent, or systematic about that reading/listening process, except, perhaps, the systematic workings of misunderstanding. This is what de Shazer (1991, p. 51) presumably means when he says "one cannot read, one can only misread." For him, all reading is therefore inherently problematic.

Let us now return from that digression into literary theory to the question that heads this section, namely, how to go about constructing therapeutic narratives—how to use language itself—to produce the maximum possible impact on the client's understanding (or narratives) of his life and so, ultimately, on his extralinguistic behavior. Note that this question is relevant to therapy to the extent that we accept its implicit assumption that the truth claims about the therapeutic effects of language made within the postmodern narrative therapy movement are indeed true. Let us first rehearse those claims once more: (a) stories/narratives about life events can cause the experience of problems; (b) interventions such as deconstructing/challenging/questioning old narratives cause the co-construction or reconstruction of new stories/narratives about those same life events; (c) these new stories/narratives can cause the experience or perception of new options and potential solutions, which in turn can cause the enactment of new behavior—that is, cause new life events themselves. To return to our question, we may ask how language as a system itself may be used to produce narratives that are intelligible and, because of that intelligibility, have effects on both the generic listener's understanding and, ultimately, her behavior/life. Put differently, this question concerns itself with how to understand not only language itself, but, more relevant to therapy, the *relationship* between, on the one hand, language use — the production of narratives that generate meaning/understanding/intelligibility, and on the other hand, (extralinguistic) behavior (cf. Gerrig, 1993). The point of this understanding is the generation of rules (i.e., a system) to guide the process of problem resolution, of therapy itself, for any and all clients.

Narratology

The disciplines of literary theory and criticism, which include narratology, and the discipline of rhetoric itself[5] can, according to narrative therapists, help answer that question. In his influential work, *Reading for the Plot: Design and Intention in Narrative*, Brooks (1992) considers a "'universal grammar' of narrative" (p. 17) but concerns himself more with "how narratives work on us, as readers, to create models of understanding" (p. xiii). Since narrative therapists only rarely incorporate the *specifics* of literary theories into their own theoretical systems, let us now consider in some detail the concept of narrative structure.

Eagleton (1983) discusses several schemes for classifying the structures or component parts of narrative. He begins, in a structuralist spirit, with the Russian Formalist Vladimir Propp's reduction of folk tales to (among other "elements") a total of seven "spheres of action" (e.g., the "hero," "helper," "villain," "person sought-for") which could be combined in particular ways to produce any one folk tale (p. 104). According to Eagleton (1983, pp. 104–105), A. J. Greimas, in his *Sémantique structurale* (1966), used the concept of an "actant" — which is a "structural unit" rather than a specific narrative or a character — to increase the level of abstraction of his narrative system. Eagleton states, "The six *actants* of Subject and Object, Sender and Receiver, Helper and Opponent can subsume Propp's various spheres of action and make for an even more elegant simplicity" (p. 105).

Eagleton also discusses Genette, who, in his well-known book *Narrative Discourse: An Essay in Method* (1980), emphasizes the way language structures events temporally and how authors may manipulate time structures to establish certain (real) effects in the reader. He cites Genette's use of the narrative distinction between "*récit*" (plot), "*histoire*" (story), and "*narration.*" *Récit* refers to "the actual order of events in the text," *histoire* to "the sequence in which those events 'actually' occurred, as we can infer this from the text," and *narration* to "the act of narrating itself" (p. 105). It may, as Eagleton suggests, produce more dramatic effect for the reader if a murder mystery, for instance, begins with the discovery of the body and works backward in time "to expose how the murder happened" (p. 105) than if the text simply reports the events in the chronological order in which they occurred.

Eagleton summarizes Genette's five basic categories of "narrative analysis." "Order" indicates the operation of "time-order" in the narrative, which may consist in "prolepsis (anticipation), analepsis (flashback) or anachrony" ("discordances between 'story' and 'plot'") (p. 105). "Duration" concerns how the narrative may "elide" or "expand" episodes, "summarize, pause a little and so on" (p. 105). "Frequency" refers to "whether an event happened once in the 'story' and is narrated once . . . [or] narrated several times, [or whether the event] happened several times and is narrated several times . . . [or] narrated only once" (p. 105). "Mood" includes "distance" (e.g., whether the narrative is told in direct or indirect speech) and "perspective" (e.g., does the narrator know more or less than the characters?) (pp. 105–106). "Voice," the act of narrating, concerns the implied type of narrator and narratee (e.g., Do you "tell of events before, after, or . . . while they happen"? Is the narrator "absent from his own narrative" or "inside his narrative as [e.g.] in first-person stories"? [p. 106]) (see also Groden & Kreiswirth, 1994, entry on Narratology, pp. 524–527).

It is noteworthy that Eagleton makes a process/content distinction about discourse not unlike the one I discussed in terms of therapy systems in Chapter 3: "[Genette's classifications alert us to] the difference between *narration*—the act and process of telling a story—and *narrative*—what it is you actually recount" (p. 106). Eagleton finds these are not so clearly distinguished: he uses the example of an autobiographical story about himself to indicate how "the 'I' who does the telling" seems to be both identical with and yet different from "the 'I' whom I describe" (p. 106). Indeed, it seems fair to say that how you say something, the way you manipulate narrative structures to make your point, [6] can never be completely independent of the particular words and expressions you use to make it, that is, its content (cf. Groden & Kreiswirth, 1994, pp. 524–527). Thus, to argue that the important process for therapeutic change consists in knowing and manipulating clients' narratives or, more specifically, narrative structures or components (however they may be defined) is at once to say something about the content of therapy, however general that content may be, and however much the therapist strives to let that content be client determined. Again, one cannot speak of therapeutic process, in this case how to go about the business, the *act*, of questioning and challenging clients' narratives to maximize therapeutic impact, without also speaking, at least implicitly and generally, of content, what to focus on or change. In this case that most general content consists in narratives or aspects/components of narratives themselves.

In any case, Proposed System 1 consists in a call to develop a theoretical system of therapy informed by narrative therapy concerns, by conducting empirical research to answer the question of how narrative may best be structured systematically to produce, that is, cause, therapeutic effects for the generic listener. Thus, the components of this system are not particularized in relation to distinct client or problem types (Component C), as they could and would be in a matrix paradigm approach; therefore, the system itself is likely to cause any practice of therapy guided by it to be more systematic than individualized.

Sarbin (1986), a psychologist, provides ideas that are relevant to the question posed just above (i.e., relevant to Proposed System 1) in his edited book *Narrative Psychology: The Storied Nature of Human Conduct*. In the second chapter of that book, Gergen and Gergen (1986) state that narrative "structure[s] events in such a way that they demonstrate, first, a connectedness or coherence, and second, a sense of movement or direction through time" (p. 25). Narrative must therefore "*establish a goal state*" (e.g., a protagonist's well-being) (pp. 25–26), "*select and arrange events*" in a way that makes that goal state "*more or less probable*" [all italics in original] (p. 26), and make available "causal linkages" between the components of the story (p. 26). Here we see a generic prescription for intelligibility itself, which, recall, is fundamental to a narrative therapy view of therapeutic change. Gergen and Gergen ask what narrative forms arouse and compel audiences—that is, produce "dramatic engagement." They conclude that it is not the events themselves, but the *relations* among events, the causal connections (cf. Spence, 1982), that produce this engagement (p. 28). There again is that focus on causal connections, which is also the focus of narrative reconstruction in narrative therapy. Gergen and Gergen, therefore, may be useful to that enterprise.

Gergen and Gergen (1986) provide "three prototypical or primitive narrative forms," namely, "progressive," in which progress toward a goal is enhanced (positive slope), "regressive," in which progress toward a goal is impeded (negative slope), and "stability narrative," in which no change occurs (flat slope) (p. 27). They also claim that three characteristics of narrative form are necessary for the creation of dramatic engagement: (a) *"acceleration of the narrative slope,"* or increasing the rate of moving toward or away from some valued state, (b) *"alteration in the direction of narrative slope,"* or "change in the evaluative relationship among events," and (c) "indication that the story line could change rapidly" or move in a different direction, by "sudden acceleration and/or shift in the opposite direction" of the narrative slope from "its present course." This, they claim, creates "suspense," a "potential or anticipated series of events" (pp. 30–31). Again, note that these narrative devices are generic in that they are put forth as operative in all cases of listening.

In the final analysis, the literary distinctions of theorists like Genette and Gergen and Gergen may not prove to be of use in the actual practice of therapy. Only empirical investigation (and time) will tell. But the narrative therapy movement must nonetheless accept that narrative forms themselves are a real component part of its theoretical system of therapy, if that movement wants to specify just what its narrative interventions consist in. If it accomplishes that, it can then say something more precise about the process of therapy than its ubiquitous but amorphous call to "deconstruct," "question," and "challenge" old narratives in general, and "reconstruct" or "co-construct" new ones. That greater precision in theory should allow narrative therapy to become more systematic in its practice. That is, by predetermining what distinct *aspects* of clients' narratives may be problematic, or preventing the perception of new options, the narrative system of therapy can give the therapist more guidance about what her narrative interventions might entail. Thus, the theory of problem causation is no longer so general—"stories/ narratives cause problems"—as to place no practical constraints on what the object of the intervention process can be. It is no longer narratives in general that are the focus of therapy, but rather the determination of those distinct, predetermined *aspects* or forms of narratives that should provide the focus of therapy.

In what I now call a generic narrative system of therapy, for lack of a better term, the therapeutic intervention itself (Component B) may still consist in questioning, challenging, and ultimately, rearranging or reconstructing narratives. But now those same acts of intervention will have as their object (i.e., their content) predetermined narrative components, forms, or structures, for instance, the way events in the client's narrative are arranged *temporally* (see Genette), or the rate and direction of the narrative slope (see Gergen and Gergen). These changes are made in the belief that they will enhance dramatic engagement, and so will better affect understanding and ultimately behavior itself. The content of therapy (Component A) is thus more precisely defined, specified, or particularized in this system than in the existing descriptions of narrative therapy. That specification or particularization constrains the practice of therapy more, thereby making that practice more rule-governed, and so more consistent/replicable, across cases, that is, it makes that practice more systematic.

Although the use of predetermined narrative forms, structures, or components places more constraints upon the content of therapy, it still allows each client to determine the (particular) content of each form. For instance, attention to the temporal organization of events recounted in every client's narrative predetermines attention to the time factor in restructuring all narratives. But that attention does not at all predetermine the events themselves that are important to recount in the narrative, as would be the case in some more conventional (A B C) system of therapy, which might, for example, look to instances of acceptance or rejection by significant others in the client's past as the events that have caused the current problem.

In short, Proposed System 1 consists in a call to produce a system of those real, specified, predetermined narrative forms or structures that have been shown to play some causal role in the experience of problems (Component A), and so should be the focus of narrative interventions (Component B). Again, we are here taking the business of narrative perhaps more seriously—certainly more precisely—than has generally been the case in the narrative therapy movement. The discerning reader will anticipate that a matrix paradigm cannot, therefore, be far behind.

Rhetoric

I do not attempt an overview of rhetorical theory, even a most simple-minded one like that which I provided for narratology just above, since rhetorical theory as such is well beyond the scope of this book. I mention rhetoric in this section only because the proposal under consideration—to determine how to use language or construct narrative in therapy so that it may have the maximum effect on the client's understanding and behavior/ life—is one that defines the discipline of rhetoric itself. According to *Webster's*, rhetoric is "the art or science of using words effectively in speaking or writing, so as to influence or persuade." In his edited book *Rhetoric and Philosophy*, Cherwitz (1990, p. 1) states, "Since the 5th century B.C. there has been a fascination with 'rhetoric,' a concept encompassing the manner in which humans symbolically influence one another. . . . [or] the way the content and form of language affects individual experience and social order." Thus, the linking of language and persuasion or influence is common to both therapy—all therapy, but most explicitly to narrative therapy—and rhetoric. Certain therapists (e.g., Frank, 1973, 1987), have even explicitly claimed, however unconvincingly to some, that therapy *is* the art (or science) of rhetoric.

I have simply assumed that one's narrative or language use must have some degree of intelligibility to influence behavior, and I know of no therapist or rhetorician who would dispute that assumption. Indeed, a central claim of the narrative therapy movement is that narrative changes behavior by way of changing the understanding or meaning of life events, that is, their intelligibility. To recall White and Epston (1990, p. 3), "it is the meaning that [family] members attribute to events that determines their behavior." To quote therapists we have not heretofore reviewed, let us now consider a quotation from Eron and Lund (1993):

> Bogdan (1986) . . . clarif[ies] the link between meaning and action . . . . He notes that "it cannot, strictly speaking, be the case that behaviors . . . are maintained by other *behaviors*. I have no access to your behavior per se, only to my representation or interpretation of it. Therefore, it must be my *interpretation* of your behavior, not your behavior per se, that maintains my own actions" (p. 35).
>
> The above statement is in line with constructivist/postmodern [and, I would add, antirealist] thinking on the subject of the interconnection between meaning and behavior.[7] (Eron & Lund, 1993, p. 295)

Given the pervasiveness of this line of thinking, I will continue to work with the assumption that meaning affects behavior (but I do not, of course, accept Eron and Lund's, and Bogdan's, antirealist assumption that we cannot have direct access to overt behavior/action itself). I nonetheless emphasize the point that the intelligibility of any narrative can be argued to have something substantial to do with its realism. That point runs counter to the claims of narrative therapists. Recall (from Chapter 5) that they claim it is only the (internal) coherence, or *narrative* fidelity, of the story, rather than its extralinguistic truth, that determines its intelligibility and so its potential effect on the client (cf. Spence, 1982; Omer & Strenger, 1992).

In his work on rhetoric and realism, Hikins (1990) argues that all good rhetoric is persuasive by virtue of supplying facts in addition to rhetorical style (or form). He argues that "narrative fidelity" and the "coherence of a story," concepts not alien to both literary theory and narrative therapy, are derived from the the narrative's relation to the world, in a realist sense: "if we are to avoid the dizzying descent from intersubjectivity [or what I call social constructionism] to subjectivity [or what I call constructivism] and, ultimately, to solipsism, we must grant that *some external criteria of facticity must be available against which to test the factual claims of any discourse*" (p. 49). Note here that Hikins argues that there is something *external* to, independent of, the discourse in use to which we may appeal to test the truth of the discourse. This is similar to Pols's claim that the empirical pole in science must be independent of the theoretic (or linguistic) pole, if theories are to be tested in a way that is independent of the theory, and so if science is to advance by means of successive approximations to the extratheoretically real. Of course, the social constructionism/antirealism of postmodernism, including the postmodern narrative therapy movement, denies the independence of theory/ language and empirical observation. For members of those movements, recall, theory/language makes, constitutes, constructs, or at least alters/distorts in language, whatever reality we encounter, or attend to, in life. That position is therefore nothing less than a form of antirealism itself.

We find a similar convergence between rhetorical and at least some types of literary theory when we compare Brooks and Hikins. In his book *Reading for the Plot*, Brooks (1992) may be seen to echo the realist sentiment of Hikins when he states, in consideration of constructions that arise within psychoanalytic treatment, that good narrative works by creating the conviction that the events "derived from it must be right" (pp. 321–322). Although Brooks, unlike Hikins, is not a self-proclaimed realist, both help make the case that for a narrative to be convincing to any reader/listener (i.e., for it to work its effects on the reader), it must somehow bear *some* proper relation to the extralinguistically real. Postmodern social constructionists/antirealists would certainly be quick to point out that being convinced that the events in the narrative are right has to do only with the coherence of the narrative (cf. Spence's, 1982, concept of "narrative truth") and not its report of any extralinguistic reality. But in doing so they miss the point that the truth of the central causal claim of postmodernism—that narratives themselves (even antirealist ones) may, if constructed well, (causally) affect the listener in *some* way—depends at the least upon a modest realism that acknowledges direct secondary rational awareness of narratives and other linguistic entities that have a real, independent existence as linguistic entities. It also depends on direct primary rational awareness of real listeners and the ways in which they reveal the real effects on them of narratives, however those effects are assessed. Thus, there is some reality to the stable existence and stable effects of "narrative truth" itself. In the next section I examine that concept and the claims made about it.

Psychotherapy

Turning to psychotherapy literature itself, Frank (1987), who himself adopts the postmodern "patient as text" (p. 297) analogy, also appeals to rhetorical devices to enhance persuasion in therapy: "the therapeutic power of any form of psychotherapy depends primarily on its persuasiveness. In this a psychotherapeutic method resembles a literary production more than applied science" (p. 300). There is much in that quotation, and I have more to say about the question of therapy as an art vs. a science in Chapter 8. But note here the equation between persuasion, literature, and therapy.

Spence (1982), in his influential book *Narrative Truth and Historical Truth*, also makes reference to the artistic and rhetorical components of therapeutic interpretation/narrative when he states,

> Freud's "tally argument" ([Grünbaum], 1979, p. 465) [is] that an interpreta-
> tion, to be effective, must *tally* with what is real in the patient—and that only
> accurate interpretation, so defined, can mediate veridical insight and only such
> insight can cure the neurosis.... [A]s he [Freud] became more clinically
> experienced, he began to back away from this model and adopt a more moder-
> ate stand about the historical truth value of his analytic work, and in his final
> paper on the topic, he [says] ... that "an assured conviction of the truth of the
> construction ... achieves the same therapeutic result as a recaptured memory"
> (1937, p. 266). If a creative interpretation can bring about that kind of
> assurance, then perhaps a strict correspondence with the specific past event is
> no longer necessary.... If an interpretation is seen as an artistic product, we
> might argue further that it achieves its effect through something analogous to
> the well-known *suspension of disbelief* [italics in original]. *An interpretation may*
> *produce the desired result because the patient, supported by a belief in the analyst and*
> *reinforced by the power of the transference, may allow himself to suspend disbelief in*
> *the literal meaning of a given interpretation and thereby make himself accessible to its*
> *artistic and rhetorical surround.* [italics added] (pp. 288–289)[8]

An interpretation, then, may bring about a positive effect not because it corresponds to a specific piece of the past but because it appears to relate the known
to the unknown, to provide explanation in place of uncertainty.... [C]ertain
kinds of pragmatic statements can produce changes in behavior simply by virtue

of being stated. . . . [I]nterpretations may be effective without necessarily being "true" in a strict historical sense. (p. 290)

There is more in that quotation than I have room to comment on in this book. But before I make some comments about it, let me say why I find it necessary in this chapter to consider Spence, along with a very few other narrative therapists, more extensively than most I have reviewed so far. In short, Spence is, in my view, the first in a line of narrative therapists who are struggling admirably, by virtue of attending more precisely to the use of language/narrative, to attain a systematic therapeutic enterprise without losing sight of the client's individuality — and all within the confines of a professed antirealist philosophy. Thus, as I now intend to demonstrate, with Spence we find that the two core issues of my critique — the realism/antirealism problem (i.e., oscillation) and the individuality/systematic problem — connect in an unprecedented way. Put differently, I find Spence to be the first of some very few antirealist/narrative therapists who seem, in some (but not all) ways, to be struggling to defy what I have called the antisystematic aspirations of many such therapists.

Let us therefore begin this analysis by returning to the above quotation of Spence. First, note the attention to art (presumably literary) and rhetoric as components of successful interpretation and hence successful therapy. Second, note that therapeutic interventions, in this case interpretations, need not be realist to affect behavior; even antirealist stories/interpretations can presumably have an effect on behavior — a real effect — *if they have real narrative truth*, or the internal coherence and so forth that Spence spoke of earlier. Moreover, antirealist narratives, ones with narrative rather than historical truth, are alleged really or truly to create their real effect on real behavior by means of creating in the client a real, assured conviction of their truth. That conviction is attained by way of a real belief in the analyst, the real power of the transference, and hence the real "suspension of disbelief" alleged to be necessary to create the effect of the interpretation. These truth or reality claims about problem resolution are no less true because they propound the effects of antirealist stories.

But the question we must now ask is this: how, if Spence is right about the effects of narrative truth, does one form interpretations or stories or narratives in therapy that have these real (i.e., extralinguistic) beneficial or therapeutic effects on the client's life? Put differently, how does one go about achieving narrative truth? Can we appeal to the use of distinct, predetermined narrative forms or structures, along the lines that I have been suggesting, to do so? Here Spence indeed confronts a problem. It is not so much the problem of an oscillating realism/antirealism (although that problem certainly persists[9]). Rather, there is the problem of trying to keep the practice of therapy highly individualized, and so thoroughly antisystematic, while trying to construct a theoretical system of therapy.

Thus, Spence lays out a perfectly general concept for the successful doing of all therapy—the attainment of narrative truth. But he then goes on to tell us that there can be no general rules for its attainment in practice, since narrative truth is always particular to the uniquely detailed nuance of each and every clinical encounter. (So, in effect, he lays out his antisystematic aspirations systematically.) Let us consider a few more of his statements that make this difficulty apparent.

> If validation seems out of reach, how do we arrive at a general theory? The answer may be a long time coming—because of the *particular* [italics added] nature of narrative truth. If interpretations are creative rather than veridical and if the analyst functions more as a pattern maker than a pattern finder [I take this to mean that there can be no predetermined content in therapy], then we may be faced with a glaring absence of general rules. . . . If the impact of a particular interpretation is contingent . . . on the specific texture of time and place, the rules for it being true are just as much out of reach as the rules for any other kind of artistic masterpiece [note therapy is likened to art and not science]. . . .
>
> The widespread belief in this general theory may actually interfere with our clinical work. To the extent that the analyst is guided by certain kinds of presuppositions, he will tend to understand the material in a more restricted fashion [note how the use of predetermined theory constrains therapy]. . . .
>
> Working within a tradition of narrative truth, . . . we would not assume that we are establishing general laws. (1982, pp. 292–294)

Even though Spence is all too keenly aware of the antisystematic implications of his abandonment of general laws for the creation of narrative truth, he seems to lose sight of one fact: that positing a causal relationship between (a) the attainment of narrative truth (i.e., antirealist stories with real narrative truth) and (b) therapeutic effects on the client's behavior *is* a general (causal) law itself. Nonetheless, he himself appears more invested in the individuality side of the individuality/systematic tension, although his struggle with that tension is heightened in the last pages of his book.

[I]f we are shifting to a more relativistic notion of truth, then the discoveries we make in our clinical work . . . do not necessarily generalize to other patients. Our discoveries, in other words, may be highly situational and need to be understood in their immediate context; it would be a mistake to reduce them to some general law because, by doing so, we might lose the very ingredient that made them effective in the specific case. (p. 295)

Still, the admirable struggle between the unique, or individualized, and the general, or systematic, may be seen in this last quotation:

If the specific detail of the clinical happening is what makes all the difference, then it becomes all the more important to carry out a systematic unpacking of each clinical encounter. . . . to find ways of naturalizing[10] each encounter in a *routine* [italics added] and *systematic* [italics added] manner [is Spence here seeking a Component B—a general, indeed universal, theory-cum-method of problem resolution?] and to take precautions *not* to reduce a complicated happening to a stereotyped "law". . . . If narrative truth is the source of our clinical success, then it should be taken seriously in all of its specific detail; it will not survive translation into something more general. (pp. 295–296)

In short, it again seems that Spence is suggesting that we go about attaining our antisystematic aspirations systematically. Systematic and antisystematic aspirations in closer proximity to each other surely cannot be found.[11]

There are other psychotherapists and psychotherapy researchers who speak to the question of how best to construct narratives to achieve therapeutic effects. Omer (Omer, 1993, 1994; Omer & Strenger, 1992; Strenger & Omer, 1992), whom we have considered in the context of both the integrative/eclectic and the narrative therapy movements, exemplifies work in the tradition of Spence to make therapy with an antirealist premise as systematic as possible by attending more explicitly to the specifics of narrative construction. As he himself states in his book *Critical Interventions in Psychotherapy*, "Pluralism and relativism are not the same as anarchy, and quality judgment is still possible without a world of fixed beliefs (Strenger & Omer, 1992)" (1994, pp. 8–9). Later in this same book he states,

The shared features between the psychotherapeutic and the literary crafts [e.g., "semantics," "syntax," "poetics," "narratology," "characterology," "dramatics," and "theory of form" (p. 66)] have often been adumbrated, but hardly ever specified. (1994, p. 65)

A deeper awareness of the similarities, however, will allow us to perform the task not only intuitively, but intentionally and professionally. The quasi-literary side of psychotherapy should not be relegated to fickle inspiration. On the contrary, if well defined it could lead to a better understanding of the component skills that make psychotherapy a *craft* [italics added]. (1994, p. 67)

Omer (1994) has relevance for a generic narrative system insofar as he prescribes, in the context of his "psycho-editorial principles," some general guidelines for the construction of any therapeutic narrative. He (1994, p. 49) is careful in his advocacy of pluralism to disclaim their *universal* effectiveness, but he puts them forth as "particularly valuable" to keep in mind nonetheless. Therapists should therefore (a) "gain a narrative foothold," by which Omer means that therapists should start with their patients' premises/self-narratives and only carefully move away from them (pp. 49–51), (b) "detrivialize suffering," which speaks to the importance of the events in the patient's life (pp. 51–52), (c) "invest the patient as hero," which focuses on the patient as the protagonist of her own story (pp. 56–57), and (d) "create options by a new character," by which Omer means adding characters to the therapeutic narrative who serve an "unbalancing function" (pp. 60–61). Taken together, the second two principles in particular are designed to change "the experience of life as a spate of occurrences irrelevant and indifferent to one's wishes, values, and acts" (p. 56).

Although his own work does not follow in Spence's (1982) tradition as much as does Omer's, Russell (1987a, 1987b, 1989) nonetheless also advocates a postmodern/linguistic approach to therapy research (and therapy itself) by claiming that all self, being, and becoming is constituted in narrative (1989, p. 510), and that language mediates all "construals," that is, all that is known (1989, p. 509). He even proclaims the postmodern "world-making [rather than world representing or reflecting] function of language" (p. 508). Thus, Russell clearly endorses the applicability to therapy of a typically postmodern antirealism. Indeed, he presents the idea of a "linguistically constructed world of subjectivity, of identity, and . . . of social interaction" (1989, p. 511) as nothing less than the very stuff of therapy itself. But unlike most psychotherapy researchers of any theoretical persuasion, Russell proclaims the importance of deploying only those theories that *explicitly* link language and therapeutic process. To use his words, we must, in conducting psychotherapy research, concern ourselves with "the detailed specification of the rationale linking a specific view of therapy to a specific view of language use" (p. 513). That rationale is, for Russell, all too rare. Or, to put it another way, according to him we need a "souped-up science of language as a plausible instrument-cum-theory for investigating the process of therapy" (p. 512). [12]

It is beyond the scope of this book to explore Russell's proposed research strategies in detail. But he nonetheless proposes rule-governed formalisms, derived from the unitizing and categorizing of language use in therapy, to organize our understanding of how the process of therapy works in language. Thus, he strives to give us the kind of general rules of language use in therapy that could, in at least some of their manifestations, comprise a generic narrative (structure) approach. As Russell himself states, we could design a research program that could "use the corpus of obtained language data to reconstruct the rules that speakers use to create and that listeners use to understand the actions conveyed by surface linguistic forms such as statements, commands, questions and so on" (1989, p. 516). For him, since "discourse [*itself* may be viewed] as a rule governed behavior" (1989, p. 517), we should "make explicit and formalize the rules that *constrain* [italics added] the possible sequences of actions carried out in conversation" (p. 516). For instance, we might want, using an interactional view of both language and therapy, to determine the probability with which a "client insight statement followed a therapist interpretive statement" (p. 515). [13] But Russell also suggests a more explanatory system of rules than that example, which is only descriptive. For instance, he suggests defining the general rules that explain the production of "valid requests for action" that can be understood—that is, received—as valid requests.

Russell is clearly not defining his narrative categories in the ways suggested by Genette and Gergen and Gergen, who propose attention to the use of temporal arrangements and narrative slope, respectively, to achieve narrative coherence, intelligibility, and therefore dramatic engagement. Still, there is nothing about Russell's suggestions that precludes the incorporation of any variable that may contribute to the determination of narrative style, form, or structure, insofar as *that* has therapeutic relevance. As he himself states,

> Of particular interest has been the exploration of [such larger units as] the narrative or episodic description as a viable unit for [therapy] process research (e.g., Russell, 1985; Schafer, 1980; Spence, 1982). The conjecture is that there are adaptive and nonadaptive styles of narration . . . . (1987b, p. 347)

Two points about Russell's efforts are important. First, despite the post-modern narrative therapy movement's professed concern with the explicit attention to language use in therapy, few of its members have engaged in the kind of slow, painstaking research that Russell himself does and advocates. Thus, those members do not seem to take their own theory to heart, since their theory implies a meticulous attention to language use in therapy and in research, including attention to the research findings of those who engage in that meticulous, painstaking research.[14] As Russell himself puts it,

> Even if the search for curative factors is restricted to the domain of client and therapist *talk* [italics added], the relevant phenomena to be investigated are forbiddingly numerous and complex. . . . [A]ny analysis of the forms and functions of language usage can expect to be a lengthy and arduous task, spanning across many individual research careers. . . . This lack ["of truly programmatic research"] is prompted by the fact that granting agencies are not "terribly excited" by studies of psychotherapeutic talk, . . . that progress is slow, and thus hazardous to beginning researchers, . . . and that most graduate students choose, or are advised, not to pursue such research as topics for dissertations. (1987a, pp. 2–3)

Second, Russell is himself taking the business of language in therapy seriously by attempting to define a system of language use that describes and explains the process of all therapy—that is, "therapy talk," in all its generality. But he is nonetheless careful about the general/particular distinction. According to him, we should always begin by describing "the language data in terms of local and specific rules [note a microevents-type analysis; see Chapter 2] and then to attempt to posit a more abstract set of general rules" (1989, p. 517). Russell defines a three-step process in pursuit of those rules: (a) "identify episodes in the hour that have had fairly obvious therapeutic value. . . . The idea is to accumulate a set of therapeutically significant episodes, preferably *spanning across* [italics added] types of therapies, clients, and therapists" (note the generality here; the processes should be common to all change events); (b) by way of "microanalytic study" of therapist/client interchange, identify the "process commonalities ingredient in each of the episodes"; and (c) systematically determine the (causal) role of these commonalities "in achieving therapeutic change" by means of controlled studies (1987b, p. 345).[15]

There can be no question, then, that Russell is attempting to give us, in scientific terms, a theoretical system that helps us organize or systematize the way we think about and practice therapy. That system should tell us how the language of therapy/change works for—imposes constraints on—clients (and therapists) in general. In this respect, he is clearly more comfortable in his search for the generalities that can make the practice of therapy systematic, that is, rule-governed and so scientific, than is Spence (1982), who makes no bones about his preference for the art of individualizing therapy—an art that always functions at the expense of those generalities that constitute a (scientific) theoretical system. Again, we find that tradeoff between the individualized and the systematic, which is now seen in terms of the artistic and the scientific, respectively. But no matter how general or particular Russell's ultimate system (of constraints/rules for language use in therapy) may be, he is—despite his own postmodern antirealism—surely claiming something real about how the language of therapy itself really or truly works for all speakers of that language. Those modestly realist claims obtain for Russell whether or not that therapeutic language provides any extralinguistic reality, a question that I find is not answered by him with clarity. [16]

Three observations about a call to develop a comprehensive "generic narrative (structure)" system of therapy can be made. First, knowledge from such disciplines as rhetoric and narratology (and again, linguistics, psycholinguistics, sociolinguistics, among others) may help to inform the theory and practice of therapy, which itself ultimately aims to create beneficial effects through the use of language or narrative. Second, there is a modest realism in all of those disciplines: (a) At the most modest level of realism, linguistic forms or structures are, once produced by the formative function of rationality, real, and they can be known directly *as* linguistic entities (that exist independently of any particular knower) by way of secondary rational awareness. This is true even if those entities give us no indirect knowledge of any extralinguistic reality. Disciplines like narratology and rhetoric, for instance, can tell us what those real, stable structures or forms are, and how we may arrange them to heighten the reader's (dramatic) engagement, to use Gergen and Gergen's term. But notice, once again (see Chapter 5), that the claims about how to enhance both the reader's engagement and the behavioral consequences of that engagement, are claims made by narrative therapists about the real effects of certain kinds of language use on that which is extralinguistically real—namely, behavior itself. (b) A less modest realism can be seen in the argument that good rhetoric, narrative, or language is persuasive—that is, it causes an effect in the listener—only if it refers adequately to an extralinguistic reality. Of course, some aspects of that reality—temporospatial entities in our size range, for instance—can be known directly by way of primary rational awareness.

Third, it should be noticed that an approach to therapy based on a system of narrative structures that enhance (real) dramatic engagement and persuasion and so have consequences for (real) behavior is not necessarily compatible with a matrix paradigm (although it certainly points toward one). In proposing that we work to determine rules about the therapeutic workings of language that hold true for (i.e., transcend) all speakers and listeners, I do not imply that clients need be assigned to distinct client/problem categories or types (Component C) for the purpose of narrative intervention selection (Component B). However, there is nothing in what I have suggested that would prevent that kind of particularization within whatever (linguistic) system of therapy anyone works to establish. Still, there need be no emergence here of such rules as "if client complains of problem x or produces a narrative with linguistic style, structure, or content y, apply linguistic intervention z," although, again, the theoretical system could certainly evolve in that type of particularized way. To quote Spence (1982, pp. 40–41),

> Good literature approximates reality because it provides the reader with just enough of the right kind of information in just the right sequence to permit a controlled appreciation of the passage in question. . . . A finished piece of writing, because it controls the background associations of the reader, will bring about a roughly similar series of reactions in *all* [italics added] readers; we say that it is *publicly accessible.*

However, if the narrative therapy system did not evolve in a way that linked particular narrative structure, style, or meaning types produced by clients (C) with particular narrative interventions provided by therapists (B), the proponents of eclecticism could protest that that generic narrative system falls victim to the old "uniformity myth." That myth, recall, consists in the belief that certain interventions, in this case, interventions based on rearranging narratives to enhance the client's dramatic engagement, work for all clients equally well (see Chapter 2).

To be sure, this is the uniform approach to therapy that the eclectic therapy movement sought to eliminate in its pursuit of individuality, by means of employing in practice a system of therapy that indeed linked distinct, predetermined client/problem categories or types (Component C) to the use of distinct, predetermined interventions (Component B). There is the compromise or balance between an individualized and systematic approach to therapy proffered by the technical/systematic eclectic therapy movement. But there is also a linguistic or narrative version of the traditional matrix paradigm of technical eclecticism, and it is to that possibility that I now turn.

PROPOSED SYSTEM 2: HOW TO CONSTRUCT THERAPEUTIC NARRATIVE TYPES TO AFFECT THE BEHAVIOR OF CLIENTS WITH DISTINCT NARRATIVE TYPES: A LINGUISTIC/ NARRATIVE MATRIX PARADIGM

In the previous proposed system, I called upon therapists to determine how narrative or language may best be structured to produce systematic therapeutic effects on the generic client, or listener. In Proposed System 2 I suggest that clients can be classified into distinct (predetermined) *narrative* categories, either categories of narrative form/style/structure or categories of content/meaning.[17] These narrative categories could then carry with them implications for different types of narrative interventions. This idea is almost implicit in a generic narrative approach, in that I think its realization is practically inevitable, as I soon demonstrate. But here I again emphasize that the use of categories or components of narratives to predetermine client (C) and intervention (B) types rests on our ability to take seriously the claims of the narrative therapy movement: that the *way* one narrates one's life affects the options or solutions one perceives and therefore, ultimately, affects the behavior one enacts—that is, the way one actually *lives* one's life. Thus, the whole point of a linguistic/narrative matrix paradigm is to use the power of language to maximize therapeutic effects. That effort surely entails making the practice of therapy as individualized as possible and, if we want to claim there is some science in our enterprise, as systematic as possible.

Although I am now suggesting a (predetermined) "if-then" rule system like that found within the traditional matrix paradigm, Proposed System 2 differs from that tradition in one important respect: here *all* categories, both for classifying clients and for classifying interventions, *may* be taken as existing solely in the domain of language, or narrative. This makes Proposed System 2 more modest in its realism than the traditional matrix paradigm, which uses dimensions and categories in the usual way, namely, to convey the extralinguistic realities of the client's life. For instance, Beutler's dimension of client coping style, which contains the category of externalizing/acting out, and the therapeutic intervention of teaching coping skills, which are often linked to that style, have real, extralinguistic referents that are the object of interest for technical eclectics. Language use as such is therefore deemphasized in a traditional matrix paradigm, which accordingly uses language in a traditional, realist way to report or reflect some extralinguistic reality.

To be sure, antirealists may take solace in the possibility that these categories may give us no extralinguistic reality (although I of course think they can and do in at least some instances). But they nonetheless must face the fact that these categories are still real, stable, linguistic entities that have an existence independent of any particular knower. Therefore, they can be known directly *as* linguistic entities by way of secondary rational awareness — known, that is, without danger of alteration or distortion caused by the mediating use of some *other* theory/language to get at them. And as we find in the traditional matrix paradigm, distinct, predetermined linguistic/narrative categories of clients/problems (C) and interventions (B) are linked by way of scientific investigation, that is, by the traditional process of theoretic-empirical cycling. The purpose of the linguistic/narrative matrix paradigm, then, is identical to that of the traditional matrix paradigm: to strike a balance or compromise between the attainment of individuality in a therapy practice that still manages to be rule-governed. Those goals are certainly no less real in their attainment for being achieved by the dedicated and explicit attention to real narrative or real language use itself.

I have found few proponents of the postmodern narrative therapy movement who advocate this kind of rule-governed system: recall that anything systematic is by definition generalized, at least to some extent, and so is anti-individual or antilocalized in any extreme sense. Anything systematic is, therefore, ultimately antipostmodern; rather, it is modern from the viewpoint of postmodernists. But I again emphasize that narrative therapists nonetheless hold to the belief that once the client's — *any* client's — narrative is changed, change in the experience or perception of options and solutions, and so in behavior/action or life itself, may follow. That is, the change that results from altering the client's narrative of her life experience occurs in the client's *linguistic productions* (i.e., her narrative itself) and, ultimately, in the client's *extralinguistic behavior/life*. Recall again that that is why attention to life stories or narratives is important in the first place. Let us now consider some postmodern narrative therapists who I believe are indeed moving in the direction of a "linguistic/narrative matrix paradigm," although they do not appear to think of their theoretical system in that way and might even object to my use of that terminology.

Omer and Strenger (1992) and Sluzki (1992) provide what I have found to be the clearest moves toward what I now call a "narrative matrix paradigm," although, again, they do not use that expression to characterize their "systems" of therapy. I put the word "systems" in quotation marks to emphasize the fact that in the very act of proposing a system to guide the practice of therapy, these authors paradoxically disclaim the provision of anything so generalized, so constraining, so anti-individualized, as a true theoretical system. Sluzki (1992) denies that his proposed system to guide therapy practice is just that. Moreover, he makes a paradoxical call (p. 229) for therapists to learn a system (i.e., "conceptual tools") of therapy to guide their practice, but then to "forget" what they have learned, lest it be too constraining, or deindividualizing. Sluzki (1992, p. 221) is quite emphatic about the fact that therapists do not follow the "steps" or "sequence" of even his own proposed theoretical system, "by design." Rather, for him,

> the therapist's behavior is guided by a set of overall stances (for example, openness, empathy . . .) and conceptual guidelines (privileging stories . . . about family of origin . . .), but the process of the consultation "happens" in rather *idiosyncratic* [italics added] ways and is affected by many family, therapist, and context variables. However, the reconstructive blueprint or sequence proposed above allows one to track the *shadow of a design* [italics added] that underlies almost every session . . . . (1992, p. 221)

There is, for Sluzki, no design, only its shadow. We can easily see, in his use of the term "shadow of a design," his struggle (not unlike Spence's) to practice therapy systematically in the context of an antisystematic, individualized agenda. Omer and Strenger's (self-described) paradoxical call (1992, pp. 259–260) for therapists simultaneously to believe but yet not to believe the systems of therapy that guide their practice is another illustration of this ambivalence within narrative therapy about the generalized use of (predetermined) therapy systems, including systems proposed by narrative therapists.

Omer and Strenger (1992) have proposed what they call a "store" of meaning categories (p. 256), categories that reflect ways to understand the client's or therapist's narrative. Note that these categories are ones that give meaning to – provide some explanatory focus for – the client's life experiences, much like the content categories (within Components A and C) in complete, conventional therapies, but unlike the categories defined by narrative style, structure, or form in the generic narrative system I first proposed. Also note that Omer and Strenger propose several meaning categories, any of which can be used flexibly as a function of the best fit for any particular client's difficulties. They therefore can certainly individualize therapy more than what we find in a conventional (A B C) therapy system, which often has only one, generalized way of explaining, or giving meaning to, clients/problems (A and C). Omer and Strenger certainly can, moreover, individualize their therapy at least as well as what may be achieved in a traditional, less modestly realist matrix paradigm.

Because their predetermined categories constrain the ways to understand clients, Omer and Strenger's therapy cannot be as individualized as therapy guided by a "system" that does not predetermine anything (about the nature of problems). But that very constraint surely increases the systematization of their practice, which is, to recall the quotations from Omer (1994) provided earlier in this chapter, an explicit goal. Also recall that Omer and Strenger's professed epistemology is social constructionist, or antirealist (see Chapter 4, pp. 100–101), so that their categories can allegedly give us no (knower) independent, extralinguistic reality; we therefore, as with Spence, find in them the admirable attempt to systematize practice in the context of an antirealist philosophy. However, here I must again ask the reader to recall from Chapter 3 a central point of my argument: the realism or antirealism of categories in a theoretical system (that is, whether the categories give us any extralinguistic reality, and not the reality of the categories as linguistic entities themselves) bears no necessary relation to the individuality/systematic tension; it is the degree of completeness of the (predetermined) theoretical system used to guide the practice of therapy—and not how much that system gives us any extralinguistic reality—that determines one's balance or compromise between the two poles of that tension. Thus, the categories or components of the system themselves are always real and stable as categories, that is, as linguistic entities. Therefore, they can be known directly by way of secondary rational awareness, as indeed can the system itself as a whole. It is precisely that knowledge that permits in therapy practice the consistent or replicable, the systematic, use of those categories (and the system that comprises them as a whole).

To turn now to the categories themselves, Omer and Strenger (1992, pp. 256–259) propose that meaning may be defined in the following ways: (a) meaning as the "covert origin of behavior" or its hidden causes, for instance, revealing the unconscious conflicts behind symptoms (as in psychoanalysis); (b) meaning as the "emotional charge" of events/experience, for instance, giving mundane events such as a typical family transaction more emotional charge, or making a seemingly catastrophic event or fear appear more trivial (as in gestalt therapy); (c) meaning as the covert future "purpose or outcome," the teleological goal, of an act/symptom, for instance, discussing how a symptom such as anorexia has meaning because it may work to strengthen the family's bond (as in existential therapy); (d) meaning as the "mental associations evoked by a stimulus," that is, the connecting patterns or associational nets of the problem, for instance, expanding the context in which a symptom is understood by asking where else it occurs, how it may be understood in the context of dreams or broader cultural events, etc. (as in Jungian dream interpretation); and (e) meaning as the "moral of the story" or the "typical mistakes" that problems may reveal, for instance, showing how an attempted solution to some life difficulty actually perpetuates it or makes it worse (as in strategic/systemic therapy).[18]

What about all this, then, lends itself toward the construction of a linguistic/narrative matrix system? Let us consider the *act* of transforming or shifting clients' narratives (by means of questions, comments, challenges) to be the (problem resolution) process of therapy applied generally, or across all cases (Component B). Let us also consider the *aspects* of narratives targeted for such transformation to be the content of therapy, or the client narrative type (Component C). We are now in a position to form a matrix that links more refined narrative transformation processes with distinct or particularized client narrative types.[19] That the same general intervention process—transform narratives by means of questions, comments, challenges—applies to all clients without exception is deindividualizing, to be sure. But that problem resolution process can now itself be refined, or particularized, in relation to different client narrative types. This individualizes therapy as a function of the degree to which the predetermined matrix of client narrative types is particularized (i.e., the number of distinctions among client types it makes). Moreover, because there is a (predetermined) matrix of client narrative (C) and narrative intervention (B) types, this format provides a more complete system of therapy than what is typically found within the narrative therapy movement: recall that it usually explicates only one, general, systemic component (i.e., Component B). That more complete theoretical system must make the practice of therapy more rule-governed, or constrained, and so more consistent or replicable—more systematic. A matrix system based on Omer and Strenger's categories is illustrated in Figure 7.1.

Note again that, for Omer and Strenger, the categories within the matrix system are defined by meaning: they provide a taxonomy of (problem) explanatory categories, and not a taxonomy of narrative-structure, form, or style categories (see Omer, 1993, 1994, for the latter). Omer and Strenger reveal their matrix tendencies—that is, their desire to link (but in a flexible way) distinct narrative intervention types (B) with distinct client/problem narrative types (C)—when they state, "The process of reinterpretation [B] should not be an exchange of like for like [C]," by which they mean the client's meanings should *not* be "substituted by those of the therapist's in the *same* [italics added] category"

C	B
Client Narrative Types	*Narrative Intervention Shifts*
1. Covert Origin	1. Shift C1 meaning to C2, 3, 4, 5
2. Emotional Charge	2. Shift C2 meaning to C1, 3, 4, 5
3. Covert Future Purpose	3. Shift C3 meaning to C1, 2, 4, 5
4. Mental Association	4. Shift C4 meaning to C1, 2, 3, 5
5. Story's Moral	5. Shift C5 meaning to C1, 2, 3, 4

**Figure 7.1 A Narrative Matrix System Based on
Omer and Strenger's Meaning Categories**

(1992, p. 259). Rather, they explain how therapy can progress more skillfully if the therapist deliberately steers the client's narrative away from her typical categories. They suggest, for example, that therapists may discuss outcomes (Category 3) with clients who are preoccupied with the origins of behaviors (Category 1) or may expand associations (Category 4) when clients are persevering on teleological themes (Category 3) (p. 259).

Thus, we see quite clearly a rule emerging from Omer and Strenger's matrix system: a particular category in B never employs the corresponding category in C as its object of intervention. For example, B1 can create a narrative shift by using the meanings of C2, C3, C4, C5, but not of C1; B2 uses C1, C3, C4, C5, but not C2 (and so forth; see Figure 7.1). Although they do not say so explicitly, Omer and Strenger imply that one meaning category will dominate a client's narrative and so will be the primary target of a narrative shift. However, there is nothing in what they say that precludes the possibility of applying more than one meaning category to any one client, especially since the categories are not mutually exclusive.

As I suggested earlier in this chapter, there is indeed a problem in using the term "matrix paradigm" to characterize what Omer and Strenger propose, even if it is one that is qualified by the term "narrative/linguistic." That is because Omer himself, in his recent (1994) book, objects to the efforts of such technical/systematic eclectics as Beutler (who, recall, advocate the matrix paradigm) to solve the individuality/systematic problem. Omer's own advocacy of pluralism makes those efforts *both* too universal/general and too realist for him. Those problems are apparent when he states,

[S]ystematic eclecticism (Beutler, 1986; Norcross, 1986) . . . proposes to make the therapy fit the patient according to a method well grounded upon a metatheory, a common psychotherapeutic language, or an unimpeachable body of fact. Unfortunately, the invisible worm of pluralism gnaws at the heart of metatheories, common languages, and what counts as acceptable fact, just as it did with the schools' theories, languages, and "facts." (1994, pp. 115–116)

Note, in particular, Omer's use of quotation marks to call into question the truth or reality of facts.

Nonetheless, there is in Omer's (1994) book more evidence of a move toward a linguistic/narrative matrix. In his chapter on "Narrative Reconstruction" he offers what he calls a "typology of flawed narratives," of which there are three: (a) "patchy and chaotic narratives," which contain "gaps and leaps" such as missing episodes, stages, and causal connections (p. 46); (b) "closed narratives," which consistently eliminate good options and promote bad endings. Here Omer cites Gustafson's (1992) delineation of three types of closed narratives, namely, "subservience stories," in which people allow themselves to enact servitude while becoming resentful, "delay stories," in which people put off living life to avoid feeling pain, and "overpowering stories," in which people domineer and so create hostility; and (c) "meaningless narratives," which may create such feelings as "absurdity," "triviality," and "inauthenticity" (p. 47).

The point of Omer's typology is to guide the process of "narrative reconstruction" in a systematic way. But unlike his more generic "psycho-editorial principles" (e.g., "detrivialize suffering"), here he suggests, in a matrix-like move (again, a flexible one), the use of distinct narrative interventions for distinct narrative types. In Omer's (1994, pp. 48–49) own words,

> A typology of flawed stories implies a set of psycho-editorial principles for their repair. For example, "establish continuities" . . . , "search for missing links," and "bring about thematic unity" . . . are possible rules for dealing with chaotic and patchy stories; "challenge the story's assumptions," "focus on unique outcomes" (White & Epston, 1990) are prescriptions for addressing closed narratives; "increase emotional involvement," "search for hidden meanings," "strive for a sense of purpose," "find a moral for the story," . . . are all possible avenues to the meaningless narrative. From a pluralist perspective, any rule may prove helpful in some cases but damaging in others.

Note in that last sentence that Omer tells us that no rule should be used in practice in any hard-and-fast, absolutist way; his pluralism presumably sensitizes him to individuality even in the face of rules/generality. According to him (perhaps in an echo of Spence's aforementioned struggles), we therefore should be systematic, but not *too* systematic. Note also that the prescriptions for "meaningless narratives" constitute the "basic store of meaning categories" that were provided by Omer and Strenger (1992) and that I used to construct the narrative matrix system based on them (see Figure 7.1). Presumably, with sufficient particularization of the client-narrative (Component C) and narrative-intervention (Component B) categories, we could construct such a matrix system for each of the other two types of flawed narratives defined by Omer (1994). The same holds for Gustafson, who in his (1992) book, *Self-Delight in a Harsh World*, describes different ways of responding therapeutically to "subservience" (pp. 33–39), "bureaucratic delay" (pp. 40–48), and "overpowering" (pp. 49–57) stories.

Sluzki (1992) also gives indications of moving toward a linguistic/narrative matrix paradigm, although he, too, does not use that terminology to characterize his work. He calls the categories he uses to guide the reformulation of narratives (Step 3 in his "blueprint") "dimensions," to reflect the fact that each dimension has its own set of opposing poles. Some of those dimensions incorporate the notion of narrative structure or form; they are not, therefore, necessarily meaning, or content, dimensions/categories in the strictest sense, as we found in Omer and Strenger (1992). Rather, they are what Sluzki calls "intrinsic components of narratives" (p. 228)—structural dimensions that may be manipulated to alter the meanings clients obtain. Sluzki's system is more extensive than the one outlined in Omer and Strenger (1992); I therefore list his six narrative dimensions and only some of the "transformative shifts" that may take place within each, and then give an illustration or two. Note that Sluzki also states that his dimensions are not mutually exclusive, but rather may support each other.

The six dimensions are:

(a) Transformations in Time—here narratives may shift around the poles of (1) static vs. fluctuating (shifts between descriptions of symptoms/events that do and those that do not present "temporal fluctuations"/instability [p. 222]), (2) nouns vs. verbs (shifts between descriptions of people/symptoms/traits/events that suggest static/immutable states and "descriptions of actions" [p. 223]), and (3) ahistoric vs. historic;

(b) Transformations in Space—here narratives may shift around the poles of (1) noncontextual vs. contextual (shifts between narratives with and those without "spatial context" or "scenario" [p. 223]);

(c) Transformations in Causality—here narratives may shift around the poles of (1) cause vs. effects (shifts between stories about the assumed causes of problems and stories about the "ongoing effects" of problems "on self or others" [p. 224]);

(d) Transformations in Interaction—narratives may shift around the poles of (1) intrapersonal vs. interpersonal ("shifts between descriptions of a person's attributes and descriptions of patterns of interaction" [p. 224]), (2) intentions vs. effects ("shifts between attribution of intent to a person . . . and discussion of the effect of that person's behavior" [p. 224]), (3) symptoms vs. conflicts ("shifts between a story based on 'expressions of mental disorder' and one based on the reciprocal behaviors" [p. 225]), and (4) roles vs. rules (shifts between stories that assign to people role attributes and stories that emphasize "interactive rules" or "interpersonal patterns" [p. 225]);

(e) Transformations in Values of the Story—narratives may shift around the poles of (1) good intent vs. bad intent, (2) sane vs. insane, and (3) legitimate vs. illegitimate (shifts between stories that are reasonable/logical and those that are not [p. 226]); and

(f) Transformations in Telling the Story—narratives may shift around the poles of (1) passive vs. active (shifts between stories in which the storyteller is the passive "object" or "victim" and stories "in which the speaker is an agent and is thus accountable" [p. 226]), (2) interpretations vs. descriptions, and (3) incompetence vs. competence.

Sluzki is explicit and adamant about the fact that therapy works by shifting a client's narrative to *either* pole within any dimension. Thus, no pole is inherently good or bad for therapeutic purposes. Rather than ensuring that narrative reflects some extralinguistic reality, as would be the case in more conventional, modern therapies, the goal here—true to the claims of postmodern narrative therapy—is to create a narrative *shift* that produces new meaning, new options/solutions, and, ultimately, new behavior. As Sluzki puts it, "therapists may choose to enhance particular features of stories when they estimate that the potential shape of the new narrative will broaden the patient's or family's range and quality of options for resolving problems" (p. 228). Thus, Sluzki's matrix-like "if-then" rules can supposedly work back and forth between the poles of any dimension, as needed, to produce a narrative shift. For example, if the client's narrative stresses the cause of a problem, then the therapist might attend to its effects; but if the client is caught up in a problem's effects, a therapist might want the client to shift her attentions (and resulting narrative) to problem causation, to open new meaning. The decision is strictly utilitarian.

It is noteworthy that this value-free, pragmatic shift toward either pole within a dimension is abandoned when we encounter the dimension called Transformations in Values of the Story. On that dimension the therapist is enjoined always to shift the client's narrative toward the positive pole: good intent is always favored over bad, sanity over insanity, and legitimacy over illegitimacy (of people's behavior). Values are not as relative, or value-free, as other aspects of narratives, it seems. Also noteworthy is the modest realism of this enterprise, especially given Sluzki's (1992) own professed social constructionism/antirealism (see Chapter 4, p. 100). Again, narratives themselves, as well as the dimensions found within them, are real and stable linguistic entities and can be known directly as such. Moreover, Sluzki's proposed narrative shifts are set forth with the claim that they really, or truly, cause desirable effects in clients—that is, they really help to solve clients' problems, linguistic or extralinguistic. These narrative shifts are therefore not only useful, but are *truly* useful.

Ellis (1989, p. 158), the author of *Against Deconstruction*, the book we considered in Chapter 4, argues that "theory exerts its pressure on the status quo" by pushing for ever more constraint, clarification, and differentiation. Thus, for narrative therapy to become more theoretical—that is, to establish itself as a theoretical system of therapy—it must encourage the use of distinctions or discriminations of the sort that we have seen in the recent contributions made by Omer (Omer, 1993, 1994; Omer & Strenger, 1992), Sluzki (1992), and Gustafson (1992). But most important for my purposes are two observations: first, the compatibility of the narrative and eclectic approaches found within a "narrative matrix paradigm"; second, the fact that, although the client's type of story or narrative is privileged, and although the therapeutic intervention consists in the therapist's provocation, through questions and comments, of narrative shift itself, (a) the narrative categories are real as linguistic entities, (b) the narrative shifts or transformations that are caused by therapeutic intervention are real linguistic shifts or transformations, and (c) most important, those shifts or transformations are presumed to cause real, extralinguistic effects in the lives of the clients who undergo narrative therapy. Thus, for most narrative therapists, something more than the client's story is ultimately changed.

PROPOSED SYSTEM 3: HOW TO
CONSTRUCT THERAPEUTIC
INTERVENTION TYPES TO AFFECT THE
BEHAVIOR OF CLIENTS WITH DISTINCT
PROBLEM TYPES: A TRADITIONAL
MATRIX PARADIGM WITH A
LINGUISTIC TWIST

This question reflects none other than the traditional matrix paradigm derived from the technical or systematic eclectic therapy movement. Clients are assigned to predetermined categories on such dimensions as diagnosis, coping style, resistance potential, and so forth. Note that these dimensions may not be mutually exclusive, that is, each client may be assigned to one category on each dimension. The categories within any dimension are, however, mutually exclusive. For instance, a client may have a diagnosis of depression, have a coping style that is internal, and have a resistance potential that is high—all of which contribute to the selection of an intervention. But he may not simultaneously have both a high and low resistance potential (see Beutler, 1991, p. 227 and Chapter 2 for a complete description). The purpose of such classification is the use of interventions (such as supportive vs. insight vs. action-oriented therapies) that are selected on the basis of what has been shown empirically to work best for each client type. Because this is a description of a traditional matrix paradigm, these dimensions and categories are meant to be taken (in a realist sense) to reflect some extralinguistic feature of the client's being; they are not *merely* linguistic entities.

I refer to the traditional matrix paradigm again in this section for two reasons. First, nothing about it precludes assigning clients—in addition to the traditional matrix categories just illustrated—to the kinds of narrative categories seen in my proposed linguistic/narrative matrix paradigm. Indeed, interventions within the traditional matrix could certainly incorporate the use of different types of (predetermined) narrative forms or moves, although I know of no such explicit use of narrative therapy ideas by Beutler or other matrix paradigm proponents. The traditional matrix paradigm, then, is potentially more general than the narrative matrix paradigm: its explicit attention to aspects of narrative—that is, to linguistic entities themselves as nothing more than linguistic entities—could constitute only one of many ways to predetermine types of clients and types of interventions. Second, the traditional matrix paradigm, operating out of a modern scientific rather than a postmodern mindset, is compatible, in its underlying epistemology, with the realism I have been proposing. Its proponents have none of the implicit or explicit difficulty, seen in narrative therapists, with the assertion that therapeutic interventions, whatever their type, are real themselves and work systematically to affect the client's extralinguistic behavior, as well as his linguistic productions. In short, therapy really or truly helps people change real (independent of the knower) thoughts, feelings, and actions, including how and what they *say*, that is, narrate, about those thoughts, feelings, and actions.

CONCLUDING COMMENT

The three modestly realist systems of therapy (with built-in research programs) that I have proposed reflect my serious attention to narrative therapists' own modestly realist claims about the therapeutic workings of language. I proposed those three systems to suggest some possible ways to make therapy systems with the emphasis on language found in the narrative therapy movement more complete systems (and also more specified or particularized systems)[20] than the ones we now tend to find within that movement. Only then can the practice of therapy guided by them be more systematic. Note, however, that none of the proposed systems is fully complete in that none contains all three (A B C) component parts. Also note that the second two (matrix) proposed systems are more likely to produce an individualized practice than the first (generic) proposed system. In any case, in each of the proposed systems the reader will find that I take for granted that there are indeed contributions to be made to the practice of therapy by attending to the way language gets used in therapy, as the narrative therapy movement has ardently professed.

But unlike that movement, I believe those contributions can be made only if we accept the use of language in a more realist way than narrative therapists now want to accept. (In this chapter, then, the realism/antirealism debate does indeed meet up with the individuality/systematic dilemma.) Therefore, I began and end my description of these three proposed systems with a very general proposal: that narrative therapists explicitly acknowledge the modest realism that implicitly permeates their own theorizing, regardless of the system they ultimately adopt.

CHAPTER 8

Ethical and Other Practical Implications of Postmodern Antirealism in Therapy

Questions about the ethics of therapy and the reality/nature of therapist expertise are now commonplace in the literature of postmodern narrative/social constructionist therapy (e.g., Anderson & Goolishian, 1988, 1992; Atkinson, 1992, 1993; Atkinson & Heath, 1990; Hare-Mustin, 1994; Hoffman, 1990; Nichols, 1993; Simon, 1992; Solovey & Duncan, 1992). There are good reasons for the appearance of these questions: the antirealist tendency of the movement calls into question the very existence—the reality—of ethics in therapy, just as it questions the accessibility and sometimes the very existence of any extralinguistic reality; and the antisystematic aspiration of the movement calls into question both the nature and the existence of expertise in therapy. It is obvious, moreover, that it is often impossible to separate questions about ethics from questions about expertise, so much so that it would seem that it is unethical—or so I argue—to take up at least one position about expertise that we shall be looking at in the course of this chapter.

In the previous chapters of this book I emphasized the failure of the postmodern narrative therapy movement to achieve theoretical consistency because of its oscillation between realism and antirealism, an oscillation brought about by its attempts to solve the individuality/systematic problem. In this final chapter I turn my attention to the ethical and other practical consequences of this complex theoretical issue.[1]

ETHICS IN THERAPY

Truth vs. Lies in Antirealist Therapies

The problem of conscious/intentional deceit. If we take the antirealism of the postmodern narrative therapy movement seriously, an ethical question at once leaps out at us: if there is no objective, independent truth to be known about anything, how can there be any lies told—either by therapists or by clients—in the practice of therapy? Since my focus in this chapter is on the ethics of doing therapy, let us confine that question to the telling of truth or lies on the part of the therapist. Let us also agree to accept the definition of a lie that Bok (1989) provides in her now famous book *Lying*—"an intentionally deceptive message in the form of a *statement*" (p. 15). The "intention to mislead" (p. 8) is important for Bok's definition and for this discussion; an agent who unwittingly communicates an untruth can hardly be put in the same moral boat as one who intentionally does so.

Duncan and his colleagues (Duncan, Solovey, & Rusk, 1992; Solovey & Duncan, 1992), who consider the ethics of therapy in the context of a constructivist, or antirealist, epistemology, call for the elimination of all "conscious deceit" in therapy. That is a reasonable request, and I know of no therapist who would endorse the conscious or intentional use of lies to help a client achieve his goal, no matter how important or virtuous it seemed.[2] Duncan and his colleagues provide a typical postmodern/social constructionist answer to the question how one can profess to speak only the truth if one believes we have no access to any single, independent truth. They claim that because there are many "truths" or "representations of reality" available in any therapy or life situation (note the language of pluralism here), the therapist need only select the one she finds to be a good fit for any particular set of circumstances, that is, the one that she believes to be a *possible* explanation for the client's difficulties.

But in order to select an explanation that is possible because it fits the client's particular life circumstances, the therapist must appeal to—must know—something about the client's life circumstances—something that he believes to be true about those circumstances. The members of the Duncan group have no problem with that requirement, and are again perfectly consistent with social constructionist thinking when they appeal to the client's personal "meaning system" and the "facts" of the case as the data upon which to base one's selection of an explanation. To quote them directly,

> From a constructivist viewpoint, theoretical language and content are somewhat arbitrary metaphorical representations [i.e., "views of reality rather than undeniable truths" (p. 55)] which explain and organize the therapist's reality. . . . This perspective permits selective ascription of meaning without a belief in the inherent truth of the selected meaning *across* situations [note the antigeneral, and hence antisystematic thrust]. The therapist need only believe in the selected meaning's applicability in the specific context in which it is used. This

implication, however, does not afford the freedom to say anything at all to clients and remain ethical (or even credible) [note the similarity to the social constructionist aphorism "not just anything goes"], nor does it allow a therapist to concoct or impose meaning in a haphazard fashion with no regard for its ramifications. (Solovey & Duncan, 1992, p. 55)

Duncan et al. clarify the "ethical responsibility" that accompanies the "freedom to select meaning" afforded by the adoption of a constructivist epistemology:

First, the selected meaning must satisfy the criterion of honest representation; that is, the therapist must believe that the selected meaning is a *plausible* and *credible* explanation of the client's circumstance. . . . The selected meaning must also be congruent with the client's stated meaning system, as well as fit the "facts" of the situation. The therapist should attempt to match the client's beliefs, values, and the emotional context associated with the presenting problem. (Duncan, Solovey, & Rusk, 1992, p. 219)

Here we find the by-now-familiar realist/antirealist oscillation that characterizes the narrative (social-constructionist) therapy movement, even though Duncan and his colleagues do not call themselves by that name. First, note the familiar but paradoxical postmodern/social-constructionist/constructivist call to believe but yet not to believe one's particular case formulations, or explanations (cf. Omer & Strenger, 1992; Sluzki, 1992; Spence, 1982). But there is also for Duncan's group (as for Sluzki, Omer and Strenger, and Spence) equivocation about the need to believe the claims about how therapy *in general* works, that is, claims about the underlying theoretical system itself, as distinct from a particular case formulation. That too, according to Duncan, should apparently be believed, but not too much. Second, note that although there allegedly are only multiple *views* of reality, there nonetheless are aspects of reality that the therapist can—and must—know in order to produce an explanation that is possible and credible in any particular case. In particular, the therapist is assumed to know (a) the meaning systems of clients as they really, independently exist, and (b) the "facts" or circumstances of the client's life—although the Duncan group's use of quotation marks around the word "facts" suggests that these authors are, like others we have encountered, equivocal about the reality of facts.

To permit knowledge of (a) and (b) without the contradiction introduced by the authors' simultaneous appeal to a constructivist/antirealist doctrine, Duncan and his colleagues disavow the common antirealist definition of constructivism found in narrative therapy circles:

Constructivism, not in the radical sense, but in the common sense variety applied to therapy, does not deny the existence of objects, events, or experiences, but rather provides a challenging commentary on the relative and context-bound nature of meanings ascribed to those objects, events, and experiences by an observer. (Duncan et al., 1992, pp. 13–14)

Note that although an independent reality allegedly *exists*, the knower cannot, true to antirealism, *know* that reality as it exists, independent of the knower. A page earlier in their same book, Duncan and his colleagues provide that common, antirealist definition of constructivism:

The philosophical position of constructivism and social construction theory from psychology (Gergen, 1985) both suggest that reality develops phenomenologically, emerging from the constructs of the observer-describer and his or her interaction with the environment. Reality is therefore invented, not discovered (Watzlawick, 1984) and is evident only through the constructed meanings that shape and organize experience. (pp. 12–13)

Thus, in both of these typically antirealist versions of constructivism, all knowledge of reality is alleged to be mediated by language/meanings which alter or shape in experience its true, independent nature. Nonetheless, for Duncan, Solovey, and Rusk (1992), the therapist, in addition to knowing (a) and (b) as they really, independently, exist, can also apparently know (c) "the client's beliefs, values, and the emotional context associated with the presenting problem" (p. 219), not to mention knowledge of the presenting problem itself, and not least of all knowledge of (d) the theoretical system Duncan et al. try to persuade us to adopt.

Duncan and his colleagues are worthy of our attention not because they are particularly extreme in their epistemological oscillation, for they are rather typical in that regard. But they are exemplary in their struggle to confront directly the problem of truth as it pertains to the ethics of therapy in the context of a doctrine—constructivism—that is thoroughly antirealist, however much they (sometimes) disclaim that antirealism. They are also important because, in their struggle to arrive at an ethical antirealist therapy, they distinguish between particular case formulations and the general theoretical systems that underlie them. But there is a simpler remedy for the oscillatory ailment that afflicts them and other therapists within the constructivist/constructionist (i.e., antirealist) camp: simply concede or accept the necessity of allowing direct (theoretically unmediated) knowledge of some aspects of reality—even if that directly knowable reality is limited to the client's personal meanings and the therapist's theoretical system.

The problem of unconscious (self) deceit. If therapists agree that we should not consciously or intentionally deceive our clients, it follows that they ought to agree that we should not deceive ourselves. Although the definition of self-deception is by no means a simple one,[3] it must include the principle that the deception of the self is in some way unconscious or unintentional—hence, self-"deception" cannot be defined by way of bad intentions. I raise the issue of self-deception here because I fear that it may be implicit in the pervasive acceptance of a constructivist or antirealist doctrine within psychotherapy. That possible "self-deceit," in my experience, takes the explicit form of what I consider to be simulated or excessive humility on the part of therapists. By simulated humility I mean nothing more than a failing (or reluctance) to acknowledge *to ourselves* what we *actually do believe* to be the case about how best to go about helping people solve their problems—that is, how best to be truly useful to others, or at least useful enough to deserve payment.

I suspect that a form of "self-deception" may be taking place when postmodern narrative or constructionist/constructivist therapists disavow—in the name of "humility" about the limits of knowing—the truth, or reality, claims they themselves make, believe, promote, and try to persuade others to adopt. For instance, Sluzki exhibits this mental sleight-of-hand when he, apparently aware of the impending contradiction, speaks of the social constructionist doctrine: "Our social world is constituted in and through a network of multiple stories or narratives (the 'story' that our social world is constructed in or through multiple stories or narratives being one of them)" (1992, pp. 218–219). In other words, the claims of the postmodern narrative movement are just another antirealist "story" that we should believe enough to use in therapy, but not believe too much.

Efran and Clarfield (1992, p. 201) also show such "humility" when they ask that constructivist claims be regarded as nothing more than personal or subjective "preferences" or shared "opinions," which everyone, they argue, must be allowed to have without being accused of having made a contradictory reality claim. Unfortunately, they do not then go on to tell us how we can distinguish mere personal preference, or even social/consensual opinion, from truth/knowledge—a situation especially troubling in a profession that purports to help others in a way that merits real payment.

Recall that others within the constructivist/constructionist camp, for instance, Omer and Strenger (1992), Duncan, Solovey, and Rusk (1992),

Spence (1982), have also asked therapists to believe—yet not believe—their case formulations and the entire system of therapy that guides their particular case formulations. Yet my quotations of those authors reveal how hard they must work to convince themselves, if not us, that they do not believe what they in fact believe—and do not know what in fact they do know—about the process and the content of therapy. I call this "believe but don't believe" maneuver a "failing (or reluctance) to acknowledge" to themselves rather than a pretense because I do not believe the mental gymnastics required to make it are done with the conscious intent to deceive. Rather, I think they are done out of an unarticulated need to avoid the impending contradiction whose half-felt presence discomforts those who have adopted postmodern antirealism but who nonetheless wish to speak with conviction or authority about the human condition. But to avoid that contradiction therapists must expend much energy to convince themselves that they do not believe what they actually do believe, or that they do not know what they actually do know about reality. We saw those oscillatory efforts in the quotations of Chapter 5. Being an antirealist is apparently no easy occupation.

If the realist/antirealist oscillation so typical of postmodern narrative therapy (see Chapter 5) does not reflect any intent on the part of those therapists to deceive clients or themselves about what they truly believe to be the case about therapy, they at least reflect an unintended—that is, unconscious—attempt to deny (a) what we truly know about an independent reality, and (b) what we truly believe about the knowability of an independent reality. This includes, in its most modest form, the direct knowability of (a) some entities and events themselves—certainly here and now entities and events that we can observe as they exist or occur—and meanings about those current and past events in the client's life, and (b) the theoretical system of therapy in use.

A healthy skepticism about whether any therapy system (or scientific theory) can survive unaltered over time in no way subverts the direct access to those temporospatial and nontemporospatial aspects of reality that primary and secondary (direct) rational awareness, respectively, have always afforded us, and that narrative therapists, like scientists, rely upon both to construct their theoretical system and to make their case for the truth of its claims. To be sure, we cannot have direct access to all aspects of reality. For instance, knowledge of causal connections between events requires indirect or inferential knowing by way of constructed theories that may not, in the final analysis, turn out to be adequate to the reality under investigation. But that fact does not mean we should deny the direct access to those aspects of reality that we do have and usually take for granted. It is precisely that denial that is endemic to—indeed, defines—postmodern narrative therapy in particular, and postmodernism in general.

What in all this concerns the ethical issues particular or unique to psychotherapy? First, therapists must practice what they preach. If narrative therapists really or truly believe that stories/narratives affect all clients' perceptions of options and solutions, and in so doing affect behavior, then they must take their own story about that effect seriously, that is, without the equivocation and disclaimers (the "self-deception") that now accompany that claim. But if narrative therapists are really or truly serious about their antirealism, that is, if they really or truly believe that narrative therapy has no real, objective effects, then at least two problems emerge. The first is accepting real, objective money, be it from clients themselves or their third-party payers, for an antirealist activity, that is, one in which the therapist finds no extralinguistic or independent truth. (We shall return to that problem in the final subsection of this first section, "Ethical Implications of the Conception of Therapist Expertise in Antirealist Therapies.")

The second problem is one that I myself have heard mentioned only once, by Gergen (1991b) no less, who (I think) is himself not a therapist but who has nonetheless promoted a most extreme antirealism both in the articulation of his own social constructionism (1985) and in that doctrine's application to therapy (Gergen & Kaye, 1992). But that problem is a serious one, and Gergen must be commended for pointing it out. It is this: if narrative therapists are truly antirealists (and so not engaged in what I myself would call "self-deception" about their antirealism), then isn't it wrong or problematic for a narrative therapist to help a client co-construct a new narrative, or story, that the therapist takes to be antirealist but then allows, if not encourages, the client to take to be the objective truth or reality about his life?

I find that question to be a highly compelling one, yet I know of no narrative therapist who has raised it. I also know of no reactions to it in the narrative therapy literature. I find this shocking, since the ethical implications of Gergen's question are profound. For Gergen may be suggesting that therapists who claim we have no access whatever to any independent reality—that is, antirealist therapists, which is what postmodern narrative therapists claim to be—are consciously deceiving their clients if they do not teach their clients that the new co-constructed story, like the old one, is thoroughly subjective or antirealist: it has no objective reality or truth in it. Despite the fact that I myself am a realist, I find much merit in Gergen's concern.

Of course, Gergen's solution to this ethical dilemma is an antirealist one, and so it of necessity opposes mine. Whereas I ask narrative therapists to accept the realism which I find in their position but which they deny, Gergen asks that narrative/social constructionist therapists literally teach their clients to *be* antirealists. This is not done merely to achieve a higher standard of ethics, although Gergen appears concerned with that. Rather, it is done because Gergen seems really or truly to believe that teaching clients to adopt an antirealist epistemology is the surest route to mental health. (Note the realism implicit in that claim.) Let us consider these closing remarks of his, some of which we first encountered in Chapter 4 (p. 128) and Chapter 5 (p. 143).

> [A]ttention must be drawn . . . to the role that can be played in therapy by the exploration of experience from multiple perspectives, by sensitizing another to the relational context in which behavior is situated, and by a thorough *relativizing* [italics in original] of experience. . . .
>
> These are but a few examples [see Chapter 4, p. 128] of means by which people can be enabled to construct things from different viewpoints, thus liberating them from the oppression of limiting narrative beliefs and relieving the resulting pain. In this way those turning to us in times of trouble may come to transcend the restraints imposed by their erstwhile reliance on a determinate set of meanings and be freed from the struggle than [sic] ensues from imposing their beliefs on self and others. For some, new solutions to problems will become apparent, while for others a richer set of narrative meanings will emerge. *For still others a stance toward meaning itself will evolve; one which betokens that tolerance of uncertainty, that freeing of experience which comes from acceptance of unbounded relativity of meaning.* . . . [italics added] (Gergen & Kaye, 1992, p. 183)

Of course, that new "stance toward meaning itself," to which clients must be sensitized and shifted, is nothing short of antirealism itself.

To be sure, there is a more moderate solution to Gergen's dilemma. It is the one we have seen expressed by those who themselves seem more tentative than Gergen about the antirealism of social constructionism and postmodernism. Instead of explicitly teaching clients that there *is* no truth, which is what Gergen evidently proposes, Duncan (Duncan et al., 1992; Solovey & Duncan, 1992), Atkinson (1992), and Simon (1992),[4] for example, recommend that therapists be honest (humble) about the limitations of their own knowledge by putting their particular case formulations, their case narratives, to their clients as (tentative) hypotheses or opinions based on their own informed views. As Duncan et al. (1992) state, "An honest tentativeness in presentation of the meaning [i.e., of possible explanations in therapy] permits the client to understand that the therapist is not absolutely certain of the meaning's applicability, as well as allows the client the freedom to disagree" (p. 219). Atkinson (1992) is explicit about his ethical stance given what I take to be his own social constructionism,

> Simon's [1992] paper has stimulated me to attempt to clarify more specifically what I believe is required of constructivist or social constructionist therapists who intend to be straightforward in sharing their ideas and suggestions with clients. . . . Therapists should be careful to present their views as their opinions, not objective facts, and avoid words like "obviously" or "clearly." . . . Therapists should invite each client to evaluate the therapists' ideas based on how sensible they are to the client, not based on how authoritative or confident therapists seem to be. (p. 390)

Several comments about these suggestions may be made. First, as a practicing clinician and a realist, I have no problem with a tentative or modest view of the case formulations we present to clients and for which we have at best only inconclusive or limited evidence. After all, the therapist as well as the client may have direct knowledge of any particular act the client engages in (e.g., not adhering to his commitments), but they can only speculate about, that is, derive theories that give us at best indirect knowledge of, the causes and effects of those acts. To be sure, the theories can be tested informally, as I discussed in Chapter 6. But they cannot be tested formally/scientifically, and so it is only right—only realistic—that we remain tentative, open to revision, about that which we cannot know directly. That fact, however, does not commit the knower to antirealism/social constructionism, since, recall, the theories that give us indirect knowledge are always constructed on the basis of what can be known directly.

Note that both Duncan et al. and Atkinson feel the client should be invited to disagree with the therapist's formulations. In Atkinson's case, that disagreement should be based on what seems "sensible" to the client. Surely what seems sensible has to do, at least in part, with aspects of reality that the client knows directly, aspects that therefore provide components of the causal explanation, the theory, that the therapist and client are working to construct to make sense of the problem. For instance, the client can know directly, and can report to the therapist directly, that she has not completed all her assignments in a series of jobs, and that in each new job, after failing to complete her assignments for several weeks, she is fired. Neither the therapist nor the client can know directly, and so both can only infer by way of theory, that it is the failure to complete assignments, and not some other factor/event, that is actually causing the series of job losses that has brought this client into therapy.

That last illustration brings me to my second comment about the suggestion to be tentative in therapy. It is this: we must distinguish between a theoretical formulation—a causal explanation or account—the therapist devises for a *particular* case (hence my use of the term "case formulation"), and the theoretical system, with all *its* causal accounts, that the therapist has adopted in practice for *general* use across cases. In the case of the Duncan group at least, that theoretical system of therapy fits within (but is not identical with) what I have been calling the narrative therapy movement: those authors endorse the narrative therapy claim that changing meanings in therapy can cause the experience of new options, which can result in new actions. (They also, importantly enough, claim that change can work the other way around—from new behavior/actions to new meanings.) Thus, whereas they may be honestly tentative about the theory/story they tell a particular client to explain her particular or unique behavior, they cannot be honestly tentative, or at least not *so* honestly tentative, about the theory/ story they tell themselves and others about the real workings of change—of therapy itself—in general. In short, two different levels of uncertainty are operating here. Perhaps the confusion between these two levels of explanation again has to do with the discomfort of acknowledging the creation and use of a real theoretical system, with real causal claims or propositions, in the context of an intellectual climate—social constructionism/antirealism/post-modernism—that tries to be both antisystematic and antirealist.

But even if we accept the Duncan group's and Atkinson's solution to the problem of therapist authority and conviction, we are faced with another problem we considered in the previous chapter. What if conviction about the soundness of one's therapeutic interventions—whatever their type—indeed turns out to be a necessary (common factor) component of all therapeutic change? Recall that Frank (1973, 1987), among others, has spoken of the provision of hope as a key ingredient in all therapy cases. Can a tentative therapist, one who does not truly believe in his theoretical formulations, act in a way that elevates a despairing client's level of hope? To answer that question, we must once again keep in mind the distinction between a theoretical formulation for a particular case, that is, a case formulation, and the theoretical system that a therapist uses to guide therapy across all cases, in general. It seems clear to me that Gergen, in all his extreme antirealism, and the Duncan group, in their more moderate version of antirealism, truly

believe the basic claims of the narrative therapy movement's system of therapy—a theoretical system that informs all their cases. So they are on firm
footing with regard to conveying conviction about that underlying theory, to
the extent that they manage or want to do so in therapy.[5]

Ironically, however, Gergen's extreme antirealism may produce better effects in therapy than Duncan's and Atkinson's more moderate position on the
truth of case formulations or causal accounts given to a particular client. It
seems the latter therapists would like to give the best, most true account they
can, but feel they must be honest about the limits of their realism/knowledge.
But that very honesty must compromise the amount of conviction they can
convey to clients, and so it may compromise what makes therapy work.
Gergen, by contrast, has no such problem. He seems to think there is no
truer or falser account in the first place, because he more fully than the others
believes we cannot know *any* independent reality. That is, he appears more
radical or extreme in his antirealism than the others. But he also believes that
teaching clients to be "thoroughgoing relativists," or antirealists, like himself,
really or truly lifts their "oppression and pain," to use his own words. So he
can convey to clients all the conviction needed for therapeutic, hope-inducing
purposes because he is convinced and can, if pushed, say without qualification
that he is convinced that it is perfectly true that we cannot know anything
real, and that that state of affairs is moreover good, that is, it is a *therapeutic*
reality. The problem with all this, however, is that in Gergen's conviction
there lurks an implicit claim about what in life really or truly causes problems
(namely, being a realist) and what really or truly causes solutions (namely,
being an antirealist).

There is, however, another problem with Gergen's radical position. Gerrig
(1993), in his book *Experiencing Narrative Worlds: On the Psychological Activities of Reading*, uses cognitive psychology findings to support his claim that
any narrative that engages the reader—whether factual or fictitious—can, by
"transporting" her to the "narrative world," have effects on the reader's "real-
world" attitudes, beliefs, and even behaviors. Gerrig supplies solid research to
show that fiction has the same effects on readers as nonfiction, *so long as the
reader does not expend explicit, or intentional, effort to understand the fiction as only
fictional* (p. 240). Once the reader does that, argues Gerrig, the real-world
effects of the narrative are eliminated.

How does this finding apply to Gergen's claim? On the one hand, it
supports Gergen's, and the narrative therapy movement's, antirealist contention that nonrealist stories (i.e., fiction) can affect real-world human understanding and behavior. But on the other hand, it suggests that if people are

explicitly taught or told or led to understand a story as merely fiction – which is, after all, what Gergen apparently wants therapists explicitly to teach clients about their own and all life stories – then that effect on real-world attitudes, beliefs, and behaviors vanishes. For people in the real world, the distinction between fact and fiction is evidently an important one, with real consequences.

Help vs. Harm in Antirealist Therapies

It is practically impossible to discuss the question of what constitutes help and harm in antirealist therapies without discussing the related question of what constitutes therapist expertise, which I consider in the next section. It is also evident to me that one cannot speak of help and harm in therapy without providing a discussion of human nature/existence itself (ontology), and what constitutes good and bad in human existence (ethics) – the very stuff postmodern narrative therapists hope to avoid when pursuing their antisystematic aspirations.[6] Given the history and scope of these topics, I shall not try to address them here. Rather, I limit myself to one question of central concern to the antirealist position in therapy: on what basis should we select theories for use in therapy, if no theory is more or less true (or *inherently* better) than any other?

Gergen (1985), again speaking about matters of theory construction and use in general, makes a postmodern/social constructionist argument that I find particularly troublesome. In brief, he claims that since (a) theories can never give us any independent, or extratheoretic, reality, and since (b) the belief that some theories are true has consequences that are usually negative for – that are oppressive of – many, (c) we should therefore select theories solely on the basis of their effects or consequences, that is, their utility, and not on the basis of their (independent) truth status. This argument sounds strikingly like the one we see promoted in the postmodern narrative therapy movement: therapists should construct and/or select theories that have a beneficial effect on the client's life. They therefore should not oppress clients by imposing ones that are put forth as the unitary truth.

To quote Gergen again,

Unlike the moral relativism of the empiricist tradition, constructionism reasserts the relevance of moral criteria for scientific practice. To the extent that psychological theory (and related practices) enter into the life of the culture, sustaining certain patterns of conduct and destroying others, such work must be evaluated in terms of good and ill. The practitioner can no longer justify any socially reprehensible conclusion on the grounds of being a "victim of the facts"; he or she must confront the pragmatic implications of such conclusions within society more generally. (1985, p. 273)

The discerning reader will immediately see a problem leap out at her, namely, how we can know the real effects, the actual pragmatic implications, of our actions—be they good or bad effects, helpful or harmful—in the context of a philosophy that denies our access to *any* independent truth? That problem is simply another variation of the contradiction I have worked to illuminate in the course of this book. But apart from the problem of *knowing* from an antirealist perspective whether a client is being helped or harmed— knowing the pragmatic consequences of one's theories—there is the funda- mental problem of *who* decides, and by what criteria *anyone* decides, what constitutes help vs. harm in the therapy relationship.

Most narrative/social constructionist therapists say it is the client who decides for himself what the goals of therapy are (i.e., what the content of therapy should be, which must never be predetermined), and therefore whether he is being helped or harmed in the therapeutic process. Thus, the client is the expert about his own life (e.g., Anderson & Goolishian, 1988; Duncan et al., 1992), a position that has some good common sense (and so some truth) in it. But as we have seen in the course of this book, therapists cannot—indeed, if they want to be called experts, should not—be completely neutral about the nature of problems (Component C) and their causes (Com- ponent A), and hence the goals of therapy—that is, its content. Recall from Chapter 3 that in adopting a theory of problem resolution to guide the intervention process, therapists automatically define something, however gen- eral, about what the object or target—the content—of that (intervention) process should be. There is, moreover, the problem of clients who engage in behavior which is not necessarily seen as problematic by the client herself, but which the therapist finds problematic—that is, harmful to the client's self or to others. Even therapists who aspire to place therapeutic content com- pletely in the hands of the client have limits in those cases, and with good reason. As Duncan, Solovey, and Rusk (1992) themselves state,

> There are several somewhat extreme, but obvious, situations that preclude elevating the client's meaning system and not insisting upon the validity of the therapist's point of view. Examples include sexual abuse, any act of violence, or involuntary hospitalization. (p. 229)

It seems that the reality of at least those extreme situations conflicts with the antireality of constructivism.

I want here to inspect more closely the harm potentially brought about by those who take the antirealist agenda most seriously in therapy—for instance, those, like Gergen, who exalt antirealism to the point of advocating that we literally teach clients to *be* antirealists in their own lives, by helping them to recognize the nonsubstantial, evanescent, now-you-see-it-now-you-don't quality of all aspects of being. Gergen (1991a) focuses particular attention on the nonsubstantial, evanescent, *unreal* nature of the "self," which for most postmodernists pops in and out of being as a function of ever-changing linguistic/interpersonal contexts. This fast and loose, "playful" stance vis-à-vis the self may work perfectly well for clients who already have some good sense of who and what they are (and are not) in life. But as Glass (1993) warns us in his book *Shattered Selves*, that stance can actually damage those who suffer from forms of mental illness—schizophrenia or multiple personality disorder, for instance—that deprive the individual of what each of us not so afflicted can playfully afford to take for granted. For clients suffering from real, intractable (i.e., stable, enduring) disorders or problems, there is no reason to assume that an antirealist theory or approach to therapy (which is inconsistently taken to be true or truly/really helpful) will be any less oppressive or harmful than an incorrect realist theory that is taken to be true. Incidentally, my critical view of adopting a playful attitude in the face of serious matters is hardly original, as these lines, attributed by Plutarch to the third century B.C. (minor) philosopher Bion, make clear: "Boys throw stones at frogs for fun, but the frogs don't die for 'fun,' but in sober earnest" (Bion, cited in Plutarch, *Moralia*).[7]

Let us conclude this section with a comment about the relationship between truth and morality itself. Pols (1992b) has argued that it is immoral not to seek the truth to the best of our ability. The fact that there are limits to that quest does not mean the quest should be abandoned. Nowhere is this admonition more pertinent than in the enterprise we call therapy, where our task is nothing less than helping to alleviate real pain and suffering, so that people can lead better lives. I therefore believe that it is our moral obligation as therapists to seek, as best we can, the truth about human nature, including the truth about what causes and alleviates the psychological problems to which life gives rise. To say or (as I have put it) to propound, as do postmodernists on some occasions, that there is no truth whatever to be had in that pursuit—or that the pursuit of truth is itself oppressive—is in my view a form of "self-deception" with grave moral consequences, however unintended it may be. It also undermines the very idea of real or true therapist expertise.

Ethical Implications of the Conception of
Therapist Expertise in Antirealist Therapies

There is much discussion about the nature of therapist expertise now taking place within the literature of those therapies that have been swayed by postmodern antirealism/constructionism. Not surprisingly, that discussion has fixed itself on a struggle to define expertise, authority, knowledge and so on for therapists working in a theoretical climate that equates truth with power and oppression, and so rejects all that smacks of power, authority, hierarchy, and indeed, truth itself. The solutions to that dilemma, which are sometimes informed by feminist thinking, usually involve minimizing the predetermined content the therapist brings to therapy (to maximize individuality), and limiting the intrusiveness of his "intervention" process (so as not to abuse his power). (I put the term "intervention" in quotes because that idea, which connotes authority of some sort on the part of the therapist, is objectionable to many therapists working within a postmodern climate.)

In place of those unacceptable behaviors, postmodern/social constructionist therapists have been asked to take "not knowing" positions about their clients (Anderson & Goolishian, 1988), to be self-monitoring and self-revealing so as not to impose or intrude upon the client in hierarchical ways (Atkinson, 1993; Hoffman, 1993), to be more intuitive than deliberate in their therapy practice (Atkinson, 1992; Atkinson & Heath, 1990; Hoffman, 1990). Many within the postmodern narrative therapy movement also agree that therapists should be "experts" only in the sense of being "master conversational artists" (Anderson & Goolishian, 1988, p. 384). They should therefore follow Rorty's call to "keep the conversation going," without predetermining or directing by virtue of their "expertise" the content of that conversation. In short, they should be experts in (therapeutic) conversational process, but not content—an impossible task, as I pointed out in Chapter 3.

None of these ideas is necessarily wrong or bad in certain therapeutic contexts (although I know of no way to be deliberately nondeliberate—a problem duly noted by Atkinson). But there is surely a contradiction to be faced by these authors when they attempt to deny or minimize the expertise that they also apparently want therapists to have—that therapists must indeed have to legitimate their activity as a profession/discipline. We therefore see, in the postmodern narrative therapy movement, an expertise/nonexpertise oscillation similar to its realist/antirealist oscillation. These two kinds of oscillation are by no means independent: if there is no truth or reality to be had, there can be no true or real expertise. In that case, the practice of therapy is truly individualized—in regard to both therapists and clients. But if therapy is fully individualized, it is also of necessity antisystematic, since the therapist then brings no (expert) system of therapy to all cases to guide her practice.[8] Therapy practiced in the absence of expertise is also, therefore, not a discipline, which by definition requires real expertise of some sort.

I do not believe the notion of a truly expert-free therapy is one any practicing therapist—modern or postmodern—would want to adopt explicitly; hence we find equivocation about therapist expertise in the context of postmodern antirealism. Nichols (1993), in his commentary on an article about the problem of therapist hierarchy, which he aptly titled "The Therapist as Authority Figure," evidently felt strongly enough about this equivocation to say what should have been obvious to all, but which evidently needed saying:

> [I]t's the therapist's separateness from the others and willingness to stand for something—to be an expert (not on life but on calling attention to what's going on)[9]—that enables him or her to function as the leader of the process of treatment. (p. 163)

> If arranging and hosting conversations were all that a therapist did, that person should be called a mediator, or the opposite of a talk-show host (whose aim is to arrange conversations that are nasty and abusive). The therapist as host neglects the role of teacher—a much maligned but essential aspect of any transformative therapy. Therapists teach not by telling people how to run their lives, but by helping them learn something about themselves. (p. 164)

Nichols continues,

> Are therapists and clients partners in a joint undertaking? Are they equals? No. Clients are, to paraphrase George Orwell, "more equal" when it comes to whose point of view ultimately counts. Therapists are, or should be, more equal when it comes to training, expertise, and objectivity—*and* taking the lead in what happens during the therapy hour. It's fine to criticize power—if what's meant by that is domination and control; it's not so fine to abdicate leadership. (p. 165)

Even those who try to minimize the predetermined content of therapy (Components A and C) to maximize individuality adhere in a realist sense to the general truth of their process of therapy (Component B)—that co-constructing new narratives or stories or meanings with all clients really or truly causes the alleviation of pain or problems. Not to believe at least that factor to be therapeutic on the basis of real, rational reasons is to liken therapy to mere hocus-pocus. And I know of no postmodern/narrative/constructionist therapist who claims that we co-construct new narratives in therapy because it somehow seems to help people solve their problems, but that we have no idea whatever why that is or might be the case; I know of no therapist who says this action is merely a pragmatic move with no theoretical rationale behind it that can be rationally articulated and assessed.

But of course, there is a rationale behind that pragmatic therapeutic behavior. It is called a system of therapy with a theory of problem causation (A), a definition of problems in general (C), and a theory-cum-method of problem resolution (B). The system is real as a theoretical system and can be known directly (by secondary rational awareness) as such. It also makes claims about reality that can at least in theory be assessed under more or less systematic, controlled circumstances. All that is why we can take payment for what we do, including third-party payment. All that is why we can consider therapy to be either a science or an art but, in either case, a real discipline.

THERAPY AS AN ART VS. THERAPY AS AN APPLIED SCIENCE: THE DEBATE REVISITED

The debate about whether therapy should be understood as an art or as the application of principles derived from a scientific psychology is almost as old as the discipline of therapy itself. It is certainly as old as psychoanalysis, whose founder believed his creation to be nothing less than a new science. The theoretical and empirical research efforts of the technical/systematic eclectic therapy movement have now been in place for some 25 years, and the scientific investigation of psychotherapy process and outcome has a good half century behind it. My aim in this section is not to rehash the debate about whether therapy is a science or an art, but to consider the implications of postmodern antirealism for that question.

As I stated in the previous section, both science and art are disciplines. *Webster's* defines a discipline as "a system of rules or methods." That definition is very broad. But it is precise enough to tell us that any enterprise which claims status as a discipline, as does therapy, must have something systematic about it. One cannot be a scientist and function in just any way. The same goes for artists, even revolutionary/modern or postrevolutionary/postmodern artists. In either case, science or art, there are traditions/theories/methods and so forth to be learned; there are always constraints on one's efforts. To be sure, we can change or abandon what does not suit our purposes, but we cannot do so freely without consequence for our standing in whatever scientific or artistic communities we wish to locate ourselves. Although some may disagree, even modern and "postmodern" artists have standards for admittance into their territory.

I shall not attempt here to undertake anything so monumental as a definition of science and of art. I want instead to make one fundamental distinction. Science purports to get at an independent reality, to eliminate the subjectivity of the scientist or knower to the fullest extent possible. Although (linguistic) philosophers speak of antirealist or postmodern science as building nothing more than antirealist/subjective theoretical systems—i.e., systems with no extratheoretic or extralinguistic truth, scientists themselves, as the quotation in Chapter 6 of the physicist J. Polkinghorne reminds us, view their enterprise as nothing less than realist every step of the way. As for art, that too may tell us something true, either about the artist, or the world, or both. In any event, subjectivity in that enterprise is no problem; indeed it is not only accepted but usually exalted. Even in that latter case, however, there are real objective standards to which any aspiring artist must adhere, no matter what her school, movement, or philosophical persuasion.

We are now in a position to consider the point I wish to make in this section. The antisystematic aspirations of the postmodern narrative therapy movement are also antiscientific. One cannot be systematic, controlled, and so scientific in one's investigations of reality if one refuses to put forth one's view of reality as a rational claim about how something in reality works, an effort that is nothing less than the construction of a theoretical system that is open to empirical test. Fortunately, as I demonstrated in Chapters 4, 5, and 7, the postmodern narrative therapy movement's antisystematic aspirations have not been fully realized: narrative therapists have managed despite themselves to put forth at least a set of claims about the way therapy actually works, if not a complete and comprehensive theoretical system. But these claims may nonetheless be put to some empirical test—one which contains direct observations that are in no way mediated by the theoretical claims being tested (see Chapter 6). How controlled and rigorous that test can possibly be is a question all psychotherapy research has struggled with, and the typical answer to that question given by researchers, namely, "not as much as we would like," is surely the reason many consider therapy to be an art. Those who take the therapy-as-art position therefore argue that we simply cannot categorize types of clients/problems, types of therapists, and types of therapies or interventions consistently, or reliably, enough to control our variables for scientific purposes, nor should we seek to do so.

The therapy-as-art proponents usually appeal to the uniqueness of each and every therapy client/situation to make their antisystematic/antiscientific case: any phenomenon that is found to be completely unique in each and every instance, and so is ever changing, does not allow any generalizations to be derived from the observation of it. But science requires the construction and testing of theoretical systems that are composed of general rules or propositions based on our observations of some aspect of the world. To the extent that those rules hold up under empirical scrutiny, they may be applied in different contexts: for instance, the application of the rules of the narrative therapy movement (e.g., co-construct a new narrative to solve problems) in all therapy cases. There is that old tradeoff again: a therapy practice that is completely individualized vs. one that is systematic. Antiscientific, therapy-as-art proponents—a category that comprises many if not most postmodern therapists, among others—want to advocate the individuality side of that tradeoff, and so they are compelled to argue that therapy must be viewed as an art form. For them, there is no alternative.

But there is an often overlooked twist to that argument. If the practice of therapy is too individualized and antisystematic to be a scientific enterprise, it may be too individualized and antisystematic to be an artistic enterprise as well. If art of any sort is a discipline, and therapy is a particular type of artistic discipline, then by definition there must be some order, regularity, organization—that is, something systematic—in its realization. Omer (1993, 1994) is surely responding to this controversy when he calls upon us to consider therapy to be a "craft."

I now turn once again to Spence's (1982) valiant struggle along these lines, because I believe he best reveals the daunting difficulties therapists face when we try to solve the individuality/systematic dilemma by construing therapy as an art rather than a science. First, let us consider the anti-rule-governed, antisystematic side of his struggle, in which he equates therapy with art:

> If validation seems out of reach, how do we arrive at a general theory? The answer may be a long time coming—because of the particular nature of narrative truth. If interpretations are creative rather than veridical . . . , then we may

be faced with a glaring absence of general rules. . . . If the impact of a particular interpretation is contingent . . . on the specific texture of time and place, the rules for it being true are just as much out of reach as the rules for any other kind of artistic masterpiece. (pp. 292–293)

Spence then goes on to discuss the consequences of there being "less established theory than we like to assume":

First, it makes each analyst even more alone than he is already; if there are almost no guidelines, then the risk of going wrong is sizably increased. If . . . an interpretation [is seen] as primarily a creative act, then the analyst, like it or not, is engaged in an artistic struggle with the patient and with all of his colleagues. Seen in this light, the impossible profession becomes even more so. (p. 294)

Our discoveries, in other words, may be highly situational and need to be understood in their immediate context; it would be a mistake to reduce them to some general law because, by doing so, we might lose the very ingredient that made them effective in the specific case.

In the hands of our most gifted colleagues, the discovery and creation of narrative truth may in fact operate so smoothly and so successfully that it appears lawful, giving the impression that our general theory is more advanced than is actually the case. (p. 295)

Again, we are left to wonder how any endeavor this antisystematic, this anti-rule-governed, this unique to every case, can be a discipline in any sense, artistic or scientific. But even if Spence is right about the uniqueness of the artistic struggle, he is, recall, not quite comfortable about abandoning entirely those more general, systematic aspects of analysis that allowed at least Freud to believe he was working in nothing less than a scientific tradition. A final quotation from Spence, the last paragraph of his important book *Narrative Truth and Historical Truth*, strikingly illustrates that struggle—a struggle, incidentally, with a great deal of realism behind it.

It may be time, once again, to reaffirm the tentative nature of our theory, thinking of it more as metaphor than established fact; to spend less time searching for confirmation (which is usually based on soft pattern matches) and more time accumulating data; and to begin to look at particular clinical events—events that come as close as possible to representing the original encounter of analyst and patient in all of its complexity [note the realism of direct rational awareness here]. As we learn the ways in which truth emerges from the psychoanalytic dialogue and leads to changes in understandings, we may slowly replace our metaphors with something more substantial and make a beginning toward formulating a *science of the mind* [italics added]. (pp. 296–297)[10]

Whether therapy is best understood as an art or as a science, two things are certain. First, it must function as a real discipline, that is with something systematic behind it that guides its practice toward desirable/therapeutic effects. To the extent that a system of therapy can, when used in practice, maximize individuality without eroding the basis for the existence of the discipline itself (i.e., its generality), so much the better. Second, the desirable/therapeutic effects of the discipline of therapy are real (and directly knowable in their reality). We should therefore not deprive our discipline either of systematic ways to enhance that reality or of that reality itself.

BACK TO REALITY: A CALL FOR A
MODEST REALISM IN PSYCHOTHERAPY

The problem of keeping the practice of therapy both individualized and systematic has been an organizing theme of this book. I have argued that the recent proliferation of postmodern narrative or social constructionist/constructivist therapies reflects an attempt to solve that very problem by virtue of an appeal to the antirealism that is central to the postmodern movement in general. But, as I have demonstrated throughout this book, the objective of an individualized yet systematic approach to therapy cannot be achieved by virtue of an appeal to antirealism of any sort. Rather, that objective requires a clearer understanding of the nature and use of theoretical systems in therapy — systems that are perfectly real and so directly knowable (by secondary rational awareness) as theoretical systems, and that also can in principle give us indirect knowledge of an independent, extratheoretic reality.

By way of the three modestly realist therapy systems outlined in Chapter 7, I hope to have convinced the reader that the narrative and eclectic therapy movements each have something to contribute toward finding ways to make the practice of therapy both individualized and systematic. Once more I emphasize my claim that both movements have some modest degree of realism in their background. That realism is usually just assumed or implicit in the matrix paradigm of the technical/systematic eclectic movement as it has traditionally been articulated. But, as I have demonstrated, there is both an implicit and sometimes an explicit realism within the narrative therapy movement as well. That realism is either denied in the context of the antirealism the narrative movement explicitly promotes or unwittingly expressed, and so it gives rise to the oscillation between realism and antirealism that exists within that movement's own narratives about itself.

The realism expressed within the postmodern narrative therapy movement consists in a set of quite general truth claims—claims that transcend the particularities of each unique client or therapy context. Those claims are nothing less than the narrative therapy movement's own modestly realist narrative or story about itself. It is simply this: the nature of the client's narrative is what keeps him stuck in a problem, discomfort, or difficulty in life. It is therefore necessary for narrative therapists to help the client co-construct or co-create a new narrative, by means of narrative interventions such as questioning and challenging the old narrative, in order to help the client get unstuck. In the narrative therapy literature, "unstuck" typically means "help the client perceive/experience new options in life, and then act on them." Hence, the narrative intervention is believed to change both (a) the linguistic aspects of the client's life—her narrative, which may or may not accurately reflect her true mental state, or her feelings, thoughts, and attitudes (which are themselves not always or clearly described in that movement to be *merely* linguistic); and (b) the extralinguistic aspects of the client's life—her behavior/actions apart from her narrative. [11]

Of course, social psychologists have known all along that narratives—factual or otherwise—can change the way people actually think and feel, which in turn may affect the way they actually act. Cognitive psychologists, as well as the cognitive/behavioral therapists we considered briefly in Chapter 7, are not uninterested in those effects either (e.g., Gerrig, 1993). But postmodernism by definition rejects any appeal to science that purports to get at the really real. And so it goes with the postmodern narrative therapy movement, which vehemently divorces itself from the research tradition and findings of a scientific psychology—a psychology that has searched for nothing less than what is true about human behavior/nature in its very broadest sense (e.g., Anderson & Goolishian, 1988). [12]

I have made much of the fact that a movement which puts so much stock in the internal coherence or consistency of a story (i.e., its "narrative truth") cannot itself produce one that is internally consistent. That failing is certainly not unique to the postmodern narrative therapy movement; it inheres in any discipline that adopts an antirealist doctrine and then tries to say something real or true about how some aspect of the world *is*. It therefore also inheres in postmodernism itself, which is, as I first stated in Chapter 1, defined by an antirealism of one sort or other.

Not surprisingly, my observations about this inconsistency in the narrative therapy movement's underlying philosophy have brought protest. One form of protest argues that we only know thoughts, feelings, and attitudes, if not actual actions, by virtue of what the client says (narrates) about them, and so we never leave the supposedly reality-altering effects on knowing of language in the first place. Although on first glance that seems a reasonable rebuttal, it is inadequate for two reasons: (a) First, it does not eliminate the fact that the narrative therapy movement makes clear reality claims about how therapeutic language itself really or truly works its beneficial effects on the linguistic productions (i.e., narratives) of clients. And recall Pols's argument that we can, after all, know linguistic propositions about the world (which are real as propositions whether they turn out to be true or false) just as directly as temporospatial objects in the world. Moreover, although clients may reveal their thoughts, feelings, and attitudes by virtue of what they say in life (again, those statements being directly observable as linguistic entities), we may also infer their feelings and attitudes by virtue of how they act or behave quite apart from the content of their linguistic utterances. For instance, vocal intonations, facial expressions, and body postures and movements may all contribute to a valid inference of an internal mental state. They may, in fact, easily contradict the content of what a client is saying about himself. For example, a client who says "I love you" while grimacing is in all probability not communicating the (whole) truth about his feelings. (b) Second, that rebuttal denies the *explicit* statements found in the narrative therapy literature that refer to an extralinguistic reality—refer, that is, to how therapeutic language really or truly works its effects ultimately on something more than the client's story.

Finally, a last word about my call for a modest realism in psychotherapy. That realism must be modest because although there are many things about the world we can know (either directly or indirectly), there are also many things about the world (including the world of therapy) we may have to go a very long time without knowing, if indeed we can ever know them at all. Nonetheless, I hope to have demonstrated in this book that all therapy systems, realist by admission or not, at least claim to tell us something real or true about what causes change, solutions, or the alleviation of problems or pain (Component B). Because those claims always contain some degree of generality, they must by definition transcend the particularities of each unique client/problem/context. They must therefore compromise individuality when used in practice, but they also provide a justification for the additional claim that the practice of therapy is itself systematic. In any event, because those claims are put forth as real or true—that is, independent of the knower—they purport to get at something that is not merely a local, linguistic creation on the part of some particular knower (constructivism) or some particular group of knowers (social constructionism).

To the extent that theories of problem resolution have implications for what has caused or is now maintaining the problem (e.g., if a new narrative gets us unstuck, the old narrative must be keeping us stuck), we may be able to say something real, however limited or modest, about problem causation/maintenance (Component A) as well. But theories of problem causation that are historical and etiological—that ask what caused the problem to begin with—are more problematic: we simply cannot have the direct knowledge of the past that we can potentially have about here and now events. The latter are events that clients can know directly in their daily lives, and that therapists can know directly in the therapy session either as an actual here and now client behavior (which is known by primary rational awareness) or as a client's report of his extratherapy behavior (which is known by secondary rational awareness).[13] Since theories, recall, are always constructed on the basis of some direct knowledge, we—both therapists and clients together—may not have *enough* direct knowledge of past events to formulate theories that can give us reasonably valid indirect (causal) knowledge. That limitation holds both for the accuracy of particular case formulations and for the accuracy of the more general propositions that constitute the theoretical systems therapists use across cases.

In an interview on C-Span's Booknotes (televised 11/7/93) about his new book, *Playing God: Seven Fateful Moments When Great Men Met to Change the World*, Charles Mee, Jr. (1993) discussed how history is replete with instances of the failure of world leaders to appreciate the real limits of their knowledge about the historical field in which they were called upon to act. But Mee did not call the acknowledgment that we often enough lack sufficient knowledge to insure that our actions will have their intended consequences "antirealism." Rather, he called that state of affairs "metarealism"—knowledge of the true limits of access to knowledge or, as he put it, knowledge of the "limits of realism itself." It seems implicit in Mee's argument that the fact that we cannot know everything, or, as he claims is the case in political endeavors, the fact that we cannot know enough to ensure that our actions/interventions will have the desired consequences, does not mean we know nothing at all, or that we should deny what it is we do know about any situation. My own claims about therapy endeavors are parallel to Mee's claims about political endeavors. However, in drawing that parallel I do not mean to imply, as do many postmodernists, that all endeavors, and the knowledge that results from them, are essentially political in nature.

Because what we know about problem causation is (still) so very limited, and because clients know more about the particularities of their lives than do therapists, I believe members of both the narrative and the eclectic therapy movements are right to limit (but not eliminate) their use of general, predetermined theories of problem causation in therapy, and to emphasize instead each client's own personal theory as the basis for a therapeutic discussion. Nevertheless, in that discussion therapists must accomplish at least three objectives if they are to conduct ethical and effective therapy:

(a) Therapists must be willing to take their clients' personal stories seriously, that is, as providing some extralinguistic reality about their lives, even if, in the case of a thoroughly psychotic client, that reality is limited to the client's real pain and suffering.

(b) Therapists must be willing to acknowledge their employment of whatever general, predetermined theories of problem causation they believe to be true. This acknowledgment applies even to a theory that is as highly abstract and so as nonconstraining as the narrative therapy movement's own truth claim about the effects of narratives on problem creation.

(c) Therapists must be willing to acknowledge their employment of whatever general, predetermined theories-cum-methods of problem resolution they believe to be true—for instance, how challenging old narratives to co-construct new ones causes beneficial changes in both meanings and behavior.

In addition, painstaking empirical investigation of the relationships that obtain among these three factors could produce the specification or particularization (of the component parts of therapy systems) that indeed maximizes the potential for practice that is both individualized and systematic and, therefore, effective.

It is my hope that, in the quest to make therapy more effective, therapists of all types will devote more time to reconsidering the composition of the theoretical systems that guide their practice and less time to extolling the virtues of antirealism as a foundation for therapy. I also hope that some of that time gets spent making those systems as extratheoretically true as possible. After all, my argument throughout this book is consistent with postmodern theory on at least this one point: that language, including the language of therapy systems, matters precisely because it affects the extralinguistic reality we all must cope with. Surely this reality is important for therapists of any philosophical persuasion. It is therefore time for all of us to get back to reality about what it is we do as therapists.

Notes

CHAPTER 1. AN INTRODUCTION TO POSTMODERN THEORY

1 The term "humanistic" refers here to the disciplines traditionally known as the humanities (e.g., literature, philosophy, languages) and not to humanistic/existential psychology. I distinguish postmodern humanities from traditional humanities by use of the term "postmodern," which I define later in this chapter.

2 Readers will note that I am deliberately excluding Kant's sense of objectivity; for Kant, objectivity was subjective in origin and therefore phenomenal. Hence, although he took scientific knowledge to be objective, he also thought that reality, as it is "in itself," was not attainable by the knower. For Kant, then, the terms "objectivity" and "reality" were not equivalent.

3 There are more radical antirealists than those I just described, in that they reject even the existence of any mind-independent reality. They therefore usually see their own mental constructions as the only reality, and so for them their theory or language can play no intervening or mediating role, because there is nothing out there—beyond mind—to be mediated by their knowing processes. That is, they presume there is no independent ontological reality to be known. I return to this point a little later.

4 Whether that therapist knows such client behaviors as pacing, arm waving, and uttering sentences as *they* really or independently exist apart from the therapist's *interpretations* of them is a problem for all antirealists. Many of them seem to be saying that the theory one holds makes or constitutes or brings into being the reality one encounters *itself*. Therefore, they claim, one never experiences what is actually there, however directly observable it may *appear* to be. I return to this problem in Chapter 6.

5 To be more precise, discourse analysis is thought to be an antirealist effort in that it considers how *ideas* (whether they are true or untrue) that dominate or are marginalized in public and private language have consequences for what constitutes knowledge and thus for thoughts and actions themselves. Discourse analysis is therefore allegedly concerned with language use, and not with the ability of language to reflect any extralinguis-

tic reality. I discuss some of the problems associated with this type of effort in Chapter 6.

6   The term "extralinguistic reality" means reality as it exists independent of the knower and the theory, language, narrative, constructs, or discourse used by the knower. For example, in therapy, the extralinguistic reality refers to how the client actually acts, thinks, or feels, which may or may not be accurately reflected by what the client says about how he or she acts, thinks, or feels. The terms "extralinguistic reality" and "extratheoretic reality" have a somewhat common meaning, and so I will use them interchangeably, depending upon my intended emphasis.

7   The term "modernist" (or "modern") has of course a long-standing general meaning outside the field of therapy. In that wider setting, modernists are not necessarily realists. The twentieth century was, in general, dominated by the notion of modernism up until the invention of postmodernism, and the realism/antirealism debate already existed during that whole "modernist" period. I equate modernism with realism in this book for two reasons: (a) to contrast it with postmodernism, which strives always to take an antirealist position, and (b) to reflect the general postmodern view that it departs from modernity on the realism/antirealism issue. For postmodernists, then, modernists are taken to be realists, even though not all modern philosophy may be so characterized. Incidentally, so-called modernist therapies (those that were conceived prior to the postmodern revolution), like modernism in general, contain antirealist elements; consider, for example, the phenomenological movement that spawned the so-called humanistic/existential therapies, which emphasized the client's personal, subjective experience or "reality." But unlike the postmodern narrative movement, the humanistic movement did not deny the truth of its own general claims about problem causation and problem resolution.

8   See Pols (1992a, p. 5) and Note 7 in Chapter 6 of this book for an explanation of the equation or conflation between theory and language made within antirealist (linguistic) philosophy.

9   See Suleiman (1980) and Tompkins (1980), especially their comments on Holland and Iser, who represent less extreme views.

10 See Note 1 for the distinction between humanities and postmodern humanities.

11 I remind the reader that I am not implying that all modern philosophers of science have been philosophical realists. See Note 7.

12 See Rosenau (1992, pp. 54–56), for the postmodern distinction between the subject and the individual.

13 For three such exceptions, see Sass (1992, pp. 174–175), Glass (1993), and Rosenau (1992).

14 See Chapter 3 for a discussion of the distinction between theories of problem resolution and the methods that are derived from them, in most systems of psychotherapy. See Chapter 2 for a description of the debate within the integrative/eclectic therapy movement about how theory should be either integrated with or kept distinct from therapeutic method.

15   The term "predetermined" is used to convey the idea that categories and conceptualizations have been determined within a theoretical system prior to their use in any *particular* therapy case. See Chapter 3 for a discussion of this point and the linking of the term "general" with the term "predetermined."

CHAPTER 2. THE ECLECTIC THERAPY MOVEMENT

1   The term "systems" here refers to distinct theoretical systems of therapy of any sort, and not to any particular type of theory of therapy, such as family systems theory/therapy.

2   Although many consider the common factors approach to be a distinct type of eclecticism in its own right, some see it as more closely aligned with the integrative movement. In any case, a brief distinction between integration and the common factors approach mentioned above will be provided in due course (see Note 5). That distinction is not, however, central to the arguments I make in this book.

3   I illustrate the oscillating antirealism of their argument in Chapters 4, 5, and 7.

4   The adoption of the term "metatheory" by the discipline is a problematic one; a particular integrative theory is not, strictly speaking, a metatheory. However, I use this term to be consistent with terminological conventions within eclecticism.

5   Mahoney (1993) includes the "common factors" of change mentioned above within the integrationist attempt. Most writers on the subject, however, see the common factors approach as distinct from the integrative form of eclecticism. Arkowitz (1991), in his editorial introduction to the new *Journal of Psychotherapy Integration*, defines integration as the attempt to combine or synthesize the *discrepant* aspects of disparate therapy systems into one unified metatheory. By contrast, the common factors approach seeks to determine the *commonalities* among all therapy systems.

6   The stages of change could actually constitute one of the components of a generic model of all therapy systems (which I present in Chapter 3), namely, categories or types of clients/problems. In that way they can be used to guide the selection of interventions, or processes of problem resolution.

7   Consider, for example, the title of the recently (1991) founded *Journal of Psychotherapy Integration*.

8   Put differently, an "if-then" system of rules for therapeutic intervention as a function of client type would be created.

9   We may add to this list a treatment-phase variable, such as Prochaska and his colleagues' five stages (or categories) of change, which I described earlier in this chapter. Note here that the therapist-type variable has received the least attention.

CHAPTER 3. THE STRUCTURE OF THERAPY SYSTEMS

1   See Orlinsky (1989, p. 431), for a description of a very different kind of "generic model of psychotherapy."

2   If nothing else, to propound a particular method in therapy is to claim that its use will

cause certain desired effects; this is a causal claim that is in a sense itself a minimal theory, or theoretical claim, since it goes beyond direct observation. The question of what constitutes theory in therapy is, as we saw in Chapter 2, a thorny one. I am taking a position contrary to those who claim to be atheoretical in their practice by virtue of simply doing what works. I believe the process of discovering what works (i.e., empirical research) is always guided by some instance of the theoretic-empirical cycle of science in general. I also believe the resulting claim about what works is never completely devoid of causal/explanatory principles: I know of no therapists who state they use a certain approach because it works, but that they have no idea whatsoever about *why* that might be the case, and thus why they selected it in the first place.

3   There is a distinction within theories of problem causation between full problem causation, which embodies the notion of etiology or the original, historical cause of the problem to begin with, and mere problem maintenance, which considers only current factors that determine or perpetuate problems already set in motion (cf. Sluzki, 1981).

4   According to Miller (1969), "a *system* is a set of units with relationships among them" (p. 68). "The word *set* implies that the units have common properties. The state of each unit is constrained by, conditioned by, or dependent on the state of other units" (p. 68). See my definition of "system" in Chapter 2.

5   It is important to recall that the particulars (e.g., client/problem categories) of technical eclecticism are not so subsumed by any universal notion of problems (C) and so they are not linked to a universal theory of problem causation (A), as we find in psychoanalysis. In any case, the point is that here the particulars do not prescribe the use of *different* methods (Component B), as they do in technical eclecticism.

6   Rogerian, or client-centered, therapy perhaps provides a simpler example of a universally applied A B C system. In that system, all problems are defined as the presence of a poor self-concept (C), which is caused by a lack of positive regard from significant others in one's past (A) and which is treated by a therapeutic relationship that supplies the missing positive regard (B).

7   I think it is fair to say that the matrix paradigm of the eclectic movement is conventional in the sense that its designers have adhered to the conventions of a systematic, (modern) scientific approach to theory construction and application. However, it is seen within the field of psychotherapy as less conventional than the complete, conventional A B C systems to which its designers responded. It is also seen in that field as more conventional than the highly incomplete postmodern narrative therapy "system." The reasons for this will become apparent in the paragraphs that follow.

8   In fact, Szasz himself, in his famous article, "The Myth of Mental Illness" (1960), pointed out the circularity behind the use of underlying psychopathology (A) to account for problems in living defined in behavioral terms (C). I refer the reader directly to Szasz for elaboration.

9   Recall that most integrative eclectics, who—unlike technical/systematic eclectics—embrace theory, explicitly include Component A in their systems of therapy. For example, consider Prochaska and DiClemente's five levels/theories of problem causation—symptom/situational factors, maladaptive cognition, interpersonal conflicts, family/system

conflicts, and intrapsychic conflicts. These five factors of problem causation are put forth as realist by Prochaska and DiClemente, who therefore share the same epistemological position as technical/systematic eclectics, even if they do not share technical eclecticism's antitheoretical stance. See Chapter 2 for more detail on the ways in which technical eclectics do indeed work with the benefit of theory.

10 The use of quotation marks around the word "problem" refers to the antirealist view that problems are linguistic creations (with no extralinguistic reality), rather than real defects in some extralinguistic, functional domain, for instance, biological, cognitive, affective, or interpersonal domains. However, as I go on to explain in Chapter 6, they are perfectly real *as linguistic entities*.

11 The client's own view/narrative of his personal experience has been called, by me and in psychology as a discipline, the client's (or subject's, if the domain is one of scientific investigation) "informal theory." Because the terms "formal" and "informal" have implications for the structure, organization, coherence and wholeness of the theory itself, I now prefer to speak only of the client's personal theory, which may be more or less formal according to those criteria. Thus, I employ the term "personal theory" to mean the client's unique, personal views about the nature, causes, effects—that is, the meanings or implications—of her unique experience.

12 Predetermined theories, those that constitute the component parts of a system of therapy, are general by definition—they must apply to more than one client or case situation, if the system is to be at all useful. Hence, I use the terms "general" and "predetermined" together, to remind the reader of that fact.

13 Postmodernists are inconsistent on this point. Sometimes general theories are seen as merely local, linguistic constructions that give us no extralinguistic reality. This constitutes the antirealist doctrine of social constructionism I discuss in Chapter 4. At other times, however, generalities are equated with the objectivity or realism that postmodernists find to be oppressive and just plain wrong; and so the generalities are themselves rejected in favor of unique, personal, antirealist stories or theories. In any case, unique, personal stories or theories are, for postmodernists, always local, contextualized, antirealist stories, or, in the usual terminology, nonrealities.

14 Here I remind the reader of the point, made in Chapter 1, Note 7, that in the modern age realist and antirealist philosophies of science coexist. Nonetheless, in keeping with the postmodern view of itself as antirealist and of modernism as more typically realist, I here again take the liberty of equating the modern with realism, and the postmodern with antirealism.

15 To know the effect of an event is to know the event itself as the cause of yet another event. Thus knowledge of effects is also causal knowledge.

16 Note that a unique, personal description of problems and theory about their causes can apply to therapists as well as to clients. Therapists can therefore impose their personal views/theories on a client, or on many clients, just as they can impose the general, predetermined components of their therapy systems. But if the therapist applies her unique views generally, that is, to all her therapy cases, her practice will be just as constrained and so just as systematic, but just as deindividualized, as a practice that

applies to all clients the same theories derived from a complete, conventional therapy system.

17   This difference is sometimes called the "theory to therapy gap."

18   Including content derived from the therapist's own unique, personal views, insofar as they may be separated from her adopted system of therapy.

19   I ask the reader to note the distinction here between (a) the particularization of a component part of a therapy system, such that not all particularities within that component part apply to all clients (which is the case in the matrix paradigm, where different particularities are selected for different clients), and (b) the particularization of a component part of a therapy system, such that all particularities within that component part do indeed apply to all clients. It is the latter case that I am discussing here. The purpose of this discussion is to demonstrate that it is not just the degree of completeness of therapy systems that determines the degree of individualization vs. systematization obtained in practice; rather, it is also the degree of specificity, or particularity, of that system's component parts that affects the individuality/systematic tradeoff. Nonetheless, to keep the concepts "completeness" and "specificity/particularity" distinct, I will say that the systematization of practice is affected both by the completeness of the theoretical system in use and by the specificity, or particularity, of the (one, two, or three) component parts that appear in the system. I return to this point again in Chapter 7, when I propose the first of three modestly realist therapy systems.

Here I ask the reader to remain clear about my use of the words "particularization" and "specification" to apply to two different types of therapy systems, namely, matrix and non-matrix systems. The nature of the relationship between the particularity/specificity of the component parts of the system and the individualization vs. systematization of practice is a complex one, for both matrix and non-matrix systems. That relationship could therefore benefit from further scrutiny.

20   Note here the antirealist view of experience itself. Thus, the nature of experience, like knowledge, is allegedly determined by the subject "for reasons of his or her own," rather than by any independent, objective reality.

21   I think it is precisely that coupling of the uniquely personal with antirealism that is behind some of the narrative therapy movement's epistemological confusion—a confusion which results in its oscillation between realism and antirealism. I provide specific examples of that oscillation in Chapter 5.

22   The question of what constitutes real therapeutic expertise is no small matter when we consider such issues as therapeutic efficacy/outcomes, ethics, and payment, third party or direct. I therefore take up these concerns in Chapter 8.

CHAPTER 4. THE NARRATIVE THERAPY MOVEMENT

1   See Note 10 in Chapter 3, concerning the use of quotation marks to suggest that problems and their causes exist only in language, that is, they have no extralinguistic, or real, referent. Also recall that, for postmodernists, generality is equated with "objectivity," uniqueness with subjectivity.

2   Whether the story/theory one holds affects only the *interpretation* of experience, the experience itself remaining what it would have been had the theory never been held, or whether it affects the actual *texture/experience* of the experience itself, is a question about the applicability of Kant's doctrine to these matters; such philosophy has yet to address the question adequately (see Pols, 1992a, pp. 116–121). For instance, does holding a theory about how an apple tastes change the actual taste of that apple or only the way one interprets in language the taste, which is itself uniform regardless of the theory held?

3   The term "constructivism" has been used within psychotherapy—especially in family/systemic therapies—to represent a highly individualistic, antirealist doctrine. We shall examine its meaning more precisely in the next section of this chapter, including its relationship to the term "social constructionism," which is a less individualized, more generalized, form of antirealism.

4   See Pols (1990, 1992a) for an overview of what he calls the "linguistic consensus" that dominates much of late twentieth-century antirealism.

5   The hidden realism that motivates that parenthetical statement and that causes the epistemological oscillation, or inconsistency, within the narrative therapy movement is examined later in this chapter.

6   Mahoney (1991, pp. 111–112) attempts to distinguish radical from critical constructivism on the basis of the nonexistence of an independent reality (radical) vs. the existence of an independent reality we cannot know but that nonetheless affects us in real ways we also cannot know (critical). Despite his apparent belief that the second is a more realist position, both in fact are equally antirealist, since fundamental to any antirealist doctrine is that knowledge of an independent reality—whether it exists or not—is not available to the knower. See Held & Pols (1985a) for elaboration of this point.

7   This observation forms the basis for the constructionist claim that, despite its antirealism, "not just anything goes." Rather, the narrative must have internal coherence and external congruence with the construct/meaning system of the social/consensual discursive context in which it emerges. These are the coherence and the social congruence theories of truth that we shall consider in terms of realism and antirealism in Chapter 5.

8   Note the circularity operating here: the social/cultural/linguistic context shapes experience, which gives rise to theories/understandings of the world that in turn shape, or become part of, that same social/cultural/linguistic context. As social constructionists have pointed out, the context is, therefore, always fluctuating, again allegedly preventing the stability that is so antithetical to postmodern thought.

9   Recall that Kant claimed that we must experience the world as we do—that is, in terms of the categories of understanding (e.g., causation) and of forms of sensibility (space and time)—because mind can only experience what it has itself formed or constituted. Thus, all knowing is universal and necessary; it cannot under any circumstances be anything but that. But knowing is also fundamentally subjective or antirealist: for Kant, objectivity is subjective in origin. Mind is so constructed that *it*, rather than some independent extramental reality, determines or gives the structure of what we experience. We therefore can never, according to Kant, have access to what he calls the thing in itself. Social constructionism may therefore have a slightly more Kantian slant than constructivism

(although it would be wrong to consider Kant a social constructionist). In constructivism, knowledge is relative to each knower—each knower misses the thing in itself in his own unique way. In social constructionism, knowledge is relative to each social/cultural/linguistic group of knowers—each group of knowers misses the thing in itself in a shared/consensual way.

10   That assumption of universal discursive practices would obtain if we believe there are no differences in the way members of disparate cultures experience the world, and then organize that experience in language, because all mind is so constructed that it must give us the same experience/categories of experience, regardless of cultural conditioning. This is, again, related to a Kantian view. However, unlike Kant's emphasis on the structure of mind, within social constructionism we find an emphasis on the structure of language, which, presumably, can be seen as reflecting the structure of mind. That latter argument, however, is a more structuralist than Kantian one.

11   The reader may note an impending contradiction here. According to social constructionism the linguistic/discursive context—including, especially, the dominant discourses within that context—always imposes some constraints on the way all of its members experience life. Problems must therefore allegedly be constructed in ways predetermined by, or consistent with, that discursive/linguistic/cultural context. Given that "fact," problem stories must be shared somewhat with others in that context, even if the therapist (who is also a member of that linguistic/discursive context [see Goldner, 1993; Hare-Mustin, 1994]) works explicitly, as do narrative therapists, to avoid the use of any predetermined system of therapy with predetermined client/problem categories. We shall return to this problem later in this chapter.

12   We must stop here and consider the possibility that each person's story/narrative can be unique to the extent that his social/discursive/linguistic context is unique to him—that is, he relates to his own unique set of people, a set itself shared by no one else. But that solution to the problem of uniqueness found within social constructionism subverts the social consensus, the shared understandings in language, that form the foundation of a social constructionism, rather than a solipsistic constructivism. In fact, V. Fish (1993), in an article in which he criticizes, but endorses, the use of deconstruction in psychotherapy, finds for the stability of "interpretive contexts" when he states, "Derrida does not suggest that there are no meanings, nor that interpretive contexts are necessarily unstable. On the contrary, a task of deconstruction is to investigate the relative stability of given interpretive contexts (Derrida, 1988, pp. 143–150)" (Fish, 1993, p. 232).

13   See Chapter 1, Note 7, for my reasons for equating modernism with realism, despite the existence of both realist and antirealist philosophies within the whole of the modernist period.

14   See Culler (1982) and Eagleton (1983) for two introductory texts on the matter.

15   Gergen, incidentally, edited, along with Shotter, a book entitled *Texts of Identity*, the title of which could not make the self/text equation more explicit.

16   This connectedness of one story to all stories within a discursive context is similar to the concept of "intertextuality," which is found in postmodern literary theory and philosophy. According to Rosenau (1992), "intertextuality" means that "everything [or what I

consider to be all texts, since for postmodernists texts are the only things we have] is related to everything else." There is, therefore, "'... no prospect of ever arriving at or being halted at an agreed point' (Bauman 1990: 427)" (p. xii). Of course, intertextuality, which allows no extralinguistic reference or meaning, has a fundamental antirealism behind it. It also means no story can be uniquely individualized, contrary to the antisystematic (anti-generality) strivings of postmodern narrative therapists.

17   White and Epston's use of the term "unique" is imprecise and so confusing. Sometimes "unique" seems to mean something experienced only by a particular individual, as it is distinct from the experiences of others. At other times, however, "unique" seems to mean an experience that is a new one for a particular individual, regardless of whether others have had that same experience. The term "performance of meaning" is also unclear. Is it the act of constructing the new, unique story itself that constitutes the performance of meaning, or the new, unique actions that result from that new story that constitute the performance of meaning? Stiles (1987) calls upon three distinctions in "speech act theory" that may apply here: (a) "An illocutionary act is the speech act performed *in* making an utterance. For example, . . . a question; . . . a request; . . . an assertion" (p. 137); (b) "*Locutionary* acts . . . consist of simply uttering words" (p. 137); and (c) "*Perlocutionary* acts . . . consist of producing some effect on the actions or attitudes of others" (pp. 137–138), by virtue of an utterance.

18   There appears to be some danger here of a return to the old "uniformity myth"—namely, the belief that we can determine what interventions work for all clients. Recall that it was this myth that prompted the emergence of the eclectic movement/matrix paradigm, with its emphasis on specificity, or antiuniformity, in the first place (see Paul, 1967).

19   See such postmodern feminists as Hare-Mustin (1992a), Hare-Mustin and Marecek (1990b), and Riger (1992), as well as other critics (e.g., Glass, 1993; Rosenau, 1992; Speed, 1991), for expressions of that concern. Postmodern feminists therefore seem more aware than many other postmodernists of the contradiction between postmodern antirealism/relativism, on the one hand, and the real workings of power, on the other hand, when they call attention to the need for any theory to take into account the subordinate position and "material conditions of women's daily lives" (Hare-Mustin & Marecek, 1990b, p. 197).

CHAPTER 5. EPISTEMOLOGICAL OSCILLATION IN NARRATIVE THERAPY

1   Within psychology there is some debate about whether the term "behavior" should refer not only to overt, directly observable actions but also to the mental states traditionally known as thoughts (i.e., cognition) and feelings (i.e., affect)—states which are typically inferred from what can be observed directly. Here I use the term "perception/experience" to refer to such (internal) mental states, and, to make my case about narrative therapy's references to and claims about extralinguistic behavior, I use the term "behavior" in its more limited sense to refer to actions and interactions. I do so because knowledge of actions is less open to dispute than is knowledge of mental states. However, I am suggesting that postmodern narrative therapy, like all therapy, affects all three

realms of human functioning and that all three realms have a real existence. The nature of mental states, and their relation to language, is a topic that exceeds the scope of this book.

2   By directly known I mean known without any theory/language that mediates between the knower and the known (a point I introduced in Chapter 1 and explain in some detail in Chapter 6). Therefore, there is no chance of theoretical/linguistic distortion or alteration of that reality in experience—a distortion that, according to antirealists, affects all knowing. Recall, however, that a realist doctrine allows, when needed, indirect knowing by way of theories that do not necessarily distort *in experience* the true, independent nature of the reality to be known. (Again, see Chapter 6 for a full discussion.)

3   I refer here again to the use of the term "performance of meaning" in the postmodern/narrative therapy literature, especially as it has been used by White and Epston (1990). There is again some ambiguity about the meaning of this term: it seems to refer either to the act of creating meaning (or narrative itself) from observed events, or to the actual behavioral effects or enactments of that created meaning or narrative, or else to both. See Note 17, Chapter 4 for a fuller discussion, including distinctions made within "speech act theory" that are pertinent.

4   See Brooks (1992, pp. 12–13), Spence (1982, pp. 249–250), and Bruner (1986, p. 7) for the distinction between two fundamental components of narrative: "fabula," or the linear sequencing of events as they actually occurred, and "sjuzet," or the way the story arranges those events.

5   Greenwood (1991), in his introduction to *The Future of Folk Psychology*, makes a similar argument when he points out, by quoting Ramsey, Stich, and Garon (1991), that "propositional attitudes . . . 'play a *causal role* in the production of other propositional attitudes, and ultimately in the production of behavior'" (p. 9). Here we find examples of the idea that one thought or story can give rise to another thought or story, either or both of which can ultimately affect extralinguistic behavior.

6   The ontology of mental states and their relation to language is a highly complex matter that exceeds the scope of this book. Nonetheless, I again take the position that such mental states as thoughts and feelings are no less real than are overt behaviors.

7   As I explain in Chapter 6, the *act* of co-constructing a new narrative on the part of the therapist (and client) is an extralinguistic behavior (e.g., moving one's mouth to speak, or moving one's hand to write on a chalkboard, computer, or notepad). This act is distinct from the *content* of the narrative, which is itself a linguistic proposition. But that linguistic proposition, or product, surely refers, more or less correctly, to some extralinguistic events in the client's life.

8   Recall that for many postmodernists there is no distinction between the self (in any extralinguistic sense) and the language, or linguistic context, that constitutes it in any given moment.

9   Ironically, Spence, who holds to the antirealist view of the content of interpretations, is not (in my opinion) as adamant in his antirealism as many of the narrative therapists whose quotations we have considered and who invoke his name in support of their more extreme antirealism.

10   The concept of direct knowing in general, and direct knowing of a linguistic proposition *as* a linguistic proposition—that is, in independence of its truth status—is explained in Chapter 6.

CHAPTER 6. AN ALTERNATIVE PHILOSOPHY OF KNOWING

1   Here is a more precise way to say this: theory/language/discourse must of necessity alter our experience of what purports to be an independent object of knowing, so that the object is not in fact an independent object of knowing. Put somewhat differently, the knower's theory/language always constitutes and reconstitutes in each and every knowing experience, or act of knowing, the thing to be known.

2   The reader should remember that a metaphysical claim is a very general reality claim, but that such a reality claim is not necessarily a claim about something *beyond* the physical. Scientific materialism is as much metaphysics as is, say, idealism.

3   For details on the distinction between rational awareness and the formative function, together with the interaction between the two functions, see Pols (1992a, Chapter 5, pp. 122–151).

4   I discuss this point later in this chapter.

5   For details on what Pols calls the rational-experiential engagement characteristic of direct knowing, see Pols (1992a, pp. 33–35, 130, 138–44, 176–79).

6   Antirealists think that theory/language/discourse is *all* we can ever attend to, or know. But their monolithic antirealism prevents direct knowledge even of *that* aspect of reality. I return to that point later in this chapter.

7   Pols (1992a, p. 5) explains the antirealist conflation of theory and language by linguistic philosophers in the opening chapter of his book, and it is worth quoting him here to clarify this most subtle and abstract problem:

> There are many academic philosophers today—perhaps a majority of the English-speaking ones—who would object that the distinction between direct and indirect knowing is not sound, for the simple reason that there is no direct knowing whatsoever, and so no direct knowing of persons—or, for that matter, of cats, dogs, squirrels, trees, flowers, and so on. All knowledge, they would say, is a function of the theories we hold and the languages we use. Those philosophers seem to think of the holding of a theory as a kind of language use. Curiously, they also tend to think of language use as a kind of theory holding. In short, they blend what, on the face of it, are separate notions or concepts, 'language' and 'theory.' To speak more bluntly, they confuse or conflate the two notions. Let us say that they make all knowledge a function of language-cum-theory, so much so that for them there is no way to get outside language-cum-theory and know *anything* directly.

8   For detailed criticism of this position, see Pols (1992a, Chapters 3 and 4).

9   For more detail on indirect knowledge, see Pols (1992a, pp. 146–151, 156–160).

10   This point reminds me of a conversation I recently had with a colleague who is a psychologist and who has adopted social constructionism. She illustrated the social constructionist claim that language mediates between the knower and the known by pointing to the example of color perception: in particular, she argued that we would not

have the experience of the color red if we did not have the word, or linguistic concept, of that color. Hume's treatment of the color blue notwithstanding, the problem with her argument lies in the comparative psychology and developmental psychology evidence. In these disciplines researchers have demonstrated that animals with no known human linguistic processes can distinguish colors, as can human infants at least as young as four months of age. My colleague quickly rescinded her social constructionist stance regarding color perception, but not regarding all other aspects of knowing.

11   See Chapter 2 and Pols (1992a, pp. 32–33, 73, 82, 156–63) for a full discussion of the cycling back and forth within scientific inquiry between a body of theory (theoretical pole) and the observations that test the theory but are known directly, independently of the theory (empirical pole). Pols explores in some detail the general cooperation of rational awareness and the formative function in science and other rational enterprises in Chapter 6 (pp. 152–174).

12   This use of a framework or system of meaning categories for a content analysis of the themes in a story is not automatically to take the *next* step often taken in content analyses: to infer that the existence of a theme in a story reflects the storyteller's underlying (extralinguistic) psychological state, for instance, a feeling of helplessness or inadequacy or anger. Such a state may be hypothesized to motivate the person's overt behavior. That state can only be known indirectly by inferring that the theme of the story, which can be known directly, reflects or gives evidence of it. Nonetheless, that inference may be a sound one if the stories that are found to reflect a certain underlying psychological state do indeed predict the known overt manifestations of that state—for instance, if stories that reflect themes of anger predict, or correlate with, the overt expressions of anger on the part of their authors. In that case, we may say that the application of the system of content categories to the subject's linguistic productions in the experiment constitutes a valid, indirect measure of anger. It is therefore important to note that Propositions 3 and 4 as I have stated them make claims only about the holding of a story, and not necessarily about the actual, underlying (extralinguistic) state of the person holding the story, even though postmodern narrative therapists often go on to make that unwitting inference about stories.

13   The so-called "interpretive contexts" used by postmodernists and social constructionists to explain the nonstability of meaning have much more stability than many postmodernists/social constructionists seem, in their enthusiasm for the locality and indeterminacy of meaning, to notice. Narrative therapists are indeed attracted to those arguments about the ever-changing meaning of language as a function of change in interpretive context— which is alleged to be so localized as to be two different reading moments of the same text by the same person (see de Shazer, 1991, p. 52). But those same narrative therapists have nonetheless shown themselves to be aware of the stability of said contexts across persons, place, and time. I discuss this point later in this chapter (also see Fish, 1993, Note 1).

14   They therefore belong to a larger class of what Pols (1992a, pp. 43–44, 78, 117, 146, 154, 166, 170–71) calls *entia rationis* (beings of reason): entities at least part of whose structure originates in the formative function of rationality.

15   See J. Polkinghorne (1989, pp. 158–176) for an exposition of his rebuttals of the

antirealist argument about science. For a caustic critique of postmodernists' attacks on science in general, including a critique of the postmodern/antirealist agenda and the internal contradictions that characterize it, I refer the reader to Gross and Levitt (1994), *Higher Superstition: The Academic Left and its Quarrels with Science*. For a discussion of scientific objectivity, I refer the reader to Kitcher (1993), *The Advancement of Science: Science without Legend, Objectivity without Illusions*.

16 The conflation of the rational awareness and formative functions of rationality reflects a traditional Kantian position. According to Pols (1987), "The conflation . . . is characteristic of the linguistic consensus that has dominated English-speaking philosophy for at least the past half-century. For that consensus, attending is in effect a linguistic constituting. Hence the common view that we linguistically 'make' a variety of different worlds, and that the only 'realities' we can attain are propositional 'realities'" (p. 6).

17 Then again, doesn't a general theory about how reality is negotiated tell us something about the real operation of mind in that process?

18 The word "other" as it is used here suggests that these "activities" are somewhat distinct from descriptions and explanations, which themselves therefore do not constitute *all* human activity. That is, there is an extralinguistic domain of behavior. (See comments about "speech act theory" in Chapter 4, Note 17, and Chapter 5, Note 3.)

19 Ellis (1989), in his attack on deconstructionism, makes clear that meaning is always bounded by the constraint of the language in which the text is written:

> There is one obvious constraint that operates on all texts: the language they are written in. No text in English can escape from the fact that it is in English, not another language. An English text means what it does because it uses the system of communication that is the English language; its meaning is bounded by that constraint; and no theory that denies the need to know how to operate in English and to show a mastery of its conventions in order to understand that text can possibly achieve credibility or command intellectual respect. Total freedom (and textuality if so understood) is therefore an impossible notion. (p. 120)

Presumably, English, like other languages, has its own stable operations and conventions that are independent of any *particular* reader or user of it.

20 The question of whether each and every act of knowing/attending/"reading" constitutes its own linguistic context and so constitutes the object of knowing has not been worked out in antirealist circles, including linguistic philosophy and postmodern theory in general. We may therefore ask whether (a) we each linguistically create or construct or constitute the object or nonreality itself in each and every instance of knowing/attending, or (b) we merely bring or make use of some *other* previously created theory/language in some "linguistic context" to mediate between the knower (us) and the object of knowing. Social constructionists seem to suggest the latter, but they make statements that indicate the former. The confusion or conflation on their part of statements (a) and (b) makes it difficult to understand their claim about the nature of knowing. More precisely, there is a subtle but complicated distinction to be made here: Do we attend "directly" to the nonreality we have just linguistically constituted? Or do we attend to (real) reality indirectly by attending directly only to the reality-altering theory/language we have ourselves constructed or borrowed in any particular act of knowing?

CHAPTER 7. THREE PROPOSED
MODESTLY REALIST THERAPY SYSTEMS

1   Here I use the word "behavior" in its broadest sense to include the client's thoughts and feelings (internal or mental states/events/activity) as well as her directly observable overt actions. Sometimes I use the term "behavior/life" to indicate that broader meaning.

2   Recall that for postmodernists, all events are nothing more than texts themselves. Therefore, texts and contexts cannot be distinguished. As de Shazer (1991) said,

> Since a word or a sentence can appear again and again in new contexts where its meaning differs, however slightly, from its meaning in any previous context (even if only because this is now and that was then), in order to understand each appearance in its difference we must study its context (Derrida, 1978). . . . However, the distinction between "text" and "context" is difficult to mark. Context is just more text; the meanings of the "context" are just as indeterminable and therefore can produce the same sort of ambiguities. (p. 52)

3   Recall that in Chapter 3 I argued that the degree to which one's therapy practice is individualized vs. systematic is not a function of the realism or antirealism of one's theoretical system, but rather a function of the completeness of that system: the more complete the system (in terms of the three component parts, A B C), the more systematic the practice, but the less individualized the practice can then be across cases. Here I refine that statement with the qualification that realism in the form of secondary rational awareness of stable linguistic entities is necessary for the establishment of a therapy system and hence a systematic practice.

4   Note that this same optimism obtains for postmodern feminists, who may believe that the postmodern rejection of independent truth allows female voices, indeed all who have been "marginalized" in discourse, to have as much legitimacy and so as much right to be heard as male. This is a dubious cause for celebration, however, in that it subverts the reality claims of feminists that must be taken seriously, in particular, that women have indeed been oppressed within our culture.

5   Among other disciplines, e.g., linguistics, psycholinguistics, sociolinguistics, anthropology—see Russell (1987a, p. 3) for a more complete list.

6   Here I distinguish narrative structure from the "paralinguistic" features of your narrative, such as facial expression. I use the word "paralinguistic" here to distinguish it from "extralinguistic" as I have been using it. Paralinguistic thus refers to nonverbal movements and facial expressions that accompany and give meaning to utterances. Extralinguistic events certainly include these, but go well beyond them to include events that are in no way associated with speech acts.

7   Note here that Eron and Lund appear to use the word "behavior" in the narrow sense of action, rather than the broad meaning which includes thinking and feeling, or internal states/events, as well as overt actions. Note also that in taking a realist perspective, I disagree with their antirealist claim that we cannot have direct knowledge of/access to overt actions *themselves*, but rather must rely on our interpretive representations of them, interpretations which presumably distort the real reality in experience. In addition, it is unclear from the White and Epston quotation that precedes the Eron and Lund one just how broadly or narrowly they are using the term "behavior."

8   The well-known phrase (of Coleridge) is "that *willing* [italics added] suspension of disbelief for the moment, which constitutes poetic faith"; that's an important difference. Coleridge, who was speaking of poetry, does not mean that the reader accepts something as the literal truth. Freud, and Spence, apparently did not have such a reservation about interpretation. We shall encounter this idea again in Chapter 8. There I summarize Gerrig (1993), who discusses the active, or willing, nature of suspending disbelief in understanding fiction *as* fiction.

9   In his new book, *The Rhetorical Voice of Psychoanalysis: Displacement of Evidence by Theory*, Spence (1994) at least implicitly invokes questions about realism and antirealism when he calls for more consideration of how language is used "as a means of representing the world" (p. 146), in order to provide a stronger evidentiary base for psychoanalysis. It is not clear from this analysis, however, that he has resolved the epistemological oscillation that I find in his earlier text. Indeed, he explicitly supports a coherence rather than a correspondence (with reality) theory of truth (pp. 69–74).

10   Spence (1982) defines the process of naturalizing a text as follows:

> We can define the process of adding private commentaries to the psychoanalytic transcript as the process of *naturalizing* the text. This step provides the link between privileged and normative competence. ["*Normative* competence belongs to all members of the psychoanalytic community. . . . *Privileged* competence belongs to the analyst at a specific time and place in a particular analysis" (pp. 215–216).] Once a session has been naturalized by the treating analyst with all (or most all) of its implicit meanings painstakingly unpacked, it then becomes accessible to someone with normative competence. (p. 218)

Here once again we see surfacing a tension between individuality and generality.

11   This struggle between the general and the specific, the systematic and antisystematic, is echoed throughout Spence's 1994 book, *The Rhetorical Voice of Psychoanalysis*. For expressions of this struggle see Spence (1994, pp. 69–74, 162–163, 203–204).

12   Russell's requests that units, categories, and descriptive systems in therapy research be based on a theory of language use that is compatible with a theory of therapy, and not simply ease of use, is not unlike Beutler's request that the dimensions and categories within his matrix system be selected on the basis of theory, and not ease of use. However, Russell is not proposing a matrix paradigm in Beutler's sense.

13   Note that this is an example of the microevents paradigm discussed in Chapter 2 (see Stiles et al., 1986), in which sessions are understood utterance by utterance, however utterances may be unitized and then classified, or categorized.

14   Spence (1994) is one important exception to this rule. In his new book, *The Rhetorical Voice of Psychoanalysis*, he reports his own research on the relation between the "co-occurrence rate of [the client's] shared pairs of pronouns" (p. 190) (i.e., when the client refers to both himself and the therapist) and the timing and rate of therapist interventions. As Spence himself put it,

> It would appear that at the same time the analyst in the session is responding to problems of drive and defense, transference and countertransference, he is also responding to subtle changes in the patterning of the patient's speech that tell him when it is safe (and fruitful) to enter the analytic space. (1994, p. 191)

15   Neuro-linguistic Programming is a system of therapy that provides particularized, nuanced descriptions of language use in therapy. Although it has received little if any attention from narrative therapists, it should at least be noted here. For a complete account, see Bandler and Grinder (1975), *The Structure of Magic I: A Book about Language and Therapy*, and Grinder and Bandler (1976), *The Structure of Magic II*.

16   This quotation of him makes that question apparent:

> The meticulous investigation of transitions between particular client states of mind (e.g., self-disgust, competitiveness, etc.), as expressed in and through language, promises to help illuminate both cognitive and emotional factors associated with change . . . . (Russell, 1987b, p. 345)

Does the fact that mind states, and perhaps cognitive and emotional factors, are expressed in and through language mean that they have no extralinguistic ontological status, independent of what the client may say, or even know, about them? (The question of the nature of consciousness cannot of course be completely avoided here, but that is well beyond the scope of this book.) Moreover, it is not clear whether Russell thinks that language is important in therapy because it affects extralinguistic behavior as well as linguistic productions of clients. At times he makes reference to extralinguistic effects, for instance, when he states,

> The strategies used to study the communication between therapist and client have *not* [italics added] been devised with the principal intent of discovering regularities in speech and speech-related phenomena alone. [Rather, they have been used to study] . . . topics of obvious significance for the conduct of psychotherapy, and for the understanding of normal and abnormal patterns of adjustment. (1987a, p. 5)

But he later refers to patterns of adjustment in terms of adaptive and maladaptive communication styles or language use/behavior itself (1987b, pp. 342–344). Then again, he also suggests that more evolved communication styles should be seen as both highly differentiated and an integrated component of successfully pursuing "behavioral or interactional goals" (p. 343). In short, I find his distinction between linguistic and extralinguistic events to be at best unclear.

17   The distinction between narrative form/structure/style and narrative content/meaning as the object of change is not very clear. This will become apparent when I propose some possible narrative matrix systems of therapy, based mostly on meaning categories. These potential systems reflect ideas now emerging within the postmodern narrative therapy movement.

18   The reader has probably noticed that these categories are not mutually exclusive. For example, to consider the emotional charge, the future purpose, or the mistake in a client's problem/narrative of her life experience is always, in some sense, to talk about causal, or explanatory, factors which may be hidden from view prior to the therapy (Category 1). That makes sense, since I have argued that meaning itself is about how one perceives causal connections between events in one's life, and how that perception works to explain or make sense of them (cf. Spence, 1982).

19   Recall from Chapter 3 that one cannot specify a process of change without defining, at least in a general way, what the object, content, or target of that change process should

be. To specify a change process is therefore to say something about what is causing/ maintaining the problem to be changed.

20 Here I remind the reader that the completeness of the system refers to the extent to which it contains all three (A B C) components of a generic system as I laid them out in Chapter 3. The specification or particularization of the system refers to the extent to which each of the component parts is itself specified or particularized, for instance, by way of the mutually exclusive categories we find in a traditional matrix system.

CHAPTER 8. ETHICAL AND OTHER PRACTICAL IMPLICATIONS

1 The tradition that ethics is the sphere of *practical* reason goes right back to Aristotle. It is still a very lively tradition in philosophy.

2 The use of conscious deception in the early days of the strategic therapy movement has been renounced by all concerned. See Solovey and Duncan's (1992, p. 54) discussion of Haley's (1987) position on lies.

3 Bok (1989, p. 291) elaborates on the problem of explaining self-deception:

> Self-deception offers difficult problems of definition. Is it deception or not? Intentional or not? Is there even communication or not? If a person appears to deceive himself, there are not two different human beings of whom one intends to mislead the other. Yet, arguably, two "parts" of this person are involved in a deceptive relationship. Are there times when the right hand does not know what the left hand is doing? And times when the left hand is in fact deceiving the right hand? New research on brain function may show that there is then not so much a deceiver and a deceived, but rather two different processes coordinated by the brain. Whether these processes should properly be called deception is a question discussed since Plato, and taken up anew by contemporary philosophers.

4 See Simon's (1992) paper for an interesting attempt to merge the constructivist view that language creates "reality" with the endorsement of stability within that "reality"; more specifically, that language itself has some stability and so must allow for stability within the "reality" (e.g., social systems) it allegedly creates. Although I have endorsed the stability of a real (independent) reality throughout this book, I of course have many problems with Simon's formulation precisely because of its constructivist assumptions.

5 The question of whether therapists should make their underlying, guiding system of therapy—with all its assumptions—explicit to clients is an interesting one. Although that act may be considered a form of self disclosure, it is not the kind of self disclosure that the literature on the effects of therapist self disclosure usually addresses.

6 Recall that the antisystematic aspiration of postmodern narrative therapists manifests itself in the attempt to eliminate from their theoretical system predetermined content, or descriptions of problems (Component C) and theories about their causes (Component A). Without these, it is hard to imagine a general notion, or even particular notions, of what is to be avoided in life, and therefore what constitutes the helping vs. harming of therapy clients.

7 I am grateful to Dr. Henry Grunebaum, who brought this quotation to my attention, and to Professor Barbara Weiden Boyd, who helped me locate these lines in Plutarch, *Moralia* (Loeb Classical Library Edition, edited and translated by H. Cherniss and

W. C. Helmbold, Harvard University Press, Vol. 12, p. 355), "Whether Land or Sea Animals are Cleverer," 7, p. 965.

8   Recall that for therapy to be systematic, the therapist must know and use—across cases—a theoretical system that is at the very least real and directly knowable as a theoretical system. That is true whether or not the system gives an adequate account of some extratheoretic reality.

9   One quibble here: isn't "what's going on" part of life? Note the attempt to avoid predetermined content, to be an expert about the process of calling attention to what's going on, which should apparently be determined by the client. The attempt to avoid predetermined content in the therapeutic system is seen later in this quote.

10   I again refer the reader to Spence's (1994) new book, *The Rhetorical Voice of Psychoanalysis: Displacement of Evidence by Theory*, for the continuation of his struggle with the individuality/systematic problem. Incidentally, Spence (1994) argues for a coherence theory of truth and against a correspondence theory of truth precisely on the basis of the uniqueness of every therapeutic encounter (pp. 69–74).

11   Recall from Chapter 6 that the *act* of speaking or writing itself is an extralinguistic behavior with temporospatial status; it therefore can be known directly by way of primary rational awareness. The *content* of the speaking or writing is, however, a linguistic entity that therefore must be known directly by way of secondary rational awareness.

12   By behavior in its very broadest sense I again mean not only overt, directly observable actions, but also the mental states/events—e.g., attitudes and feelings—that are thought to motivate them (see Chapter 5, Notes 1 and 6). The ontology of mental states—whether they exist as biochemical/physical events, linguistically mediated events, or in some other unspecified way—is of course nothing less than the mind/body problem itself, and, relatedly, the problem of consciousness. I refer the reader to Pols's work-in-progress, *The Causal Structure of Embodied Mind*, and Flanagan's (1992) book, *Consciousness Reconsidered*, for cogent discussions of those very problems, respectively.

13   Recall that knowledge of reports *as* linguistic entities or reports is direct. The report usually refers to some other event, some extralinguistic reality (usually in the past), that the receiver of the report (in this case the therapist) cannot know directly, unless she happened to be there to observe it, which is unlikely in the case of therapy. Then the report gives the receiver of the report—the therapist—indirect knowledge of that extralinguistic event.

References

Alford, C. F. (1991). *The self in social theory: A psychoanalytic account of its construction in Plato, Hobbes, Locke, Rawls, and Rousseau.* New Haven: Yale University Press.

Anderson, H., & Goolishian, H. A. (1988). Human systems as linguistic systems: Preliminary and evolving ideas about the implications for clinical theory. *Family Process, 27,* 371–393.

Anderson, H., & Goolishian, H. A. (1989). Dialogic rather than interventionist: An interview by Lee Winderman. *Family Therapy News,* November/December.

Anderson, H., & Goolishian, H. (1992). The client is the expert: A not-knowing approach to therapy. In S. McNamee & K. J. Gergen (Eds.), *Therapy as social construction* (pp. 25–39). Newbury Park, CA: Sage.

Arkowitz, H. (1989). The role of theory in psychotherapy integration. *Journal of Integrative and Eclectic Psychotherapy, 8,* 8–16.

Arkowitz, H. (1991). Introductory statement: Psychotherapy integration comes of age. *Journal of Psychotherapy Integration, 1,* 1–3.

Atkinson, B. J. (1992). Aesthetics and pragmatics of family therapy revisited. *Journal of Marital and Family Therapy, 18,* 389–393.

Atkinson, B. J. (1993). Hierarchy: The imbalance of risk. *Family Process, 32,* 167–170.

Atkinson, B. J., & Heath, A. W. (1990). Further thoughts on second-order family therapy—This time it's personal. *Family Process, 29,* 145–155.

Ayoub, N. C. (1993, June 30). Nota bene [Review of the book *Shattered selves: Multiple personality in a postmodern world*]. *Chronicle of Higher Education, 39(43),* p. A10.

Bandler, R., & Grinder, J. (1975). *The structure of magic I: A book about language and therapy.* Palo Alto, CA: Science and Behavior Books.

Bauman, Z. (1990). Philosophical affinities of postmodern sociology. *The Sociological Review, 38,* 411–444.

Best, S., & Kellner, D. (1991). *Postmodern theory: Critical interrogations.* New York: Guilford.

Beutler, L. E. (1983). *Eclectic psychotherapy: A systematic approach.* New York: Pergamon.

Beutler, L. E. (1986). Systematic eclectic psychotherapy. In J. C. Norcross (Ed.), *Handbook of Eclectic Psychotherapy* (pp. 94–131). New York: Brunner/Mazel.

Beutler, L. E. (1989). The misplaced role of theory in psychotherapy integration. *Journal of Integrative and Eclectic Psychotherapy, 8,* 17–22.

Beutler, L. E. (1991). Have all won and must all have prizes? Revisiting Luborsky et al.'s verdict. *Journal of Consulting and Clinical Psychology, 59,* 226–232.

Beutler, L. E., Machado, P. P., Engle, D., & Mohr, D. (1993). Differential patient x treatment maintenance among cognitive, experiential, and self-directed psychotherapies. *Journal of Psychotherapy Integration, 3,* 15–31.

Blum, J. D. (1978). On changes in psychiatric diagnosis over time. *American Psychologist, 33,* 1017–1031.

Bogdan, J. (1986). Do families really need problems? Why I am not a functionalist. *Family Therapy Networker, 10(4),* 30–35, 67–69.

Bok, S. (1989). *Lying: Moral choice in public and private life.* New York: Vintage Books.

Booknotes (aired Nov. 7, 1993). C-Span. Interview with Charles L. Mee, Jr. about his book *Playing God: Seven fateful moments when great men met to change the world.*

Bouchard, M. A., & Guérette, L. (1991). Psychotherapy as a hermeneutical experience. *Psychotherapy, 28,* 385–394.

Boyd, B. W. (1991). Personal communication.

Brooks, P. (1992). *Reading for the plot: Design and intention in narrative.* Cambridge, MA: Harvard University Press.

Bruner, J. (1986). *Actual minds, possible worlds.* Cambridge, MA: Harvard University Press.

Cade, B. (1986). The reality of "reality" (or the "reality" of reality). *American Journal of Family Therapy, 14,* 49–56.

Chaiklin, S. (1992). From theory to practice and back again: What does postmodern philosophy contribute to psychological science? In S. Kvale (Ed.), *Psychology and postmodernism* (pp. 194–208). Newbury Park, CA: Sage.

Cherwitz, R. A. (1990). The philosophical foundations of rhetoric. In R. A. Cherwitz (Ed.), *Rhetoric and philosophy* (pp. 1–19). Hillsdale, NJ: Lawrence Erlbaum.

Coleridge, S. T. (1817/1983). *Biographia literaria.* In J. Engell & W. J. Bate (Eds.), *The collected works of Samuel Taylor Coleridge (Vol. 7): Biographia literaria II* (Bollington Series LXXV). Princeton: Princeton University Press.

Cornsweet, C. (1983). Nonspecific factors and theoretical choice. *Psychotherapy: Theory, Research and Practice, 20,* 307–313.

Coyne, J. C. (1985). Toward a theory of frames and reframing: The social nature of frames. *Journal of Marital and Family Therapy, 11,* 337–344.

Culler, J. (1980). Prolegomena to a theory of reading. In S. R. Suleiman & I. Crosman (Eds.), *The reader in the text: Essays on audience and interpretation* (pp. 46–66). Princeton: Princeton University Press.

Culler, J. (1982). *On deconstruction: Theory and criticism after struturalism.* Ithaca: Cornell University Press.

Cushman, P. (1990). Why the self is empty: Toward a historically situated psychology. *American Psychologist, 45,* 599–611.

Dell, P. F. (1985). Understanding Bateson and Maturana: Toward a biological foundation for the social sciences. *Journal of Marital and Family Therapy, 11,* 1–20.

de Man, P. (1979). *Allegories of reading.* New Haven: Yale University Press.

Derrida, J. (1978). *Writing and difference* (A. Bass, trans.). Chicago: University of Chicago Press.

Derrida, J. (1981). *Positions* (A. Bass, trans.). Chicago: University of Chicago Press.

Derrida, J. (1988). *Limited inc.* Evanston, IL: Northwestern University Press.

de Shazer, S. (1991). *Putting difference to work.* New York: W. W. Norton.

de Shazer, S., & Berg, I. K. (1992). Doing therapy: A post-structural re-vision. *Journal of Marital and Family Therapy, 18*, 71–81.

de Shazer, S. (1993). Creative misunderstanding: There is no escape from language. In S. Gilligan & R. Price (Eds.), *Therapeutic conversations* (pp. 81–90). New York: W. W. Norton.

Doherty, W. J. (1986). Quanta, quarks, and families: Implications of quantum physics for family research. *Family Process, 25*, 249–263.

Duncan, B. L., Solovey, A. D., & Rusk, G. S. (1992). *Changing the rules: A client-directed approach to therapy.* New York: Guilford.

Eagleton, T. (1983). *Literary theory: An introduction.* Minneapolis, MN: University of Minnesota Press.

Efran, J. S., & Clarfield, L. E. (1992). Constructionist therapy: Sense and nonsense. In S. McNamee & K. J. Gergen (Eds.), *Therapy as social construction* (pp. 200–217). Newbury Park, CA: Sage.

Efran, J. S., Lukens, R. J., & Lukens, M. D. (1988). Constructivism: What's in it for you? *Family Therapy Networker, 12(5)*, 26–35.

Efran, J. S., Lukens, M. D., & Lukens, R. J. (1990). *Language, structure, and change: Frameworks of meaning in psychotherapy.* New York: W. W. Norton.

Ellis, J. M. (1989). *Against deconstruction.* Princeton: Princeton University Press.

Epstein, E. S., & Loos, V. E. (1989). Some irreverent thoughts on the limits of family therapy: Toward a language-based explanation of human systems. *Journal of Family Psychology, 2*, 405–421.

Eron, J. B., & Lund, T. W. (1993). How problems evolve and dissolve: Integrating narrative and strategic concepts. *Family Process, 32*, 291–309.

Fish, S. E. (1980). Literature in the reader: Affective stylistics. In J. P. Tompkins (Ed.), *Reader-response criticism: From formalism to post-structuralism* (pp. 70–100). Baltimore: Johns Hopkins University Press.

Fish, V. (1993). Poststructuralism in family therapy: Interrogating the narrative/conversational mode. *Journal of Marital and Family Therapy, 19*, 221–232.

Fishman, D. B., & Franks, C. M. (1992). Evolution and differentiation with behavior therapy: A theoretical and epistemological review. In D. K. Freedheim (Ed.), *History of psychotherapy: A century of change* (pp. 159–196). Washington, D.C.: American Psychological Association.

Flanagan, O. (1992). *Consciousness reconsidered.* Cambridge, MA: MIT Press.

Frank, J. D. (1973). *Persuasion and healing: A comparative study of psychotherapy* (Rev. ed.). Baltimore: Johns Hopkins University Press.

Frank, J. D. (1987). Psychotherapy, rhetoric, and hermeneutics: Implications for practice and research. *Psychotherapy, 24*, 293–302.

Freud, S. (1937/1976). Constructions in analysis. In J. Strachey (Trans. & Ed.), *The standard edition of the complete psychological works of Sigmund Freud,* Vol. 23. New York: W. W. Norton.

Garfield, S. L. (1980). *Psychotherapy: An eclectic approach.* New York: Wiley.

Garfield, S. L., & Kurtz, R. (1977). A study of eclectic views. *Journal of Consulting and Clinical Psychology, 45*, 78–83.

Genette, G. (1980). *Narrative discourse: An essay in method* (J. E. Lewin, trans.). Ithaca: Cornell University Press.

Gergen, K. J. (1981). The meagre voice of empiricist affirmation. *Personality and Social Psychology Bulletin, 7*, 333–337.

Gergen, K. J. (1985). The social constructionist movement in modern psychology. *American Psychologist, 40*, 266–275.

Gergen, K. J. (1991a). *The saturated self: Dilemmas of identity in contemporary life*. New York: Basic.

Gergen, K. J. (1991b). *Narrative in/of relationships*. Paper presented at Narrative and Psychotherapy: New Directions in Theory and Practice. Houston-Galveston Institute. Houston, TX, May 10–12.

Gergen, K. J. (1992). Toward a postmodern psychology. In S. Kvale (Ed.), *Psychology and postmodernism* (pp. 17–30). Newbury Park, CA: Sage.

Gergen, K. J. (1994). Exploring the postmodern: Perils or potentials? *American Psychologist, 49*, 412–416.

Gergen, K. J., & Gergen, M. M. (1986). Narrative form and the construction of psychological science. In T. R. Sarbin (Ed.), *Narrative psychology: The storied nature of human conduct* (pp. 22–44). New York: Praeger.

Gergen, K. J., & Kaye, J. (1992). Beyond narrative in the negotiation of therapeutic meaning. In S. McNamee & K. J. Gergen (Eds.), *Therapy as social construction* (pp. 166–185). Newbury Park, CA: Sage.

Gerrig, R. J. (1993). *Experiencing narrative worlds: On the psychological activities of reading*. New Haven: Yale University Press.

Glass, J. M. (1993). *Shattered selves: Multiple personality in a postmodern world*. Ithaca: Cornell University Press.

Goldberg, D., & David, A. S. (1991). Family therapy and the glamour of science. *Journal of Family Therapy, 13*, 17–30.

Goldfried, M. R. (1980). Toward the delineation of therapeutic change principles. *American Psychologist, 35*, 991–999.

Goldfried, M. R. (Ed.). (1982). *Converging themes in psychotherapy: Trends in psychodynamic, humanistic, and behavioral practice*. New York: Springer.

Goldfried, M. R., & Newman, C. (1986). Psychotherapy integration: An historical perspective. In J. C. Norcross (Ed.). *Handbook of eclectic psychotherapy* (pp. 25–61). New York: Brunner/Mazel.

Goldner, V. (1993). Power and hierarchy: Let's talk about it! *Family Process, 32*, 157–162.

Greenwood, J. D. (Ed.). (1991). *The future of folk psychology: Intentionality and cognitive science*. Cambridge: Cambridge University Press.

Greimas, A. J. (1966). *Sémantique structurale*. Paris: Larousse.

Grencavage, L. M., & Norcross, J. C. (1990). Where are the commonalities among the therapeutic common factors? *Professional Psychology: Research and Practice, 21*, 372–378.

Grinder, J., & Bandler, R. (1976). *The structure of magic II*. Palo Alto, CA: Science and Behavior Books.

Groden, M., & Kreiswirth, M. (Eds.) (1994). *The Johns Hopkins guide to literary theory and criticism*. Baltimore: Johns Hopkins University Press.

Gross, P. R., & Levitt, N. (1994). *Higher superstition: The academic left and its quarrels with science*. Baltimore: Johns Hopkins University Press.

Grünbaum, A. (1979). Epistemological liabilities of the clinical appraisal of psychoanalytic theory. *Psychoanalysis and Contemporary Thought, 2*, 451–526.

Gustafson, J. P. (1992). *Self-delight in a harsh world: The main stories of individual, marital, and family psychotherapy.* New York: W. W. Norton.

Guterman, J. T. (1991). Letter to the editor. *Journal of Marital and Family Therapy, 17*, 315–316.

Haley, J. (1987). *Problem-solving therapy* (2nd ed.). San Francisco: Jossey-Bass.

Hare-Mustin, R. T. (1992a). Cries and whispers: The psychotherapy of Anne Sexton. *Psychotherapy, 29*, 406–409.

Hare-Mustin, R. T. (1992b). Meanings in the mirrored room: On cats and dogs. *Journal of Marital and Family Therapy, 18*, 309–310.

Hare-Mustin, R. T. (1994). Discourses in the mirrored room: A postmodern analysis of therapy. *Family Process, 33*, 19–35.

Hare-Mustin, R. T., & Marecek, J. (1990a). Gender and the meaning of difference: Postmodernism and psychology. In R. T. Hare-Mustin & J. Marecek (Eds.), *Making a difference: Psychology and the construction of gender* (pp. 22–64). New Haven: Yale University Press.

Hare-Mustin, R. T., & Marecek, J. (1990b). Beyond difference. In R. T. Hare-Mustin & J. Marecek (Eds.), *Making a difference: Psychology and the construction of gender* (pp. 184–201). New Haven: Yale University Press.

Harland, R. (1987). *Superstructuralism: The philosophy of structuralism and post-structuralism.* London: Methuen.

Held, B. S. (1990). What's in a name? Some confusions and concerns about constructivism. *Journal of Marital and Family Therapy, 16*, 179–186.

Held, B. S. (1991a). The process/content distinction in psychotherapy revisited. *Psychotherapy, 28*, 207–217.

Held, B. S. (1991b). Constructing constructivism: A reply to Oz. *Journal of Marital and Family Therapy, 17*, 193–195.

Held, B. S. (1992). The problem of strategy within the systemic therapies. *Journal of Marital and Family Therapy, 18*, 25–34.

Held, B. S. (in press). The real meaning of constructivism. *Journal of Constructivist Psychology.*

Held, B. S., & Pols, E. (1985a). The confusion about epistemology and "epistemology"—and what to do about it. *Family Process, 24*, 509–517.

Held, B. S., & Pols, E. (1985b). Rejoinder: On contradiction. *Family Process, 24*, 521–524.

Held, B. S., & Pols, E. (1987a). Dell on Maturana: A real foundation for family therapy? *Psychotherapy, 24*, 455–461.

Held, B. S., & Pols, E. (1987b). The philosophy of Dell and Maturana. *Psychotherapy, 24*, 466–468.

Hikins, J. W. (1990). Realism and its implications for rhetorical theory. In R. A. Cherwitz (Ed.), *Rhetoric and philosophy* (pp. 21–77). Hillsdale, NJ: Lawrence Erlbaum.

Hoffman, L. (1990). Constructing realities: An art of lenses. *Family Process, 29*, 1–12.

Hoffman, L. (1993). *The connecting voice: A collaborative approach to relationship therapy.* Presentation at the Family Institute of Maine, Portland, Maine, September 18.

Howard, G. S. (1991). Culture tales: A narrative approach to thinking, cross-cultural psychology, and psychotherapy. *American Psychologist, 46*, 187–197.

Karasu, T. B. (1986). The specificity versus nonspecificity dilemma: Toward identifying therapeutic change agents. *American Journal of Psychiatry, 143*, 687–695.

Kelly, G. A. (1955). *The psychology of personal constructs*. New York: W. W. Norton.

Kiesler, D. J. (1966). Some myths of psychotherapy research and the search for a paradigm. *Psychological Bulletin, 65*, 110–136.

Kitcher, P. (1993). *The advancement of science: Science without legend, objectivity without illusions.* New York: Oxford University Press.

Krieger, M. (Ed.). (1987). *The aims of representation: Subject/text/history*. New York: Columbia University Press.

Kugler, P. (1988). From modernism to post-modernism: Some implications for a depth psychology of dreams. *Psychiatric Journal of the University of Ottawa, 13*, 60–65.

Kvale, S. (Ed.). (1992a). *Psychology and postmodernism*. London: Sage.

Kvale, S. (1992b). Introduction: From the archaeology of the psyche to the architecture of cultural landscapes. In S. Kvale (Ed.), *Psychology and postmodernism* (pp. 1–16). Newbury Park, CA: Sage.

Kvale, S. (1992c). Postmodern psychology: A contradiction in terms? In S. Kvale (Ed.), *Psychology and postmodernism* (pp. 31–57). Newbury Park, CA: Sage.

Lambert, M. J. (1989). The individual therapist's contribution to psychotherapy process and outcome. *Clinical Psychology Review, 9*, 469–485.

Lax, W. D. (1992). Postmodern thinking in a clinical practice. In S. McNamee & K. J. Gergen (Eds.), *Therapy as social construction* (pp. 69–85). Newbury Park, CA: Sage.

Lazarus, A. A. (1967). In support of technical eclecticism. *Psychological Reports, 21*, 415–416.

Lazarus, A. A. (1986). Multimodal therapy. In J. C. Norcross (Ed.), *Handbook of eclectic psychotherapy* (pp. 65–93). New York: Brunner/Mazel.

Lazarus, A. A., & Messer, S. B. (1991). Does chaos prevail? An exchange on technical eclecticism and assimilative integration. *Journal of Psychotherapy Integration, 1*, 143–158.

Leitch, V. B. (1983). *Deconstructive criticism: An advanced introduction*. New York: Columbia University Press.

Løvlie, L. (1992). Postmodernism and subjectivity. In S. Kvale (Ed.), *Psychology and postmodernism* (pp. 119–134). Newbury Park, CA: Sage.

Luborsky, L., McLellan, A. T., Woody, G. E., O'Brien, C. P., & Auerbach, A. (1985). Therapist success and its determinants. *Archives of General Psychiatry, 42*, 602–611.

Luborsky, L., Singer, B., & Luborsky, L. (1975). Comparative studies of psychotherapies: Is it true that "Everyone has won and all must have prizes"? *Archives of General Psychiatry, 32*, 995–1008.

Mahoney, M. J. (1989). Scientific psychology and radical behaviorism: Important distinctions based in scientism and objectivity. *American Psychologist, 44*, 1372–1377.

Mahoney, M. J. (1991). *Human change processes: The scientific foundations of psychotherapy*. New York: Basic.

Mahoney, M. J. (1993). Diversity and the dynamics of development in psychotherapy integration. *Journal of Psychotherapy Integration, 3*, 1–13.

McGinn, C. (1993, June 28). Logic and sadness [Review of the book *Charles Sanders Peirce: A life*]. *New Republic, 208(26)*, 27–30.

McNamee, S., & Gergen, K. J. (1992). Introduction. In S. McNamee & K. J. Gergen (Eds.), *Therapy as social construction* (pp. 1–6). Newbury Park, CA: Sage.

Mee, C. L., Jr. (1993). *Playing god: Seven fateful moments when great men met to change the world*. New York: Simon and Schuster.

Russell, R. L. (1989). Language and psychotherapy. *Clinical Psychology Review, 9*, 505–519.

Ryan, R. M., & Wild, T. C. (1993). Tools for ascribing meaning to narratives [Review of the book *Motivation and personality: Handbook of thematic content analysis*]. *Contemporary Psychology, 38*, 912–914.

Sarbin, T. R. (1986). The narrative as a root metaphor for psychology. In T. R. Sarbin (Ed.), *Narrative psychology: The storied nature of human conduct* (pp. 3–21). New York: Praeger.

Sass, L. A. (1992). The epic of disbelief: The postmodernist turn in contemporary psychoanalysis. In S. Kvale (Ed.), *Psychology and postmodernism* (pp. 166–182). Newbury Park, CA: Sage.

Schafer, R. (1980). Narration in the psychoanalytic dialogue. *Critical Inquiry, 7*, 29–53.

Schafer, R. (1992). *Retelling a life: Narration and dialogue in psychoanalysis*. New York: Basic.

Shotter, J., & Gergen, K. J. (Eds.). (1989). *Texts of identity*. Newbury Park, CA: Sage.

Simon, G. M. (1992). Having a second-order mind while doing first-order therapy. *Journal of Marital and Family Therapy, 18*, 377–387.

Singer, M. G. (1971). The pragmatic use of language and the will to believe. *American Philosophical Quarterly, 8*, 24–34.

Sluzki, C. E. (1981). Process of symptom production and patterns of symptom maintenance. *Journal of Marital and Family Therapy, 7*, 273–280.

Sluzki, C. E. (1992). Transformations: A blueprint for narrative changes in therapy. *Family Process, 31*, 217–230.

Smith, D. S. (1982). Trends in counseling and psychotherapy. *American Psychologist, 37*, 802–809.

Smith, M. L., & Glass, G. V. (1977). Meta-analysis of psychotherapy outcome studies. *American Psychologist, 32*, 752–760.

Solovey, A. D., & Duncan, B. L. (1992). Ethics and strategic therapy: A proposed ethical direction. *Journal of Marital and Family Therapy, 18*, 53–61.

Speed, B. (1984). How really real is real? *Family Process, 23*, 511–517.

Speed, B. (1991). Reality exists O.K.? An argument against constructivism and social constructionism. *Family Therapy, 13*, 395–409.

Spence, D. P. (1982). *Narrative truth and historical truth: Meaning and interpretation in psychoanalysis*. New York: W. W. Norton.

Spence, D. P. (1994). *The rhetorical voice of psychoanalysis: Displacement of evidence by theory*. Cambridge, MA: Harvard University Press.

Stiles, W. B. (1987). Verbal response modes as intersubjective categories. In R. L. Russell (Ed.), *Language in psychotherapy: Strategies of discovery* (pp. 131–170). New York: Plenum.

Stiles, W. B., Shapiro, D. A., & Elliott, R. (1986). "Are all psychotherapies equivalent?" *American Psychologist, 41*, 165–180.

Strenger, C., & Omer, H. (1992). Pluralistic criteria for psychotherapy: An alternative to sectarianism, anarchy, and utopian integration. *American Journal of Psychotherapy, 46*, 111–130.

Strupp, H. H. (1973). On the basic ingredients of psychotherapy. *Journal of Consulting and Clinical Psychology, 41*, 1–8.

Strupp, H. H. (1986). The nonspecific hypothesis of therapeutic effectiveness: A current assessment. *American Journal of Orthopsychiatry, 56*, 513–520.

Suleiman, S. R. (1980). Introduction: Varieties of audience-oriented criticism. In S. R. Suleiman & I. Crosman (Eds.), *The reader in the text: Essays on audience and interpretation* (pp. 3–45). Princeton: Princeton University Press.

Suleiman, S. R., & Crosman, I. (Eds.) (1980). *The reader in the text: Essays on audience and interpretation*. Princeton: Princeton University Press.

Szasz, T. S. (1960). The myth of mental illness. *American Psychologist, 15*, 113–118.

Tompkins, J. P. (1980). An introduction to reader-response criticism. In J. P. Tompkins (Ed.), *Reader-response criticism: From formalism to post-structuralism* (pp. ix–xxvi). Baltimore: Johns Hopkins University Press.

von Foerster, H. (1984). On constructing a reality. In P. Watzlawick (Ed.), *The invented reality* (pp. 41–61). New York and London: W. W. Norton.

von Foerster, H. (1985). Apropos epistemologies. *Family Process, 24*, 517–521.

von Glasersfeld, E. (1984). An introduction to radical constructivism. In P. Watzlawick (Ed.), *The invented reality* (pp. 17–40). New York: W. W. Norton.

Walsh, W. H. (1958). "Plain" and "significant" narrative in history. *Journal of Philosophy, 55*, 479–484.

Watzlawick, P. (1984). (Ed.), *The invented reality*. New York: W. W. Norton.

Watzlawick, P., Weakland, J. H., & Fisch, R. (1974). *Change: Principles of problem formation and problem resolution*. New York: W. W. Norton.

Webster's new universal unabridged dictionary (2nd ed.). (1983). New York: Simon & Schuster.

Wessler, R. L., & Wessler, S. H. (1986). Cognitive appraisal therapy. In W. Dryden & W. Golden (Eds.), *Cognitive-behavioral approaches to psychotherapy*. London: Harper & Row.

Wetherell, M., & Potter, J. (1988). Discourse analysis and the identification of interpretive repertoires. In C. Antaki (Ed.), *Analysing everyday explanation: A casebook of methods* (pp. 168–183). Newbury Park, CA: Sage.

White, M. (1993). Deconstruction and therapy. In S. Gilligan & R. Price (Eds.), *Therapeutic conversations* (pp. 22–61). New York: W. W. Norton.

White, M., & Epston, D. (1990). *Narrative means to therapeutic ends*. New York: W. W. Norton.

Wittgenstein, L. (1953). *Philosophical investigations* (G. E. M. Anscombe, trans.). New York: Macmillan. (Omer & Strenger, 1992, cite a 1958 edition published by Blackwell.)

Index

Material from endnotes is marked with *nx*, where x represents the note number.

coast country, called the *litera*. The traveller reposes on the cushioned floor of the oblong body, covered with an arched weatherproof top, this is supported midway on tough and flexible shafts, projecting before and behind, and suspended by simple harness from the backs of mules. A couple of stout-looking Indians, with whips in their hands, walked by the side of the mules, directing their gaits, whilst the luxurious passenger lolled on his back and sides, lazily expelling the smoke from a half-lit *cigarrito*.

Manga de Clavo, the hacienda of Santa Anna, lies to the left of the road, and is barely visible through the forest glades that separate it from the highway. This estate, though embracing an immense quantity of land, is greatly inferior in cultivation and adornment to many contiguous to it; the Dictator's military and civil engagements engrossing too much of his time to bestow the necessary care for its improvement. When overwhelmed by the disasters that occasionally beset his eventful career, he hies him to this friendly and remote retreat, finding, in a circle of devoted friends and neighbours, sympathy for his misfortunes, and encouragement to renew the struggle of his destiny. Within its sheltering solitudes has he again and again buried himself from public scorn and indignation, till the auspicious moment has arrived to resume his authority and popularity with his countrymen.

A ride of twelve miles more brought me to Vera Cruz, and terminated my wanderings on Mexican soil.

This city, once the most renowned of any in the new world for its trade and commerce, extends along the low and sandy Gulf shore for more than two miles. Since the divorce of Spain and her colony, its prosperity has suffered a material reduction, having lost more than half of its commerce, and a still greater amount of its population.

Its present census is estimated above seven thousand, and being destined for ever to continue the most important sea-port of the country, any change in the future must be one of advancement in wealth and numbers.

The streets are regular and clean, and the buildings massive and tasteful; indicating a high degree of luxury and elegance in their interior finish. The cupolas and towers of the churches, and the battlements of the castle, present an imposing effect when viewed from the sea, but greatly exaggerate the real dimensions of the place.

The castle of San Juan de Ulloa, so renowned for its strength, is built on an island, near a mile from the town, and is said to have cost the Spanish Government near *forty millions of dollars* in its construction. It was the last foothold of Spain in the country, and when surrendered to the French, in 1838, was manned by but a tenth of the force requisite to garrison it properly. In compliment to their own valour in reducing it, they have christened it by various titles, implying a degree of impregnability its age and imperfect accessories of defence do not entitle it to.

The Plaza is small, but surrounded by noble edifices, amongst which are the governor's palace, and various civil and military offices. A much larger square has been selected as the site for the new custom-house; the granite for which has been brought from the United States, and will constitute the exclusive material to be used in its erection.

The Mole is a work of great solidity and convenience, being furnished with broad stairs of masonry, and cranes to facilitate the landing of cargoes during the prevalence of storms that drive the waves entirely over it.

Amongst the shipping in the harbour, the United States cutter Woodbury, lay moored about three miles distant; being on the eve of sailing, after a month of fruitless detention, for an instalment of the American Indemnity.

Through the politeness of Mr. Dimond, late United States consul at Vera Cruz, (whose disinterested humanity and untiring kindness to my comrades and self, whilst in Perote, can never be forgotten,) a passage was secured for me in the cutter to New Orleans. Going on board immediately, I was most cordially and hospitably received by her gentlemanly commander, Captain Foster. The next morning, July the 12th, we left our anchorage, with a fair wind, but it was not until the following evening that the towering peak of Orizaba had melted behind the line of the western horizon.

Concluding Remarks

And now, gentle reader, I am once more in the land of my boyhood, in my native state, Kentucky, and as you may be anxious to know how my release from imprisonment was procured, I will close this Journal by gratifying that curiosity. It came upon me like the light of day returning upon one that had long been blind. It was as the manna that descended from heaven to feed the hungry Jews; the hand that besought it was unknown, the individual that procured it was to me unknown. I had no conception how it happened that I should be the favoured of the many, and my liberty given me, while all my comrades in arms and fellow-soldiers were still doomed to wear away their days in this horrid prison. I did not know that while I was in chains, and suffering from want and a loathsome imprisonment, that I had a friend that neither spared pains, trouble, nor money, to have me released; but such was the fact, as I have learned since my return to the United States.

General Milton Stapp, of Madison, Indiana, who is my father's brother, after trying every expedient that he could think of, to procure my release, through Judge Eve, the American Charge to Texas, and General Thompson, the American minister to Mexico, hit upon the plan of going in person to General Almonte, the Mexican minister to the United States. This he did in April, 1844, and after several interviews with General Almonte, was successful in getting that gentleman's interest in my behalf. This done, success was certain, and at the request of the Mexican Minister, I was released as before stated, on the 16th day of May, 1844.

I am under many obligations to General Almonte for his kind interference for me, and respect Santa Anna for listening and giving his approbation to the application of my friend, and the recommendation of his minister, and some would say that gratitude would dictate other language than that which I have used toward Santa Anna in the foregoing narrative, but to such I have to reply that these are facts that belong to the history of the country, and cannot

be given in exchange even for life itself. But should Santa Anna or General Almonte ever be placed in the position that I occupied in the prison of Perote, and it is in my power to administer to their comfort or relief, they will not find me ungrateful or unmindful of their past favours.

THE END.